Egypt's Occupation

EGYPT'S OCCUPATION

Colonial Economism and the Crises of Capitalism

Aaron G. Jakes

STANFORD UNIVERSITY PRESS
Stanford, California

STANFORD UNIVERSITY PRESS
Stanford, California

Printed in the United States of America on acid-free, archival-quality paper

Library of Congress Cataloging-in-Publication Data

Names: Jakes, Aaron, author.
Title: Egypt's occupation : colonial economism and the crises of capitalism / Aaron Jakes.
Description: Stanford, California : Stanford University Press, 2020. | Includes bibliographical references and index.
Identifiers: LCCN 2020019962 (print) | LCCN 2020019963 (ebook) | ISBN 9781503607194 (cloth) | ISBN 9781503612617 (paperback) | ISBN 9781503612624 (epub)
Subjects: LCSH: Capitalism—Egypt—History | Egypt—Economic conditions—1882-1919 | Egypt—History—British occupation, 1882-1936 | Egypt—Economic policy
Classification: LCC HC830 .J327 2020 (print) | LCC HC830 (ebook) | DDC 330.962/04—dc23
LC record available at https://lccn.loc.gov/2020019962
LC ebook record available at https://lccn.loc.gov/2020019963

Cover image: Egyptian stock certificates and financial instruments, early 1900s. Collection of Aaron G. Jakes.

Book design by Kevin Barrett Kane

Typeset at Stanford University Press in 10/15 Brill

TO MY SIX NIECES:

Miriam, Evelyn, Lourdina, Ruby, Amalia, and Phoebe

CONTENTS

Acknowledgments ix

Note on Transliteration xv

INTRODUCTION. Colonial Economism 1

1 Infrastructures of Occupation 32

2 Egypt's Colonial Interior 58

3 Fields of Finance 84

4 Gilded Speech 113

5 The Many Agents of Azmah 141

6 Unions of Mass Mobilization 167

7 Punjab on the Nile 193

8 The Material Occupation 219

CONCLUSION. Economism Militarized 246

Notes 255

Bibliography 305

Note on Illustrations 333

Index 335

ACKNOWLEDGMENTS

The academic monograph is a strange commodity. Like other goods for sale on global markets, a book like this one obscures from sight a multitude of distinct ecologies, labor processes, and acts of exchange that have together produced the tangible object in the hands of its reader. In flipping through the pages, that reader will learn nothing of the tall forests from which they were logged, or of the men and women who turned trees into paper and chemicals into ink. If, as is increasingly likely, this reader purchased the book with the click of a button, the cardboard box that arrived mere hours later would bear no traces of the hands that ushered it along that breakneck sprint from warehouse to doorstep.

But if in this regard it differs little from the sweater, frying pan, or harmonica the same money might purchase, in several others the academic book is unusual. For one thing, the proceeds of its sales are unlikely ever to approach its real costs of production. This book in particular has benefited from the immense generosity, both monetary and otherwise, of a great many people and institutions over the dozen years it took me to write it. Most recently, a fellowship from Yale's Program in Agrarian Studies gave me the time and space to produce the first full draft. I'm especially grateful to James C. Scott and Kalyanakrishnan Sivaramakrishnan for making "ag studies" such a welcoming space, and to Adriana Chira, John Lee, and Holly Stephens for a wonderful year of conversations. Grants from the New School's Heilbroner Center for Capitalism Studies and the Eugene Lang College Dean's Office provided the funding that made the final stages of my research possible. A fellowship from George Washington University's Institute for Middle East Studies in 2014–15 allowed me to start figuring out how the pieces would fit together. Before that, the research that made its way into this book was supported by grants from the American Council of Learned Societies, the American Research Center in Egypt, the Social Science Research Council, Fulbright Hays, and the Center for Arabic Study Abroad.

As I write these words, the administrations of some of the world's wealthiest universities, Stanford foremost among them, are threatening the very existence of academic publishing by insisting that their own presses should operate in the black like any other business. The variety of cost accounting that underlies such arguments is profoundly misleading and made in immense bad faith. I have felt tremendously fortunate to work with my editors Kate Wahl, Leah Pennywark, Faith Wilson Stein, Caroline McKusick, and Gigi Mark as they have ushered this project through to completion. But I am all the more grateful for the role that the staff of Stanford University Press have played in fighting battles both great and small to defend the place of the academic press against these latest attacks.

Beyond its incongruous relation to capitalism's value form, the monograph is also special in that it can make visible at least some of the accumulated labor that gave rise to the final product. Within the constraints of the publisher's word count, many of my intellectual debts to the brilliance, creativity, and hard work of others are documented in the endnotes. But here at the beginning, I can name at least some of the vast crowd of people whose insight, instruction, care, laughter, and love have left their traces throughout this book.

For more than a decade now, Zachary Lockman has been a source of constant inspiration and gentle guidance. He offered both the encouragement and the incisive criticism that allowed me to find my own way. Without Khaled Fahmy's tireless support, I might never have entered the Egyptian National Archives, let alone known what to do there. His commitment to writing history that is as elegant as it is politically engaged remains a model I can only aspire to emulate. Manu Goswami often saw where this project was going before I did. Her well-timed suggestions changed both how I read and how I think about the historian's craft. At key points along the way, David Ludden and Neil Brenner both helped immensely with thinking through the wider implications of this work.

Since returning to New York a few years ago, I have been especially grateful to Andrew Sartori for his jovial mentorship and his careful reading of the manuscript. Andrew Zimmerman pointed me in the right direction when I first started thinking more about economism. Jason W. Moore has several times provided encouragement when I needed it most. At one time or another, every single member of the Department of Historical Studies at the New School has read and commented on parts of this book and made them better. I could not have dreamed up a better group of colleagues than Emma Park, Federico Finchelstein, Julia Ott, Jeremy Varon, Natalia Mehlman Petrzela, Oz Frankel, Elaine Abelson, Eli Zaretsky, Claire Potter, Laura Palermo, and Amanda Bellows. Through workshops at the Heilbroner Center and elsewhere at the New School for Social Research, I have also benefited from the comments and suggestions of Will Milberg, Janet Roitman, Koray Çaliskan, Benoit Challand, Nancy Fraser, Rachel Sherman, Rachel Heiman, Sebastian Conrad, Carlos Forment, McKenzie Wark, Clara Mattei, Quentin Bruneau, Robert Brenner, Anwar Shaykh, Cinzia Arruzza, Andrew Arato, Victoria Hattam, Paul Kottman, and Ann Stoler.

For their assistance and considerable patience, I would like to thank Dr. Muhammad Sabir ʿArab, Dr. ʿAbd al-Wahid al-Nabawi, Madame Nadia Mustafa, and the staff of the Egyptian National Archives. I am also grateful to Muhammad ʿAfifi, Narmin Khalil, and their team of researchers for helping me to navigate the Egyptian Public Records Office. In the United Kingdom, the Mohamed Ali Foundation was kind enough to grant me access to the Abbas Hilmi II collection. Jane Hogan and the staff of the Special Archives and Collections at the Durham University Library did much to make my time there both pleasant and productive. I would also like to thank the staff of the British National Archives, the London Metropolitan Archives, the British Library, Oxford's Middle East Centre Archive, the Bank of England, Barclay's Bank, ING Bank, the Library of Congress, the Hoover Institution Library, and the Uttar Pradesh State Archives for everything they did to make this research possible.

I was able to write this book because I never had to do so alone. Since we met in Cairo in the spring of 2011, Hussein Omar and I have spoken pretty much every day about what quickly became a sprawling research collaboration on the histories of political and political-economic thought in modern Egypt. In similar fashion, I learned to start making sense of capitalism and revolution by talking to Ahmad Shokr. The writing we have done together proved crucial to the framing of this project. Matthew Ellis and I found our way into Egyptian history together, and I'm especially glad I took his advice about how to restructure the early chapters of the book. I've been following David Huyssen's lead since we shared neighboring desks in the first grade, and I feel incredibly lucky that we are still working together all these years later. From lunches on the steps of the archives to long hours on the phone, Samantha Iyer has been an invaluable sounding board, critic, and exemplar of clarity. Since our first long strolls in Lucknow, David Boyk has shown me it's possible to learn with the same voracious gusto one brings to a delicious meal. Charles Anderson shared his uncompromising rigor and underlying warmth as I worked through some of the most challenging moments in the writing process. In addition to reading and commenting on countless drafts, Sherene Seikaly has provided a model of critical practice that is as generous as it is incisive. For years now, Jennifer Derr has been the person I call to talk about all things Egyptian agriculture. Since we decided to organize a conference together a couple of years ago, Meghna Chaudhuri, Matt Shutzer, and Emma Park have become constant companions in thinking about histories of global capitalism and much more. I could not have hoped for a better research assistant than Deren Ertas. And I would not have been able to write the Introduction without the insight and intellectual creativity that the graduate students in our States of Taxation seminar shared last spring.

More people than I can probably count have read and commented on parts of this project over the years. For their criticism, guidance, friendship, and suggestions, I would like to thank David Rainbow, Thomas Fleischman, Omar Cheta, Hollian Wint, Masha Kirasirova, Samantha Seeley, Natalie Blum-Ross, Shana Minkin, Sam Dolbee, Micrea Raianu, Walter Armbrust, Lucie Ryzova, On Barak, David Wachsmuth, Daniel Aldana Cohen, Hillary Angelo, Eric Schewe, Joseph Prestel, Elizabeth Holt, Jason Frydman, Emad Abou-Ghazi, Nady Abdal-Ghaffar, Zoe Griffith, Greta Marchesi, Jatin Dua, Abbas Amanat, Peter Perdue, Alan Mikhail, Marshall Watson, Max Weiss, Angela Creager, Natasha Wheatley, Robert Tignor, Peter Wirzbicki, Matt Karp, Christine Walker, Brendan O'Malley, Kristen Alff, Muriam Davis, Ziad Fahmy, Daniel Stolz, Eric Tagliacozzo, Kirsten Weld, Shaul Mitelpunkt, Adrian Gregory, Tim Lorek, Ziad Abu Rish, Bassam Haddad, Jonathan Levy, Beshara Doumani, Nader Atassi, Esmat Elhalaby, Katherine Halls, Neil Ketchley, Hannah Deuchar, Isaac Miller, John Chalcraft, Saba Mahmood, Fahad Bishara, Will Hanley, Hannah Archambault, Diane Singerman, Mona Atia, Ilana Feldman, Dina Khoury, Marc Lynch, Shana Marshall, Elizabeth Williams, Nora Barakat, Michael Gilsenan, Arang Keshavarzian, Greta Scharnweber, Peter Hill, Marilyn Booth, Tony Gorman, Toby Jones, Laleh Khalili, David Harvey, Wendy Wolford, Marc Edelman, Nathan Sayre, James Vernon, Joel Beinin, Adam Hanieh, Julia Elyachar, and Ritu Birla.

For their kindness, commiseration, edification, humor, criticism, guidance, and encouragement in the long years of travel, research, writing, and revolution, I would also like to thank Anjali Kamat, Heba Morayef, Lina Attalah, Liam Stack, Muhammad Shoman, Muhammad Mabruk, Hussein Elsayed, Bahaa Mohamed, Elhosseini Hammad, Hanan Kholoussy, Pascale Ghazaleh, Ahmed Harfoush, Miguel Merino, Adam Miller, Andre Segone, Hesham Galal, Samer George, Mitko Dmitrov, Rami Attallah, Diaa and Ehab Tass, Djodi Deutsch, Scott Nelson, Rawya Rageh, Caitlin McNary, Ashraf Fahim, Sameen Gauhar, Naseem Surhio, Danika Swanson, Maxine and Robbie McClintock, Amir Moosavi, Mohamed Elshahed, Abigail Hauslohner, and Reuben Heyman-Kantor.

My family has grown much larger since I started this project. My parents, Karen and Peter, have managed to support me at every step along my meandering path to finishing this book. Their willingness to endure years of monologues about caterpillars and credit networks has been nothing short of remarkable. My big sister Susan has been my best friend and favorite interlocutor since before I could speak. I learned to learn from her, and she usually knows what I am trying to say when I do not. Her husband, Jeffrey Prescott, has become a better older brother than I could have conjured from my own imagination. Amber Abbas, Jamison Warren, Rahilla and Don Shatto, and Cynthia Abbas managed to make me feel welcome in their family from the moment we all met. My nieces Miriam, Evy, Lulu, Ruby, Amalia, and Phoebe made me want to finish this book faster so that I could spend more time with all of them. It has been one of the unexpected delights of revising the manuscript to realize that its pages are so closely connected in my mind to memories of watching them all grow into the remarkable people they have become.

I met Tania Abbas right when I moved back to Cairo to start the research for this book. I had a ridiculous mustache at the time, and she talked to me anyway. She has been reminding me that a better world is possible and worth fighting for ever since.

NOTE ON TRANSLITERATION

Throughout this book, I have employed a modified version of the Library of Congress style for Arabic transliteration. While the *International Journal of Middle East Studies* style guideline is far more common for research and publications using Arabic sources, its usage introduces the added complication of rendering bibliographic information in a format different from that by which the source materials may be located in library catalogs throughout the United States. Because the bulk of the Arabic transliterations in this book reside in the endnotes and the bibliography, I have used the LOC standard with full diacritics in those places. Within the body text of book, to reduce complications for nonspecialists, I have simplified the LOC style by omitting diacritics except for the ʻayn (ʻ) and hamzah (ʼ). Where more common English spellings of place names (Cairo, Alexandria), persons (Mehmed Ali, Gamal Abdel Nasser), and common terms (feddan, kantar) exist, I have retained them. Where other transliteration styles are used in original source materials, I have preserved them as written.

Unless otherwise noted, all translations in the book are my own.

Egypt's Occupation

Introduction

COLONIAL ECONOMISM

LORD CROMER WAS AN UNRELIABLE NARRATOR of Egypt's past, present, and future. Through a quarter century as Great Britain's agent and consul-general in Cairo, he exercised minute control over the official narrative of the peculiar regime he was charged to oversee.[1] British forces invaded the country in 1882 to secure payment on Egypt's crippling foreign debts and to quash the movement for fiscal sovereignty and constitutional rule that had formed under the Egyptian military officer Ahmad 'Urabi Pasha. The legal status of the ensuing occupation was murky at best. Formally, Egypt remained a semiautonomous territory of the Ottoman Empire, ruled by the sultan's khedive (vice-regent) and his Council of Ministers. Backed by the resident threat of their troops garrisoned in downtown Cairo, a small British staff exercised effective control over government policy as "advisers" to the various ministries.

Cromer understood that the case for this "veiled protectorate" would rest upon the results it could deliver. From the moment he became consul-general until his final years in England, he was an assiduous curator of the occupation's public image. He obsessed over the annual reports that showcased the "progress of reforms."[2] He forbade subordinates from airing their disagreements with his policies.[3] After leaving Egypt in 1907, he ordered the staff of the British consulate in Cairo to burn his papers.[4] And upon his return to England, he set about publishing the volumes that would comprise his own authoritative account of the occupation's accomplishments.

Writing from London in January of 1915, he congratulated himself on the enduring results of his long tenure. The outbreak of World War I had stoked fears in some quarters that the "spurious Nationalist movement of recent times" might rile Egyptian support for Britain's enemies. Nothing of the sort had transpired. "Why is it," he asked, that "there was never any really serious danger that Egyptian affairs would get thoroughly out of hand?" He allowed that Britain's military "unquestionably counts for much in explanation of these very singular political phenomena."[5] But the "true reason" lay elsewhere. That "no general discontent prevailed of which the agitator, the religious fanatic, or the political intriguer could make use as a lever" was the ultimate vindication of "a policy for the initiation and execution of which I am myself mainly responsible."[6] Arriving at the heart of the matter, he explained that "in the absence of ties, such as community of race, language, religion, and social customs, the only link between the governors and the governed is to be found in material interests, and amongst those interests by far the most important is the imposition of light fiscal burdens."[7]

As a forecast of things to come, Cromer's reassurance would weather poorly. Though he did not live to see it happen, in the spring of 1919 Egyptians from both town and country would undertake a mass insurgency of the very sort he had deemed unthinkable. As a characterization of Egypt's recent history, Cromer's pronouncements likewise strained against even the short chronicle of political events that he provided. Over the previous decade, the constituencies of the nationalist movement he dubbed spurious had grown far more vocal and numerous. Against an opposition capable of mobilizing substantial popular support, the occupation had responded with ever more frequent recourse to the use of force. Just weeks before Cromer put pen to paper, the British government had imposed martial law and at last declared Egypt a full-blown protectorate.[8] "After hanging in the balance for a period of thirty-three years," the aging administrator acknowledged, "the political destiny of Egypt has at last been definitely settled. The country has been incorporated into the British Empire. No other solution was possible."[9]

Questionable as his claims to success may have been, however, Cromer did here offer a faithful introduction to the theory of rule that guided British policy in Egypt over the course of his long tenure. While he did not elaborate in this instance, his comments about the primacy of "material interests" and "light fiscal burdens" condensed several important ideas at once. First among these was the notion that a sensitivity to material interests was the most significant trait shared amongst an otherwise differentiated humanity. If it was the differences—of "race, language, religion, and social customs"—that Cromer often invoked as reason for some peoples to rule over others, it was by focusing on this basic commonality that the "government of subject races" could be sustained.[10] Second was an assertion about the appropriate functions of government itself: where the population in question lacked a capacity to construe their interests in more expansive ways, the state should limit its ambitions to the promotion of material gain. To be sure, the case for streamlining what Cromer called the "machinery of government" aligned neatly with Egypt's new regime of imposed austerity.[11] That these claims were about something more than rationalizing budget cuts, however, was evinced by his confidence in the merit of "light fiscal burdens."[12] By insisting, as he so often did, that a reduction in taxes would be entirely compatible with the imperative of debt repayment, Cromer suggested that the Egyptians whom he otherwise held in famously low regard could play a productive role in their country's economic regeneration.

Although he may have ranked among their more influential adherents, Cromer was by no means the first or the only person to articulate this cluster of claims. As was the case for so many of his public statements, his pretensions to originality were more self-serving than true. But to a degree that has largely escaped the notice of subsequent generations, Cromer's brief gloss on the "corner-stone" of his policy does capture something foundational about Egypt's long era of "hanging in the balance" under British rule.

THE ARGUMENT OF THE WORK

This book tells the story of Egypt's occupation. It argues that British efforts to treat the government as a machinery for advancing material interests proved transformative in at least three respects. First, they informed the specific policies that Egypt's "advisers" pursued and altered the institutions of the Egyptian state in significant and lasting ways. Second, they created conditions for a massive, if short-lived, financial boom and thereby changed the character of material interests themselves. Third, thanks in no small measure to the frequency and consistency with which Cromer and his supporters propounded their theories about imperial rule, they made Egypt the arena for a sprawling debate about the relationship between economics and politics. In time, that debate would prove crucial to both the animating concerns and the distinguishing objectives of the nationalist movement Cromer was, to the very end, so eager to dismiss.

Across the three decades from the military invasion of 1882 to the outbreak of World War I in 1914, the British occupation of Egypt was defined by the discourse I refer to as *colonial economism*. Given its mandate to represent the demands of foreign bondholders, it might seem unsurprising that this de facto colonial regime elevated "economic development" as its foremost priority. But as Cromer's brief retrospective begins to indicate, colonial economism was not simply an ideological cover for those extractive arrangements. Because it informed the decisions that British officials made about how to govern and how to generate financial prosperity from the materials of a bankrupt polity, the discourse of colonial economism affected how processes of state formation and capital accumulation unfolded. As the British explained it in the early years of the occupation, the pursuit of economic growth—in the form of larger crop yields, higher land values, and increased foreign investment—was about much more than fiscal restructuring. Rather, it represented a necessary stage on a singular trajectory of civilizational progress, a trajectory that European countries like Britain had already marked out and that Egypt would need to follow before imperial rule could end. By the 1890s, as their endeavors appeared to be paying off, the British began to make a stronger assertion: that popular support for their rule was growing with the economic gains it could deliver. Material prosperity, they now alleged, had won them the active approval of the Egyptian people.

Notions about the primacy of economic forces are hardly unique to the British occupation of Egypt. To this day, they feature prominently in social commentaries about both good times and bad across much of the globe. In calling the central premise of British rule in Egypt colonial economism, I do not, therefore, intend to imply that these ideas have a uniquely colonial genealogy. As I explain below, the generic term *economism* captures a wide array of discourses, many with no discernible origin in colonial situations. Colonial economism was distinctive in that its truth claims were resolutely particular, not universal. That is, its proponents described the economic determination of politics as a defining feature of specific human populations that rendered them unqualified to govern themselves and thereby made political tutelage both necessary and legitimate.

At its core, colonial economism entailed a set of manifestly experimental propositions about the character of "Oriental" subjects. The discourse took shape in the context of a sweeping reevaluation of classical liberalism that preoccupied officials across the British Empire in the latter half of the nineteenth century. In the decades following the Indian uprising of 1857, an earlier optimism about the amenability of colonial populations to liberal reform gave way to a new uncertainty about which aspects of human nature were universal and which were not. Having judged some of the differences separating putatively discrete races to be insurmountable, colonial administrators set out to map and measure what shared attributes remained. While never without its detractors, colonial economism expressed one clear hypothesis: in a country like Egypt, the core principles of liberal political economy could, under a just government, hold true. Liberal political theory could not. In other words, Egyptians possessed a basic capacity to recognize and act upon their own material interests; for that reason, they would benefit from heightened access to the transactions and institutions of modern commercial society. What they purportedly lacked was the wherewithal to reason beyond the calculus of personal profit and loss. And it was only that comprehension of a greater public good that qualified some communities of people to govern themselves.

This generic characterization of the Egyptian as a human type narrowly oriented toward economic gain figured prominently in both diagnoses of the khedivate's failings and plans for the country's regeneration. On the one hand, Cromer and others explained the fiscal and political turmoil that had preceded the British invasion as an "orgy of corrupt and despotic misrule."[13] A ruling class bent upon lining its own pockets at public expense, they claimed, had emptied the state's coffers and driven the country into bankruptcy. On the other hand, they identified Egypt's oppressed rural majority as the motor force of economic revival. Endowed by nature with a propensity to toil in service of their own material gain, the peasantry could become the agents of their own prosperity and their country's economic development. Through a long series of institutional adjustments and innovations, all of them dubbed "experiments," British officials singled out the peasant smallholder as the intended beneficiary of Egypt's occupation. Politics as such, however, required an ability to construe a greater good beyond individual wants and needs. That was an ability Egyptians of all ranks and classes supposedly lacked. As the argument went, a peasantry driven by material interests would seize upon the occupation's agrarian improvements and produce enough wealth to satisfy the bondholders and themselves at the same time. The varieties of popular discontent that the occupation's critics mistook for political consciousness, meanwhile, would evaporate as the country prospered.

Rather than simply justifying the various measures that the occupation imposed under the mantle of "reform," then, the discourse of colonial economism was engineered into the specific design of the policies themselves. Acting upon the assumption that peasants could not think beyond the horizon of their immediate self-interest, British officials worked to shut down the limited avenues for political participation that had existed under the khedivate. The resulting evisceration of local politics would prove to be one of the most enduring and pernicious legacies of British rule. Even as it figured into new mechanisms of political exclusion, however, this same conception of a subject closely attuned to material interests provided the basis for a distinctly optimistic portrait of the *fallah*, the Egyptian peasant, as an economic actor: when supplied with adequate access to water, he would toil to raise revenue-generating crops; when freed from the burden of exorbitant taxation and conscription, he would direct his funds and labor time into remunerative improvements rather than leisure and extravagance; when granted secure title to land and better means of borrowing money, he would likewise employ credit as farm capital.

By the time British officials began in earnest to act upon that last claim in particular, it was anything but commonplace. Instead, it represented one clear position in a major controversy over the problem of peasant indebtedness that preoccupied provincial administrators and political economists across the British Empire. And from the mid-1890s, that utopian vision of the fallah as a petty agrarian capitalist-in-waiting gave rise to a series of institutional innovations that together aimed to make Egypt an appealing target for the relocation of financial capital from Europe.

The decade-long financial boom that resulted from these efforts has until now attracted little notice from historians of modern Egypt.[14] For the better part of the last fifty years, the central paradigm of nearly all existing economic histories of British rule has been one of qualitative continuity and quantitative expansion: Egypt had already become a major exporter of raw cotton before 1882; British control simply ensured that more and more of the country's arable surface would be devoted to growing fiber to supply England's industrial mills.[15] As the socialist writer Theodore Rothstein put it in 1910, in one of the earliest systematic elaborations of this argument, "Just as the geese at Strasburg are fed and fattened until they turn all into liver, so has Egypt been fed by irrigation, in order that it may all turn into cotton."[16]

The British themselves presumed that an influx of foreign finance would simply complement their other plans for agrarian improvement. Himself a scion of Baring Brothers, one of Britain's leading financial houses, Lord Cromer (born Evelyn Baring) sought to promote "the employment of European capital" to bolster and accelerate a program of economic development centered around the reclamation of farmland and the expanded cultivation of cotton.[17] The investment of foreign capital through private enterprise was all the more appealing because the arrangements controlling repayment of Egypt's existing foreign debts constrained the government's ability to contract new loans of its own with foreign creditors.[18] In one way or another, the rapid inflation of land prices, the sudden multiplication of joint-stock companies, and the frenetic proliferation of credit arrangements that many identified as the boom's most distinctive features all had their origins in British policies that aimed to increase cotton production. By the early 1900s, the occupation's boosters were proclaiming that Egypt had become the site of a profitable new symbiosis between metropolitan banking and colonial agriculture.

On closer examination, however, the dynamics of the boom fit awkwardly at best within conventional narratives of Egypt's peripheral status as a supplier of raw cotton to metropolitan industries. As a major target for European investment and a site for the experimental elaboration of novel instruments and institutions—colonial-era precursors to the subprime loans, mortgage-backed securities, and credit insurance of our own times—Egypt played an altogether different and more central role in the worldwide financial expansion of the late nineteenth century.[19] Indeed, while most subsequent histories of the period have either ignored the boom or treated it as a simple continuation of long-standing patterns, many observers by the early 1900s, both within Egypt and abroad, described the unprecedented influx of financial capital—and the increasingly uneven, abstract, and ephemeral forms of wealth it seemed to generate—as a striking departure from the country's prior course of economic development. The new banks that raced to extend their operations day by day seemed to construe their role in the country in ways that the occupation had hardly anticipated. The soaring valuations of company shares on the stock markets of Cairo and Alexandria turned out to be a dubious metric for the well-being of the Egyptian public whose interests British officials claimed to represent. As these dynamics unfolded, the relationship between the country's new financial fortunes and the livelihoods of peasant producers proved sometimes ambiguous and at other times profoundly antagonistic.

The chapters that follow argue that this financial boom and the crises it unleashed cast the history of the occupation as a whole in a different light than conventional narratives about the long-term continuities of the cotton economy. Egypt's reputation as a "field for banking business" and its status as a gigantic cotton plantation located the country within distinct, if sometimes overlapping, geographies of capital.[20] From the vantage of financial investors in London, Paris, and Brussels, what mattered most was not the specific purpose of a given venture but the relative rate of return it promised.

That structural indifference to the particular objects through which financial capital flowed had at least two significant consequences for the character of Egypt's fin de siècle boom. First, it meant that the country's new banks and mortgage companies were fickle partners in the occupation's agrarian development schemes. Their decisions about how and where to invest intensified the very patterns of rural inequality that the British had promised to alleviate. When other, more lucrative opportunities appeared beyond the cotton fields, the banks moved their money elsewhere. Though British officials may have liked to suggest otherwise, the relationship between metropolitan finance and Egyptian agriculture was always fraught and deeply contradictory. Over time, the pressures of Egypt's multilayered debt obligations would undermine both the social and the ecological conditions for intensive cotton cultivation. And at a crucial moment in the frenzy of financial speculation, it was the rising value of Egypt's cotton crop itself that would throw global capital markets into turmoil.

Second, the complex interconnections of the financial networks that stretched out across the globe in these years meant that the livelihoods of ordinary Egyptians were ever more vulnerable to shifts in the demand for money in other distant locales. While the British heralded the country's newfound prosperity as evidence of their own success, less sanguine observers cautioned that such fortunes might be fleeting. Their concern was well warranted. In the spring of 1907, Egypt was among the first countries hit by the cascade of financial crises that sent asset values into free fall across many parts of the globe.[21]

Well before that devastating reversal, Egyptian critics of the occupation had noticed that British officials treated their own measures of economic improvement as self-evident proxies for popular opinion. Writing in December of 1905 for *al-Liwa'*, the official newspaper of the country's leading nationalist organization, the young journalist Ahmad Hilmi coined a pithy moniker for an official discourse gaudily adorned with references to rising wealth. "Gilded speech" he called it. Hilmi would soon play an exceptional and influential role in the fledgling movement against British rule. But he was by no means alone in understanding what was at stake when British officials boasted about "the rapid progress of this country in its material life . . . every time the sun comes up or a new year begins."[22] Many critics of the occupation recognized in its closely managed statements a reductive contention that most Egyptians were capable of no more and no less than a bare recognition of their own material interests.

From the moment an organized opposition to British rule took shape in the early 1890s, its protagonists sought to rebut that claim on both normative and empirical grounds. But they also understood that those grounds were shifting beneath their feet. In the heady years of the boom, they worked to demonstrate that prosperity was no substitute for sovereignty and that the effects of foreign investment were not what the British claimed. The advent of the crisis in 1907 changed the terms of that argument, lending new weight to counternarratives about the ravages of an illegitimate occupation. At the same time, the patterned, globe-spanning character of the crisis also suggested that British rule had introduced problems that political independence would no longer, on its own, prove adequate to address. It was only by forging a complex of institutions that would insulate the country from the vagaries and volatilities of global capital, the proponents of a new economic nationalism argued, that Egyptians could begin to exercise a meaningful control over their own collective conditions of life.

These ongoing reflections contributed to a vigorous, creative, and many-sided conversation about the relationship between economic and political development as well as the adequacy of the political-economic theories British officials invoked to explain the momentous upheavals their experiments were inducing. In this regard, Egypt's self-proclaimed nationalists were not mere passive consumers of a ready-made political-economic discourse imported from abroad. Often writing in fragmentary form and developing their ideas in newspaper articles rather than in book-length treatises, these figures reworked political-economic concepts to elaborate their own critical accounts of boom and bust.[23] The voluminous archive of their thought and praxis—long ignored or dismissed as so many bad copies of a European original—brings to light a set of sophisticated and troubling meditations on the deeper contradictions of capitalism and the very meaning of freedom in a capitalist world.

ECONOMISM IN THEORY AND HISTORY

The British Empire was nothing if not a vast apparatus for pilfering the labor of others. It should come as no surprise, then, that one of its most outspoken defenders showed little compunction about taking credit where it was not due. Cromer's ideas were not, of course, shared by every British subject across the Empire. In their sheer volume, his official statements often had a particular effect of drowning out the actual diversity of British people in Egypt and the opinions they held.[24] But neither did colonial economism emerge fully formed from the mind of the imperious proconsul. While Cromer's efforts to act as the singular voice for British rule in Egypt did often lend a focus and clarity to the critical thought of his detractors, he was not alone responsible for the discourse that became the common sense of so much Anglophone commentary on Egyptian affairs.

As generations of postcolonial scholarship have emphasized, the brute fact of colonial rule situated disparate territories within comparative frames of thought and practice that made empire workable.[25] In the case of Egypt, the arrival of British troops in the summer of 1882 meant that intellectual traditions that had before then figured only vaguely in the government of the country suddenly took on a different weight. When they wrote and spoke about Egypt, British officials drew upon ideas that originated elsewhere and addressed themselves to audiences well beyond Egypt's borders. Explaining the wider context out of which colonial economism emerged therefore requires something of a preliminary detour outside of Egypt.

The meaning of *economism* has shifted significantly over the past century. In the early 1900s, it served mainly as a term of denunciation among European socialists. For those who wielded the label, economism named the error, both political and theoretical, of trade unionists and others who sought to restrict the ambitions of class struggle to improving wages and living conditions while abandoning or postponing any concerted political movement for revolution.[26] At stake in this moment was a question of strategy. In his famous pamphlet of 1902, "What Is to Be Done?" Vladimir I. Lenin railed against "the fundamental error that all the Economists commit, namely, their conviction that it is possible to develop the class political consciousness of the workers *from within* the economic struggle, so to speak, i.e., making the economic struggle the exclusive, or, at least, the main starting point, making the economic struggle the exclusive, or, at least, the main basis." Such political consciousness, he went on to argue, "can be brought to the workers *only from without*, that is, only outside of the economic struggle, outside of the sphere of relations between workers and employers."[27] A century later, the term has, somewhat ironically, reappeared on occasion as a label for the fallacies of neoliberal ideology.[28] But its predominant usage today occurs within academic circles, as shorthand for the varieties of economic reductivism and mechanistic determinism that many critics identify with older traditions of Marxist thought.[29]

In what follows, I use economism broadly to denote forms of thought that treat the economic as a discrete, self-contained domain of social life and that assign analytical or causal primacy to that domain. But why adopt an unfamiliar term that already carries a complex and freighted history? I have chosen to do so here for two reasons, one methodological, the other historical.

First, I employ the term to mark a certain considered distance from the conventions and presuppositions of economic history. The recent and widespread reemergence of capitalism as an object of critical inquiry has roused some legitimate concerns that these "new" approaches to histories of capitalism, capitalism studies, or critical political economy might simply rehearse the problems of economism that several generations of social and cultural historians worked very hard to overcome. It bears mentioning, in this regard, that for many scholars of the postcolonial world a generation ago, the choice to write within the genre of economic history represented a critical intervention in its own right. Well before the publication of Edward Said's *Orientalism*, the universalist idiom of quantification offered a powerful analytic with which to rebut the kinds of exceptionalism and essentialism that had long characterized the field of "Oriental studies" and that gained a new patina of authority with the advent of Modernization Theory.[30]

Such critical uses of economic history have played an important role in challenging the ethnocentrism and cultural determinism that still inflect both popular and scholarly attitudes toward the global South. But they have often done so by reinscribing a sharp line between the economic and other putative domains of social existence.[31] By contrast, one overwhelming point of agreement among the various "new" approaches to the study of capitalism has been a pronounced and generative skepticism toward that way of dividing up the world and making sense of it. Despite other differences of theory and method, work by heterodox Marxists, cultural political economists, critical geographers, actor-network theorists, and new materialists has, consequently, shared a basic point of departure in the argument that capitalism is not, or at the very least not exclusively, a self-enclosed economic system.

This heterogeneous project to specify and explore capitalism's more-than-economic characteristics has, in turn, yielded several significant insights that inform both the arguments and the empirical content of the chapters that follow. Relative to the conventions of economic history—best exemplified in the case of Egypt by the unrivaled oeuvre of Roger Owen—the range of sources and topics covered here may seem surprising. Those differences are deliberate. Central to any meaningful distinction between economic histories and histories of capitalism is the proposition that the various processes and practices commonly labeled economic depend for their perpetuation on what the political theorist Nancy Fraser has called capitalism's "background conditions."[32] Commodity markets, regimes of property, and media of exchange do not simply emerge from some natural and self-propelling dynamics of commerce. Rather, their existence and normalized operations require the establishment and maintenance of a whole host of legal regimes, regulatory agencies, and material infrastructures that typically fall within the responsibilities of the state.[33] Moreover, capitalism's historically specific ways of construing and enumerating the material wealth of human communities entail a series of constitutive distinctions between those varieties of work that count as economic and others that do not.

The production of surplus value through *exploitation* of wage labor in the "hidden abode of production" has, in actual historical practice, been sustained by diverse arrangements of *expropriation* that serve to drive down the costs of production that capital is forced to pay through direct acts of market exchange. For present purposes, that dynamic between exploitation and expropriation has at least two further implications that loom large across the history of British rule in Egypt. First, capitalism is better understood not as an economic system with various pronounced and discernible ecological effects but rather as a "way of organizing nature."[34] The profitability of commodities for sale on global markets—be they industrial goods like cotton thread or even raw materials like the cotton fiber itself—depends upon the continuous production of geographic arrangements through which repositories of uncapitalized or undercapitalized nature may be claimed as "free gifts" for capitalist enterprise.[35] In the case of Egypt, the occupation's contention that British rule could boost payments to the bondholders and enrich the peasantry at the same time was premised on a belief that British technical expertise could seize upon the fabled gifts of the Nile where the khedivate had squandered them. Capital accumulation, in other words, is always both a social and an ecological process.

Second, the boundary between exploitation and expropriation, between commodified and uncommodified forms of work, has articulated closely with other systems of domination and ways of elaborating distinctions among groups of human subjects.[36] From this perspective, the discursive production of categories of difference has been crucial to capitalism's history as an institutionalized social order. As several generations of radical feminist scholars have shown, the mapping of gender onto a division between social reproduction and "production proper" has set the terms according to which some work becomes wage labor and much work does not.[37] Likewise, processes of racialization on a worldwide scale have been integral to the systematic cheapening of work without which the accumulation of capital cannot proceed.[38] The recent and welcome surge of efforts to excavate what the sociologist Maria Mies once called the "underground of capitalist patriarchy," namely the "subordination of women, nature and colonies," has thus helped to snap the cordons that once held "economic" and "cultural" history apart.[39]

The second reason for adopting economism as the central category of this study follows from and builds upon these insights. The various approaches to an expanded conception of capitalism mentioned above have gone a long way toward explaining both the methodological and the political hazards of economism. They have had less to say, however, about why it has been such a recurrent and pervasive feature of modern social thought in the first place. In this sense, economism is not only an analytical disposition to be corrected by better theories, methods, and narratives. Rather, it is a way of apprehending the world particular to the history of capitalism itself. If one aim of this book is to pursue a history of capitalism in Egypt that draws from recent methodological critiques of economism, then another is to show that economism merits critical scrutiny as an object of historical analysis in its own right.[40]

To the extent that historians have sought to explain economism, rather than simply debunk it, they have usually done so by way of political or ideological affiliation. Whether the blame is laid on Marx himself or his subsequent interpreters, the Marxist tradition in particular has acquired a special ignominy as a font of economistic ideas. For well more than a century, Marx's use of the "base-superstructure" metaphor—to describe the interaction between relations of production, on the one hand, and "definite forms of social consciousness," on the other—has been treated as the hallmark of a deterministic mode of analysis that assigns primary, or even singular, importance to economic forces.[41] It was this reputation, already well entrenched by the 1930s, that the Italian Marxist Antonio Gramsci sought to address when he mused that "it should be considered whether economism, in its most developed form, is not a direct descendant of liberalism."[42] For present purposes, the importance of Gramsci's remark lies neither in ignoring the kinds of crude determinism that many self-identified Marxists have espoused nor in defending one intellectual tradition by shunting blame to another. Though couched in overtly partisan terms, Gramsci's observation instead suggests both that economism is a recognizable tendency within multiple, even opposing, intellectual traditions and that its prevalence predated the work of Marx himself. That longer and more diffuse history calls out for a different kind of explanation.

Gramsci went on to condemn economism as a grave "theoretical error," but his comments on the subject described an error of a peculiar and contradictory kind. "The ideas of the Free Trade movement," he explained, were "based on a distinction between political society and civil society, which is made into and presented as an organic one" such that "economic activity belongs to civil society, and that the State must not intervene to regulate it."[43] The proponents of free trade thereby treated as timeless and inviolable a series of conceptual divisions that were instead specific to capitalism's peculiar social topography. In arguing that "*laissez-faire* too is a form of State 'regulation,' introduced by legislation and coercive means," Gramsci was insisting that other ways of organizing human communities were both possible and desirable. By affirming the distinction between the economic and the political and insisting on the primacy of the former, his interlocutors thus made the error of naturalizing what was historically produced and ripe for contestation. On that basis, he discerned a role for economism not simply as an analytical disposition but as a mode of governance instrumental to capital's ongoing self-expansion. At the same time, it would make little sense to speak of economism in a context where the economic was not already widely understood to contain a discrete subset of social life. The very plausibility of economism as a way of understanding the world was contingent upon the appearance of that very distinction as an "organic" feature of modern societies. In this respect, what Gramsci described as a "theoretical error" also expressed something essential about how capitalism differs from other institutionalized social orders.

BETWEEN THE ECONOMIC AND THE ECONOMY

At this point, some brief clarification may be necessary. Among studies of modern Egypt, few have proven as influential as the political theorist Timothy Mitchell's *Rule of Experts*. Among the book's most cited findings is Mitchell's observation that the "idea of the economy in its contemporary sense did not emerge until the middle decades of the twentieth century."[44] The subtle and unremarked appearance of the definite article, he explains, indexed the emergence of an entire complex of new calculative practices and technologies that first made "the economy" available as an object of expertise and political intervention. The historically recent "making of the economy," in turn, exemplifies a longer history of entanglements between the rise of mainstream social science and the violence of colonial domination.[45] The European empires of the late nineteenth century, Mitchell shows, served as the laboratories where new disciplinary methods for developing universalist claims about humanity could be tested. The abstract categories of the social sciences, economics chief among them, made possible new techniques of power that, in their very claims to scientific objectivity, "ignored the importance of a larger structure of empire" and thereby treated the particular historical experiences of the West as models for social development everywhere.[46]

It would be difficult to overstate the generative impact of Mitchell's scholarship. Well beyond the field of Middle East studies, his interrogation of the economy has played a key role in reinvigorating the critical study of capitalism, both historical and contemporary.[47] In questioning the taken-for-granted status of the master categories that continue to organize social-scientific inquiry, Mitchell's work moreover represents a signal contribution to the methodological critiques of economism outlined above.

As a set of historical claims with obvious theoretical implications, however, Mitchell's arguments about the economy require some qualification. The particular dating he assigns to the appearance of the definite article has elicited occasional disagreement from historians of economic thought.[48] But Mitchell is surely right to locate in new methods of national income accounting and techniques for measuring the totality of transactions within a bounded national territory a series of conceptual shifts with broad and lasting importance to the politics of the twentieth century. More questionable are two subsidiary interpretations he attaches to the economy's surprising novelty. The first is a conflation of the economy with the economic. On this basis, Mitchell asserts that "[through] these novel forms of political rationality and practice it became possible to imagine the economy as a self-contained sphere, distinct from the social, the cultural, and other spheres." He thus contends that to "create the economy meant also to create the non-economic."[49] The second is a characterization of political economy prior to the 1930s that relies upon that same conflation. Noting that the term *economy* in the eighteenth and nineteenth centuries still meant "thrift" and the " 'proper governing' of the community's affairs," Mitchell asserts that " 'political economy' refers to this economy, or governing, of the polity, not to the politics of an economy."[50]

The crucial point here is that the conceptual distinction between the economic and the political long preceded the invention of the economy as a discrete object of expertise. Without some prior notion of that division, it is difficult at best to explain how European socialists could become so exercised about a problem they called economism several decades before the economy existed. In the case of Egypt, it would seem similarly puzzling for the occupation's apologists to emphasize "economic development," "economic progress," or "economic reform" without already having in their minds a way of distinguishing those achievements from the effects of British rule in other possible spheres of social existence. Likewise, while the language they used to describe it could vary, the leading figures of classical political economy were quite clear in delimiting their object of inquiry as an identifiable subset of social phenomena, one that appeared to be governed not by the management of any state but by its own seemingly automatic movements and laws.

Rather than a simple scaling up of ideas about resource management from the household or community to the polity, political economy emerged as a recognizable discourse out of efforts to grapple with a set of profound historical transformations that for the first time rendered the economic meaningful and intelligible.[51] In the broadest sense, those changes concerned the conditions under which a society's surplus wealth was produced and distributed.[52] To be sure, practices of trade, moneylending, and manufacture had existed across much of the world since ancient times, but as historical theorists of capitalism have often argued, in all prior social formations, the appropriation of the social surplus had occurred mainly through overt forms of interpersonal domination. It was in this sense that Karl Polanyi wrote of the "embeddedness" of the market, that Joseph Schumpeter insisted on the fundamental modernity of "the tax state," and that Karl Marx remarked about medieval Europe that "the social relations between individuals in the performance of their labour [appeared] at all events as their own personal relations."[53] By contrast, what the early political economists of England and France, from at least the late seventeenth century, referred to as "commercial society" was characterized by radically novel forms of objective social interdependence. For the first time, growing numbers of people were drawn or forced into a field of commodity exchange whereby the products of their labor and their labor itself became the means not of fulfilling their own immediate wants and needs but of acquiring the products of others. Under these conditions of growing market dependence, the production and distribution of social wealth began to exhibit patterns of macroregularity that seemed to exist beyond the will or intention of any individual. In other words, as Ellen Meiksins Wood explains in her classic and incisive account of this historical separation, the economic came to designate an expanding terrain of generalized social practices whereby the "allocation of resources and labour does not, on the whole, take place by means of political direction, communal deliberation, hereditary duty, custom, or religious obligation, but rather through the mechanisms of commodity exchange."[54] It was the peculiar, law-like operation of those mechanisms that the discourse of classical political economy sought to investigate and comprehend through abstract categories such as value, capital, and rent.

With the benefit of the historian Andrew Sartori's helpful clarifications, the long historical caesura between the advent of the economic and the making of the economy might also be understood in terms of the difference between two modes of abstraction. The abstraction that concerns Mitchell is a kind of generalization from the otherwise unmanageable complexity of lived experience; abstract categories like national income and GDP are ways of counting some phenomena and not others.

The central concepts of political economy, by contrast, are not "merely aggregations of concrete particularities. Rather, they seek to grasp real abstractions—social practices that are, in some sense, themselves abstract."[55] The economic thus acquired its meaning as a way of naming "a whole constellation of social practices" in which growing numbers of people were implicated by their mundane acts of exchange.[56] It was this thickening fabric of objective interdependence that Adam Smith famously described when he observed, "It is not from the benevolence of the butcher, the brewer, or the baker, that we expect our dinner, but from their regard to their own interest. We address ourselves, not to their humanity but to their self-love, and never talk to them of our own necessities but of their advantages."[57]

FROM LIBERALISM TO COLONIAL ECONOMISM

This conception of the economic as a plausibly separate domain of human affairs brought with it an array of problems and questions that have animated studies of capitalist social formations ever since. In the most general sense, once it became possible to think about society as comprising a number of distinct spheres, it also became necessary to ascertain how those spheres might relate to each other. The leading proponents of the discourse of political economy often likened the movements of commerce and production to the workings of a machine, a machine that operated according to its own autonomous processes.[58] Convinced by the potentialities of that self-governing machinery to drive the improvement of society and the general increase of material wealth, they sought to demarcate, through scientific inquiry, the optimal boundary between the terrains of political and civil society. While many of the formative texts of political economy addressed themselves directly to the needs of the state, their guidance now concerned not simply how best to govern but also what not to govern. Michel Foucault identified the novelty of this bifurcation between the political and economic when he noted that "political economy was able to appear as the first form of this new self-limiting governmental *ratio*."[59] This is also what Gramsci meant when he described liberalism as the main progenitor of economism. By mistaking the historical peculiarities of capitalist social relations for the unfolding of natural laws, the liberal proponents of laissez-faire advanced a "form of State 'regulation' " that actively expanded the domain of the economic into which the state "must not intervene."[60]

According to this new vision of human development, the progress of civilization would require a narrowing of the ambit of the political. While direct, sovereign claims upon the social surplus continued to exist—as taxes, tariffs, and rents—they now appeared as so many deductions from a natural self-expansion of wealth unfolding within the sphere of the economic.[61] On this basis, David Ricardo judged it "certain that, but for taxation, this increase of capital would have been much greater. There are no taxes which have not a tendency to lessen the power to accumulate."[62] Nevertheless, the new principle of limitation did not, on its own, translate into a conviction that the "power to accumulate" was or should be the sole end of social life. Instead, the leading figures of classical political economy evinced a profound ambivalence about following their own arguments through to that conclusion. In an irreverent set piece toward the end of *The Wealth of Nations*, Smith sought to demonstrate that Britain's courts, universities, and churches would all function better if judges, professors, and priests were stripped of endowments or fixed salaries and forced to compete for their compensation.[63] While he thereby insisted that the free pursuit of economic interest could secure the "proper performance of every service," Smith clearly understood justice, education, and spiritual guidance as social goods distinct from material wealth.[64] The public interest for Smith continued to exceed the economic.[65] In similar fashion, Jeremy Bentham's theory of utilitarianism derived "principles of morals and legislation" out of techniques of commercial accounting: "Sum up all the values of all the pleasures on the one side, and those of all the pains on the other. The balance, if it be on the side of pleasure, will give the good tendency of the act upon the whole."[66] But Bentham also insisted that the pleasures and pains so tabulated were more numerous and varied than wealth alone.[67] Utility could be made to increase like money without being reducible to it.

Lurking throughout these efforts to adjudicate the relationship between the economic and the political was a set of further questions about the human subjects adequate to each domain. The political economists were notoriously fond of time travel back to a state of nature. In deriving their theories of value from imagined scenarios in "the early stages of society," they claimed for political economy the status of a universal science grounded upon enduring features of human existence.[68] In these moments at least, the human species was reimagined as *homo oeconomicus*, Smith's creature endowed with "the propensity to truck, barter, and exchange one thing for another."[69] It was that supposedly innate human tendency to pursue self-interest through production and exchange that could, when freed from constraint, facilitate a limitless expansion of social wealth.

From that confidence in the promise of political economy followed at least two arguments that would become essential to the development of liberal political theory. First, whereas an older tradition of English republicanism had held that the pursuit of wealth could have a corrupting influence upon politics and that political subjects should therefore exercise a civic virtue cautiously divorced from material considerations, the discourse of political economy provided a basis to reconceive the polity as an apparatus for acknowledging, balancing, and channeling the diverse "interests" of individuals who together comprised the public.[70] Second, the mundane transactions of generalized commodity exchange offered their own practical basis for liberal norms of equality, freedom, and rights. The defining act of commercial society, as the political economists understood it, was one in which free individuals posited their formal equality by treating the objects of their respective labors as equivalent.[71] Universalist claims about the self-interested subject of political economy thus could and did provide grounds for universalist claims about the free and equal subject of liberal political theory.

Even when dealing with their own contemporary society in Britain, however, these same thinkers found reason to doubt that the translation between the economic and the political was always so simple.[72] For one thing, the same process of accumulation that gave new normative force to concepts of freedom and equality from one angle was, from another, premised on the existence and intensification of unfreedom and inequality. Marx, of course, faulted the political economists for restricting their analysis to the "sphere of simple circulation," that "very Eden of the innate rights of man" where "alone rule Freedom, Equality, Property, and Bentham." Without entering the "hidden abode of production" and locating "the secret of profit making" in the exploitation of labor, they failed to comprehend the fundamental contradictions of a social order that systematically undermined the very ideals that it simultaneously rendered meaningful.[73] They did, however, notice the problem. As the anthropologist Julia Elyachar has noted, Smith's political economy grew out of an "immersion in debates of moral philosophy about the rights of private property versus the rights of the excluded."[74] He may have exhibited great confidence that the division of labor would contribute to a general increase of wealth. Yet he also fretted that "the man whose whole life is spent in performing a few simple operations . . . generally becomes as stupid and ignorant as it is possible for a human creature to become. . . . Of the great and extensive interests of his country he is altogether incapable of judging."[75] The self-interested subject of political economy, he thus suggested, might not always possess the requisite capacities to act as the self-governing subject of a liberal polity.

Such reservations about the universality of their theories became all the more consequential when these same thinkers turned their gaze abroad. Liberal political theory could and did sometimes provide normative grounds from which to mobilize opposition to colonial rule. But as the rich and growing body of postcolonial scholarship on liberalism and empire has shown, the universalist abstractions of liberal thought also furnished a powerful idiom for treating human diversity as so many deviations from a singular ideal of progress that colonial rule would serve to advance.[76]

In elaborating a theoretical armature for that liberal accommodation with empire, the figure of John Stuart Mill played a particularly significant, if far from singular, role. Having followed his father's footsteps into a career in the political department of the East India Company, Mill famously argued that there are "conditions of society in which a vigorous despotism is in itself the best mode of government for training the people in what is specifically wanting to render them capable of a higher civilization."[77] Building on his lifelong project to develop a science of character formation—what he called *ethology*—Mill saw British rule as the institutional framework through which a long-term pedagogical project would develop India's "national character" toward the eventual realization of self-rule and representative government.[78] By substituting a malleable, historically contingent conception of race for one of rigid, biological determination, Mill thus furnished the case for an ambitiously interventionist project of utilitarian "reform."[79]

Like the larger body of literature to which they belong, existing critical histories of Mill's apologia for colonial rule have tended to treat the relationship between liberalism and empire mainly as a problem of and for political theory. Almost entirely absent from consideration, as a result, is the corpus of Mill's contemporaneous writings on political economy. Whereas many of his predecessors had questioned the economic benefits of the Empire for Britain, Mill concluded his *Principles of Political Economy* by making the case for a lucrative symbiosis between colony and metropole.[80] By recognizing the promise of the colonies as targets for the relocation of idle capital and labor, Mill explained, metropolitan investors could realize healthy profits for themselves while at the same time funding the large-scale infrastructures that would deliver higher levels of development to colonial populations.[81] The linkage between Mill's writings on political economy and political theory, however, went well beyond such complementary justifications for the "vigorous despotism" of Britain's imperium.[82] Rather, running throughout Mill's vast oeuvre is a subtle but consistent line of argument that refigures the relationship between the economic and the political in terms of a developmental hierarchy between "savage" and "civilized" peoples.[83] To put matters more bluntly, Mill sought to resolve this long-standing ambiguity by recourse to a crude (if necessarily "contingent") taxonomy of racial types.[84]

In his *Essays on Some Unsettled Questions of Political Economy*, Mill set out to delimit the "nature and object" of political economy as a science that "traces the laws of such of the phenomena of society as arise from the combined operations of mankind for the production of wealth, in so far as those phenomena are not modified by the pursuit of any other object."[85] As the political theorist Wendy Brown has noted, Mill understood the laws of human nature as partible. If nineteenth-century political economy represented the human subject as *homo oeconomicus*, it was not because its practitioners believed that all people were motivated solely by economic gain. Political economy, Mill explained, did not deal with "the whole conduct of man in society. It is concerned with him solely as a being who desires to possess wealth, and who is capable of judging of the comparative efficacy of means for obtaining that end."[86] For Brown's purposes, Mill's acknowledgment of this "entire abstraction of every other human passion or motive" is significant precisely because it implies that other passions or motives can and should exist.[87] Whereas classical liberals like Mill preserved a distinction between *homo oeconomicus* and *homo politicus*, Brown observes, the neoliberal discourse of our own times has peddled a radically narrowed conception of the human as a financialized subject driven by capital appreciation.[88]

Brown is correct to suggest both that the political subject of classical liberal thought "must literally subdue the creature of self-interest and self-absorption" and that many variants of neoliberal discourse tend toward a "specific eclipse of *homo politicus*."[89] But elsewhere in Mill's writings, this same distinction took on an altogether different significance. In his essay on "Civilization," Mill declared that the most "accurate test of the progress of civilization" was "the progress of the power of co-operation."[90] There, as in his later work, he did observe that higher-order forms of cooperation—exemplified by the division of labor, large-scale manufacturing, and the joint-stock corporation—would confer immense economic advantages.[91] But he went on to equate the progress of cooperation with the development of government and to insist that the essence of civilization lay in the constraint of individualistic self-interest through conscious recognition of the public good. Among the diverse "inducements to call forth energy of character," Mill held that the "only one of them which can be considered as anything like universal, is the desire of wealth."[92] Civilization, as he defined it, entailed the "concentration" of that innate desire "within the narrow sphere of the individual's money-getting pursuits."[93]

Mill thus explained the relationship between the economic and the political in terms of a historical ascent from the former to the latter. This early essay was by no means the only place where he did so. In his various writings on utilitarianism, he faulted Bentham for an undifferentiated universalism that took "next to no account of national character and the causes which form and maintain it."[94] To the extent that Mill's own utilitarianism required that its practitioners be "familiar with the fact of co-operating with others, and proposing to themselves a collective, not an individual, interest," it was a mode of reasoning only available to higher orders of civilization.[95] In *Considerations on Representative Government*, he furthermore described a "good despotism" as one in which "the intelligence and sentiments of the whole people are given up to the material interests, and when these are provided for, to the amusement and ornamentation, of private life. But to say this is to say, if the whole testimony of history is worth anything, that the era of national decline has arrived: that is, if the nation had ever attained anything to decline from. If it has never risen above the condition of an Oriental people, in that condition it continues to stagnate."[96]

Mill thus proposed that the self-interest of *homo oeconomicus* was universal while the self-limiting cooperative capacity of *homo politicus* was particular and historically contingent. This way of resolving the structural tensions between the economic and the political onto a vague and underspecified hierarchy of racial types resonated powerfully with the ambitions of the colonial state in India during the middle decades of the nineteenth century. On this understanding, an expansive program of legal, institutional, and infrastructural reforms under the "good despotism" of the East India Company's rule would contribute to the increase of general wealth and, in turn, prepare the way to the formation of a national character as yet unequipped for representative self-government.

Influential as it was, however, Mill's was by no means the only way of addressing these questions. By the 1860s, this version of imperial liberalism was facing a powerful backlash from within the channels of official opinion. In the long aftermath of the Indian uprising of 1857, a new cohort of colonial administrators charged that the interventionist methods of the Utilitarians were rending the fabric of a tradition-bound society and causing social dislocation so extreme as to undermine the very foundations of Britain's presence. Among the proponents of this conservative turn, none would prove more influential for subsequent strategies of colonial rule—not just in India but across the Empire—than the jurist Henry Sumner Maine.[97]

If Mill had taken his forebears to task for neglecting "national character," Maine followed that historicist impulse toward a thoroughgoing critique of liberal universalism as such. He reserved some of his harshest language for "the English political economists" who "throw aside, under the name of *friction*, all the extraneous influences which clog the action of those wheels of social mechanism to which economical science, with much more justification in the West than in the East, confines almost wholly its attention."[98] It was crucial to the colonial politics of Maine's intellectual project that he did not regard all forms of abstraction merely as partial generalizations from the rich concreteness of lived experience. He noted in particular that the market mechanism so central to the "great deductive science of Political Economy" presumed an indifference to the specific objects of exchange and a profit motive that is "sufficiently general to make it safe for practical purposes to treat it as universal."[99] Where, as in England, those conditions did obtain, abstract economic categories like price and rent would have real analytical purchase. The problem, as Maine understood it, was that "it is most difficult for a citizen of western Europe to bring thoroughly home to himself the truth that the civilization which surrounds him is a rare exception in the history of the world."[100] Liberal reformers had misconstrued that "rare exception" as a universal norm and imposed institutions particular to their own historical circumstances where they did not belong. Recent events had demonstrated that the "perpetual change" they advocated was "not in harmony with the normal forces ruling human nature, and is apt therefore to lead to cruel disappointment or serious disaster."[101]

For Maine and the cohort of officials who sought to implement his ideas, this heightened emphasis on the durable sedimentation of human difference did not lead to a repudiation of Britain's colonial ambitions. On the contrary, their efforts to investigate and codify the diversity of local practice would provide what the political theorist Karuna Mantena has called a new "alibi of empire."[102] Maine and his followers still regarded the institutions of the free market and representative democracy as hallmarks of civilizational progress. Their conservatism was not, in that sense, premised upon a nostalgia for Europe's own distant past. They nevertheless warned that for people still living under the sway of "custom," the encounter with modern institutions would be hazardous and disruptive. The task of the colonial state, then, was to manage the interface between the "age of progress" and a diverse multitude of customary social groupings exemplified in India by the village community.[103]

From the closing decades of the nineteenth century, this ethnographic turn provided the basis for practices of "indirect rule" that sought to identify and enlist "native" leaders as the ideal intermediaries of the colonial state.[104] It moreover engendered a pronounced aversion toward the unqualified extension of free markets for land, labor, commodities, and capital in "Eastern" countries. Bewildered by the mounting incidence of phenomena that the "deductive science" of political economy had failed to predict—from rising rates of indebtedness to rural insurgencies and cataclysmic famines—colonial conservatives began to advocate new kinds of protective, paternalistic legislation to insulate village communities from the transactions of a modern world they were now deemed unequipped to comprehend.

It was in the context of this empire-spanning debate over theories of imperial rule that the discourse of colonial economism in Egypt emerged. When Cromer and others referred to their policies as experiments, they implied that Egypt might become a laboratory in which to settle those greater questions of the Empire. Viewed in this light, their working hypothesis also helps to explain an apparent paradox of recent efforts to situate the occupation within the genealogies of British political thought: whereas Mitchell, among others, has characterized British rule in Egypt as an exemplary case of the immanent relationship between liberal universalism and colonial domination, Mantena describes the very same colonial regime as an early instance of the conservative, ethnographic turn against liberal universalism.[105] Neither is exactly wrong, but each offers a one-sided analysis of a discourse that was centrally concerned with the relationship between political economy and political theory.

The British occupation's persistent and ubiquitous claims both about the necessary historical progression from the achievement of economic development to the viability of self-government and about the narrow economic self-interest of Egyptians as human subjects bore an obvious resemblance to Mill's civilizational schemas. The influence of Mill's thought is similarly apparent in the archives of the occupation, through direct references to his publications and casual usage of his terminology, as well as the broadly utilitarian logic of efforts to quantify, document, and circulate evidence of the improvements British rule was delivering.[106] In the confidence with which they championed the principles of political economy in the Nile Valley, Cromer and his supporters were likewise at odds with Maine's acolytes in India. Those differences would have profound consequences for the policies they adopted. Making this position as explicit as possible, Alfred Milner wrote of Egypt in 1892 that "for a political economist I can imagine no experience more interesting or more instructive than that of practical contact with Egyptian affairs. . . . Economic causes produce their theoretically correct results with a swiftness and exactitude not easily visible in other lands."[107]

Milner worked as the British financial adviser in the late 1880s, and he would remain closely involved in Egyptian affairs over the next three decades. As he went on to explain, Egypt would serve as the testing ground "not of economic doctrines only, but of the deeper laws, which connect economics with politics and with morality."[108] It was in their working conception of these "deeper laws" that the British in Egypt departed in subtle but significant ways from the views of their liberal predecessors. Like Mill, they did often describe the connection of "economics with politics" in terms of a historical progression. Ironically, their favored metaphor for doing so was the very one that would gain the Marxist tradition its reputation for economism. British rule would need to shore up the "foundation" of economic development before it could "pass on to more attractive and imposing superstructure."[109] But whereas the Utilitarians of an earlier generation had sought to hasten that progression through a sweeping program of reforms, the officials at the helm of occupation shared Maine's skepticism about the prospects for movement in that direction. Far from proposing to mold a population of self-governing subjects in the image of an abstract, liberal ideal, they expressed doubt about where such a governmental project might lead. The "transformation of national character," Cromer warned, "must necessarily be a slow process."[110] He opposed unreservedly the notion that Egypt's peasant majority would ever be prepared for representative self-government, and from the mid-1890s onward, the occupation moved to shut down existing avenues of popular political participation. Convinced that the gravest threats to stability and prosperity resided in the latent "fanaticism" of Egypt's native population, the British likewise avoided interference with what they understood to be the traditional institutions of Islam.[111] On this understanding, the forms of popular discontent that had erupted in the 'Urabi revolt were evidence not of political consciousness but of unreasoning religious prejudice. And for a people narrowly oriented, by their nature, to material interests, the danger of such upheavals would recede as a direct function of the prosperity that the occupation could deliver. Economic development might remain a necessary precondition of self-rule. But in a country like Egypt, or so the British claimed, the achievement of the former would cause most demands for the latter to vanish.

NATIONALIST THOUGHT IN THE AGE OF IMPERIAL FINANCE

That Egypt became a proving ground for this racialized theory of the relationship between the economic and the political was overdetermined by the particular circumstances that culminated in the British occupation. The long-term economic effects of the occupation have made it all the easier to dismiss the content of British statements as so much self-serving verbiage. When read backwards, in terms of its outcomes, the era of the veiled protectorate can seem to represent a mere extension of prior trends of economic peripheralization and deepening inequality. The country grew and exported more cotton in 1914 than it did in 1882, and the wealthiest landowners possessed more of the country's surface in larger properties as the population of landless peasants continued to grow. But around the turn of the century, matters looked quite different. To contemporary observers both within Egypt and abroad, what stood out most were not the continuities with earlier decades of the nineteenth century but how very much seemed to be changing. As financial capital poured in from abroad, Egypt attained the global reputation of a model case for colonial development. In a moment when the British could and did claim that their policies had succeeded, ignoring the discourse of colonial economism was a luxury that the occupation's critics could not afford.

This was the conundrum that the young journalist Ahmad Hilmi named when he suggested that the British spoke as if money were coming out of their mouths. In its heyday, "gilded speech" placed the opponents of British rule in a double bind. It forced them to engage with the occupation on its own terms even as they argued that these were the wrong terms upon which to establish a political order. From the moment an organized opposition emerged in the 1890s, its members recognized and bemoaned the distinctiveness of a regime that reduced the role of government to economic development and alleged that Egyptians cared about little else. In response, they sought both to defend a range of alternative criteria for political legitimacy and to document evidence, in a wide array of media and genres, that the occupation's chosen indicators of material prosperity were a deceptive stand-in for the lived experiences of Egyptians under British rule. At the same time, they recognized the hazards of accepting the official measures of material prosperity at face value. From the late nineteenth century onwards, they analyzed the political-economic transformations that British policy had introduced with an eye toward substantiating more critical assessments of the occupation's vaunted achievements.

Neither the substance of this sustained critical engagement with colonial discourse nor the globe-spanning processes of capitalist transformation amidst which it took place has received much attention in existing histories of Egyptian nationalism. Among the various consequences of the continuity narratives mentioned above has been the relegation of political economy to the "background" sections of works that cover the occupation era. If the fundamental coordinates of "the cotton economy" underwent no significant change throughout this period, there could be little reason to investigate any kind of relationship, whether deterministic or otherwise, between processes of capital accumulation and the dynamic vibrancy of Egyptian thought and culture.[112]

This notion of a qualitatively static economic history has only been reinforced by a more general trend in approaches to the study of nationalism. Since the publication of Benedict Anderson's *Imagined Communities*, many works on the topic have accepted, at least implicitly, his assertion that "unlike most other isms, nationalism has never produced its own grand thinkers."[113] Following this line of argument, scholars of modern Egypt have offered important insights about how diverse discourses of nationalism served to reconfigure collective identities,[114] gender norms,[115] class relations between town and country,[116] hierarchies of scientific knowledge production,[117] conceptions of selfhood and sexuality,[118] and everyday practices of engagement with the law.[119] They have likewise probed the role that mass media played in opening avenues for the creativity of vernacular culture and in organizing new kinds of popular politics.[120] But in approaching nationalism mainly as a discourse of individual and collective subject formation, these same works have left unchallenged Anderson's claims about "the philosophical poverty and even incoherence" of nationalism.[121] They have likewise tended to skirt questions about why growing numbers of Egyptians came to see the political form of the nation as a compelling object of their aspirations or about what they believed the establishment of national institutions would accomplish.[122]

There was never only one answer to those questions. In Egypt, as in much of the colonial world at the time, the promise of nationalism captured a spectrum of hopes and ideals so broad as to point sometimes in opposing directions.[123] Moreover, not all Egyptians saw reason to oppose British rule, and among the growing numbers who did, not all of them saw nationalism as the most appealing alternative.[124] It is nevertheless the case that by the end of the first decade of the twentieth century, nationalism in Egypt was beginning to assume the character of a popular movement capable of mobilizing its constituencies through a quickening schedule of rallies, marches, demonstrations, and strikes. By the spring of 1910, the British were sufficiently alarmed by the prospect of a mass revolt that they staged a dramatic crackdown. To the extent that they register at all in histories of this period, these developments have sometimes been explained as the political effects of underlying economic causes.[125] In this version of things, the crisis of 1907 brought about a range of material grievances that found their expression in political parties and unions that pledged their support for national independence. As I argue at some length in the latter half of this book, the financial turmoil of these years did mark a turning point in the history of the occupation, and the reverberations of the crisis were particularly devastating for Egypt's poorer classes. But reading the popular appeal of the nationalist movement as an index of economic hardship falls well short of capturing the creativity and complexity of the ideas that animated this moment of political effervescence. It also risks reproducing the economistic dismissal of Egyptian nationalism that saturates the colonial archive.

The advent of what contemporary reporting, in both Arabic and European papers, dubbed "the financial crisis" rearranged the terms of the mounting struggle over the occupation in several ways at once. Having leaned heavily on the promise of prosperity, the British were reluctant to acknowledge the extent of the downturn or move to counteract it. Once the problems became impossible to ignore, they interpreted the crisis not as evidence of their own missteps but as an indication that their optimistic assessments of Egyptians as economic actors had been misplaced. It was at this point that British officials began to draw more directly on the ethnographic conservatism of Henry Maine. For the occupation's critics, meanwhile, the significance of the crisis went well beyond the losses that vindicated their warnings about the fleeting nature of financial gains. Because the crises of 1907 were a worldwide phenomenon, their occurrence furnished an opportunity to compare Egypt's experience under British rule with those of other independent states whose governments had responded differently. Rather than the insular domains that official discourse held them to be, the crisis revealed that the economic and the political were necessarily connected. This nationalist critique of economism as such, moreover, resonated with a core premise of the labor militancy that began to occur with increased frequency in these years. Unlike the European trade unionists whose economism Lenin was lambasting at roughly the same time, the Egyptian workers and students who organized themselves into unions and went on strike linked their grievances directly to the political exclusions of imperial rule. They protested not simply for improved wages but for a collective role in determining their own conditions of life.

Even as the diverse manifestations of crisis added force to arguments that only a government controlled by Egyptians themselves would respond to their needs and desires, however, those same phenomena raised questions about the preconditions of independence itself. As many observers noted at the time, this crisis was a problem of an elusive and unsettling kind. While its proximate causes might be localized and specific parties blamed for failing to dampen its effects, its far-flung ramifications revealed patterns of social practice in which large numbers of Egyptians were themselves now deeply involved. Nationalist critics might attribute the tangling of credit relations, the acceleration of land transactions, or the spread of speculation in complicated financial instruments to specific policies the occupation had imposed. But those policies drew Egypt into a set of dependencies that had long since exceeded the particular institutions, colonial or otherwise, that first set them in motion.[126]

The result, more concretely, was that growing segments of the Egyptian public had come to depend on regular flows of foreign capital to sustain their everyday lives. So long as that remained the case, the independence Egyptians demanded could no longer be construed in narrowly political terms. In that apprehension lay a fundamental contradiction of Egyptian nationalism as it existed on the eve of World War I. The very social transformations that had made nationalism into a popular political project also gave new weight to arguments that the national public as a whole would need to conform to the dictates of national capital formation. In the 1890s, the founding figures of the Egyptian National Party railed against a project of colonial development that collapsed all of politics into a balance sheet of monetary profit and loss. Two decades later, emboldened by the devastation of a prolonged economic crisis, Egypt's foremost nationalist writers and strategists were no less committed to terminating British rule. But whereas once its opponents had sought to establish the autonomy of the political against the occupation's economistic pretensions, they now insisted that the economic and the political were intimately intertwined. The chapters that follow tell the story of how that intertwining came to be.

Chapter 1

INFRASTRUCTURES OF OCCUPATION

TODAY, the Arabic term *istiʿmar* is the standard translation for "colonialism." That usage was already extant a century ago. But at the time, the word still retained another meaning. Given its overwhelmingly negative connotations in the present, instances of the older usage can be jarring. In 1900, for example, a short biography of Mahmud Sabri Pasha, then governor (*mudir*) of Manufiyah province, praised the seasoned administrator for "his noble inclination toward *istiʿmar*."[1] By this turn of phrase, the author ʿAbd al-Latif Shukri al-Iskandari was not implying that Sabri Pasha was a British flunky. Here *istiʿmar* instead meant something more akin to "infrastructural development," a process of building out provincial territory with roads, railways, canals, and schools.[2]

There is little suggestion in the text that the double entendre was deliberate. The very content of al-Iskandari's biographical sketch, however, evokes a tension between these two meanings of *istiʿmar* that posed a fundamental problem for the occupation at its inception. Sabri Pasha's career in government service was testament to a history of Egyptian state-building that long predated the arrival of British troops in 1882. In justifying their continued presence, the British could not, therefore, claim to be introducing the institutions and infrastructures of modern government where none had existed before. Under these circumstances, as the French historian Jacques Berque once put it, "imperialism lacked that which elsewhere guaranteed its sway: a monopoly of technical and cultural innovation. This had been under way in Egypt for the past half-century. The basic insecurity resulting from this was reflected in manifold political difficulties."[3]

The earliest articulations of colonial economism as the common sense of Egypt's new British "advisers" were closely bound up with efforts to address those difficulties in both thought and practice. If what Cromer called "the machinery of government" was already up and running, then something else would need to distinguish the occupation from the putative despotism it promised to rectify. From the moment British officials began to formulate plans for the country's future in the autumn of 1882, their responses to that dilemma turned upon a series of assertions about how Egyptians perceived and responded to their material interests. On the one hand, the British interpreted the catastrophic insolvency of the khedivate as evidence that Egypt's ruling classes had drained the coffers of the state for their own ends. The "machinery," such as it was, had been misassembled and operated to advance private gain at public expense.[4] On the other, it was the orientation of Egypt's peasant majority toward their own self-interest that would allow the occupation to succeed as both a program of fiscal rehabilitation and a system of rule. Ignorant of the abstract concepts and ideals that animated political theory in Europe, the fallahin would recognize Britain's "reforms" as a break with the past through the immediate experience of their own material conditions. Well beyond the mandate to enforce Egypt's foreign debt obligations, the measures of economic improvement would thus mark out the distance between the isti'mar of khedivial statecraft and the isti'mar of Britain's "veiled protectorate."

Explicit in even the most preliminary formulations of this governing agenda was a particular class analysis of Egyptian society. But the class that the British identified as their primary constituency was not the one most accounts of the period have named. Since at least the 1950s, histories of the occupation have often suggested that British officials aimed to cultivate the support of Egypt's large landlords as the willing intermediaries of colonial exploitation. The claim that foreign powers "occupied the country, assisted by these traitors" loomed especially large in the state propaganda that Gamal Abdel Nasser's government produced to accompany its land reforms.[5] But it also became an animating thesis for the influential corpus of agrarian social histories produced in subsequent decades.[6] In a compact distillation of this argument, Roger Owen once observed that "the major beneficiaries of British policies were the large landowners who saw a huge increase in the value of their properties, in their ability to borrow money and in their incomes after 1882. Here, if anywhere, was the alliance which safeguarded imperial interests in the countryside."[7]

Owen and others were certainly correct that the class of landowners who controlled the largest holdings, those of fifty *feddans* or more, owned more of Egypt's cultivable land in larger properties in 1914 than they did in 1882.[8] In this respect, they were "the major beneficiaries" of British rule. Later chapters of this book explore in considerable detail both the social processes and the specific measures enacted by the British that contributed to that intensification of rural inequality. But the assertion that the occupation from the outset pursued an alliance of convenience with the landed elite reads those outcomes backwards as evidence of a deliberate strategy. The notion that British officials sought to bolster the dominance of the large landholding class moreover stands at odds with a sizable archive of sources in which they claimed to be doing just the opposite. With remarkable consistency, it was the peasant smallholder that the British held out as the worthy beneficiary of their policies. Key features of the occupation's agrarian development agenda in its early years were specifically crafted around a conception of the smallholder as an industrious individual strongly motivated by the narrow pursuit of economic gain. When the British mentioned the large landowners, they were most likely to condemn them as the social stratum responsible for the disasters of the 1870s and the main obstacle to Egypt's recovery.

That histories of the occupation have generally ignored this line of commentary on the smallholder or dismissed it as mere falsehood is probably best explained as an instance of a more widespread misconception of the smallholding as a last redoubt of normative virtue and resistance to agrarian capitalism.[9] Colonial administrators in many parts of the worldwide "empire of cotton" would have likely found that association confusing.[10] For many of them, the small family farm, with its heavy reliance on the uncompensated labor of women and children, seemed entirely compatible with the cultivation of cheap agricultural commodities to supply metropolitan industry.[11] Indeed, John Stuart Mill devoted two full chapters of his *Principles of Political Economy* to a thoroughgoing defense of "peasant proprietors." He concluded that "no other existing state of agricultural economy has so beneficial an effect on the industry, the intelligence, the frugality, and prudence of the population, nor tends on the whole so much to discourage an improvident increase in their numbers."[12] There was nothing inherently more altruistic or less exploitative, in other words, about an agrarian policy that sought to promote cash-crop cultivation on small properties rather than on or alongside large estates. In Egypt as well, British officials regularly championed the peasant smallholding as a viable site for the realization of foreign capital's interests, whether in the form of raw cotton or debt repayment.[13]

When the British invoked the fallah, it was most often to the owner of a small family farm that they were referring. That reduction of "peasant" into the figure of the adult male smallholder obscured large swaths of rural society. Perhaps most obviously, it rendered women and the labor they performed invisible.[14] It also meant that, for several decades at least, the Egyptian government remained largely agnostic to the sizable and growing populations who worked the land as tenants, sharecroppers, or day laborers. To the extent that the British aimed to address the condition of smallholders, they moreover did so within decidedly narrow bounds. They did not contemplate measures that might actively redistribute land or rectify the histories of violence and dispossession by which many larger properties had been acquired.

It was nevertheless this particular figure of the fallah who became the target of the occupation's most consequential agrarian policies throughout its first decade. The repair and expansion of irrigation infrastructures, the suppression of state labor conscription through the corvée, and the standardization of property rights all took as their object the smallholding farm as a repository of untapped productivity. In each case, the engineers of these policies held that a peasant subject closely attuned to material gain would seize upon these changes to deliver the economic growth and political stability that the occupation proclaimed as the rightful ends of good government.

BUILDING TOWARD BANKRUPTCY

The khedivate, as the British found it in 1882, was the product of an ambitious project of state-building that had been taking place since the turn of the previous century. Following the Anglo-Ottoman campaign in 1801, Egypt was ruled by the man who had served as deputy commander of the forces sent by Istanbul to expel Napoleon's army from this vital Ottoman province. In an effort to secure an autonomous dynasty for himself and his heirs, Mehmed Ali Pasha established a novel military-fiscal regime.[15] He built a disciplined conscript army and waged a series of campaigns that ultimately won him the concessions he desired from the Ottoman sultan. To fund this war-making enterprise and the attendant expansion of the government's bureaucracy, the Pasha mobilized the growing coercive powers of the state and compelled peasants across the Nile Delta to begin farming cotton for sale on the world market.[16] That decision would prove immensely consequential in at least two respects. First, it meant that Egypt's new regime sought greater room for maneuver within the Ottoman Empire by actively cultivating closer ties to Britain.[17] Second, it entailed a significant shift in the objectives of the labor that peasants performed. In the past, Istanbul's main interest in Egypt's grain crops lay in their utility as food. By contrast, the purpose of growing cotton was to exchange it for money that could then be used to cover an infinite variety of expenses.

From the outset, turning cotton into increased state revenue entailed a number of other changes that would hold lasting importance both for the reordering of social relations within Egypt and for the country's gradual subordination within the capitalist world economy. Although the choice to cultivate cotton may have been voluntary from the vantage of Egypt's ambitious rulers, the same was hardly true for those who actually worked the new crop. To force this labor-intensive fiber on an unwilling peasantry and to implement a more efficient system of revenue extraction, the ambitious Pasha required a loyal power base of local agents. He gathered support by making land grants to his own extended family and to the existing rural notability, who together constituted an emerging class of large landowners.[18] The new cotton crop also demanded a wholesale reconfiguration of rural landscapes, from the construction of new dams, canals, and railways to the installation of steam-powered irrigation pumps and cotton gins.[19] Mehmed Ali and his heirs managed to offset the enormous costs of this environmental transformation by intensifying the state's reliance on the corvée. Through this annual tax upon labor time, the government conscripted hundreds of thousands of peasants each year to build and maintain public works for free.

Throughout Mehmed Ali's reign, these methods of appropriating labor and revenue allowed the government to cover its expenditures without making recourse to foreign debt.[20] Yet as the scope of his heirs' engineering feats grew, the capital expenses of these monumental projects outstripped the government's available resources.[21] To meet the shortfall, Egypt's rulers turned to the banking houses of Europe. As it turned out, their new willingness to borrow coincided with a new eagerness to lend. In a prelude to the more dramatic financial expansion that would occur at the century's end, the European economic crisis of 1847–48 had spurred a search for profitable new outlets toward which growing pools of unemployed surplus capital might flow. The outcome was an unprecedented proliferation of debt-financed infrastructures and built environments not only within Europe but across much of the globe. Most famously, this novel "spatial fix" to the crisis of the mid-century provided the basis for Baron Haussmann's authoritarian reconstruction of modern Paris.[22] But Haussmannization was neither exclusively Parisian nor even exclusively French. Aided in many cases by the lopsided political arrangements of empire, European banks facilitated a massive reinvestment abroad that, in turn, served to bind distant regions into a single, if highly uneven, global space of intensified commodity production and exchange.[23]

Mehmed Ali's successors seized upon the ready availability of foreign credit and thereby inaugurated the cycle of borrowing that reached its climax in the reign of Isma'il, who assumed power in 1863. At the time, the global shortage of cotton due to the American Civil War had created a windfall for other cotton-producing countries like Egypt.[24] To enhance his dynasty's autonomy from the Ottoman sultan through the purchase of the new title khedive (vice-regent) and to finance a range of major projects including the completion of the Suez Canal and the construction of downtown Cairo (hailed as a "Paris on the Nile"), Isma'il borrowed lavishly from banks in London and Paris against the inflated revenues of the cotton market.[25] When the war ended and cotton prices fell, his government faced a serious fiscal shortfall.

Despite drastic attempts to squeeze ever more tax revenue from its rural subjects, by 1876 Isma'il's government had defaulted on its loans.[26] With the backing of their respective governments, Egypt's European creditors imposed harsh austerity measures under the auspices of a new Caisse de la Dette Publique (Commission of the Public Debt). The distributed burden of the debt fueled widespread unrest which culminated in the revolt led by the military officer Ahmad 'Urabi Pasha.[27] Fearing that Egypt would not pay if the revolt succeeded, Britain intervened and quashed it.[28]

THE BANKRUPTCIES OF ORIENTAL DESPOTISM

In the immediate aftermath of the invasion, Egypt's future status became the topic of vigorous debate in London. Domestic political conflicts, concerns over the escalation of imperial rivalries, and disagreements about the underlying causes of the uprising all contributed to uncertainty about how long the occupation should last and what role it should play. At the end of October 1882, the British Cabinet sent a mission under the Earl of Dufferin, then serving as ambassador in Istanbul, to develop a proposal for Britain's best course of action.[29] After three months of tours and interviews, Dufferin submitted his "General Report" to the British Foreign Office.[30]

Carefully crafted to navigate the political hazards of the moment, the report offered an ambiguous answer to the looming question of the occupation's duration.[31] The opening passages foresaw a system of rule that "ought not to differ in any great degree from those which have been found advantageous in other countries, namely, national independence and constitutional government."[32] Dufferin judged that even the Egyptian peasant had "shown himself not only equal to the discharge of some of those functions of which none but the members of the most civilized communities were thought capable, but unexpectedly appreciative of his legitimate political interests and moral rights."[33] On this basis, he had overseen the drafting of a new Organic Law that would mark "a far more bold and generous move in the direction of self-government than anything the most revolutionary Indian statesman has hitherto dared to suggest for that country."[34] Dufferin's proposal would be ratified as a khedivial decree several months later.[35] The new Organic Law of May 1883 established a Provincial Council for each *mudiriyah* (province) comprising representatives from the villages, a consultative Council of Legislation containing both elected members and government appointees, and a larger elected General Assembly that would likewise offer nonbinding opinions on new laws but also enjoy an absolute right of veto over any new taxes.

As Dufferin explained their design in the opening sections of the report, these new institutions would help to prepare a return to Egyptian self-rule. But as he moved on to his account of current conditions, he offered the caveat that the country was not "ripe for pure popular government."[36] Devising a program of reform to address the immediate problems of an indefinite interim would require a frank and systematic analysis of the circumstances that had "compelled us to enter Egypt single-handed."[37]

Each subsequent section of the report etched deeper the contrast between a long and bleak history of "despotism" and the new age of "justice" that Britain would inaugurate. So grave and extensive was the "accumulation of difficulties," he determined, that "native statesmanship, even though supplemented by the new-born institutions, will hardly be able to cope, unless assisted for a time by our sympathy and guidance."[38]

For Dufferin, bankruptcy was the logical and inevitable outcome of Oriental despotism. While noting that the khedivate's debts had translated into a mounting demand for tax revenue, he refrained from suggesting that European lenders might bear some responsibility for Egypt's current predicament.[39] Instead, he presented Egypt's agrarian order as a systematic and disastrous violation of utilitarian principles. At every turn, the khedives and their retainers had enriched themselves to the detriment of the public good. Not only had these practices contributed to untold human suffering and fueled popular outrage. They had also thwarted Egypt's immense productive potential. "The aggregation of land in large farms is not suitable to Egypt except where the sugarcane is cultivated," he explained, "whereas 'la petite culture' is eminently adapted to soil and climate."[40] Far from endorsing an alliance of convenience with the large landholding class, Dufferin cast them as the foremost impediment to both political reform and economic revival. He went on to enumerate the wasteful exactions of "the rich landed proprietors, the owners of pumps, the regulators of the 'corvée,' and every one who makes money out of the present discreditable state of affairs."[41]

Dealing in turn with the issues of agricultural labor, control and distribution of water, revenue assessment, and access to credit, Dufferin built his case that the interests of a privileged few had undermined the rightful prosperity of the many. The use of corvée for vital public works "not only inflicts the greatest hardship on the peasantry, but obtains a minimum of result for a maximum of effort."[42] To make matters worse, Egypt's ruling classes often diverted conscript labor to work their own estates. The irrigation system, in similar fashion, served as the lynchpin of class power in the countryside. "There are perhaps more abuses in the distribution of water," Dufferin mused, "than in any other branch of the irrigation service."[43] Rich proprietors exercised disproportionate influence over the government's engineers. The widespread use of pumping stations and mobile steam engines to manage the movement of water was, moreover, a symptom of deficient engineering, a parasitic drain on the state's finances, and a dangerous enticement to the wrongful monopolization of the Nile's waters.[44]

While Egypt's wealthy proprietors hampered agricultural production by misappropriating labor and water alike, they also bore the lightest burden of the state's fiscal demands. Observing that the "cruel and illegal exactions perpetrated by former Governments" had translated into alarming rates of rural indebtedness, Dufferin questioned "the degree to which the assessment of the land tax, representing an annuity of about £E 5,000,000, may be considered as compatible with the well-being of the cultivators."[45] A more just allocation of taxes would depend upon a careful assessment of each property, but to date no such "scientific discrimination of the relative value of land" had taken place. Instead, the wealthy and the powerful often enjoyed preferential rates granted long ago by the khedives. As a result, "the inequalities of assessment are glaring, and the dissatisfaction of those who pay the higher ratings is proportionate. The decreasing fertility of the soil, from over-cropping, and from the growing scarcity of the water supply, is rapidly reducing the value of land, on which the assessment, though originally fairly applotted, is now unduly onerous."[46]

Finally, among the most worrisome consequences of these inequities was the rising indebtedness of the fallahin. In an early instance of the comparison that would characterize debates about agricultural credit in both countries for decades to come, Dufferin opined that "a similar problem confronts us in India." In both cases, the existing legal systems had once afforded rural moneylenders with only limited recourse against delinquent debtors. The advent of European legal codes had "on the one hand, stimulated the [peasant's] borrowing instincts by constituting his holding a legal security, and on the other they . . . armed the mortgagee with far too ready and extensive powers of selling up the encumbered owner."[47] In Egypt, during the debt negotiations of 1876, the European powers had secured the creation of a new system of Mixed Courts, which employed a modified Napoleonic code and held jurisdiction over all cases involving parties of differing nationalities. Registered debts at the Mixed Courts had mushroomed by more than a factor of ten in just a few years. If nothing was done to arrest this process, the outcome would be the steady dispossession of the peasantry. "Such an operation," Dufferin warned, "could scarcely take place without producing an agrarian crisis, which would prove equally disastrous to the creditors, the debtors, and the Government."[48]

Altogether, Britain's emissary provided a narrative of Egypt's recent history in which the moral, political, and economic failures of the old regime were tightly intertwined. By this line of reasoning, rooting out the "injustice," "corruption," and "abuse" he had witnessed would quickly restore conditions for steady repayment of the debt and the overall advancement of agrarian prosperity. Yet for all the confidence with which he delivered his findings, Dufferin concluded his report with two crucial qualifications that would leave his successors wide room for maneuver. First, he cautioned that a "great part of what we are about to inaugurate will be of necessity tentative and experimental."[49] In both the near and long term, that understanding of the occupation as a laboratory would help to accommodate what might otherwise appear as glaring disagreements between the statements and policies of other British officials. Second, having opened with the promise of "national independence and constitutional government," Dufferin closed by leaving that moment of arrival uncertain. If the new administrative system was to succeed, it "must have time to consolidate, in order to resist disintegrating influences from within and without."[50] Far from resolving the question of its duration, the report conferred upon the occupation the sole discretion of judging Egypt's eventual readiness for self-rule.

SILK PURSE AND SOW'S EAR

Officially, this plan for Egypt's reorganization was to serve as Cromer's guide when he became Britain's agent and consul-general on September 11, 1883. During the early phases of Egypt's debt negotiations, Cromer had worked as the British member of the Anglo-French "Dual Control." After returning to India to serve as finance member of Lord Ripon's government in 1880, Cromer had remained in regular contact with Lord Gladstone's cabinet about Egyptian affairs.[51] In many ways, the broadly utilitarian logic of Dufferin's report aligned closely with the new consul-general's views. But although Cromer only made the disagreement explicit much later, his own assessment of Egyptian society differed in at least two crucial respects from the positions Dufferin had outlined.

First, Cromer entertained none of Dufferin's curiosity about the Egyptian peasant's capacity to recognize and act upon his "legitimate political interests." The "General Report" had alighted, in particular, upon the institution of the village election as evidence for the viability of representative government in Egypt. Dufferin had thus suggested that in "seeking for the roots," the British might employ village elections as an authentic native form out of which parliamentary government might one day grow.[52] Attacking this very idea, Cromer would later contend that "whether we deal with the roots, or the trunk, or the branches, or the leaves, free institutions in the full sense of the term must for generations to come be wholly unsuitable to countries such as India and Egypt. If the use of a metaphor, though of a less polished type, be allowed, it may be said that it will probably never be possible to make a Western silk purse out of an Eastern sow's ear."[53] In his approach to political institutions, Cromer was consistent and unequivocal about the error of applying liberal theories of popular self-government to "subject races" like the Egyptians.

The consul-general's second major disagreement with Dufferin, however, seemed to invert their positions on the spectrum of British political opinions. On questions of political economy, the "General Report" placed Dufferin somewhat closer to the conservative thinkers whose ideas were, in those same years, gaining ground in the colonial administration of British India. He did describe several possible mechanisms for improving access to agricultural credit. But in asserting that the peasant, "like a child," did not possess a fully-formed apparatus of economic calculation, Dufferin also recommended that the government should implement legal protections to "throw difficulties in the way of the fellah's outrageous habits of borrowing."[54] Regarding such "palliatives," Cromer later responded that "many of them sin against economic law, which provides that legislation intended to protect a man against the consequences of improvidence is generally unproductive of result." Steadfast adherence to the dictates of classical political economy might "have its victims, amongst whom are to some extent inevitably numbered those who do not recognize the paramount necessities of the Budget system."[55] But in Egypt, as in England, silk purse and sow's ear would need to exchange freely at their market value. As Cromer would soon make clear, he believed that the solution lay not in insulating peasant farms from the circulation of capital but in promoting forms of investment that would link the Egyptian countryside more directly into global capital markets.[56]

It was this pairing of a deep pessimism about popular self-government with a firm commitment to classical political economy that caused Cromer, on occasion, to dub himself an "Oriental liberal."[57] Both positions were rooted fundamentally in his conception of the Egyptian peasant as a racially distinctive human subject. Later on, these points of divergence from Dufferin's thinking would form the basis of two of the occupation's most distinctive and consequential policies: the abolition of village elections in 1895 and the establishment of the Agricultural Bank of Egypt in 1902.[58] But these disagreements were more a matter of degree than of kind. Dufferin, too, presupposed a world of distinct races endowed with unequal capabilities;

he simply judged the particular character of the Egyptian peasant differently. And although the "General Report" may have described an alternative trajectory for the occupation in the long term, its approach to the present problems confronting the country accorded closely with Cromer's own theory of "material interests" as the basis of imperial rule.

ENGINEERING AGAINST DESPOTISM

In the near term, the foremost challenge for the occupation was to stabilize payments on Egypt's foreign debt without exacerbating an already onerous system of revenue extraction. On one side of the ledger, this fiscal agenda entailed slashing government expenses that the British deemed superfluous. Most controversially, Cromer made sweeping cuts to the Ministry of Public Instruction and thereby gave rise to one of the most pronounced and lasting grievances of his Egyptian critics.[59] On its own, however, this winnowing of public projects and services would be insufficient to win what the occupation's foremost propagandist, Alfred Milner, called the "race against bankruptcy."[60] Dufferin had already suggested that the real solution would lie in raising agricultural productivity and thereby boosting government revenue. On that basis, he had recommended that the Indian government send "a thoroughly competent engineer with large experience of irrigation works." The first of these Anglo-Indian engineers, Colin Scott-Moncrieff, took up the post of undersecretary of state for Public Works shortly prior to Cromer's arrival.[61]

In assuming control of the Ministry of Public Works (*nizarat al-ashghal al-ʿumumiyah*), Scott-Moncrieff and the other Anglo-Indian engineers who soon followed could make no plausible claim to be introducing modern technologies from scratch. Complex hydraulic systems had been a core feature of the Ottoman imperial administration for generations.[62] Since the early nineteenth century, Mehmed Ali and his successors had overseen a dramatic multiplication of irrigation and transport infrastructures. These technical endeavors had transformed the Nile Delta into a densely engineered environment furnished with the perennial irrigation necessary for intensive cotton cultivation.[63] They had also entailed the training and employment of the bureaucrats and civil servants who filled the ministry's ranks and who were, unsurprisingly, reluctant to countenance British claims about an absence of Egyptian expertise.[64] Compounding the challenges posed to the British engineers by this prior history of developmentalism was the fiscal stringency of the government they had been hired to oversee. According to the arrangements negotiated in 1876, the Caisse de la Dette Publique—comprising representatives of Austria-Hungary, Italy, France, and Britain—not only laid claim to roughly half of the annual revenues but enjoyed veto power over changes to the government's operating budget.[65] The Caisse was understandably reluctant to authorize more borrowing.

In time, these situational constraints would themselves be adduced to support the occupation's utilitarian claims about the necessity and benevolence of British rule. The "machinery of government," as the argument went, was only so good as the hand that operated it. The khedivate may have appropriated the trappings of modern bureaucracy and purchased the instruments of modern technology, but the results spoke for themselves. Endowed with an immense natural bounty, Egypt's ruling class had lined their own pockets while driving those who tilled the soil into penury. Working with far more limited resources, by contrast, the Anglo-Indian engineers would now bestow prosperity on the country as a whole.

At the center of this narrative, throughout the 1880s, was the project to repair and improve the Delta Barrage, a massive dam spanning the two branches of the Nile where they fork, just north of Cairo. Originally designed in 1843, the Barrage was completed two decades later. Cracks had formed in the foundation during its first year of use, and in 1867, a large section over the western (Rosetta) branch had sheared off and shifted downstream.[66] Given the increasingly disadvantageous terms on which it was borrowing by the 1870s, Isma'il's government had decided to forego the estimated £E 1 million cost of repairs in favor of annualized pumping contracts.[67] When they arrived, Scott-Moncrieff and William Willcocks—another irrigation officer he had recruited from India—made their own case that the Barrage could be repaired and generate substantial savings. On the basis of their preliminary research, Cromer was able in 1885 to negotiate a new loan in Britain for £1 million, on far better terms than those available to the khedivate a decade prior.[68] Over the next five years, as the reconstruction proceeded, Willcocks and Scott-Moncrieff employed the Barrage in a limited fashion to store and release water, and they built a series of temporary dams and weirs to manage distribution within the Delta.[69]

As the irrigation officers sometimes admitted, this work was less an application of established scientific expertise than a haphazard process of tinkering with complex systems they did not fully understand. There were plenty of missteps. To prevent the infiltration of salt water into the northernmost part of the Delta in 1885, the engineer E.W.P. Foster constructed an earthen dam near the town of Mahallat al-Amir; the dam had left the city of Rashid (Rosetta) without drinking water, so tanks had to be sent daily from Alexandria by train.[70] In the dry summer of 1886, William Willcocks shut the supply of water to the Delta canals for the better part of two weeks. That decision proved "fatal to the rice crops, the interest of which it was necessary to sacrifice in order to keep the cotton alive."[71] That same year, an attempt to flush accumulated silt and mud from a major canal feeding the western Delta had caused its banks to collapse and block the channel altogether.[72]

Disastrous as these incidents may have been for specific localities, however, Scott-Moncrieff and his staff employed a form of cost-benefit analysis that refigured each mishap as a difficult choice undertaken in service of the greater good. This emphasis on aggregate improvement was fully on display in Cromer's *Report on the Administration and Condition of Egypt and the Progress of Reforms* for 1890, the first such publication in which the consul-general could proclaim that "the accounts of the Egyptian Treasury, which were formerly in a state of the utmost confusion, are now in perfect order."[73] The numbers seemed to speak for themselves. The monetary gain to the country as a whole had already outstripped the capital expended on irrigation repairs and "placed the people of Egypt in a far better position than heretofore to support the fiscal burthens imposed on them."[74] Like the engineers themselves, Cromer here relied on a particular statistical proxy for the conditions he described. Though Isma'il's government had created a Statistical Department in 1873, the British had cut its funding, and the government would not generate comprehensive statistics again until the mid-1890s.[75] In the absence of alternatives, the British charted progress in *kantars* of cotton.[76] "The 'barrage' has not much increased the area of cultivation," the consul-general conceded, "but it has very largely increased that of land bearing double crops, that is to say, the area producing cotton."[77] The annual yield over the past five years had risen by an average of 15,000 tons for an increased export value of £E 835,000 per year.[78] As Scott-Moncrieff's own reports indicated, this expansion of the cotton harvest had sometimes come at the expense of other crops.[79] Promoting Egypt's most valuable export also meant that the irrigation department tended to privilege the northern parts of the country where cotton was grown.[80] Yet by emphasizing that the overall area of cultivation had not changed, Cromer continued to build the case that rising yields were the consequence of technocratic equanimity: "In former times very great abuses occurred in connection with this subject. The water is now distributed on just and scientific principles."[81]

In the vision of the irrigation engineers, a judicious elaboration of public works would produce an agrarian landscape nourished by steady and even flows: of water, goods, credit, law, and knowledge. The despotism that others reviled in the abstract they saw inscribed in the physical features of rural space. By arranging the infrastructures they designed to promote even distributions, the officials in the Ministry of Public Works promised to unleash the productivity that the khedivial regime had squandered. As the impartial arbiters of public utility, they would counteract the hoarding of privileges that had assumed material form in the stark unevenness of the countryside.[82]

Alongside the quantification of fiscal recovery, anecdotal reporting frequently presented these productive improvements as the consequence of a change at the level of individual properties. If well-regulated infrastructures would ensure that each region received the water it required, centralized control over the release and allocation of that supply would simultaneously mitigate the class inequality between pashas and peasants. In a "Report on the Condition of the Agricultural Population in Egypt" that he wrote for Cromer's submission to Parliament in 1888, Frederick S. Clarke emphasized that "the small owners of land are all loud in their praises of the Irrigation Department, and of the justice and efficiency displayed by the officials in the supply and distribution of water."[83] By this rendering, the Irrigation Department was at once fiscally remunerative and politically effective. It was in "the improvement of the irrigation and the just distribution of water" that Egypt's rural population would recognize the contrast between "British justice" and "Oriental despotism."[84] Inflating Clarke's pronouncements two years later, another British official reported, "The fellaheen are not so stupid as not to know that these and many other things have been done by the English and that they would not have been done had the English not come into the country."[85]

In both their internal correspondence and their official publications, the irrigation engineers hinted at times that their control never reached quite so far as these hagiographic proclamations might suggest. The release of water into this or that channel was only ever part of the story. Wealthy landowners commonly possessed superior mechanical pumps that allowed them to draw more water from the canals. The ministry made several attempts to encourage registration of unlicensed machines and to ban the use of pumps during periods of low supply.[86] But swayed by warnings that removing illegal pumps en masse might threaten the summer cotton crop, the Irrigation Department took a lenient approach to enforcement.[87] And even when they were carried out, the punishments for violating the government's water rotation schedules were insufficient to deter the owners of larger estates.[88]

If the Irrigation Department's regulatory control had its limits, though, it conformed, in two key respects, with the occupation's overall conception of its mission in these early years. First, the oblique arrangements of ministerial advice provided a ready-made explanation for each deviation from some more ambitious goal. Distribution could only be so just when the engineers needed to rely on the whims of others to implement their designs. Second, colonial economism was a discourse of relative improvements not absolute ideals. The British public might judge the occupation's accomplishments against their own notions of freedom, justice, or equality, but Egypt's peasants would assess imperial rule according to an unmediated intuition of self-interest. The abstract principles that British officials sometimes mentioned in support of their policies would, on this understanding, acquire meaning for the fallah only insofar as they named a concrete experience of material change. And so long as that change registered as improvement, the consequence of British efforts would be the growing acquiescence of Egypt's rural majority. This was the conclusion that E.W.P Foster drew about the peasantry from his "four years' constant intercourse with them." Foster observed that "the word 'liberty' is travelling fast. To the initiated it means that Pashas can no longer force them to labour in their fields without payment, that they get their fair share of water, that their complaints receive equal attention, and that they are not called on to pay more than their legal taxes."[89]

CORVÉE ABOLITION REVISITED

As Foster explained "the effect of English control," peasants would apprehend "liberty" through practical experience rather than by reference to an abstract ideal.[90] Its appeal would extend only so far as it conformed to the rural population's apprehensions of their own self-interest. The economistic subjects comprising this agrarian society, in other words, would embrace their newfound freedom as a means, not an end in itself. And for no issue did this distinction prove more significant than the abolition of the corvée. As the political scientist Nathan Brown argued several decades ago, the claim that Britain abolished the corvée is doubly misleading: first, because efforts to end the state's reliance on forced labor began well before 1882, at the impetus of Egyptian officials and landowners themselves, and second, because the corvée was not entirely abandoned even after it had been outlawed.[91] Brown's revision, however, differs less from the occupation's own account of what transpired than from subsequent scholarly interpretations of it.[92] British officials readily acknowledged that efforts to suppress the corvée predated their arrival. They also made little effort to deny the persistence of labor conscription after the proclaimed abolition of corvée. Instead, they once again insisted that peasants would recognize the benefits of British rule not through the application of "liberal ideology"—about which they held no preconceptions—but through a realization of their own economic interests.[93]

For the British, the corvée exemplified the worst failings of the old regime. In his detailed *Note sur la Corvée en Égypte*, Scott-Moncrieff explained in 1886 that the spread of perennial irrigation had intensified the contradiction between the state's demand for conscripts and the farmer's need for labor on his own property. On the one hand, the new canals required massive annual outlays of labor for maintenance and cleaning. On the other, the introduction of cotton and sugar cultivation had "taught the peasant to know the value of his time; fields needed to be labored and weeded, and the rich farmers were willing to pay to have this work carried out."[94] The smallholder was no less able than the wealthy proprietor to see the state's demand for corvée as a deduction from his own earnings. But because the khedivate had deformed the machinery of government to serve the private interests of the few, it had allocated that burden in manifestly regressive ways. That the landed elite had originally raised their own objections to the corvée was unsurprising. But rather than reduce its overall reliance on forced labor, the khedivate had responded by granting selective exemptions. Under these arrangements, the wealthy and the powerful were not only allowed to retain labor on their own estates; they also found opportunities to appropriate the public work of the corvée for private gain. As F. S. Clarke explained in his 1888 report, "It was the consciousness of the injustice . . . that rendered it such a burden to the fellah. He well knew that his labour was required for the general benefit of the land; . . . but what was most galling was to see that the rich Pashas and his more influential neighbours were, through fear or bribery, enabled to evade the corvée service."[95]

Contrary to such blanket denunciations of incompetence and venality, Egyptian officials had articulated their own analogous concerns about the corvée prior to the British invasion. Writing in January of 1881, the Minister of Public Works ʿAli Pasha Mubarak deprecated the strain that the corvée placed on the rural population, "especially given the needs and requirements of agriculture." In an expression of his own technocratic optimism, he looked forward to a near future when the demand for labor might be "lifted from the people by building new works and employing various mechanical means to clear the canals." He suggested that a series of legislative "experiments [*tajarib*]" might soon "lead to a knowledge of what must be done." For Mubarak, the foremost civil engineer of the khedivate, the corvée would last only as long as it took to devise a practical alternative.[96]

Far from downplaying these earlier efforts, however, the British presented them as more evidence for the necessity of their own guidance. ʿAli Mubarak and his contemporaries might have recognized the potential of improved technology to replace so much wasted labor, the Anglo-Indian engineers argued. But they lacked the technical expertise to achieve that transformation.[97] As Cromer later put it, "Scientific knowledge could, in some degree, serve as a substitute for labour."[98] What's more, the urgency with which the Egyptian ministers now pressed their British advisers to help abolish the corvée was recruited to bolster several interrelated claims about the khedivate's catastrophic inability to adjudicate between public and private interest.

On this understanding, the notorious "three Cs"—corruption, "courbash [*kurbaj*]," and corvée—were not isolated features of khedivial despotism but interlocking parts of a destructive political-economic order.[99] It was only because they benefited from the corrupt system of exemptions that the landed elite supported the corvée. And it was only under the dreadful threat of the courbash—the hippopotamus-hide whip used for corporal punishment—that peasants were willing to subject themselves to conscription.[100] Foreign oversight of the Egyptian government had already begun to alter these arrangements. In September 1878, as part of the government's debt negotiations, a French representative, the Marquis de Blignières, was placed in charge of the Ministry of Public Works.[101] Employing a language of "equality" as justification for what amounted to a revenue-generating tactic, the new minister abolished exemptions from the corvée while introducing the option of a cash payment in lieu of service.[102] And in January 1883, shortly prior to the publication of his "General Report," Lord Dufferin had overseen the promulgation of a khedivial decree outlawing the use of the *kurbaj*.[103] That these moves to rectify two of the three Cs had rendered the third unsustainable was, according to the British, indicative of both the perils and the promise of Egyptian society. On the first count, the eagerness of the ruling class to abolish the corvée only once they lost their "corrupt" exemptions revealed an inability to separate private gain from public good. On the second, the reluctance of the peasantry to cede their labor without a threat of physical violence from the "courbash" exemplified an innate materialism that might be directed toward more positive ends.

The primary use of corvée at the time was for the annual cleaning of irrigation channels. Whereas the old methods of basin irrigation had spread the Nile's fertilizing silt across the country's fields, the canals used for perennial irrigation trapped that particulate matter as sediment. Unless it was somehow removed, the silt would restrict the flow of water. Adjustments to the design of the canals could help, but technical improvements could not eliminate the problem of canal clearance altogether. To address this residual need for labor, the British proposed a system of subcontracting. A competitive bidding process would keep costs low while also expanding the market for wage work in the countryside.[104] But replacing what amounted to a tax in labor with paid workers would require more money, and finding that money posed other troubles. Raising the land tax to cover the cost would seem to contradict the occupation's stated commitments to fiscal moderation.[105] And any changes to the budget would require approval from the Caisse de la Dette.

By the mid-1880s the French government recognized that the abolition of corvée had become a major priority for the occupation and that British administrators believed this achievement would secure the lasting approval of the peasantry.[106] In a testament to the inter-imperial rivalries that marked this opening phase of "the scramble for Africa," the French used their vote on the Caisse to obstruct British efforts. The result was a prolonged game of diplomatic chicken. When the British located funds in the budget to replace the corvée, the French leveraged their veto power to demand a variety of concessions.[107] The British retaliated by taking measures to publicly associate the continuation of the corvée with French intransigence.[108] These culminated in new legislation, backed by Prime Minister Riaz Pasha and authorized by the new General Assembly, to levy a surcharge on the land tax should the French refuse to release other monies.[109] Eventually, the French balked at the threat of this "French tax" and approved a temporary budget allocation for 1890.[110] After another two years of negotiations, the Egyptian government was able, on January 30, 1892, to issue a new decree affirming the suppression of the corvée.[111]

Despite the fanfare with which it was announced, however, this decree did not, in fact, eliminate the Egyptian government's reliance on labor conscription. In December 1891, Scott-Moncrieff clarified that "the corvée against which we all fought was the tremendous burden of cleaning out the canals and repairing the embankments." This invidious and unnecessary form of conscription, he explained, was distinct from the "Nile corvée," for which the government had summoned roughly 67,000 individuals the previous year to protect the riverbanks during the annual flood.[112] While this practice might seem inconsistent with his professed aversion to forced labor, the engineer sought to justify its continuation by referencing the peasant's own judgments about their interests. "They look on it, I think, as natural and fitting," he reported, "and for the present at least I am sure it would cause great uneasiness and would be most impolitic to commit this duty to contractors."[113]

In the coming years, British officials would continue to refine and adjust this line of argument. The employment of free labor, they explained, was not universally applicable and might, under certain circumstances, undermine the public good. William Garstin, the irrigation inspector who succeeded Scott-Moncrieff as undersecretary of state for Public Works, elaborated upon this distinction in a "Note on Payment of the Nile Corvée" that he wrote in May 1893. The variability of the Nile flood, he argued, meant that "no contractor would take this work at a rate insufficient to guarantee him against loss." The nature of the task was also such that the actions of individual contractors could cause damage well beyond their respective areas of responsibility. Like Scott-Moncrieff, Garstin suggested that "the feeling of insecurity throughout the country during a high flood, knowing that the Nile banks were being protected by means of contract labour, would be exceedingly great."[114]

The previous autumn, Arthur Hardinge, Cromer's deputy at the consulate, had reported that "the fellahin are less ignorant than is commonly supposed of public events, where these affect their interests.... Believing that every form of corvée had been absolutely abolished, the peasants claimed to be paid for their work, and the Mudirs and other authorities met with a good deal of difficulty in enforcing the provisions of the Flood Law of 1887."[115] On that basis, Garstin went on to recommend that the government should relieve "the hardship of forced labor" both by compensating the Nile guards for the materials they furnished and by paying them a wage that would not "give them profit" but nevertheless "enable them to live."[116]

If Garstin evinced little discomfort with the way this proposal might violate a pure ideal of free labor, it was because the wholesale implementation of that ideal was only ever, at most, a secondary concern. What Cromer would later refer to as "theoretical objections to forced labour, of which no one is more fully aware than myself" were always already grounded in a primary and undisguised calculus of economic interests.[117] The corvée, as it existed in 1882, was antithetical to the peasant's industrious pursuit of private gain and, consequently, an impediment to the productivity of the country as a whole. Removing that obstacle would, like the improvement of irrigation infrastructures, bring the material interests of Egyptian farmers into alignment with the requirements of their government's foreign creditors. But so long as the Nile flood remained unpredictable, the government must retain the power to compel and manage labor, and reluctant though they may have been to leave their fields, so the engineers claimed, the peasantry accepted that necessity. Under these particular conditions, what Garstin proposed as the goal of British reform was not the universalization of free labor but the compensation of labor, whether free or not. Once again, this divergence from a pure form of liberal ideology hinged upon a claim about the Egyptian peasant's intuitions of economic self-interest.

THE RULE OF LANDED PROPERTY

It was this very same premise that underpinned the last of the occupation's signature agrarian policies in its first decade. For many historians of modern Egypt, the Khedivial Decree of April 15, 1891, establishing full rights of proprietorship for all landowners has figured as a defining moment in the country's agrarian transformation under British rule.[118] In Gabriel Baer's *History of Landownership in Modern Egypt*, the decree represents the logical culmination of "the emergence of a market in land and the development of cash crops."[119] For a generation of critical social historians in Egypt, the standardization of property law was instrumental to Britain's larger objectives of expanding foreign land ownership and bolstering the power of a subservient landed elite.[120] More recently, Timothy Mitchell has narrated the consolidation of landed property under British rule as a sort of centennial reprise of the Permanent

Settlement of 1793 in Bengal. When explained as the colonial application of "principles true in every country," property law in Egypt becomes yet another instance of liberal universalism's role as an alibi for imperial expansion.[121]

On the wider implications of Egypt's emergent property regime, each of these histories offers important insights. The standardization of ownership rights was crucial to the acceleration of land transactions and the capitalization of agricultural production. The process of simplifying a complex array of relationships, rights, and obligations around land into a singular, globally recognizable form of property would indeed help to entice the investment of European capital.[122] And certainly, as Mitchell suggests, the abstraction of property law obscured, and thereby affirmed, the concrete and irreducibly particular acts of violence through which Egypt's large estates had been amassed. But each of these accounts deduces reasons for the 1891 law from its later consequences. All imply, albeit in different ways, that the occupation's motives were linked to a preference for large landholdings. None of them offers archival evidence for its arguments beyond the text of the April 15 decree itself.

In his published statements from these years, Cromer was strategically emphatic about his encouragement of foreign capital investment and his celebration of reforms that might resonate with the liberal sensibilities of British voters wary of the occupation. It is therefore striking that he chose to make no mention of the 1891 decree in his report for that year.[123] Cromer did, however, provide a brief gloss on the new property law in his correspondence with the Foreign Office. His explanation was less concerned with conferring a universal right to private property than with standardizing the state's powers to take land away. Here, once again, Cromer framed the April 15 decree as a modest, but significant, corrective to the wider pattern of inequities between pashas and peasants that would render the occupation more appealing to the latter's conceptions of justice and self-interest.

At issue was the complex system of land classifications that had developed throughout the nineteenth century. According to the legal doctrines that governed land tenure during the Ottoman era, taxable (*kharaji*) land was, at least theoretically, the property of the sultan, and the land tax represented a form of ground rent that conferred usufruct upon the landholder. In practice, many land transactions had, by the eighteenth century, come to approximate ownership far more than the manuals of legal theory might suggest.[124] The state nevertheless retained a right to expropriate *kharaji* land without compensation for "works of public utility."[125] When Mehmed Ali and his heirs began to distribute lands to their retainers and the rural notability, they created new classifications that conferred new rights to the land along with lower tax rates or complete exemption. And in 1871, hoping to boost short-term revenue, Isma'il's government introduced a scheme called the *muqabalah* (quid pro quo). By paying six years of taxes up front, participants would receive a 50% reduction on future tax liability as well as permanent tenure (*raqabah*) on their land.[126] As Dufferin's report had noted, these arrangements exacerbated an already regressive distribution of the government's revenue demands. But by the late 1880s, officials in the Ministry of Public Works had begun to raise concerns about a different issue attending this residual diversity of claims to the land.

Even for Egypt's most privileged landowners, the rights of property (*milkiyah*) were not absolute. The state retained its eminent domain and could, therefore, seize land for purposes it deemed advantageous to public utility (*al-manafi' al-'umumiyah*). Those who enjoyed permanent tenure, however, were entitled to payment. Meanwhile, as Cromer explained to the Foreign Office, "occupiers of land which had not paid the Moukabala in whole or in part, received no compensation from the Government for the land of which they were dispossessed."[127] By the early 1890s, this situation had become a problem. The distinguishing feature of their public works, the British had argued, would be to counteract forms of inequality that the khedivate's own infrastructural projects had built into the rural landscape. The existing pattern of property rights, however, seemed to portend just the opposite effect. Any expropriation for public works would likely prove most prejudicial to the very class of smallholders that the engineers named as their intended beneficiaries. The Ministry of Public Works had requested a new law governing expropriations as early as May 1888, but three years later, nothing had happened. Writing again on April 6, 1891, the ministry stressed "the necessity of promulgating a new law, upon which we might rely in this matter, that would prevent the difficulties arising from the methods employed right now."[128] The details of that legislation would not be finalized for another five years.[129] But it was as a first and necessary step toward standardizing these procedures that the government issued the brief decree of April 15, 1891, granting "the holders of *kharaji* lands who had not paid the *muqabalah* the same full rights of property as those who had."[130] While noting that this change "finally abolishes the last vestige of the theory that the state is the general proprietor of all the lands in the country," Cromer went on to stress its "practical importance."

Every proprietor from whom land was "taken up for state purposes such as railways and canals" would "now receive compensation at the same rate as others."[131]

As in the case of the corvée suppression, what the new law of property secured was not an absolute freedom but an entitlement to payment when the state exercised its residual powers of seizure. The "practical importance" of the measure lay in the corrective it delivered against the manifest disparities of the old regime. Egypt's peasants, in the estimation of British officials, were liable to judge their own experiences of the occupation not against "principles true in every country" but against the treatment of their wealthier compatriots. Procedural uniformity—what Cromer elsewhere called "a reign of order and regularity"—would demonstrate the government's commitment to the public whose interests its works were meant to serve.[132] Converting what had been acts of raw compulsion into regulated monetary transactions would allow the peasant to see government action, for the first time, as an expression of his own self-interest. Thus, the British claimed, would the stability of their occupation be secured.

CONCLUSION

Animating all of these measures was an insistence that government in Egypt should be judged by its generalized effects. That the project of khedivial state-building was a failure, Lord Dufferin had argued, was amply attested by the paired disasters of bankruptcy and mass revolt. Under the uncontested guidance of British engineers, by contrast, the institutions of the state would now be made to function as an efficient machine for maximizing the production of material wealth. The occupation's achievements might fall short of various abstract ideals. Wealthy landowners might draw more than their fair share of the Nile's waters. Peasants might remain subject to periodic conscription. Property rights might be circumscribed by the government's shifting needs for land. But for a rural population with no prior standards of liberty, freedom, or equality, it was the steady, relative improvement of their immediate economic condition that would fill such novel concepts with meaning and allow them to distinguish "British justice" from the "Oriental despotism" that had oppressed them for many long centuries.

The broadly utilitarian logic of such claims was already apparent in the content of Lord Dufferin's "General Report," and it figured prominently in the arguments that Lord Cromer and the Anglo-Indian engineers made on behalf of their early agricultural policies. On this understanding, public utility could be measured on the balance sheets of the Egyptian government and the export figures of cotton traders in Alexandria. From their mundane calculations about the quantifiable results of infrastructural improvement and new rights to land and labor, the peasantry would, in turn, learn the merits of British rule. It was on this basis that Cromer professed there to be "a much greater identity between the interests of the bondholders, properly understood, and those of the Egyptian people than is often supposed."[133]

Beyond its role in recasting a regime of financial extraction as a benefit to the debtor state, this emphasis on the markers of aggregate improvement reflected certain limitations of the occupation's influence in these early years. The British had not yet attached advisers to every ministry. Even where they had, their small staff could only exercise so much control. Colin Scott-Moncrieff may have liked to write about his "maneuvering of the water" from the canal heads as a testament to technical prowess.[134] But it was also a way of engineering around other institutions of power within which the British as yet exercised little sway. As the scope of the occupation's endeavors continued expand, those constraints became harder and harder to ignore.

The British staff of the Ministry of Public Works were all too aware that their Egyptian counterparts possessed their own prior experience of statecraft. On occasion, they refused to accept the "advice" they received in silence. One such exchange, prompted by a proposal from William Garstin to build a new network of unpaved "agricultural roads," provided a telling glimpse of things to come. In characteristic fashion, Garstin's original memorandum handed sole responsibility for charting the new routes to British engineers in Cairo while assigning the full cost of funding them to the specific localities through which they would run.[135] It soon prompted a response from ʿAli Pasha Mubarak, who was then serving as Minister of Public Instruction. In the details of Garstin's proposal, this prominent figure of *istiʿmar* in its older sense discerned a pronounced shift in both the objects and the organization of politics. "It does not appear possible," he explained, "to pose, a priori, general and uniform rules on this subject, since local circumstances, infinite in their variation, must be taken into consideration for each particular route."[136] Gesturing at a much longer tradition of thought on the categories of *maslahah* (interest) and *manfaʿah* (utility), Mubarak insisted that the "general interest" represented by such roads was not singular and uniform, as Garstin's proposal implied, but multiple and "divided" across several geographic scales.[137] In pressing back against the centralization that Garstin envisioned, the ageing civil engineer was not making a case for popular self-government. Like his British interlocutors, he was a committed technocrat. But in his reference to "local circumstances, infinite in their variation," he did suggest that the "utility" the government aimed to advance should remain open to ongoing deliberation. Howsoever subtly, he thus discerned the contours of a coming confrontation. Throughout this first decade, the British in Egypt had aimed to implement a form of rule that would be antipolitical in its effects. By the early 1890s, growing numbers of British officials had begun to suggest that the occupation should be more deliberately antipolitical in practice as well.

Chapter 2

EGYPT'S COLONIAL INTERIOR

BY NOVEMBER 1894, Muhmmad Rushdi had been spying for five months. As he traversed the Nile Delta, he penned weekly reports of his findings for the young Khedive ʿAbbas Hilmi II. Most often, he detailed the foibles and misdeeds of the provincial officials that the British had appointed to do their bidding. But prior to his foray into clandestine service, the wandering informant had worked as the manager of a large agricultural estate belonging to the current Minister of Finance Ahmad Mazlum Pasha. That previous vocation had prepared Rushdi better than his fellow spies to assess the economic condition of the countryside after a dozen years of foreign occupation. What he saw enraged him.

Writing from the city of Mansurah, a major hub of the inland cotton trade, Rushdi reflected on the implications of a recent economic slump. A bumper crop in the United States had caused Egypt's fine, long-staple cotton to lose a third of its value since the last harvest. In their determination to "make a boom for foreign countries on the back of Egypt's debts," the British had "plunged the interior of this land into a state of total poverty." Policies tailored to augment the supply of raw cotton for British mills had left a hapless peasantry more exposed than ever to the vagaries of the world market. Obliged to pay their taxes no matter the price of their crops, poor farmers found themselves trapped in a vicious cycle of debt. A credit system rigged in favor of lenders ensured that the money exchanged for Egypt's chief export flowed overwhelmingly into the hands of the foreigners who controlled the cotton trade. Before long, Rushdi predicted, more peasants would lose their farms. Reduced to the status of day laborers, Egypt's rural population would be left to eke out a precarious existence while a tiny elite of wealthy notables and European investors consolidated their ownership of the soil.[1]

Though he was plainly unconvinced that it represented any kind of progress, Rushdi did suggest that the occupation's program of economic development was proving transformative. Stepping back from the minutiae of the cotton harvest, he mused that "the pound has become the religion, the trust, and the support upon which people rely, and every person now strives to earn a bunch of pounds so that he may leave the country with them or so that he may make a living from them by keeping money out of the hands of his countrymen." So total was this change that even "the reciter who has memorized the Qur'an is forced to take up recitation as a trade, namely as a way to earn money; the learned shaykh likewise studies for the sake of making money, and no one benefits from his knowledge." To Rushdi's eyes, the occupation's so-called reforms were converting time-honored relationships into mere acts of exchange.[2]

By the summer of 1894, Rushdi and his fellow spies were well aware of British statements about the material improvements their presence in the country would deliver. Over the coming months, much of their reporting to the palace spymaster Muhammad Said Shimi Bey would document the mishaps and failings of the occupation's agrarian development projects. The timing of Muhammad Rushdi's career change from estate manager to wandering informant, however, had a different and more specific cause. In his correspondence with the young Khedive, Shimi Bey anticipated that the British were angling to consolidate their influence over the Ministry of Interior. The spymaster had hired and dispatched his new informants to traverse the countryside and monitor what he understood to be the opening moves of a British plot to infiltrate the provincial administration that lay under the Interior's control. Throughout the first decade or so of the occupation, the Interior had remained relatively free from British influence.[3] Unlike the Ministries of Public Works and Finance, the occupation had been unable to attach an adviser. In the mid-1890s, more confident in their position, the British began to alter that arrangement.

As the Khedive's informants described it, the takeover of the Interior would mark a decisive shift in the workings of the occupation. Since the early 1880s, the British had asserted that Egyptians lacked the capacity to reason beyond individual self-interest that was essential to any viable procedures of self-government. They had also proposed that rising prosperity would temper and eventually overcome any residual demands for political participation. Throughout its first decade, Lord Cromer's regime had touted the realization of the latter idea while largely skirting the implications of the former. It was in this sense that the British irrigation inspectors sometimes described public works as technologies of political engineering; by applying their dispassionate expertise to the movement of water, they promised to erode the ossified structures of khedivial misrule without needing to intervene more directly in the organization of the government itself.

A decade later, that approach had begun to encounter new problems. The more British ambitions to draw rural areas into a web of new projects and regulations increased, the more the obstacles to projecting power evenly across state territory seemed to multiply.[4] Cromer's "reign of order and regularity" would ultimately require a multitude of local agents to actuate its designs on the ground. While the ministries in Cairo observed an increasingly fine-grained division of labor, the laws and directives emanating from these many sites in the capital landed on the same small number of figures in each village. And so long as the Interior reserved a measure of autonomy, the provincial administration remained beyond the reach of British authority. While they could influence the selection of ministers in Cairo, officials at the British Consulate had little say in appointments to lower-level posts from the *mudir* (governor) of each province down to the *'umdah* (mayor) of each village. Complicating matters further was the persistence of the electoral procedures that Lord Dufferin had once identified as a promising indigenous basis for parliamentary institutions. As the occupation's agrarian programs came to rely more and more on the executive functions of the provincial administration, these residual forms of village politics appeared as so much sand jamming the gears in the "machinery of government." The British takeover of the Interior would therefore facilitate a sweeping and remarkably durable act of political exclusion. Among Eldon Gorst's first tasks as British adviser was the systematic abolition of local elections.

It was in this moment that an organized opposition to British rule first began to form. Shimi Bey and his spies were no champions of popular democracy. Adopting a language of patriotism (*wataniyah*), they affirmed established hierarchies and organized themselves around the young Khedive whose authority they hoped to protect. Nevertheless, they recognized the magnitude of what was taking place. Through the narrative thickness of their intelligence reports, they together articulated a preliminary but pointed critique of colonial economism at a decisive moment of its institutionalization. Their ribald, even voyeuristic, narrative style was likely tailored to rile the emotions of the adolescent Khedive. But that minute description of everyday misconduct, punctuated often by moments of somber commentary, delivered its own clear argument. Those who governed had not always been the grasping, self-interested individuals the occupation believed them to be. But by reorganizing the provincial administration root and branch around the singular task of making money, the British were molding Egyptian society in that image. The stories that the spies told were the endless variations on a biography of power unrestrained by any higher purpose than the wanton fulfillment of personal desire.

Even as Shimi Bey's agents produced these covert testimonies to the occupation's seamy underside, a second, more voluminous river of paper continued to wend its way toward the palace from more humble origins. Concerned with the urgent details of struggles over land and livelihood, the peasant petitioners who begged for the Khedive's intercession only rarely linked their experiences to any larger movement or confrontation with British rule. Their troubles were manifestly local. And by the late 1890s, the chances that their words might alter circumstances in the village were slim. But in both the content and the form that their communications assumed, the inhabitants of Egypt's rural interior provided their own insistent response to the occupation's accounts of rising prosperity and generalized contentment. From this expansive multitude of local vantages, British rule was not so much removing politics from Egyptian life as forcing those hoping to appropriate, direct, or resist the workings of power to seek out new avenues of expression.

GOVERNING THE COUNTRYSIDE

When British officials made plans to overhaul the Interior, they often implied that they were working upon timeless and unchanging institutions. In fact, the provincial administration they encountered in the 1880s was the product of almost a century of struggles and accommodations between the Mehmed Ali dynasty and the rural communities to whose labor and produce it laid claim. Prior to the Napoleonic conquest, the figure of the village shaykh had served as a crucial intermediary between the village community and the various tax farmers and administrators who represented Ottoman interests in the countryside. The title of *shaykh* itself was a testament to the diverse array of clans and tribes that comprised agrarian society in this period.[5] Typically, each of the local clans would designate an elder to sit on a village council. That council would in turn select one among their number—usually the wealthiest—to serve as *shaykh al-mashayikh*. In addition to adjudicating local disputes, these "premier shaykhs" served a dual role, "being at the same time community leaders and state representatives in their communities."[6]

Mehmed Ali's novel brand of military fiscalism would require a corps of local authorities more directly accountable to the regime for the enforcement of its revenue demands and its monopoly control over peasant cultivation. It was under Mehmed Ali that the head shaykh first assumed the name of *ʿumdah*, the "strut" upon which a new administrative structure would rest.[7] State centralization, in this sense, went hand in hand with an intensification of local authority. When the Pasha moved to replace the Ottoman system of tax farming with direct government assessments, he devolved responsibility for the remittance of village taxes upon the head shaykh.[8] Through successive efforts to reorganize the apparatus of public security, the ʿumdah retained responsibility for local law enforcement and oversight of the village watchmen (*ghafaraʾ*). And in the face of widespread resistance from the peasantry, the government in Cairo came to rely on these local officials to execute its annual orders for both military conscripts and corvée labor.[9]

To the extent that this new regime might be described as revolutionary, there was nothing "gentle" about it.[10] The extractive ambition and sheer brutality of the aspiring dynasty brought no shortage of detractors. Rather than accept the toll upon their bodies and the products of their labor, many peasant cultivators opted to abandon their villages.[11] In the varied terrain of Upper Egypt, some fled into the mountains beyond the irrigated plateau and formed bandit gangs that staged raids on the surrounding farmland.[12] On several occasions, these acts of refusal coalesced into full-blown agrarian insurgency.[13]

As they scrambled to respond, officials in Cairo relied on a shifting mix of penalties and incentives for a rural population that would only be pushed so far. Wealthy proprietors with the means to pay their taxes and recruit peasant labor were permitted, through a succession of new measures, to expand their holdings by taking over abandoned land.[14] By the latter half of the nineteenth century, the largest of these estates, including those owned by the Khedive himself, had begun to approximate "small communities with the appearance of private economic formations."[15] In navigating the thick tangle of its multiplying debt obligations, the government in Cairo thus saw fit to devolve, outsource, and subcontract its authority onto a variegated mosaic of arrangements for managing the territories and populations it claimed to rule.[16]

Even at its most onerous, however, the khedivate could not operate through the distribution of force alone. As the petitions that continued to flood into the ministries and the palace attest, long-established norms of justice and mutual obligation continued to inform popular responses to the exercise of power.[17] For a system of rule dependent on the probity of its intermediaries, this sanctioned mode of intercourse between the sovereign and his "flock" also furnished an important means of monitoring and disciplining the many proxies of state authority.[18] While refining bureaucratic mechanisms for processing the flow of petitions, Mehmed Ali's successors opened several new avenues for their subjects to engage with the state. Faced with mounting social conflict and fiscal stringency, Khedive Isma'il in 1866 established a new Consultative Chamber of Delegates. The chamber, which drew its elected representatives on a proportional basis from across the country, provided opportunities for native Egyptian notables—otherwise excluded by law from holding government office—to offer guidance and consultation in shaping new laws and regulations.[19]

Alongside the creation of this new consultative body in Cairo, Egypt's new Basic Law of 1866 stipulated that the village shaykhs were to be chosen *bi-raghbat al-ahali* (according to the desire of the people). On one level, this extension of electoral procedures to the village followed from the chamber's constitution as a representative body. In formalizing the shaykhs' role as representatives of their village communities, the Basic

Law designated them as village electors responsible for choosing the delegates to the chamber in Cairo. But the formal sanction of electoral procedures also provided new opportunities, from both above and below, to monitor and check the intermediaries who served as the central government's own representatives on a local level.

Like legislation from the same year that recognized elections for the shaykhs of trade guilds, this official endorsement of representative principles seems to have aimed at ensuring a higher degree of administrative accountability.[20] The new legislation certainly did not inaugurate an era of thriving village democracy.[21] In many instances the ʿumdahs and shaykhs continued to come from the same families that had occupied those positions for generations.[22] What is clear, however, is that villagers seized upon the language of elections and representation as another means of seeking redress for mistreatment at the hands of their local officials.[23] And by the 1880s, notions of the headmen's role as "spokesmen and delegates of the commune" were sufficiently well established that Lord Dufferin was able to alight upon the village elections as the ancient customary "roots" out of which a robust system of Egyptian democracy might one day grow.[24]

Dufferin invoked that liberal trajectory to denounce Oriental despotism for obstructing it. But the fact that the khedivate had itself taken steps to formalize electoral practices need not lead to an equally implausible reading of Ismaʿil's government as a champion of popular sovereignty.[25] Instead, recourse to these forms of circumscribed political participation served to counteract, or at least mitigate, the centrifugal forces that tugged ever harder against Cairo's demands. In opening spaces for maneuver within the institutions of the state, the khedivate sought to direct its subjects away from other modes of contestation and evasion that it could never fully control.

RELOCATING THE VILLAGE

It was those alternative forms of politics, in all their diversity, that erupted in spectacular fashion by the early 1880s and ultimately provided the pretext for the occupation. The suppression of the ʿUrabi revolt and the arrival of British forces quickly set the stage for a protracted tug of war over the workings of the provincial administration. In the early 1880s, as they set about "restoring stability," the British attempted to impose a sweeping overhaul of the Interior and its security apparatus, but the minister at the time, Nubar Pasha, had rebuffed what he saw as a usurpation of his prerogatives and threatened to resign.[26] Fearful of precipitating such open confrontation in these early days, Cromer and the Foreign Office relented, setting in place a tenuous division of labor.[27] A British deputy inspector-general and his staff would oversee a constabulary organized along quasi-military lines and consisting of the city police, the provincial gendarmerie, and a reserve force. But the mudirs would retain control of law enforcement in their governorates through the existing assortment of provincial officials and village guards. The provincial administration managed by the Minister of the Interior would thereafter stand as an enclave of relative autonomy from British interference.[28]

Over the course of the next decade, the main response of British officials in the other ministries was to minimize their reliance on the provincial administration. It was as an antidote to the residual powers of the mudirs, *ma'murs* (district chiefs), ʿumdahs, and shaykhs, they now argued, that the occupation's agrarian policies would deliver not only an increase of material wealth but a lasting political transformation. By this understanding, the notorious three Cs of khedivial despotism were evils that inhered in the office of the village headman, to whom Cromer referred as "the corner-stone on which the edifice of provincial society rests."[29] Eliminating corruption, corvée, and "courbash" would amount to "a social as much as an administrative revolution."[30] The same policies that would allow the fallah to realize his economic potential would thus free him from the tyranny of local officials. In a report he sent to Cromer in May 1888, William Garstin observed that "the Sheikhs dislike us, and it is only natural that they should do so." In earlier times, he explained, "the Sheikh was entirely master over the fellaheen in his village, and he made them work as he pleased." Now, thanks to the abolition of corporal punishment and the corvée, their "power and authority over their villages is not one quarter what it used to be."[31]

If standardized tax assessments, paid labor contracting, and new judicial institutions all promised to diminish the role of village officials, however, the Ministry of Interior's own endeavors in these same years tended to pull in the opposite direction. In a bid to consolidate the alternative security apparatus he had wrested from British oversight, Nubar Pasha tasked the mudirs in 1884 with establishing a special Brigandage Commission in each governorate. Operating outside the purview of the new National Court system, these commissions enjoyed broad powers to arrest and try suspects under procedures more akin to martial law.[32] While the Interior did not "invent" the problem of banditry it now undertook to combat, the commissions did mark a significant departure from earlier efforts to reduce the incidence of rural crime.[33] Now forced to compete with the British-run police force in demonstrating their effectiveness, provincial officials took up this mandate with considerable zeal.

Central to the Interior's crime-fighting agenda was an effort to reorganize rural space. Throughout the upheaval of the 1870s, growing numbers of peasants had continued to flee their villages. The label most commonly assigned to their informal settlements—*'izbah* (pl. *'izab*)—was a testament to the negative space these hamlets described. Whether for reasons of practical convenience or outright evasion, what defined the rural communities to which the name *'izbah* applied was their distance or isolation from the recognized villages that comprised the lowest level of the government's administrative hierarchies.[34] Even before the occupation, the Interior had taken steps to eliminate these holes in the territorial fabric of state power. They drafted preliminary guidelines for the construction of any new 'izab and commissioned inventories of existing settlements.[35] With the advent of the Brigandage Commissions, however, Nubar Pasha's Ministry of Interior laid out terms for a more decisive, and violent, redefinition of the 'izbah. According to the regulations promulgated on November 10, 1884, any settlement unable to pay for the legally mandated number of guards or deemed a refuge for criminals would now be destroyed. Permits for new 'izab would only be granted to properties of at least fifty contiguous feddans of land owned by a single proprietor. Peasants who had fled their villages "to escape from their public duties and from the village guards without a license" would be forcibly relocated so that they might "work toward the fulfillment of their obligations just as others like them do."[36]

The new law opened the way for a systematic and coercive simplification of rural space. The change was not instantaneous. Unsurprisingly, the residents of targeted hamlets did what they could to remain in place, often petitioning the Council of Ministers with detailed histories of their settlements and explanations for why they represented worthy exceptions to the law's strictures.[37] On occasion, the ministers in Cairo found grounds to relent.[38] But the overall effect of the new measures was clear. The previous diversity of arrangements distant from the reach of the state was forcibly reduced to a simpler correspondence between 'izbah and large estate. All individuals not employed to work the land of a recognized 'izbah would now return to the regulated domain of the village.[39]

For the rural communities who were removed from their homes and compelled to relocate, these early years of the occupation were likely experienced as a violent break with the past and one rather different from what British officials liked to describe. But within the Ministry of Interior, these efforts to reconfigure rural space still conformed to older patterns and arrangements for governing the countryside. While asserting its authority to condemn and destroy ʿizab, the Ministry of Interior relied on a variable distribution of discretion to enforce its will. Groups that had chosen to take up residence outside the village might still demonstrate the viability of their small communities. And provincial officials in each governorate retained broad leeway to decide who could stay and who must go. From the earliest moments of the occupation, it was precisely this devolution of authority that British officials identified as a primary cause of the disorder, crime, and corruption that had tainted the khedivial regime. British justice, they now insisted, would mean consistent policies applied evenly across state territory; and that uniformity would depend upon the realization of clear organizational hierarchies. Administrative restructuring would thus need to proceed in tandem with a more concerted reorganization of rural space. The Ministry of Interior was crucial to the achievement of both objectives.

ADVISER TO THE INTERIOR

The process that culminated in Eldon Gorst's appointment as adviser to the Interior in November 1894 began several years earlier with the demise of the Brigandage Commissions. If the commissions had once represented an attempt to cauterize the Interior against the spread of foreign influence, they ended by furnishing a new justification for British oversight.[40] In the spring of 1889, a report by the Belgian prosecutor-general Charles LeGrelle revealed frequent use of torture and a denial of basic legal rights to the accused.[41] LeGrelle's findings allowed Cromer to claim that Egyptians should not be trusted to manage the administrative apparatus they had been consolidating without British supervision. He condemned the commissions as "a standing reproach to the system under which justice is administered in this country" and pressed for their immediate abolition.[42] But he also seized the opportunity to frame the scandal as symptomatic of a larger problem. The reason for such abuses, he explained, was obvious: "The Ministries of Justice and of the Interior are almost entirely in the hands of Egyptians. English interference in the affairs of those two departments is, relatively speaking, very slight."[43]

While he professed an aversion to "any radical change in the machinery of the Government," Cromer reminded London that "the English Government is held largely responsible for everything that takes place in Egypt."[44] Insisting over the following year that "recourse must be had, to a greater extent than heretofore, to English Agency," he secured the appointment of a British adviser, John Scott, inside the Ministry of Justice.[45] But he stopped short of asserting the same control over the Interior. Following the abolition of the Brigandage Commissions, British officials instead began to exercise greater influence over appointments even without an adviser at the ministry. By the winter of 1890, contradicting Garstin's pronouncements from two years prior, Cromer himself expressed a new optimism that amongst the "Sheikhs and Omdehs, who constitute the squirearchy of the country," a former "sympathy with the Arabi movement . . . is rapidly becoming English sympathy."[46]

The final impetus behind a British takeover occurred several years later. And it was precisely the fear that a resurgent form of anti-British politics might saturate the lowest reaches of the provincial administration that precipitated the decision.[47] Khedive Tawfiq, who had served as a pliant figurehead since his accession in 1879, passed away on January 7, 1892. Upon taking the throne, his eighteen-year-old son 'Abbas Hilmi II adopted a far more defiant posture. Within the Ministry of Interior, the system of divided authority now started to break down. Convinced that the current Minister Mustafa Fahmi Pasha was affording the British inspector-general of police too much sway over the provincial administration, the young Khedive moved, without consulting Cromer, to appoint a new Council of Ministers.[48] Cromer quickly condemned the move as a "*coup d'état*" by a "youth of mediocre intellect who has all the arbitrary tendencies of an Oriental despot." He succeeded in forcing the Khedive to compromise on a council more in line with British wishes.[49] But this "ministerial crisis" portended more concerted opposition than the British had witnessed in a decade.[50]

In the months that followed, British officials in Cairo fretted over the continued manifestations of "anti-European and anti-Christian prejudices" that the Khedive's actions had inspired. On Cromer's request, two additional battalions of British troops were dispatched to Egypt.[51] Several of the local papers—*al-Ahram*, *al-Mu'ayyad*, and 'Abdullah al-Nadim's *al-Ustadh* chief among them—began calling on their readers to demand their rights and follow the example of other nationalist movements.[52] Consular officials in the Delta reported on public demonstrations and the circulation of rumors about the imminent arrival of French and Ottoman forces to expel the British.[53] And though they may have acquiesced on the choice of ministers, the Khedive and his palace advisers continued to exercise what influence they could over officials in the provinces.

In July of 1893, the British Chargé d'Affaires Arthur Hardinge warned of the "hostility displayed by the Khedive to native sheikhs and omdehs who show cordiality towards English officials or a desire to assist them in their work in the provinces."[54] Writing again two weeks later, Hardinge made recourse to a tried and tested distinction to argue that "the Western sentiment of nationality is of course entirely non-existent." For "the uneducated masses," there could be no properly political movement of opposition to British rule. There nevertheless remained a danger that appeals to "fanaticism" might prove more attractive than the "practical benefits they have derived from English intervention." For the time being, he judged, "the promptings of their material interests are still a good deal stronger than the influence of religious prejudice.... Nor in the case of the lowest class, who are too unreasoning to connect their material condition with any political cause, must we forget the dead weight of apathetic indifference to public questions not visibly affecting their own pockets which is the natural outcome of ignorance and long slavery."[55]

Under current arrangements, however, that reassurance was tentative at best. In the aftermath of the ministerial crisis, British officials began to fixate upon the provincial administration as a dangerous obstacle to their wider program of agrarian improvement. A cooperative Minister of Interior might continue to select mudirs who were willing to work with their British counterparts. But so long as the selection of village officials lay, at least nominally, in the hands of the villagers themselves, the lowest reaches of the administration remained susceptible to the machinations of the Khedive and his supporters. It was upon the ʿumdahs and shaykhs that the government ultimately relied for the execution of policies that would keep the peasantry attuned to the "promptings of their material interests" rather than the "influence of religious prejudice." But the procedure of the village election, however inconsistently practiced, meant that a population they judged devoid of political discernment might be manipulated into making these village officials the objects of an interminable and multisited referendum on British rule.

The opportunity to forestall this potential appearance of peasant politics where it did not belong arrived the following year. When Riaz Pasha retired at the beginning of 1894, Nubar Pasha returned for a final stint as Minister of Interior. Arguing that divided control over law enforcement had become unworkable, he now proposed to eliminate the British police inspectors and the inspector-general. All departments within the Interior would be fully under the control of the minister himself. The British acquiesced, but only in exchange for the appointment of a British adviser.[56] Eldon Gorst, who was then serving as undersecretary of state for finance and whom Cromer tapped for the new post, began meeting with Nubar to discuss the reorganization on April 18, just two days after his reappointment as minister.[57] In a confidential memo he drafted for Cromer that August, Gorst stressed the importance of British control over the appointment, promotion, and supervision of provincial administrators. While the Council of Ministers would continue to select the mudirs, he proposed that all other posts be filled by committees on which British officials would now hold seats. At the local level, he recommended that village elections should be abolished. Instead, a committee chaired by the mudir and consisting of the public prosecutor, a delegate from the Interior, and several local notables would choose the ʿumdahs and shaykhs for final approval by the Ministry of Interior itself. Altogether, Gorst's plans would secure "a permanent English control . . . over the question of appointments."[58]

By the end of October, Gorst and Cromer had finalized the new arrangement with Nubar and the Khedive. Gorst took up his new position at the beginning of November. Among his first acts in office was the drafting of a new "Statute on ʿUmdahs and Shaykhs." Closely modeled on his earlier memorandum, it set a minimum age and property requirement for the holders of each office. In place of the village elections, a newly constituted Provincial Commission would handle all appointments, dismissals, and disciplinary proceedings.[59] Over the course of the next year, these commissions inaugurated a massive turnover in the staffing of village offices, replacing 714 ʿumdahs and 1,947 shaykhs and appointing 2,968 additional shaykhs to villages in Upper and Lower Egypt.[60]

In his annual report for 1895, Cromer described these changes as the antidote to a form of political practice that did not belong in the countryside. "Village life," he proclaimed, "is no longer to so great an extent troubled by political dissensions, the result, generally, of some Cairo complication which has been misunderstood and misinterpreted. Local functionaries and notabilities need no longer, much against their inclinations, range themselves in one or other of the opposing camps of Anglophiles and Anglophobes."[61] Now strictly beholden to their superiors inside the Ministry of Interior, Egypt's ʿumdahs and shaykhs could complete their metamorphosis into the petty functionaries of British designs. "Rules and Regulations," Cromer observed, "are of small use unless applied under the direction of honest and capable officials. . . . I trust I am not over sanguine in venturing to predict that, if no breach of continuity occurs, the results of the present system will eventually be to enhance the efficiency and to elevate the whole moral standard of the Egyptian Civil Service."[62]

A DELICATE OPERATION

That was the future the British envisioned and the one they chose to see. But if the stated intention of these changes was to remove any trace of political contestation from the countryside, other voices soon began to tell other stories. While the rudiments of the khedivial spy network may have existed beforehand, both the timing of Muhammad Saʿid Shimi Bey's recruitment efforts and the content of his reporting suggest that this ramp-up of the palace spymaster's "delicate operation [*khidmah daqiqah*]" was prompted by the circulation of rumors about British designs on the Interior.[63] In the spring of 1894, Shimi Bey was working in the infractions office of the Interior's police department.[64] As an employee of the Interior, he was well placed to monitor its officers and officials within the city of Cairo. But on his own, his ability to gather intelligence about other parts of the country and other ministries was limited.

In the early summer, he began to expand the group of informants to whom Muhammad Rushdi referred as "the circle of brotherhood [*dayirat al-ikhwah*]" and "the ring of valor and manly virtue [*muhit al-muruwah wa-l-futuwah*]."[65] Drawing on palace funds to cover his salary, Shimi Bey recruited Rushdi in June to leave Ahmad Mazlum Pasha's estate in Sharqiyah. He would thereafter coordinate his efforts with a small band of other men—Hussayn Afandi Nassar, ʿAli Afandi Sulayman, al-Sayyid Ibrahim, and Ahmad Afandi Mansur—all of whom the spymaster seems to have approached at roughly the same time.[66] A number of other individuals "among the most loyal to His Highness" supplemented the reporting of these full-time agents on an ad hoc basis. Muhammad Afandi Riyad kept Shimi Bey apprised of developments within the Ministry of Public Works, while ʿAbd al-Halim Afandi Mukhbir did the same for the Ministry of Education, where he worked as a clerk. Muhammad Afandi Kamil, an employee in the Department of Corrections, leaked paperwork from the Interior to Shaykh ʿAli Yusuf's palace-funded daily *al-Muʾayyad* "because it is the one and only patriotic paper."[67] Ismaʿil Bey Jawdat, who had served as director of the Cairo police department during the ʿUrabi revolt, mobilized his contacts in the provincial administration to corroborate the findings of Shimi Bey's rural informants.

In his correspondence with the Khedive, Shimi Bey was careful to maintain the formal protocols of their relationship, always implying that this growing web of agents and informants was a product of the new sovereign's own designs. Certainly, this is how Cromer often described the emergence of a more vocal and organized opposition following ʿAbbas Hilmi II's accession to the throne.[68] Wilfrid Scawen Blunt, a persistent and outspoken critic of the occupation, likewise cast the young Khedive as a rebellious and strong-willed leader who "had managed to gather about him the nucleus of a new National party, which consisted of what elements there were in Egypt either of discontent or such patriotism as was to be found in the country, half political, half religious, which resented the presence of foreign and Christian rule."[69] A closer reading of this "delicate operation" and its sprawling epistolary archive, however, suggests that the relationship worked the other way around and that this "nucleus of a new National party" had mobilized to groom the young Khedive as a reliable ally to their cause.[70]

For Shimi Bey and his fellow spies, the moment they sought to document was pivotal. The arrival of a new khedive willing, and perhaps eager, to shed his father's servile reputation presented a rare opportunity. Yet the speed with which the British were extending their hold over the lowermost reaches of the provincial administration was ominous. In his communiqués, Shimi Bey frequently adopted the didactic tone of a seasoned counselor advising a ruler still new to the throne. To his young "master," he described the world in Manichean binaries. On the one side were the Khedive and his supporters, the faithful and upright defenders of a just government that past generations of virtuous statesmen had built. On the other were the British and their partisans, a motley horde of lecherous, greedy, and unscrupulous miscreants who betrayed their country in pursuit of bodily pleasures and personal gain. By the summer of 1894, it seemed that the latter were gaining the upper hand. What Shimi Bey described was, at root, a struggle over the institutions of the Egyptian state and the ends toward which those institutions were being rearranged. To the British discourse of material and moral progress the spymaster offered an unrelenting rebuttal in vivid narrative form. The conclusion to which he directed his young reader was neatly signaled by a deliberate spelling mistake. Adding a dot above the Arabic letter *ḥa*, Shimi Bey sometimes made "*al-iḥtilāl* [the occupation]" into "*al-ikhtilāl*," a word connoting both disorder and insanity.[71]

How did this condition of disequilibrium appear in the mundane procedures he catalogued? For the Khedive, the spymaster revealed a sprawling panorama of debauchery and corruption. In his nightly perambulations, he recorded the names and ranks of the policemen, military officers, and bureaucrats he spotted in the bars and dance halls of Cairo's Azbakiyah district.[72] Reports from his rural informants closely mirrored what he was witnessing in the city. Often, their letters were so lurid that he removed or sanitized details to maintain some semblance of formality. Even so, these curated summaries described a provincial administration overrun by philanderers, pederasts, and adulterers. All of them were drunk.[73]

Alcohol located its consumers on the wrong side of a country divided in two. To drink, in these accounts, was to have cast one's lot with the British. For Shimi Bey and his spies, the ubiquity of alcohol epitomized the erosion of an Islamic moral order that had once formed the basis of good government. In the florid salutation with which he opened each letter, Muhammad Rushdi drew a line connecting the "ring of valor and manly virtue" to which he belonged with the *futuwah* brotherhoods that had once formed to defend the faithful against the Crusaders.[74] But while the spies did sometimes employ sectarian language, their concern, as they explained it, was not simply to defend Islam for its own sake. Rather, their chronicles of everyday comportment delivered a forceful critique of British colonization as they saw it unfolding. Lamenting the incidence of drinking among "the men of the sword," Shimi Bey explained that "this is among the objectives of the occupying power. There is no doubt that it is easier for them to rule an ignorant and debauched people than those who know their own dignity, who rejoice at the good of their own country, and who feel sadness for anything that impinges upon its independence."[75]

As symptoms of such ignorance and debauchery, the petty misdeeds that filled the spies' reports betrayed a deeper and more troubling change. Even before Gorst's appointment to the Interior, the British had succeeded in filling government posts with willing collaborators. But in the stories they told, the spies conveyed the possibility that the occupation might extend well beyond this substitution of personnel. Writing to the Khedive on June 15, 1894, Shimi Bey observed of Muhammad Sa'd al-Din Pasha, the mudir of Gharbiyah Province, that "he served as mudir before this term in Tanta, and he worked in a very upright manner without taking bribes or gifts. But this time around, he himself has been permitted to accept bribes and gifts."[76] Under the occupation, even high-ranking officials showed little or no compunction about exploiting their power for personal gain and bodily gratification. The mudir's willingness to sell public offices and his open "predilection for young men" were instances of the same general problem. This was the new reality against which Muhammad Rushdi inveighed when he observed that "money has become the religion and the support upon which every person relies."[77]

The spies were not wrong, of course, to identify the occupation with a concerted effort to reorient Egyptian society toward the individualistic pursuit of material interests. But to the Khedive they presented a tableau of colonial economism as the very antithesis of their own patriotic ideals. Drawn from a cohort of mid-level civil servants with their own prior experiences of Egyptian statecraft, the spies rejected both the empirical and the normative premises that underpinned Britain's development project. On the first count, their emphasis on the novelty of the changes underway stood at odds with the occupation's claims about the immutable and racially determined nature of Egyptian character. Government, they insisted, possessed a weighty capacity to form the subjects of power and imbue them with one set of values or another. For Rushdi, the propensity to "strive to attain a few pounds" was an example of what "every person has become [*sar*]," not what he or she always was or would be.[78] On the second count, though that process of becoming was an effect of the occupation, it was anything but desirable. The British claimed that Egypt's peasants would experience the new regime of free exchange and private property as a kind of emancipation. The spies, on the contrary, described that particular form of freedom as sanction for a vicious struggle of all against all in which the powerful might now take what they wanted without restraint.

If the lineaments of this counternarrative were already clear before Eldon Gorst took his new post, the British adviser at the Interior opened the way for the occupation's *ikhtilal* to spread. Writing from Cairo in late November, Shimi Bey reported that officials within the Interior now took orders directly from Gorst, "and there is no thought of the minister or his deputy."[79] The following January, Muhammad Rushdi and ʿAli Sulayman leap-frogged each other from city to city as Gorst and his retinue made an inspection tour of Upper Egypt. With a few notable exceptions, the spies watched in horror as provincial officials vied to outdo each other in fêting the British adviser.[80] While Rushdi was hampered by "the intensity of surveillance directed toward me by the provincial government's informants," his efforts did yield two important findings.[81] First, Gorst's tour was less an evaluation of administrative practices than an opportunity to affirm that "the interior of the country is now in the hands of an English official."[82] Second, what substantive inquiries the new adviser did make revolved around "the question of the obligations of the village shaykhs."[83]

Rushdi's suspicions were soon confirmed. As the British explained it, the new "Statute on ʿUmdahs and Shaykhs" would facilitate conditions of perfect technocratic efficiency—aptly summed up by Cromer's dictum "European head and Egyptian hands"—under which local officials might soon become the dutiful and consistent executors of centrally planned designs.[84] But in tracking its implementation, the Khedive's spies suggested instead that the reappointment process had opened a vast new frontier for colonial misrule. On April 30, Ismaʿil Jawdat penned a detailed memorandum entitled "Internal Political Observations on the Statute for the Appointment of ʿUmdahs and Shaykhs." Having toured Gizah and Qaliubiyah provinces, he explained that "they carried out the appointment of the ʿumdahs and shaykhs through the agency of the mudir and his deputy and a representative of the Interior, all of whom are now the men of the English [*rijal al-inkliz*], and they did this without considering the will of the people [*bidun raghbat al-ahali*] though that had been the prevailing custom since the days of Muhammad ʿAli Pasha." On the face of it, this was exactly the change the new statute mandated. Far from improving accountability, however, the new procedures appeared to have forged new chains of exploitation and graft. Jawdat determined that "the appointment takes place with utter disregard for the text of the statute and instead according to the sum each individual provides to the mudir and his deputy, and whoever pays the most is appointed ʿumdah whether he meets the required conditions or not."[85]

The spies who denounced this provincial administration overrun by "the English party [*al-hizb al-inglizi*]" were not champions of popular sovereignty.[86] Theirs was, in the most basic sense, a conservative worldview. The central refrain of their elegy to the fragile achievements of the past was that the British were flooding the ranks of government with the wrong sort of men. Their repeated warnings that village appointments now occurred "without the consent of the people [*bi-ghayr rida al-ahali*]" were no more an endorsement of peasant democracy than Ismaʿil's original decision to formalize local elections.[87] The abolition of those elections nevertheless exemplified the condition of alien rule Shimi Bey called *ikhtilal*. In their effort to root out detractors, the British had removed both the moral and procedural restraints that oriented those in power toward the public good.

Inverting the occupation's critique of Oriental despotism, the spies protested that Britain had made government into yet another site for the individualistic pursuit of economic gain. Now assured that they might "collect from the miserable peasants many times the sums they paid," aspiring ʿumdahs and shaykhs concocted outlandish schemes to secure their appointment.[88] Hussayn Nassar noted that some individuals previously convicted of crimes or dismissed from public office had paid bribes to ensure "the improvement of testimonies about them."[89] Others had contrived to meet the minimum requirements for landownership through theft and fraud. After paying the mudir of Gizah forty pounds to become ʿumdah of al-Manawah, a man named Muhammad al-Khayri tapped his son as a village shaykh. Al-Khayri had lost his own land to foreclosure, but once appointed, he registered his son as the taxpayer for a deceased woman's property, robbing her heirs of their inheritance and ensuring that father and son would meet the ownership thresholds for their ill-begotten posts. In another case, a man named ʿAbd al-Hamid Farahat arranged with the provincial officials of Qaliubiyah to "conjure land for him out of thin air." After Farahat had paid the necessary bribes, his coconspirators had modified the tax registers to shift some government land protected as an archaeological site within the bounds of a large estate in his village. With the help of his brother, who worked on the estate, the village tax collector then recorded a sale of that land to Farahat, who thereafter appeared to own enough property to hold office.[90] Such transactions were sufficiently common that in April 1895, the Alexandria-based daily *al-Ahram* reported a dramatic increase in the registration of land sales at the provincial courts. The paper judged most of these deals to be "in truth imaginary and fleeting" and attributed the phony transactions to those seeking village office.[91]

In the estimation of Shimi Bey's spies, Eldon Gorst's Interior was fast becoming the central institution of colonial duplicity, in both senses of the word. On the one hand, the ministry as they saw it was now overrun at every level by drunkards, gamblers, philanderers, and thieves. Despite their pretensions to technocratic efficiency, the British had introduced a crowd of devious sycophants who were only too eager to betray their compatriots for the gratification of their own wants and desires. On the other, amidst all the drinking, gambling, sex, and extortion, the spies described an administrative apparatus that seemed now to lead a doubled existence. Ruthless and depraved as they might be in practice, the new cohort of provincial officials were adept at performing the work of the Interior that existed on paper. On occasion, Shimi Bey's informants suggested that "nothing of what takes place in the country escapes the English, for they have spies everywhere."[92] But whatever the extent of such knowledge, the outward performance of bureaucratic consistency now allowed the government in Cairo to proceed as if the provincial administration had become reliable hands enacting orders from an all-knowing European head.

THE RESPONSIBILITIES OF THE ʿUMDAH

Having proclaimed that the ʿumdahs and shaykhs were accountable to their own direct supervision, British officials in Cairo soon devised a raft of new measures which treated these village officials as mere bureaucratic extensions of the central state. Beginning in 1895, even before the new appointment statutes had been finalized, the British adviser to the Ministry of Justice took steps to devolve responsibility for minor criminal infractions and low-value civil disputes onto the ʿumdahs.[93] Keeping minor cases in the village, he argued, would reduce the caseload of the National Courts and spare poorer peasants the cost and hassle of travel. Some commentators in the local press invoked the principle of equality before the law to question this conferral of judicial authority on the headmen as "the restoration of despotic power to their hands."[94] But as the Ministry of Justice continued to expand the ʿumdah's jurisdiction, it defended these arrangements by insisting that "the selection of village officials is now looked after and their work is supervised."[95] Nor was the Ministry of Justice alone in augmenting the ʿumdah's bailiwick. Over the coming years, the headman's obligations mushroomed to include: maintaining up-to-date registers of births and deaths, supervising public health campaigns against cholera and cattle plague, managing village labor crews during the annual flood, monitoring the distribution of irrigation water, notarizing government documents, and keeping the village informed of all official announcements. By the turn of the century, this list of duties had become so varied and complex that a number of administrative primers emerged to guide village officials in their work. As Muhammad al-Barudi observed in the introduction to his *Dalil al-ʿUmdah* (*The ʿUmdah's Guidebook*), "Most of the ʿumdahs and shaykhs are now unable to be fully informed and cognizant of all their responsibilities because they are so numerous and they are not published in one single place."[96]

FIGURE 1: Administrative Manuals. Source: Al-Barūdī, *Dalīl al-ʿUmdah*; Rifʿat, *Wājibāt al-ʿUmdah.*

The problem this new instructional literature sought to address, however, was not simply one of organizing information. Writing two years after al-Barudi, his friend and fellow police officer ʿAbd al-Fattah Rifʿat conceded, "Many of them know nothing of reading or writing and merely inherit this important vocation from their fathers. And may the honorable ʿumdahs excuse me for saying that there are those among them who are entirely or mostly ignorant of their duties."[97] The Ministry of Interior's own internal publications from these years, moreover, betray an awareness that the ʿumdah's professional metamorphosis was not so thoroughgoing as Cromer's assurances might suggest. The Interior's *al-Nashrah al-idariyah* (*The Administrative Bulletin*), published biweekly from November 1897, dealt extensively with matters of local administration. In addition to the routine announcement of government directives, the bulletin included two sections, arranged side by side, listing "praiseworthy" and "blameworthy" deeds by government officials. While the former offered brief tales of resourcefulness and derring-do, the latter chronicled a multitude of infractions investigated and punished by the new disciplinary committees in the provinces. Common to many of these telegraphic synopses was an allegation that the headman had either conspired to obscure crimes that had in fact taken place or brought false charges against other residents of his village.[98]

This published documentation of incompetence, neglect, and outright criminality might seem to represent an acknowledgment that the appointment commissions had accomplished something less than a wholesale professionalization of village government. But from another vantage, such regularized, official reporting from within the ministry's own ranks was emblematic of the change that British efforts to reorganize the Interior had brought about. British advisers did not teach the Egyptian state to "see" or introduce techniques for surveilling the countryside where none had existed before. But the takeover of the Interior in 1894–95 did result in a subtle but significant shift in the way the "legibility" of population and territory was managed.[99] The new arrangements aimed not so much at absolute homogeneity as at strict and regular hierarchies. The steady multiplication of the ʿumdah's responsibilities rested on an assumption that power now flowed only in one direction, that the headman was the government's representative in the village, and that each official was immediately accountable to his immediate superiors.

SEEING THE COLONIAL STATE LIKE A PEASANT

According to Lord Cromer, the "effect produced by these changes on those for whose benefit they were primarily intended" was that "the peace and tranquility of the village population—that is to say, of the great mass of the inhabitants of Egypt, have greatly increased."[100] But even as British officials and the agents of an emerging opposition vied to speak on their behalf, that great mass of inhabitants continued to document their own experiences through the thousands of petitions they forwarded to Cairo each year. Unlike the writings of the Khedive's spies, their paper protests in this moment rarely employed a language of patriotism or resistance to British rule. If these peasant petitioners found fault with British control of the Interior, they evinced little nostalgia for the days before the occupation. But find fault they did. The stories they told and the act of petitioning itself stood as a practical rebuke to Cromer's confident assertions about "peace and tranquility."

The occupation's narrative of administrative reform rested on a categorical separation between the "powers" and "responsibilities" of provincial officials.[101] The erosion of the former, by this reasoning, would facilitate an increase of the latter. For the peasants actually subject to the reformed ʿumdah's local authority, however, that distinction all but disappeared. Notwithstanding the variety of particular grievances, the pattern of these petitions described two significant consequences of the

Interior's reorganization. First, the multiplication of the headman's functions and responsibilities after 1895 was not, in fact, power neutral. In the stories they told, the tasks that al-Barudi's *Guidebook* sought to order and number reappeared as so many opportunities for village officials to settle scores, vanquish their adversaries, and amass new wealth. Far from an impartial public servant, the ʿumdah who typically emerged as the villain of these narratives was above all adept at turning "responsibilities" to his own advantage.[102] Second, the petitioners alleged that in bringing both the selection and the supervision of provincial officials within the ministry's ranks, the Interior had deprived the village population of yet another means to address and rectify everyday abuses of power.

By the turn of the century, as property values began to rise, allegations about the headman's malfeasance frequently concerned the wrongful acquisition of land. In May 1903, for example, the Khedive's diwan received three petitions that illustrate variations on this theme. Fatimah Bint Salim ʿAbdullah from al-Kafr al-Sharqi in Gharbiyah claimed that the ʿumdah's nephew had stolen her personal seal to forge a document of sale for her property of 4.5 feddans. While she traveled to the provincial capital to register a complaint, the ʿumdah and his nephew had fabricated additional documents to support the phony transaction.[103] Dasuqi Hamadah from Kafr Khazzam in Asyut reported that in overseeing a public sale of government land, the ʿumdah, several shaykhs, and the village muezzin had conspired to alter the land titles to "hide" a feddan that should have been available for purchase. They divided it among themselves and forged contracts of sale before starting to build on the pilfered property.[104] Ismaʿil Muhammad claimed that the ʿumdah of Jablah in Fayyum had used his authority over water rotations to deprive his farm of irrigation and force him to sell the land for a pittance. Before petitioning the Khedive, the aggrieved villager had complained to the Ministry of Public Works, but officials in Cairo had passed the matter down to the chief engineer of Fayyum. Because the ʿumdah of Jablah sat on the provincial council and enjoyed a cordial relationship with the engineer, he had succeeded in derailing the ministry's investigation.[105]

According to the logic of the 1895 law, the Interior's disciplinary apparatus would address misconduct at all levels of the provincial administration. But Ismaʿil Muhammad was not alone in suggesting that these mechanisms were inadequate. In theory, a villager could also take the headman to court, but the ʿumdah's new judicial authority could make it harder to gain standing for what the National Courts now classified as low-value civil matters. For those of limited means, the court fees required to bring suit were often prohibitive. To rectify this potential source of class inequity in the justice system, the government had created an exemption for anyone bearing a "certificate of poverty." But the certificate itself required the signature of the plaintiff's ʿumdah.[106] When the ʿumdah himself faced the threat of litigation, he could simply refuse to sign the form. Such was the fate of two sisters named Naqdah and Nafisah from the village of Awlad al-Shaykh in Girga province. When the ʿumdah appropriated four feddans of their land, they applied directly to the mudiriyah for a certificate of poverty. Following normal procedures, however, the provincial government contacted the ʿumdah to complete the form that would have facilitated a lawsuit against himself. He denied that the two sisters met the criteria for exemption from court fees, and there the case had stopped.[107]

To those who begged mercy from the Khedive, the petition was a last and often desperate recourse. The role of such petitions had already begun to change before the British arrived. The khedivial regime had standardized methods for processing these missives as an additional source of information about the workings of its growing administrative apparatus. But formal conventions of the petition still invoked the power of the sovereign as the ultimate guarantor of justice for his subjects. It was just that exceptional authority that the occupation had denounced as despotism and curtailed. Launching their petitions as a possible means to evade the structured hierarchies of the Interior, Egypt's villagers now found that this well-trodden route around provincial authority had been blocked.

The long paper trail of a man named al-Sibaʿi al-ʿAshri offers a poignant account of that procedural closure and the forms of violence it obscured. Beginning in 1885, al-ʿAshri had served as the head watchman in the village of Jaʿfariyah in Gharbiyah. In 1898, the deputy prosecutor, district judge, and police superintendent had come from the nearby district seat of Santah to celebrate the spring festival of Sham al-Nasim. The visiting dignitaries had asked the ʿumdah to furnish "prostitutes to dance and revel with them," and the headman had obliged. While prostitution was legal at the time, it was heavily regulated. Outside of large cities and towns, many women worked in the sex trade without a government license.[108] Moreover, if the khedivial spy reports and other petitions from the period are any indication, the use of government office to perpetrate acts of sexual violence was rampant. Al-ʿAshri did not provide details, but whatever transpired that night was scandalous enough that another villager, Muhammad Tamim, notified the governorate of Gharbiyah, which opened a formal inquiry.[109]

When al-ʿAshri was called to corroborate Tamim's allegations, the ʿumdah and his powerful friends demanded that he testify to their innocence. He refused, and there his troubles began. He was dismissed from his post as head watchmen. Then the ʿumdah's "gang" had him beaten and began conspiring to steal his money and land. They also succeeded in having him sentenced to prison for a crime he did not commit, though eventually the conviction was overturned on appeal. In 1904, he had petitioned the government to investigate what he by then described as a plot involving five or six other headmen from nearby villages, the district commissioner of Santah, five local prosecutors, eight court clerks, and the mudir of Gharbiyah himself. By the closing months of 1907, his situation had only grown more dire, and he sent no fewer than four separate petitions, each more insistent than the last. From the Khedive, al-ʿAshri specifically begged for intercession from a higher authority. His earlier entreaties had been passed down through the Interior and the Ministry of Justice and "no one paid attention to them because of the ties between the ʿumdah and the men of the administration and the courts."[110]

CONCLUSION

In their sheer multitude and diversity, the petitions of villagers like al-ʿAshri delivered their own response to the occupation's economistic discourse of rule and its attendant rejection of local politics. For the very peasants the occupation claimed as the deserving beneficiaries of their presence in the country, politics had never inhered solely in the electoral procedures that the British were so eager to abolish. Attentive, by force of circumstance, to the complex and differentiated "institutional materiality" of the offices, laws, procedures, and infrastructures that together comprised the Egyptian state, politics for those subaltern populations had always entailed a more creative exploration of the chinks, crevices, and levers that might, howsoever infrequently, allow them to rebuff or evade the demands that others made upon them.[111] That those endowed with greater access to power would abuse it for their own ends was, from this vantage, axiomatic.

Unlike the Khedive's spies, the petitioners who begged mercy from their sovereign made little attempt to compare their unhappy present against a glorified past. What had changed for them was not the character or mores of the individuals who filled local offices so much as the means available to challenge them. The forced reorganization of rural settlement space and the destruction of ʿizab closed down routes that some peasants had traveled to evade the authority of village officials. The abolition of local elections, whether in rural villages or urban guilds, removed another resource that could be mobilized to check or temper the abuse of power. The bureaucratization of disciplinary procedures within the ministries radically curtailed the already limited possibilities for intervention from on high. A state that was more unified and "effective" was also one that had constrained the room for maneuver.[112]

Neither the occupation's infrastructural projects nor its takeover of the Interior succeeded in thinning the complexities of everyday life in the countryside down to the bare routines of agricultural production. If nothing else, the stories that filled the pages of khedivial spy reports and peasant petitions alike offered a continuous rebuke against the notions that government could ever be remade as a mere instrument of economic development or that power could somehow be divorced from the mundane execution of the state's directives. Cromer's grand pronouncements of "peace and tranquility" notwithstanding, the occupation did not remove politics, in this broader sense, from the countryside. And yet the restructuring of the Interior in the 1890s did effect several significant and lasting changes. On the one hand, Gorst's arrival as adviser did not so much eliminate the practices the British identified with "Oriental despotism" as hide them from view. Yet for the time being at least, this appearance of a professionalized executive hierarchy responsive to commands emanating from Cairo would provide a usable semblance of order and regularity upon which the occupation could continue to pursue its ambitions. On the other, the concerted evisceration of local elections did contribute to a more general and remarkably durable conceptual shift. Across the decades that followed, struggles for popular political representation would play out almost exclusively over national institutions. Even as recently as the constitutional debates that erupted after the uprisings of January 2011, the centralized system of provincial and local appointments that the British imposed would remain largely intact. As an organized opposition to British rule gained momentum from the 1890s onwards, the nation as a whole would thus become the predominant geographic scale of politics. Everything else was just administration.

Chapter 3

FIELDS OF FINANCE

BY THE TIME Falconer Larkworthy submitted his "Report on Egypt as a Field for Banking Business" in March of 1905, the race to plant foreign capital in Egyptian soil was quickening.[1] The Ionian Bank had already lost one of its employees to the temptations of the Egyptian boom.[2] Anxious to learn more, its board dispatched Larkworthy, the bank's chairman, to investigate the merits of extending operations to Egypt. Writing from Alexandria, he proclaimed, "The stability of the financial situation in Egypt is beyond doubt, and the credit of the country was never higher. . . . It is worthy of note that it has only taken 25 years for Egypt, under British administration, to attain its present degree of prosperity"[3] It was no surprise, then, that "so many banks are hankering after the flesh pots of Egypt."[4]

Larkworthy's assessment contained an unwitting prophecy. In the biblical passage he was referencing, the hungry Israelites begin their hankering only after they have fled the Land of Pharaoh.[5] Just two years later, the bankers Larkworthy cast as a ravenous horde would make their own exodus. But in 1905, his bullish attitude was anything but unusual. By the early 1900s, Egypt had gained the global reputation of a latter-day "El Dorado," and the country's land and credit markets were drawing new investors from all across Europe.[6] The capital that arrived from abroad between 1897 and 1907 exceeded the total amount from the previous fifty years.[7] In that same decade, the paid-up capital of companies operating in Egypt increased from £E 13,885,000 to £E 87,176,000.[8] Of those many millions, the lion's share went toward the establishment of banks and mortgage companies.[9] Between 1901 and 1907, the aggregate mortgage debt recorded in the registers of Egypt's Mixed Courts increased from £E 6.7 million to £E 42 million.[10] Land values in many rural areas grew by a factor of five, and the prices of urban properties in Cairo and Alexandria rose by as much as ten times in as many years.[11] Capturing the unwavering optimism of the moment in early 1907, the *Egyptian Gazette* observed, "A review of the trade of Egypt during the past few years has become a monotonous reiteration of continued success. Nothing occurs to check its steady expansion, and it would be difficult to imagine a calamity of sufficient importance to disturb its solid foundation."[12]

That Britain's veiled protectorate became a target for European investment in the late nineteenth century was not at all unusual. That such investment assumed the form of banks making loans directly to Egyptians themselves was. When they began in earnest to court foreign financial investment in the mid-1890s, British officials made Egypt the meeting point between two very different developments that had been unfolding thousands of miles apart since the 1870s. The first arose out of the severe economic slump that sent commodity prices tumbling across much of the globe. In the long wake of this First Great Depression of 1873–1896, European investors deputized the banks and money markets of London, Paris, and Brussels to place their idle capital wherever in the world yields were highest and most secure. The second development concerned the phenomenon of peasant indebtedness that seemed to follow the spread of cash-crop agriculture wherever it occurred. Though by no means unique to the British Raj, the problem there became a focal point of concerns over the social transformations that colonial rule had set in motion. In seeking to address what they understood as a crippling cycle of usury, distinct camps of British officials returned again and again to questions about the analytical purchase of political economy among the "subject races" of the Orient.

Inspired by one position in that Indian debate, British officials in Egypt proposed that these two stories might be made to converge. European capital in search of higher returns would become credit to peasant farmers desperate for lower interest rates. This was colonial economism in its purest form. Beginning in the 1890s, Cromer's administration adopted a range of policies that specifically targeted Egypt's smallholders as agrarian capitalists-in-waiting. Equitable revenue assessments and secure title to property would incentivize productive improvements to the land. Novel institutional arrangements would channel funds directly from the banking centers of Europe into the farthest reaches of the countryside. In 1902, these credit experiments culminated in the establishment of the occupation's most famous and significant financial innovation, the Agricultural Bank of Egypt.

By the turn of the century, financial capital was gushing in from abroad. British officials claimed Egypt's newfound prosperity as a fulfillment of their own utopian designs. But as this foreign investment gained momentum, the character and consequences of the boom grew more ambiguous. Finance was a game of interest riddled with contradictions. Initially, the relative paucity of competing institutions allowed newcomers to expect returns in Egypt well beyond what Europe's money markets could offer. However foreign Egypt's people might seem, British rule had established the conditions for credit transactions that were perfectly familiar. The decision to place capital in the Nile Valley was becoming a simple matter of calculating returns, and the occupation's reforms had made those calculations both more knowable and more enticing. At the same time, this pursuit of monetary yields and the attendant indifference to the underlying source of profit cut against the stated objectives of the occupation's agrarian programs in several key respects. First, despite the publicity around mortgage lending to smallholders, the share of foreign capital that did reach the countryside accrued mostly to Egypt's wealthiest landlords. Second, as a rising tide of farm credit drove interest rates ever lower, a growing crowd of lenders began to seek other more lucrative opportunities. The resulting frenzy of speculation muddied the relationship between paper fortunes and what many contemporaries referred to as "real wealth." Finally, the value of most financial assets in Egypt ultimately represented claims upon the future productivity of the soil and the laboring bodies that farmed it. Though the fullest consequences would become apparent only years later, the ramshackle structure of leveraged debts that Europe's financiers helped to erect would leave its impression deep in the fields.

BELLE ÉPOQUE FINANCIALIZATION

When boosters extolled Egypt's virtues, they often began by naming the problem to which the country offered a solution. The prolonged slump of the First Great Depression between 1873 and1896 had left investors in Europe with fewer appealing options. The subsequent transfer of idle capital to territories offering higher rates of profit represented a classic case of what the geographer David Harvey has called a "spatial fix" to capitalism's crisis tendencies.[13] It was a role Egypt had played before. In one sense, the fin-de-siècle boom continued a pattern that had held since the 1850s, when "Haussmannization" emerged as a global strategy for dealing with sinking profits in the metropole.[14] In Egypt (as more famously in India) the spectacular proliferation of debt-financed infrastructures had offered attractive returns while integrating remote agrarian regions more directly into global export markets.[15] When British officials proposed that foreign-funded mortgages to Egyptian farmers might offer a new fix to Europe's woes, they implied that this grand imperial symbiosis between financial and industrial capital would continue. Loans secured against Egyptian properties would furnish European financial investors with hefty returns. And by supplying farmers with funds for the improvement of their land, new sources of credit would generate more fiber for European mills. The ensuing increase in general prosperity would, moreover, secure the political conditions for future waves of investment. It was an appealing sales pitch. But by the late 1890s when it began to gain traction, there were already reasons to believe that this version of Egypt's financialized future was wishful thinking.

Foremost among those reasons were the causes of the First Great Depression itself. Even in the mid-century heyday of Lancashire's influence, the unity of industrial and banking capital was at best contingent and "stressful."[16] By the 1870s, the stress had become acute. Thanks in no small measure to the extraordinary success that Britain had won, a growing crowd of aspiring competitors sought to replicate the productive achievements of the industrial juggernaut. Manufactured goods from the developing industrial sectors of other European states as well as Japan and the United States began to flood global markets and drive prices downward. The ensuing worldwide depression was, first and foremost, a crisis of overproduction in which cutthroat competition menaced the profit margins that metropolitan industries had once enjoyed.[17] Under such conditions, many enterprises opted against further rounds of investment in the expansion of industrial commodity production and chose instead to "keep at least part of their capital liquid and let the City, via the provincial bank or directly through brokers, take care of its investment in whatever form and in whatever location of the world-economy promised the safest and highest returns."[18]

The worldwide financial expansion of the fin de siècle era represented a parting of the ways in which the major banking centers of Europe undertook to locate sources of profit that the mills and factories could no longer, on their own, sustain.[19] On a global scale, the most significant consequence of these developments was the massive redirection of capital from Britain to the United States that prepared the way for the "long twentieth century" of American hegemony.[20] Unsurprisingly, the history of this process of financialization has appeared most often as a Euro-American story. But a focus on the largest recipients of these capital transfers alone runs the risk of obscuring the truly global character of the transformations taking place. Equally important in this new era of financial ferment was both a quantitative increase and a qualitative shift in the pattern of investments targeting regions well beyond the developed core of industrial capitalism. It is only this new geography, in which colonial territories were as often the incubators for new techniques and institutions as the recipients of ready-made examples from elsewhere, that begins to explain how Egypt and the United States could undergo such similar and closely connected crises when the bubble finally burst in 1907.

For much of the nineteenth century, the large industries of Europe—textile mills in Lancashire foremost among them—had appeared as the leading edge of capitalist development. In the financial innovations of the fin de siècle, some now proposed that agrarian regions might become a new frontier for capital's onward movement. In Egypt, as in other sites of financial experimentation, this vision of capitalized agriculture was closely bound up with the standardization of property regimes. But the role that landed property would play in this new relation of capital to rural societies was somewhat different from the one commonly ascribed to it. While critical social histories of modern Egypt have long identified the consolidation of property rights in land as a marker of capitalism in agriculture, they have commonly done so by analyzing property as an instrument of enclosure whereby new relations of production were established. Property, on this understanding, provided the mechanism for separating peasants from the land and thereby established a deepening class divide between a mass of landless workers and a landed bourgeoisie who could now exploit their labor for the production of surplus value.[21]

The "interests of capital," however, were never singular and unitary. From the perspective of financial investors abroad, what Egypt's regime of property made possible was a relation to land as a "pure financial asset."[22] That is, land could be treated more and more as one among any number of revenue-generating assets through which capital in search of higher returns might circulate. In theory at least, the organization of production on the land itself could thereby become a secondary concern to the annualized yield a given loan was structured to guarantee. Whether the land in question was farmed by a peasant family or by wage laborers working the latest machinery would be a matter of relative indifference. In practice, however, those same investors understood that the land against which their loans were secured was owned by actual people, and they were far more inclined to bank on some groups of people than on others. It was in just this sense that the discourse of colonial economism opened the way for a novel convergence.

DEBATING THE INDEBTED PEASANT

The policies that first drew mortgage investors to Egypt marked the culmination of British efforts to target smallholders as the productive beneficiaries of colonial reform. Drawing on ideas he had first encountered in India, Lord Cromer made Egypt the laboratory in which to test the potential of colonial agriculture to serve as a new frontier for metropolitan finance. Although he would wait until the 1890s to launch these experiments, the problem of peasant indebtedness had loomed large in British analyses of Egyptian society from the beginning. In the aftermath of the 'Urabi revolt, a British MP named Villiers Stuart had toured the Delta on behalf of the Dufferin Commission. Stuart's published findings described a landscape ravaged by usury. Turning Khedive Isma'il's fiscal misadventures to their advantage, he explained, Greek and Levantine moneylenders had trailed the government's tax collectors and extended credit to all who could not pay. Their loans were extortionate. So extreme was the burden that the aggregate interest on private borrowing exceeded the government's annual revenue from the land tax. In this alarming figure lay a double threat. Not only was this "domestic debt" a "constant source of danger to the peace of Egypt through the discontent it occasions. But besides that, it comes into mischievous competition with the Imperial taxation and the claims of the bondholders."[23]

In his warnings about "the unintentional part we have taken in bringing back the usurers," Stuart was wading into a debate that exercised government officials, political economists, and social reformers across much of the globe in the late nineteenth century.[24] At its center was the figure of the indebted smallholder. The mounting debts of farmers in regions recently incorporated into global markets seemed to undermine the most optimistic pronouncements of classical political economy about the universal benefits of free market exchange. British colonial officials in particular had reason to regard the phenomenon as something more than an academic curiosity.

Events in India weighed heavily on the occupation's approach to this agrarian question in Egypt. Ever since the Indian Revolt of 1857, imperial administrators had been voicing fears that the pace of liberal reforms had so disrupted the foundations of the established social order as to threaten British rule altogether. The phenomenon of rural usury became something of an obsession among the new generation of colonial conservatives who followed Henry Maine in warning that continued social dislocation would ignite another agrarian conflagration. Those concerns came to a head in the so-called Deccan Riots.[25] In 1875, villagers in the districts of Pune and Ahmadnagar east of Bombay had swarmed the homes and shops of local moneylenders to demand that they surrender their ledgers and loan contracts.[26] There was little physical violence, and the disturbances were swiftly quelled.[27] Nevertheless, the sharp specificity of peasant animus seemed to confirm the fears of British officials who saw political danger in rural credit relations.[28]

Of particular concern in this moment was an effort to distinguish between beneficial lending on the one hand and usury on the other. Though all agreed that the latter was dangerous and immoral, the line between the two proved elusive. While few writers at the time seemed to notice, the confusion arose in part from the ways in which debt could render the farmer's social role ambiguous. Farming cash crops for sale on world markets depended on flows of credit almost as much as water. Because they plowed their own money into the soil at the start of the growing cycle and needed to wait for plants to ripen before retrieving it, farmers required regular access to credit.[29] Within his own property, a landowner might employ the labor of others and treat the loans he received as capital to augment production. But debt was also a mechanism of value extraction. Whether or not he paid others to work his land, the farmer was working for his creditor. The result was a situation in which the indebted farmer could occupy the peculiar and contradictory class position of the "capitalist-laborer."[30]

Whether this capitalist-laborer appeared more as the former or the latter depended to a large extent on the rate of interest he paid. That singular abstraction represented its own tangle of problems. Beyond the many arrangements by which interest might be obscured, the rate itself condensed several distinct relationships and determinations into just one number. First, it indexed a set of actuarial assessments—whether calculated outright or estimated by convention—about the reputation of the borrower and the likelihood that the loan could be recovered. Second, the rate quantified a relation of force between two parties, one possessing money, the other requiring it. That relation could be pitched toward one side or the other by the workings of the law. But it could also depend upon the social milieu of the two parties, the cultural conventions that governed their encounter, and their respective interests in the loan agreement itself. Third, as a claim upon future wealth, interest expressed an expectation of profits. In the case of an agricultural loan, the rate projected—and indeed mandated—the increased productivity of the soil and the farmers who worked it. Finally, interest represented the price of money in a given credit market at a given time. That price could fluctuate widely according to the available supply of funds and the pool of prospective borrowers.

In time, all of these factors would figure in Egypt's experience of financial boom and bust, but when colonial officials debated the indebted peasant, they tended to fixate narrowly on some aspects of the credit relation far more than others. Most often, their commentaries reduced the complexity of the interest rate to a matter of the loan's origin and the identities of the borrower and the lender. They thereby attempted to understand a shifting and contradictory bundle of relationships by assigning fixed characteristics to discrete social types. The indebted peasant was an anomaly crying out for explanation, all the more so in regions where indebtedness seemed to be rising alongside other indicators of agricultural prosperity.

Within British India, nowhere was this puzzle more glaring than in the Punjab, where several decades of infrastructural projects had established the province as an enclave of privileged agrarian development.[31] In what would become a key text for one camp in the emerging debate, the young settlement officer Septimus Thorburn warned in 1886 that although the province was "enjoying greater agricultural prosperity than its oldest inhabitants could remember," a large and growing proportion of peasant proprietors were "sinking into the position of serfs to the money-lenders."[32] Like the writings of other figures in this Punjab school of colonial conservatism, *Musalmans and Money-Lenders* was less an outright rejection of classical political economy than an effort to defend its core principles through recourse to a banal taxonomy of racial difference.

In Thorburn's analysis, the pattern of dispossession that "will eventually lose us India" had everything to do with the two racial types that encountered each other to contract the loan. British policy, he explained, had abetted a profoundly asymmetrical relation of force between "reckless and improvident" Muslim peasants who were "in worldly intelligence as stupid as plough-oxen" and Hindu moneylenders who "spend their lives in their shops, and devote all their time to money making. Being naturally shrewd and unprincipled, they are as proficient in the art as Jews or Greeks."[33]

For Thorburn, as for Villiers Stuart, rural indebtedness was the consequence of alien institutions foisted upon populations unable to handle them. It fostered ethnic and sectarian hatred between Muslim peasants and their Hindu, Greek, or Jewish creditors. When debt led to foreclosure, it swelled the ranks of disgruntled landless peasants. In actual practice, high levels of indebtedness at "usurious" rates could describe a considerable variety of arrangements, not all of which would lead toward expropriation.[34] Thorburn and his ilk, however, believed that more debt meant more dispossession. On that basis, they advocated paternalistic protections to shield peasants from their own shortsightedness and the usurers' greed. This approach provided the impetus behind a variety of new acts—among them the Punjab Alienation of Land Bill of 1900—that erected legal barriers between peasants and moneylenders and thereby barred the transfer of land away from cultivators.[35]

Alarmed by the findings of Villiers Stuart's rural tour, Lord Dufferin had on his own proposed a similar remedy.[36] Years later, British officials would revisit the idea, and when they did, they looked specifically to the Punjab for inspiration.[37] But in the 1890s, when Cromer's regime took up the question of indebtedness, it was an opposing school of thought that held sway. According to this line of thought, more credit, not less, was the answer. By forging direct links between peasant households and European investors, the proponents of this latter position saw a means to address the geographically disparate crises of slumping profits in the metropole and mounting indebtedness in the colonial countryside.

In India, the most outspoken representative of this latter position was a Scottish civil servant named William Wedderburn. A fervent critic of the Government of India's famine policies, Wedderburn later helped to establish the Indian National Congress. In the 1870s, he was serving as a district judge at Ahmadnagar, one of the two towns where the Deccan Riots had first occurred.[38] For Wedderburn, the disturbances were a consequence of structural changes that had unnecessarily set the cultivator at odds with his creditor. One problem he identified was that new fixed revenue assessments often forced peasants to pay their taxes before they had sold their crops.[39] But by the early 1880s, Wedderburn had developed a growing interest in the mechanisms of rural lending itself.

In a series of articles first written for the *Bombay Gazette* in 1881, Wedderburn offered a global survey of novel agricultural credit institutions. Implicit in this comparative framing was an assertion that the problems of indebted farmers in Europe were similar to those he encountered in India. Like his conservative interlocutors, Wedderburn grounded his analysis on an assessment of the Indian peasant's innate character, but his findings left him far more confident that the problem of indebtedness in India might be amenable to the same kinds of solutions that had recently worked in Europe. "The ryot," he explained, "has always been the proprietor of his ancestral holding. The bondage from which he suffers is recent and temporary. And all that is wanted is to restore him to his own natural and healthy condition. As soon as the bonds are severed he will stand upright, and be a man."[40]

The mechanism for achieving this "natural and healthy condition" would be a new network of agricultural banks. In this institutional innovation, Wedderburn foresaw the possibility of mobilizing the money markets of Europe to turn the recent depression to the advantage of investors and borrowers alike. Agricultural banks backed by "a flood of English capital" would liberate India's agricultural classes from their onerous debts and initiate a virtuous cycle of rising prosperity.[41] Speaking before the Manchester Chamber of Commerce in 1883, Wedderburn elaborated further:

> In India we have a fine clime, a rich soil, and abundance of agricultural labour, both cheap and skillful. All of the conditions would be favourable if the cultivator were not starved for want of capital. On the other hand, here in Europe

> accumulated capital is anxiously seeking channels for investment. . . . It is as though on the one hand we had rich but thirsty soil; on the other hand vast stores of fertilizing water. What we now wish to provide is a channel of communication, in order that all parties may be benefited.[42]

Though his idea would eventually provide yet another Indian model for an Egyptian institution, Wedderburn here marshaled evidence from Egypt as he pressed for the plan's adoption in India. Noting that in Egypt "the position of the cultivator resembles that of the Indian raiyat," he mentioned the recent formation of two "loan companies"—one English, one French—that had "done much to redeem the peasantry."[43] In enlisting this Egyptian example, Wedderburn overlooked some complicating details. The companies to which he referred were the French Crédit Foncier and the British Land and Mortgage Company, both founded in 1880.[44] Contrary to his description, the clients of the two new banks were all proprietors of large estates; neither would offer credit to "the peasantry" in the manner he was advocating. In fact, it was the overwhelming reluctance of private banks like these to countenance the risk and expense of lending to smallholders that would lead the Egyptian government, roughly a decade later, to begin experimenting with Wedderburn's designs.

Misleading though it was, Wedderburn's Egyptian detour was nevertheless indicative of the future he imagined possible. The solution to the peasant's debts, as he saw it, was not less credit but more. By channeling European finance directly into the fields, new banking institutions would realize the colonial smallholder's metamorphosis into a modernizing agrarian capitalist, applying the latest European machinery to an ever-expanding production of marketable commodities.

Like the water in his irrigation metaphor, however, money could not simply flow from Europe's banking centers to the villages of the Deccan on its own. Administering a large number of small loans in remote rural areas could be expensive and risky. To serve as a "channel of communication," Wedderburn's bank would therefore enjoy two key concessions. First, its loans would be serviced not by its own employees but by government tax collectors who would simply receive installments when the land tax came due.[45] Second, to entice wary investors, the Government of India would guarantee a minimum return on the shares and bonds issued to fund the bank. Whereas in the past the revenue collected from Indian taxpayers had been pledged against returns for capital fixed in railways, roads, and irrigation canals, Wedderburn now sought to extend that financing incentive to the yield on a multitude of loans to individual farmers.[46]

When Wedderburn began promoting his scheme, Cromer was still serving as finance member under Lord Ripon, the Viceroy of India. Though he expressed some reservations about the state's role in backing a private enterprise, Cromer supported the idea.[47] With Ripon's approval, the Government of India recommended Wedderburn's plan to London in 1883, but after several years of delay, the India Office ultimately rejected the proposal.[48] Cromer remained enthusiastic about the proposal, and eventually it provided the basis for the series of trials and experiments that led to the formation of the Agricultural Bank of Egypt in 1902.

If the bank Cromer helped to establish closely resembled Wedderburn's model, however, his underlying conception of the bank's peasant borrowers marked out a distinct position in the wider debate. It was in his approach to agrarian finance that Cromer carried the logic of colonial economism to its most dramatic conclusions. Like Thorburn and countless others, the consul-general was quick to condemn usury as a symptom of racial defects. In *Modern Egypt* he would later explain that Levantine merchants "have done a vast amount of harm by associating the name of European in the minds of the Egyptians with a total absence of scruple in the pursuit of gain."[49] His dual role as both lender and peddler of alcohol, meanwhile, marked the Greek usurer as a figure of singular disrepute. "He tempts the Egyptian peasant to borrow at some exorbitant rate of interest," Cromer charged, "and then, by a sharp turn of the legal screw, reduces him from the position of an allodial proprietor to that of a serf."[50]

Cromer's elaborate racial taxonomies may have exemplified a mode of Orientalist exceptionalism quite distinct from the optimistic comparisons that underpinned Wedderburn's plans. But he did share the latter's confidence in the transformative potential of an agricultural bank. By Cromer's line of reasoning, the bank would not only provide a more abundant supply of credit at reasonable interest; it would also remove the malign influence of the usurer and replace him with the virtuous European financier. As for the peasant borrower, Cromer's enthusiasm for agricultural banking rested ultimately on his conviction that the fallah was a human subject singularly devoted to economic self-interest. When granted the opportunity, that sober and hardworking figure could employ credit productively, plowing European capital into the land to generate rising profits for borrower and lender alike. The cycle of mutual benefit would, in turn, yield a more lasting political effect. Of the Agricultural Bank, Cromer later explained that the "principal object I had in mind" was "to create a large class of small holders who would constitute a conservative dead weight, averse to any radical change."[51]

PAPER PILLARS OF THE FINANCIAL BOOM

Throughout its first decade issues of agrarian finance lay mostly beyond the occupation's reach. The Anglo-Indian engineers may have described irrigation canals as conduits of social reform, but they recognized that the underlying regime of land ownership and taxation would prove far more contentious. While they made piecemeal adjustments to revenue rates in certain districts and attempted to augment the overall productivity of the land, they otherwise left intact the unequal system of tax classifications that Lord Dufferin and others had identified as among the most glaring injustices of khedivial rule.[52] But beginning in the mid-1890s, having consolidated a more decisive hold on the ministries, the British embarked upon a far more ambitious program to reassess taxes, register title to land, and ultimately introduce new sources of credit into the countryside. It was at this point that the occupation's fiscal agenda moved well beyond the budgetary restraint of the 1880s. As they were conceived, implemented, and publicized, these policies specifically targeted the Egyptian smallholder as an agent of economic growth. Reduced taxes and better credit, so the argument went, would together furnish the smallholder with capital for productive farm improvements.

In 1894, thanks in large part to a bumper crop in the United States, raw cotton flooded global markets, and prices in Egypt fell. It was this slump that the Khedive's spy Muhammad Rushdi took as evidence that Britain's "reforms" were driving the country into abject poverty.[53] Cromer took that same "agricultural depression" as reason to argue that the occupation had not yet done enough. For many farmers the downturn had made the government's revenue demands much harder to bear. "Although it has not been proved that the land tax, at its present amount, constitutes, in the aggregate, an unduly heavy burthen on the country," he explained "it is none the less true that the incidence of the tax, as at present assessed, is very unequal."[54] This inequality was enshrined in the khedivate's system of revenue classifications. Initially, Mehmed Ali Pasha had exempted many of the land grants he made to his family and supporters from the annual *kharaj* land tax.[55] In 1854, Muhammad Sa'id Pasha's government terminated the exemption and began to tax many of these holdings at a rate of one tenth (*'ushr*) of the annual harvest; they were thereafter referred to as *'ushuri*.[56] While the maximum tax rate on 'ushuri lands had risen over subsequent decades, kharaji and 'ushuri continued to designate a gaping disparity with little or no relation to the productivity of the soil. Condemning this older system as a manifest injustice, British officials cited extreme cases in which 'ushuri lands that rented for £E 5 per acre paid only 18 piasters in taxes while kharaji land in the same village with a rental value of £E 2 paid as much as 164 piasters.[57] As Cromer later remarked, "The most ignorant Egyptian fellah or Indian ryot can understand the difference between a Government which takes nine-tenths of his crop in the shape of land-tax, and one which only takes one-third or one-fourth."[58]

The main obstacle to a comprehensive reassessment of the land tax, as the British understood matters, was the "small but influential minority" of large landlords who enjoyed the lowest rates.[59] Their approach was therefore crafted to minimize political blowback from that privileged class. At the outset, the government announced that the aggregate sum of the land tax would be fixed at its 1894 level for the next thirty years.[60] The new measures would simply redistribute the existing tax burden, leaving landowners to pocket any subsequent increase in the value of their properties.[61]

To achieve this Egyptian variation on the permanent settlements that had once been a hallmark of liberal revenue policies in India, the government required a mass of new data about the value and ownership of all cultivated land in the country.[62] Between April 1895 and April 1897, a commission headed by William Willcocks of the Public Works Ministry produced tables of rental values village by village as well as an annual sum for the entire country.[63] The amount of the land tax collected in 1894 was divided by this countrywide total of £E 16,356,000 to yield a new uniform tax rate of 28.64 %.[64] Actually implementing the new rates would require the far more daunting challenge of a cadastral survey to certify the precise extent and boundaries of each holding, a task that would not be completed until 1907.[65]

This process of surveying land and adjusting tax rates was a massive and protracted undertaking. Unsurprisingly, it garnered extensive commentary. In the most glowing renditions, these efforts were "one of the clearest proofs of the government's progressive development and the removal of . . . the forms of tyranny and inequality that occurred in times past."[66] The Khedive's spies, by contrast, saw many signs of "disorder" in the work of British surveyors who seemed to spend more time drinking whiskey in their tents than inspecting the fields.[67] Some local papers carried stories alleging collusion between the surveyors and foreign land companies that sought to steal government property.[68] Whatever the truth of such allegations, the concern to monitor the surveys and tax reforms attests to a widespread awareness of the political stakes involved. Alert to the occupation's claims about material improvement, supporters and critics alike set out to document more closely the actual consequences of its policies.

It was in response to one particularly public and damning statement along these lines that, at roughly the same time, Cromer's administration directed its attention to the question of agricultural credit. Perhaps emboldened by the recent defiance of the young Khedive, the Legislative Council opened its budget report for 1894 with a critical preface on the problem of peasant indebtedness. The note asserted that between 1881 and 1891 the private debt registered at Egypt's various courts had increased from £E 12 million to £E 20 million.[69] In the council's estimation, these figures suggested that British rule was driving Egypt's rural majority into debt peonage.

Cromer responded by tasking Elwin Palmer—then adviser to the Ministry of Finance—to conduct his own study. After mobilizing the ministry's staff to tabulate all of the private debts registered in the courts, Palmer reported that total mortgage debt stood at £E 7,323,300, not the £E 20,000,000 the Legislative Council had claimed.[70] His tables showed that the area of mortgaged land equaled only about 8% of all private property. "In the second place," he observed, "it results from the numbers in this same table that at least four fifths of the debt are at the expense of landowners possessing an area over 10 feddans and that among the latter, the proprietors of 50 feddans or more represent on their own 71% of the total mortgage debt observed."[71] Cromer included Palmer's findings in his annual report for 1894. Rather than proving "any deterioration in the position of the small landed proprietor," he judged, the ministry's statistics "point, on the contrary, to an ever growing appreciation of land. . . . It appears, therefore, to be tolerably clear that the burden of debt weighing on the poorer proprietors is inconsiderable, while the indebtedness of the wealthier class is willingly incurred as a stepping-stone to more extended economic development."[72]

As even Cromer elsewhere acknowledged, the lopsided distribution of debt in Palmer's table could also indicate differential access to sources of agricultural

TABLE 1: Data from Elwin Palmer's Mortgage Debt Table.

Landowners Categorized by Area Owned	Number of Landowners in Each Category	Area Owned by Each Category of Landowner	Area Mortgaged (feddans)	Percentage of the Area for Each Category	Amount of Debt (£E)	Percentage of the Total Debt
5 feddans or less	513,080	933,700	21,400	2.29%	573,300	7.82%
5 to 10 feddans	75,130	552,700	16,000	2.90%	392,200	5.35%
10 to 20 feddans	39,620	560,300	20,400	3.64%	407,700	5.57%
20 to 30 feddans	13,140	326,100	19,600	6.00%	307,200	4.20%
30 to 50 feddans	8,980	347,800	25,900	7.44%	409,900	5.60%
More than 50 feddans	11,430	2,000,700	292,300	14.60%	5,233,000	71.46%
Total	**661,380**	**4,721,300**	**395,600**	**8.38%**	**7,323,300**	**100%**

SOURCE: DWQ, MNW 0075-0222991.

credit. In fact, this class fragmentation of the credit system was more pronounced than Palmer's methods allowed him to discern. The Egyptian government would not attempt a more comprehensive study for another two decades.[73] But other sources from these years offer anecdotal evidence about the world beyond the court system's contract registers. Records of probate inventory (*hasr tarakah*) in particular tended to list all of the deceased party's debts, not only those registered with the Mixed Courts.[74] Contrary to British claims about Greek, Levantine, and Jewish usurers, the figure of the foreign (*khawajah*) moneylender appeared only rarely in the lists of claimants to the estates of Egypt's poorest landowners. Variations in borrowing patterns between properties of different sizes, moreover, reveal what an approximate and misleading category "smallholder" could be. Many of those owning one feddan or less showed no debts at the time of their death. The majority of debts they did incur took the form of *shar'i* usufructory mortgages (*rahunat*) between landowners within the village.[75] Some of these loans were recorded in the registers of Egypt's shari'ah courts, while others were simply handled locally by the two parties to the transaction.[76] Oftentimes, the primary lenders were members of the borrower's immediate family. Perhaps more surprising still, many of the creditors listed were women, probably widows putting the funds from an inheritance to work.[77] What few debts to individuals with foreign names did appear were usually listed as *diyun*, that is, commercial loans secured against crops and other goods rather than land.[78]

The Palmer report, then, offered at best a partial representation of the debt relations it promised to quantify. And its findings were most incomplete for the very stratum of agrarian society around which the original disagreement turned. Despite its authoritative claims, the report's mobilization of statistical data did little to settle politically charged questions about how the occupation's policies were affecting borrowing practices in particular or the condition of smallholders in general. In his published comments on the study, however, Cromer began to gesture at a different audience for these publications that was neither the political subject seeking to gauge the progress of reforms nor the government official attempting to perfect the machine of state. They may have collapsed the lived complexities of local experience or erased the struggles involved in their collection. But published data of this kind began to render Egypt legible, accessible, and globally comparable for investors anywhere with the means and motivation to read them. And when read together, Palmer's tabulation of debts and the Willcocks commission's rent assessments provided a preliminary framework for calculating relative levels of mortgage debt on landed property, both locally and nationally. Cromer's conclusion that "the burden of debt weighing on the poorer proprietors is inconsiderable, while the indebtedness of the wealthier class is willingly incurred" was not only a public reassurance that British rule was protecting Egypt's peasants from poverty and expropriation. It was also an announcement that Egypt—like the India of William Wedderburn's irrigation metaphor—was a land of "rich but thirsty soil" calling out for the "fertilizing water" of European capital. Efforts to tailor the contents of annual reports and other government publications to the needs and interests of an investing public abroad only became more pronounced in the years that followed. This was clearly what the long-serving British police official Charles Coles Pasha had in mind when he referred to Egypt as "at one time the most advertised country in the world."[79]

THE BIRTH OF THE AGRICULTURAL BANK

Having spotted opportunity in Palmer's study, Cromer began laying the groundwork for a new agricultural bank modeled closely on Wedderburn's design. In 1895, the Egyptian government allocated £E 10,000 for loans not exceeding £E 10 apiece to proprietors of five feddans or less in several districts of the provinces of Gharbiyah and Sharqiyah. At 6%, these experimental loans carried interest well below both the legal limit of 9% and the actual rates offered by rural moneylenders.[80] The measure earned plaudits from the Arabic press.[81] Amidst calls to expand the program, Cromer clarified that "the Government has no intention of embarking upon banking operations on a large scale. . . . It will depend on the results of this experiment whether at some future time an endeavour is made to come to some arrangement with a private bank with a view to more extended operations."[82]

The opportunity for such an arrangement emerged just a few years later. In June of 1898, a khedivial decree authorized the formation of the National Bank of Egypt (*al-Bank al-Ahli al-Misri*). With a capital of £1 million, the bank was funded by the British financier Sir Ernest Cassel, who purchased half of the initial offering, and the Egyptian merchant banking houses of Ralph Suares and C. M. Salvago, each of which covered half of the remaining £500,000.[83] While established as a publicly traded company and financed with private capital, the bank enjoyed the status of a quasi–state institution; along with its regular commercial operations, it held the accounts of the Egyptian government and enjoyed the right to issue paper banknotes.[84] When the bank was founded, Elwin Palmer left his post as financial adviser to become its first governor. In that capacity, he oversaw the continuation of the agricultural credit experiments that had begun during his tenure at the ministry. In 1899, the National Bank began to make two classes of loans to smallholders in the district of Bilbays in Sharqiyah province: one-year advances of up to £E 20 to cover annual farming expenses and five-year loans of up to £E 100 for the consolidation of existing debts.[85] Both types of loans now incurred interest at the legal limit of 9%. In accord with Wedderburn's proposal, the bank was permitted to use the village tax collectors (*sayarif*) as collection agents for its loans.[86]

The National Bank soon expanded the scope of this program. By 1901, the lending operations had grown large enough that the bank's directors, in consultation with the government, decided to transfer this business to a separate entity. A khedivial decree, dated May 17, 1902, established the Agricultural Bank of Egypt as an independent company enjoying both of the concessions that Wedderburn had advocated.[87] The sayarif continued to service the bank's tens of thousands of small loans for free. And the Egyptian government guaranteed that the initial offering of shares would receive a minimum return of 3% per annum; all subsequent issues of stocks or mortgage debentures received a similar guarantee.[88]

The Agricultural Bank had little difficulty attracting investors, and the value of its outstanding loans quickly soared, from £E 1,208,200 in 1902 to £E 7,033,486 by 1906.[89] Some borrowers used the opportunity to refinance existing debts.[90] Others seemed to believe (sometimes to their detriment) that the bank's special relationship with the government would cause it to deal more leniently with borrowers than their existing creditors.[91] The bank's own reporting suggested that the loans were often taken to consolidate debts, cover basic farming costs, and purchase new land.[92]

The explosive growth of the bank's business quickly gained the venture international renown. In 1904, Frederick A. Nicholson, a member of the Board of Revenue for the Madras presidency, proposed the creation of an agricultural bank in India organized according to what he now described as an Egyptian model.[93] Though it failed to gain the necessary support, Nicholson's memo circulated widely throughout the colonial administration in India and sparked numerous inquiries into whether

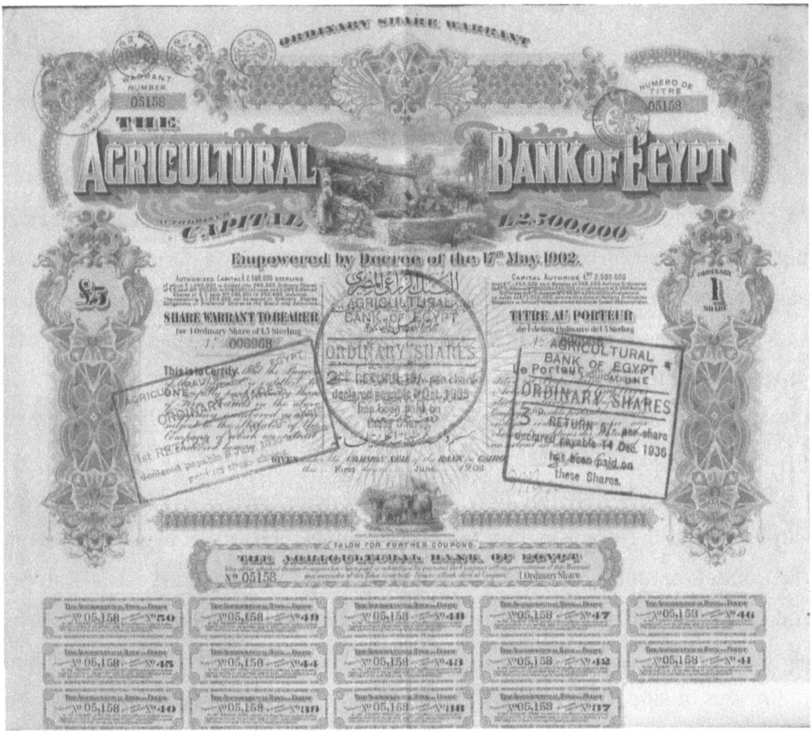

FIGURE 2: Stock Certificate of the Agricultural Bank of Egypt (1903). Source: Collection of the author.

village officials in different parts of the country could fill the role of the Egyptian sayarif.[94] The United States also commissioned a report in 1906 to determine whether a comparable institution should be established in the Philippines.[95] Making explicit the racial theories that had underpinned the Egyptian original, the *Washington Post* noted that "[the] Filipino and the Egyptian belong to entirely different races.... The Egyptian fellah is industrious and docile, making him a productive laborer and easily controlled, but the warmest admirers of the Filipino do not include among his other good qualities docility and industry."[96] Such skepticism notwithstanding, the occupation's experiments won the plaudits of the Roosevelt administration, which came to see Egypt as the model for a more progressive mode of colonial rule.[97] And although the final version differed in key respects, the Egyptian institution provided the original design for the Agricultural Bank of the Philippines that formed in June of 1908.[98]

BOOM TIMES

For all this international acclaim, the Agricultural Bank of Egypt never realized the sort of change its most zealous proponents had envisioned. At best, the bank slowed the fragmentation of small properties by lowering interest rates and, in some cases, allowing peasants to purchase new land.[99] That the loans they received did not suddenly transform Egypt's smallholders into improving agrarian capitalists or alleviate the stark class divisions in the countryside had a great deal to do with the wider context in which this much-vaunted experiment had taken place. In short, this program to channel foreign capital into loans to peasant smallholders was altogether dwarfed by the initiative of private companies to make investments they deemed more desirable and more secure.

British officials were not alone in trumpeting Egypt's virtues as an outlet for surplus capital. Beginning in the late 1890s, pamphlets and articles began to proclaim the wonders of mortgage banking in Egypt to prospective investors across Europe. Among the earliest examples of the genre was a short booklet entitled *Considerations sur les avantages et la sécurité des placements hypothécaires en Égypte*, published in Brussels in 1897.[100] Its author, Edouard Van Dieren, was a Belgian national who worked as a lawyer in the Mixed Court of Cairo. Van Dieren's text exemplifies the kind of discourse that would lead some of his more famous contemporaries to identify finance capital with a worldwide intensification of inter-imperial rivalries.[101] In an oblique reference to the lingering effects of the First Great Depression, he described a situation in which "the abundance of money accumulates so rapidly" and "the security of commercial transactions and industrial operations becomes so precarious" that "serious capitalists" were left with few appealing options in Europe. "The moment then seems to have come," he continued, "for capitalists to cast their eyes upon new lands, and Egypt among them occupies an entirely special situation."[102]

Van Dieren emphasized four factors that had gained Egypt its place as one of "the powers of premier credit."[103] First, the creation of the Mixed Courts in 1876 had established a familiar legal framework within which foreign creditors could negotiate debt instruments. Most notably, the courts operated a system of title and contract registration that could inform prospective lenders about the existing encumbrances on a given piece of land. Second, as attested by Cromer's annual reports, British rule had delivered a tremendous and ongoing increase in land values across the country.[104]

Third, foreign occupation itself was cause to reassure investors about the security of their capital. To Van Dieren's eyes, Egypt had become a colony in all but name. Even supposing that Britain should end its occupation, "there is no doubt that the powers would soon come to an agreement to create there a protectorate or an international regime which would, as effectively as today, guarantee the interests of foreigners."[105] Finally, the country enjoyed a "privileged situation in nature, which one does not encounter in any other country in the world." Mortgage investors could thus rest easy that the "prodigious fertility" of the soil would allow "the cultivator and the borrowing proprietor to meet the payments due with regularity."[106] Despite these enormous opportunities, Van Dieren observed, the mortgage sector remained mostly in the hands of just two businesses, the French Crédit Foncier and the British Land and Mortgage Company Limited.

Van Dieren was addressing himself specifically to his Belgian compatriots. But he was certainly not alone in considering the prospects of relocating an "abundance of money" to Egypt. And over the next few years, several major developments helped to bolster the sense of promise and opportunity he had sought to convey. The Anglo-Egyptian conquest of the Sudan in 1898–99 and the signing of the Entente Cordiale in 1904 seemed to confirm that British rule in Egypt would continue unchallenged.[107] A marked increase in the global price of cotton from the late 1890s onward inspired confidence that land values would continue to rise. And the completion of the first Aswan Dam in 1902, in substantially enhancing control over the supply of irrigation water, raised expectations for improvements to the productivity of existing properties and the reclamation of new terrain.[108]

This was the climate of exuberance that Falconer Larkworthy encountered when he traveled to Egypt for the Ionian Bank in 1905. Everything he saw convinced him that "wealth is rapidly increasing. There are all the constituents of economic growth, and of material happiness amongst the people."[109] The substance of his report in most respects echoed Van Dieren's case for mortgages on "high class urban properties and also estates of land."[110] Egypt's large landowners, Larkworthy noted, were figures of known reputation, and they tended to maintain good financial records. The goal in negotiating a mortgage, he reminded the Ionian Bank's directors, was both to minimize the chances of needing to seize property and to ensure that "purchasers are likely to be found in the event of the Bank having to foreclose and to realise its security."[111] But beyond the quality of the security they could offer, Larkworthy listed a new reason why the Ionian Bank should deal only with wealthy proprietors. In short, thanks to the government's concessions, any business with Egyptian smallholders "would be entirely handicapped in competition with the Agricultural Bank."[112] The same features that had gained the bank its global renown were repelling other institutions from that vast population of potential borrowers. Rather than reduce the class-specific striations of the credit system, the lending strategies of Egypt's new mortgage banks became a powerful mechanism for reinforcing and augmenting them.

FLOATING TOWARD CRISIS

If the mortgage investors who came "hankering" were reluctant to deal with Egypt's smallholders, they nevertheless saw ample opportunity in lending to the large landholders who controlled roughly two-fifths of the country's cultivable property. By the turn of the century, it was not conventional banks alone that were seeking clients among that wealthiest stratum of the population. In February 1899, a Birmingham solicitor named Robert Harding Milward approached the Alexandria branch of the Imperial Ottoman Bank about what he described as an exciting new opportunity. Milward had traveled to Egypt to monitor the investments of a British "Venture Syndicate" in several local companies. But before leaving England, he had convinced "a group of large life offices" to consider investing a portion of the float from their policy premiums in Egyptian mortgages. The insurance companies, he explained, could poach business from competing institutions by lending below the going interest rate, but they wanted an established bank to serve as a guarantor. If it agreed, the IOB would receive a commission of 0.75% per year on each loan, and the lenders would be shielded from any risk of default.[113]

The Alexandria branch manager John Reeves conveyed the proposal to his superiors in London, but they demurred. Since opening its first Egyptian branch in 1866, the IOB had played an important role in the debt transactions of the Egyptian state and the annual financing of the cotton crop.[114] The bank's statutes, however, prohibited long-term lending. Intrigued nonetheless by the idea, one of Reeves's London counterparts mused that it might be possible to establish a separate company to provide the service Milward was requesting.[115] Noting that a loan guarantee was actually a form of insurance, Reeves ran with the suggestion. Insurance companies, he reasoned, were in the business of quantifying risk, and "the proposed business has none of the hazardous nature of risks against which it is actually possible to insure, on most reasonable terms." On that basis, he proposed "the creation of a Company to be called 'The Egyptian Mortgage Insurance Co.' with a subscribed capital of say £500,000 represented by registered shares of which £100,000 might be called up."[116]

The company he envisioned never formed, and Reeves was not the first to arrive at the idea. In the United States, a small number of companies had been selling insurance policies on mortgages since at least the late 1880s.[117] During those same decades, a novel "mortgage-insurance complex" spread rapidly through the American Midwest thanks to a range of new financial instruments that securitized farm loans and insured against the risk of default.[118] Reeves's plan for an Egyptian company offering insurance policies on mortgages financed by insurance companies might not, in this sense, represent the main genealogical progenitor to the mortgage insurance giants that gained such notoriety a century later. But the fact that such an idea could emerge when and where it did is a telling indication of the role that Egypt was coming to play in the global operations of financial capital. British officials might continue to insist that the peoples of Europe and the colonies were worlds apart, the former advanced, the latter backward. The banks, however, had their own criteria for comparing one country to another. Turning the usual global hierarchy on its head, Reeves went on to reassure his superiors that "a Mortgage properly executed is, in Egypt, a more perfect security than a similar instrument executed either in France or England."[119]

A mere three years later, the insurance companies that Milward represented had reached that same conclusion. In August of 1902, the London-based Gresham Life Assurance Society began making arrangements to offer loans against landed property through their agents in Alexandria, the chartered accountants Hoare and Russell.[120] They were not alone. At roughly the same time, several other English insurance firms including the Standard Life, the Norwich Union, and the Law Union and Crown also joined the growing ranks of Egypt's mortgage lenders.[121]

By February of 1904, the Gresham's London board had decided to establish a dedicated local committee in Egypt. While they continued to sell life insurance policies, the bulk of their work over the next decade would consist of making mortgages to large landlords. In their earliest meetings, the committee members registered their concern to keep up with the "great competition in Egypt not only from Mortgage Companies such as the Crédit Foncier and the Caisse Hypothécaire, but also from a number of other Insurance Companies now established or being established in Egypt." The intensity of that competition, fueled by a rising volume of investment capital, would shape the Gresham's lending strategies in significant ways.[122]

When they made the case for foreign investment, supporters of the occupation often argued that the "resources and energy of private enterprise" allowed the Egyptian government to avoid "the indefinite deferment of projects which, with the growing needs of the community, became annually more urgent."[123] For Egypt's new mortgage lenders, the relationship more often worked the other way around; "private enterprise" quickly found ways to employ the "resources and energy" of the state toward its own ends. The volumes of standardized data amassed to facilitate the occupation's tax and credit reforms had already served a different purpose for foreign investors seeking to assess the prospects for expanded mortgage lending. The cadastral survey's printed map sheets proved so useful in facilitating land transactions that the government's printers struggled to meet public demand.[124] The very officials who had implemented those policies, meanwhile, began to divide their time or leave government service altogether in favor of more lucrative employment. Writing to his son Windham Baring in 1904, Cromer himself complained, "Private companies have now discovered the true secret of Egyptian reform. It has consisted in selecting a very small body of men most carefully, and paying them high. They now tempt my men away from me by offering terms against which no Government can compete."[125] In this regard, the Gresham's business was entirely typical. The acting chair of the local committee was Sir John Rogers, who after serving as director-general of the Sanitary Department in the Ministry of Interior from 1892 to 1899, went on to sit on the boards of at least half a dozen companies.[126]

Alongside those who populated the boards of directors, a second group of British officials began moonlighting as "valuation experts."[127] The occupation's agricultural policies had not only generated new statistics about landed property and its value. They had also produced a corps of human agents who embodied that knowledge and could mediate capital's introduction into foreign lands. Demand was particularly fierce for those who had served in the Public Works Department or taken part in the cadastral surveys and rent commissions. William Willcocks himself served as one of the Gresham's valuation experts in the earliest phase of the local committee's work, though constant requests for his services from other banks eventually forced them to find replacements.[128]

In their earliest meetings, the Gresham's local committee discussed the general framework for their new mortgage business. At the outset, the London directors had placed strict limits on their loans: a minimum of £E 5,000 and a maximum of £E 20,000 representing no more than 60% of the assessed value of properties north of Asyut in Upper Egypt.[129] Each of these guidelines represented a constraint on the risk entailed in any given mortgage. Interest rates typically ranged between 5% and 6% depending on the size of the loan and the identity of the borrower. At these rates, the 60% limit on a fifteen-year mortgage would keep the total repayment cost of the loan well below the assessed value of the security. Because the velocity of land transactions was higher in the Nile Delta than in Upper Egypt, the geographic constraint was calculated to ensure that land could be resold if necessary.[130]

The final restriction, on the size of individual loans, was the most significant of the three. The upper limit forced the local committee to spread its risk over a greater number of borrowers. The lower figure was a numerical stand-in for a class distinction: a loan of £E 5,000 implied a minimum holding of about 100 feddans. In detailing their preference for "large owners" rather than "small proprietors," the local committee made the usual references to "reputations" that were "easier to ascertain" and "proper records and accounts." More punctual payment of interest and installments "would result not only from a sense of honour or pride which is, perhaps, more developed amongst the former class, but also would arise from the fact that the former are more frequently possessed of other resources than merely the income derived from the property managed."[131] Already having money made it much easier to borrow more.

By drawing strict boundaries of class and geography, the Gresham aimed to minimize direct involvement in the affairs of its borrowers. Properly executed, each mortgage would seem to allow money to grow by itself. And yet the "flesh pots" were too tempting for such a cautious approach to last. By January 1905, the local committee judged it "very advisable that the available funds should be put out with the utmost dispatch, in order that the Society may profit by the rates of interest at present obtainable." Given "the prevailing influx of foreign capital & the many recent foundations of land & mortgage companies," they warned London that "there could scarcely fail to be a fall in the rates of interest now obtainable for mortgages."[132] Racing to act while rates remained higher, the committee requested to lengthen the term of their mortgages to twenty years, to expand operations as far south as Aswan, and to extend the upper and lower limits of their loans.[133]

The competitive dynamics of the mortgage market thus created their own incentives for lenders to court Egypt's wealthiest landowners, those whose vast estates could plausibly secure loans for tens of thousands of pounds. As the pace of foreign investment quickened, Egypt's financial boom thus intensified the class divisions that had long characterized the credit market. Interest rates on loans to wealthy landed proprietors fell much lower than they did for everyone else. And as those rates sank, at least some of these new ventures began to pursue other ways of juicing their returns.

However much the Gresham may have relaxed its standards, the company remained well on the cautious end of the spectrum of financial dealings in Egypt. As early as 1899, employees of the Imperial Ottoman Bank had expressed concerns to their superiors in London both about the willingness of other banks to assume much higher levels of risk and about the ease with which funding flowed to questionable new ventures. Convinced that the value of land would continue to rise indefinitely, some lenders began to make advances not on the land itself, but rather against the stock certificates of new Egyptian companies, many of which were themselves involved in land improvement and mortgage lending.[134] By the high point of the boom between 1905 and 1907, such speculative activity had helped to construct a teetering edifice of layered debt in which banks in Egypt borrowed money from Europe to make more and more such loans.[135]

Even as that tower began to sway, Egypt's promoters continued to insist that the promise of future profits was assured. Among the most influential and carefully argued statements to that effect came from the Belgian doctor, entrepreneur, and vice-consul Alfred Eid. These writings culminated in his 1907 study *La fortune immobilière de l'Égypte et sa dette hypothécaire*, republished two years later in Arabic translation.[136] The basic task he set himself was to calculate both the total value of urban and rural property in Egypt and the aggregate mortgage debt secured against that property. As countless others had already noted, these two figures together would offer a means to weigh the burden of existing mortgages and determine whether the country was yet "overbanked." Eid took the Willcocks rent study and the Palmer debt report as his starting point and supplemented both with additional figures, drawn largely from Cromer's annual reports. His labors yielded an exciting discovery: "the ratio between these two factors—the value of the soil and the amount of the mortgage debt—has remained nearly constant."[137] Under these condition, "Egypt could see her mortgage debt double or triple without the slightest worry."[138]

If Eid's conclusions captured the optimism of the moment, however, his study also included a more troubling analysis of the boom's consequences for different segments of Egyptian society. Toward the end of the study, Eid drew a brief comparison between two loans, one on a property of five feddans at 7.5% interest, the other on a property of fifty feddans at 6.5%. When compared with those actually offered at the time, these hypothetical rates were relatively low in the former case and high in the latter. Even so, Eid found that the two loans would have markedly different implications. The smallholder "would find himself in the identical economic position as that of a peasant who had leased a property of the same size," while the owner of the second property, simply by renting out his land at the going rate, would retain a comfortable margin above the loan's cost.[139]

When colonial officials wrote about agrarian credit relations, they often drew distinctions between usury and finance by attributing the difference to moral, racial, or cultural characteristics of the borrower and the lender involved. But for the banks actually making the loans, differing interest rates had little to do with virtue and vice. Rather, the abstraction of the interest rate reduced a whole host of determinants into a single number. While that number continued to slide downward for the largest landlords in the country, it moved far less for everyone else. So it was that a wave of financial investment actively spurred by the occupation's policies served to consolidate the very class disparities that Cromer's regime had once denounced as hallmarks of the despotism that British rule would vanquish.

CONCLUSION

In examining the conditions that gave rise to Egypt's financial boom, this chapter has highlighted the ways in which colonial policies unleashed dynamics that British officials had scarcely anticipated and were ill-equipped to control. The discourse of colonial economism located Egypt's surest route to national prosperity in a credit-fueled intensification of agricultural production. According to this vision, improved irrigation, rationalized land taxes, and mortgage capital at lower interest rates would create a society of contented smallholders invested in the steady improvement of their properties and little else. The outcomes looked very different. Rising land values contributed to wild speculation and new struggles over property. The banking sector's assessments of risk drew clear boundaries of class and geography that amplified the very forms of spatial and social inequality colonial officials claimed British rule would rectify. And the temptations of easy profit ensured that—albeit in varying degrees—the entire credit system on which Egyptian agriculture depended became shackled to a jerry-built tower of debt.

At the height of the boom, the occupation and its propagandists nevertheless continued to claim that Egypt was enjoying a golden era. Writing of "The Egyptian Boom" for *Blackwood's Magazine* in July 1907, the British financier Robert Hamilton Lang dismissed the nationalist slogan of "Egypt for the Egyptians" as the quip of those who "declare themselves hostile to a *régime* which has made the country prosperous, and which administers even-handed justice to small and great."[140] The challenge of such apparent prosperity was not lost on those Lang dismissed as irritable schoolboys. In these very same years, Indian nationalists organized their first mass mobilization around critiques of a "colonial drain of wealth."[141] In Egypt, by contrast, authors writing for nationalist organs like the Arabic daily *al-Liwa'* fretted that "wealth has now become our diversion and our consolation after the loss of our political independence."[142] Under these conditions, analyzing the character of what the journal *al-Hilal* described as *al-nahdah al-Misriyah al-maliyah* (Egypt's financial renaissance) was not simply an esoteric pastime for those intrigued by the science of political economy.[143] As land values continued to rise and new companies multiplied, the occupation's critics set out to specify the nature of the wealth that British rule had helped to create. They drew distinctions between the fictitious, ephemeral, and uneven profits of financial speculation and the tangible materiality of agricultural production. They explored the ways in which the logics of financial capital had enriched some members of Egyptian society while impoverishing others. In short, interrogating the political economy of British rule rather than taking it for granted became the central concern of a new generation seeking to articulate claims for *watiniyah* (patriotism) even as the occupation's economistic agenda seemed to be succeeding on its own terms.

Chapter 4

GILDED SPEECH

THE SPEECH MAY HAVE BEEN UNPLANNED. It was certainly no great work of oratory. On Saturday, February 4, 1905, Lord and Lady Cromer boarded a train from Cairo to Fayyum for a weekend getaway. By some accounts, the station attendants had phoned ahead to notify the governorate. The mudir then summoned a welcoming party of roughly two hundred notables and provincial officials from the neighboring villages.[1] Whether the reception that awaited him was expected or not, Cromer took the opportunity to address the crowd. Speaking in French, he expressed his delight at visiting the area for the first time and then offered some remarks on matters of recent import. He thanked the provincial administration for their vigilance in combating a locust infestation the previous year and mentioned that the government was now contemplating measures to eradicate the caterpillars that frequently threatened cotton crops. He urged the ʿumdahs and shaykhs to instruct their villagers about the benefits of postal savings banks. He reminded the audience about some new fishing regulations. He professed his eagerness to promote the spread of primary education in Arabic and lamented the incidence of drinking and gambling in rural districts. Finally, he counseled farmers against speculating on the value of their crops and reminded the crowd that the Agricultural Bank of Egypt was the best means of escaping the clutches of the usurer.[2]

To this dull litany of moralistic pronouncements, the *Egyptian Gazette* devoted a single paragraph. For the main paper of the local Anglophone community, "a speech touching on the cotton worm, locusts, irrigation, alcoholism, and many other matters" did not amount to major news.[3] Nor, it seems, did the *Gazette*'s editors see any noteworthy contradiction between Cromer's address and their own lead column that day advocating "the insular exclusiveness of a conquering race" as "one of the chief elements of England's success in the East."[4] For many of the Arabic dailies, however, the fact that Cromer was now speaking directly to crowds of Egyptians marked a significant and unwelcome change. From this perspective, his actions announced that "the Consul-General, as the representative of His Majesty the King of England, has the right to oversee the Egyptian people."[5] Having recently concluded the Entente Cordiale with France, the British now felt empowered to "chart a new course toward open, undisguised intervention in the domestic policy of the country."[6]

A decade prior, the Khedive's spies had launched their "delicate operation" against what they too saw as a consolidation of British rule. But much had changed since then. If Cromer's speech indicated that Egypt had become a colony in all but name, the response that it garnered was also a fitting testament to the obstacles facing those who professed a desire to end the occupation. Following the Anglo-French Agreement of 1904, there remained little hope that Britain's chief imperial rival might champion the cause of Egyptian independence.[7] The Khedive, for his part, though not altogether subservient, had tempered the defiance of his younger years. In the absence of any effective check against his authority, the consul-general could and did now claim that the occupation was the real agency representing the interests of the people he addressed as any sovereign would his subjects.

By 1905, rebutting that more confident claim to representation posed a formidable challenge to the critics of British rule in at least three respects. First, in their deepening hold over the information-gathering apparatus of the state, the British drew closer to enjoying a monopoly over representations of the country's condition as a whole. With its capacity to generate "statistics" in the most literal sense of the word, the occupation controlled the means by which "the progress of reforms" would be measured.[8] Second, the content of those measurements now told a story of extraordinary success. After two decades of British occupation, Egypt was gaining the "reputation of an El Dorado of which the fabulous prosperity offered something truly supernatural."[9] In pointing to the dazzling figures of economic development, British officials dismissed their detractors as a marginal group of semi-educated urbanites whose quibbles were irrelevant to the country's agrarian majority. Third, this allegation that what called itself nationalism was only ever a euphemism for the grievances of a geographically and demographically negligible minority had been commonplace since at least the 1890s. But while the numbers of those who appealed to an ideal of *wataniyah* (patriotism) had swelled by the early 1900s, both the meaning of the term and the range of groups that employed it had shifted.

On the first count, the recent manifestations of prosperity gave new urgency to questions about both the normative and empirical bases of sovereign legitimacy. Shimi Bey and his agents may have objected to the occupation's reduction of the public good to a bare calculus of monetary gains, but they also articulated their defense of the old regime against a backdrop of lingering economic hardship. Boom conditions did not altogether sideline the concerns with bureaucratic competence and moral rectitude or the appeals to territorial nativism that had once animated the spies' reports. But the signs of new prosperity did force a reckoning with the occupation's own economistic criteria for evaluating the success and popular appeal of government.

As for the social constituencies of wataniyah, in trumpeting the achievement of "economic development," British officials were making the case that these were the terms by which most Egyptians assessed the work of those in power. Numerical representations of material prosperity, they insisted, could double as proxies for public opinion. In seeking to undo that conflation, critics of British rule had long treated the press as a competing medium through which to publicize dissident voices. But here too matters had grown more complicated. In the 1890s, Egypt already enjoyed a burgeoning print culture. Daily newspapers and more specialized journals offered detailed coverage of local and international affairs and often carried extensive discussions of government policies. Some also served as semiofficial publications for distinct professional communities or confessional groups.[10] But when it came to debating the occupation, there were two papers that dominated the conversation:

the Anglophile *al-Muqattam*, published by the Syrian Christian émigrés Faris Nimr and Ya'qub Sarruf, and the palace-funded *al-Mu'ayyad*, published by Shaykh 'Ali Yusuf. In the mid-1890s, this polarization was so clear that the Khedive's agents often referred to their allies and enemies respectively as "*Mu'ayyad* men" and "*Muqattam* men." By 1905, the Arabic press had grown much more fractious. Drawing attention to this very diversity of opinion, the daily *al-Liwa'* provided a roundup of reporting on Cromer's Fayyum address so that readers might compare the positions of different journals for themselves.[11]

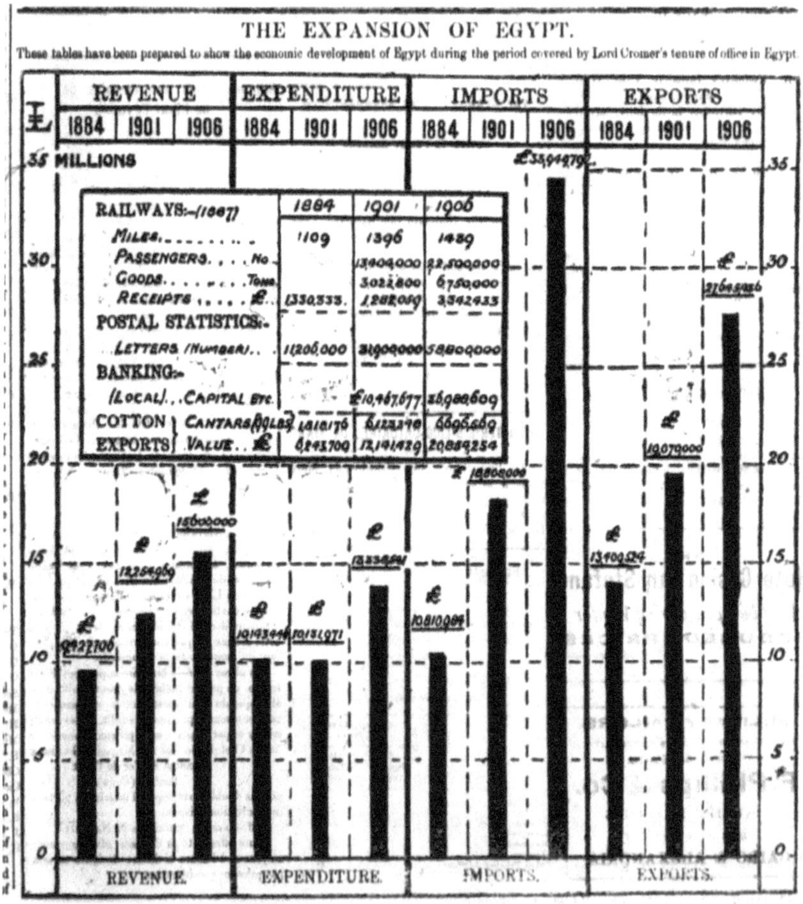

FIGURE 3: "The Expansion of Egypt." Source: *Egyptian Gazette* (November 7, 1907).

It was in the context of these mounting challenges that the young journalist Ahmad Hilmi described the occupation's public discourse as "gilded speech." Confident in their recent achievements, British officials now alloyed their language with constant references to the monetary gains they had delivered. "All outward appearances," Hilmi explained, "point toward the rapid progress of this country in its material life, and the statements of government officials affirm this fact to the fullest extent possible every time the sun comes up or a new year begins."[12] The journal *al-Liwa'* for which he served as both editor and columnist had been established in 1900 to complement the patriotic, anti-British *al-Mu'ayyad.* Its energetic founder Mustafa Kamil had, throughout his education as a lawyer in both Egypt and France, enjoyed the patronage of the Khedive, who was a mere month his senior.[13] By 1905, Kamil had secured widespread recognition as the leading voice of the movement he and his supporters referred to as *al-Hizb al-Watani* (the National Party). But his meteoric ascent had become a source of growing tension with both 'Abbas Hilmi II and the shaykh who remained his most devoted publicist.[14] Personal jealousies, however, were not the only propellants of this rivalry. Though its royal sponsor had begun to retreat from the confrontational defiance of his early years, *al-Mu'ayyad* did, at this stage, remain fiercely critical of the occupation. The rift between the two papers nevertheless signaled a difference in outlook that would only grow more pronounced in the coming years.

At its most forceful, the anticolonial imaginary of the Khedive's spies and 'Ali Yusuf's paper in the 1890s had been fundamentally retrospective. This is not to say that their nostalgia for bygone days was antimodernist. Men like Shimi Bey and his coconspirator Muhammad Rushdi were deeply committed to the khedivial project of state-building to which they had devoted their careers. Not by accident did they often describe the advent of their new British overlords as a forced movement backward in time.[15] Having discerned nothing progressive in the corrupt and corrupting influence of the occupation, these men looked to a glorified past for a historical trajectory from which British rule seemed to mark an unwelcome deviation. Both born in 1874, just a few years before the 'Urabi revolt, Mustafa Kamil and his co-editor Ahmad Hilmi were no less fervent in their desire to hasten the departure of British forces. But having come of age in the very moment when the occupation's development schemes appeared to be bearing fruit, they were keenly aware that denouncing their own colonial present from the standpoint of an idealized past was now inadequate.

As a mode of arguing about both how things ought to be and how they really were, gilded speech could no longer be dismissed as mere falsehood. At the height of the financial boom, the potential resonance of the occupation's unrestrained economism represented the single overarching problem that posed itself to any serious case against British rule. Recognizing the gravity of this predicament, the rising generation of journalists and political strategists sought to develop a two-pronged rejoinder. On the one hand, they challenged the occupation's narratives of material improvement on their own terms. Through detailed financial reporting in the press, Egyptian critics of the occupation mobilized the methods and concepts of political economy to pursue their own critical analyses of the social transformations to which boom conditions were giving rise. On the other, they continued to argue that these were the wrong terms by which to judge the success or failure of government. Tacking between these two positions, they worked to expand the terrain of anticolonial politics under conditions of apparent prosperity.

It was no accident, in this regard, that the journalist who heard danger in the occupation's gilded speech also played a pivotal role in reporting the event that, more than any other in these years, changed the conversation. As capital gushed into the country, the organs of a growing nationalist movement sought to demonstrate that, despite the occupation's command over the means of representation, the shared sentiments and experiences of the Egyptian people were irreducible to the charts and tables that adorned the pages of Cromer's annual reports. It was in driving home that normative failing of colonial economism that Hilmi and others would first discern a greater significance in the famed Dinshaway Incident of 1906. The spectacular violence of the occupation's response to the incident, they began to argue, revealed the deeper costs of British rule that no increase in wages, land values, or stock prices could ever compensate.

WEALTH FOR WHOM? WEALTH OF WHAT KIND?

In January of 1905, Mustafa Kamil posed the question for his readers, "The Egyptians and the Occupiers: How Do They Live Together?"[16] His answer summed up the dilemma of the moment: "The English in their country believe that the Egyptians are happy in the age of the occupation. And the occupiers in Egypt exert every effort to reinforce this belief so that if you asked the lowliest Englishman in his own country what England has done in Egypt, he would tell you, 'She has brought forth

[Egypt's] people from the darkness into the light and from death into life.' "[17] Kamil acknowledged the gravity of Britain's hegemonic claims and the doubled challenge of refuting them before publics both at home and abroad. "As long as Egyptians greet every incident by masking their pain and keeping silent their sadness," he continued, "this belief will only grow stronger and more deeply rooted." It was therefore imperative that they should make clear to one and all that they were not so happy as the British alleged. The enumeration of benefits the occupation had bestowed upon Egypt always obscured a more fundamental violation of national sovereignty and the rights it entailed. For "the man of reason," it was "the holiest of his obligations to call upon [the Egyptians] to hold fast to their rights, to demand them through peaceful, lawful means, and to demonstrate the power and authority of public opinion."[18] Kamil's invocation of inviolable rights here represented one possible response to the occupation's statistical representations of rising wealth. The British could claim that their rule had succeeded by its own standards. According to Kamil, these were simply the wrong standards. Economic development had no bearing on the universal and inviolable right of nations to govern themselves.

This was not a new argument in 1905, nor was Kamil alone in making it. From the occupation's inception, British officials had maintained that popular support would increase as a function of material improvement. Their critics had been rejecting that premise ever since. Parroting Britain's self-aggrandizing pronouncements, a column in the newspaper *Misr* from 1897 had declared, "Verily I am more deserving of [Egypt] because I have served her wealth and reformed her interior. (Improving a thing earns the right to possess it.)" Though the British may have delivered such gains, it was "impossible to deny that wielding power over [the country's] administration is a right belonging to the Egyptians."[19] Efforts to divorce sovereign rights from the material condition of the country, then, had been a staple of anticolonial critiques for some time. But they grew at once more urgent and more problematic amidst the explosive economic growth of the early 1900s.

Already prior to the boom, an alternative line of argument had begun to scrutinize the details of British policy to challenge the occupation's narrative of economic benefit itself. This, of course, was a critical strategy that the Khedive's spy Muhammad Rushdi had adopted in arguing that Egypt, like Ireland before it, was becoming an exploited dependency marred by "total poverty."[20] It was likewise a staple of writing in the press. Challenging the credibility of official publications, the major

Arabic dailies promised to reveal the real motives and interests behind each new government measure. One obvious flashpoint was the occupation's distribution of concessions to foreign—and specifically British—companies. In an especially strident articulation of this position, a columnist for *al-Ra'id al-Misri* declared that the government "has become like a joint-stock company for exploiting this land" and "for snatching its money and sucking the blood of the peasant."[21]

Beyond rhetorical flourish, the ability of the papers to document the distance separating official pronouncements from unadorned truth depended on the rather porous boundary between journalism and civil service at the time. The career trajectory of the young Ahmad Hilmi was, in this regard, exemplary. Raised by his uncle, a clerk in the Ministry of Public Works, he had learned to read and write Arabic prose from the specimens of bureaucratic paperwork he received to guide his studies. As a teenager in Alexandria, he took a job with a foreign company as an opportunity to learn French. Soon thereafter, he began to work his way up the ranks of the Ministry of Finance.[22] This early employment provided a grounding in political economy that some of his more well-to-do contemporaries, Kamil among them, would have received as part of their legal education.[23] But it also allowed Hilmi to serve as a conduit of information between the Ministry of Finance and the press. In that capacity, he was particularly attentive to the comportment of the British officials he encountered at work. Following the speech in Fayyum, Hilmi offered a pointed response to the consul-general's suggestion that the Egyptian farmer should "sell his cotton and other crops at the going price rather than hoard them in hope of great profit." What Cromer understood as the peasantry's propensity for gambling and speculation, Hilmi explained instead as a response to market manipulation by more powerful actors. On several occasions in recent years, he alleged, British irrigation inspectors had leaked misinformation about the Nile flood to the press in order to play the cotton futures market to their own advantage. Given the wild price fluctuations that ensued from such insider trading, the poor peasant could hardly be blamed for wondering when best to sell his crops.[24]

Hilmi was not the only one to tell such stories of blatant self-dealing. A few years earlier, Harry Boyle, the Oriental secretary at the British Consulate, had complained in a letter to his mother about "the most appalling cotton speculation going on here in consequence of the uncertainty about the forthcoming crop, caused by the state of the Nile." Remarking sarcastically, "Bless my soul what people we are in this country!"

he confided that R. Hanbury Brown, William Garstin, and Cromer himself had all made sizable fortunes by "rigging the market."[25] Well aware of these rumors, Cromer sought on occasion to address them. In his annual report for 1906, he weighed the "very special temptations to which British officials in Egypt are now exposed" against the "benefits which they have often contributed to bestow on others." Forced to accept "very moderate incomes" while "the cost of living has greatly increased," they were "naturally tempted to follow the examples of others who are not bound by any official ties." Acknowledging that "no precise rules on the subject have been framed," Cromer simply reminded his subordinates of "their duty to resist this temptation."[26]

That even his public treatment of the issue was so mild was indicative of a more general attitude toward the criticisms his administration encountered. Writing in less guarded language to his nephew John Baring (2nd Baron Revelstoke), Cromer griped, "I live in a glass house. I am in the presence of a very vigilant, very hostile and utterly unscrupulous opposition." Among his detractors, the consul-general counted not only the Khedive and his supporters but "every newspaper man whom I have refused to bribe, every incompetent place-hunter whom I have refused to employ, every corrupt official whose illicit income I have curtailed, and every unofficial scamp in this putrid heterogenous society whose infamous practices have in one form or another, been checked through my instrumentality."[27] Though Cromer reserved such vitriol for his private correspondence, his characterization of the "opposition" in this letter was quite typical of his position. Since his earliest confrontations with ʿAbbas Hilmi II, Cromer had attributed each manifestation of organized resistance to the machinations of the palace. If that accusation had once contained a granule of truth, by 1905 it smacked more of denial and conspiratorial thinking. But even as the ranks of this opposition swelled, Cromer's dismissal contained a more durable and problematic allegation. What the occupation's critics shared, he yet again alleged, was a narrow devotion to their own self-interest. At best, their patriotism was a misnomer for an unwarranted resentment toward imperial rule. If British businesses and British officials profited along the way, their own benefit was distinct from the corruption of this "unscrupulous opposition" by virtue of the economic development they had achieved for the Egyptian people.

This narrative of mutualism seemed to gain force with each new headline trumpeting "Egypt's Amazing Prosperity."[28] Apologists for the occupation dismissed both legalistic arguments about natural rights and investigative reporting about foreign profiteering as the grumblings of a small but vocal minority who downplayed the country's changing fortunes. Boom conditions thus called for a creative elaboration of critiques that engaged the occupation more directly on its own terms. Ahmad Hilmi's own response in the piece he entitled "*al-Kalam al-dhahabi*" exemplified one possible approach. There, he sought to distinguish the occupation's concern with monetary wealth from a more expansive understanding of social improvement. It was not "rapid financial progress" alone that patriotic Egyptians should desire so much as "the progress of higher knowledge." Egypt's newfound prosperity only accentuated the limitations of a regime that had accomplished so little with such vast resources at its disposal. "Is it not disgraceful," Hilmi asked, "that there should be universities in Athens and Beirut, but Egypt is deprived of one? For which of these three countries is the wealthiest and the most fertile?"[29]

In his focus on unrealized possibilities, Hilmi left intact the proposition that Egypt was indeed becoming a wealthy country. But as the pace of foreign investment quickened, that fundamental premise of the occupation's gilded speech became an object of closer scrutiny. A common line of argument challenged the occupation's narrative of mutual benefit by raising questions about distribution. Egypt's new wealth, these critics observed, flowed disproportionately into the coffers of foreign banks and companies, leaving Egyptians themselves with little gain. A column in *al-Liwa'* thus remarked, "The foreign companies have pitched their tents all across Egypt and deposited their burdens upon the necks of their servants; they have deprived the people of their money and prohibited them from enjoying the benefits of their country and the blessings of their homeland."[30]

While articles of this kind refigured foreign investment as a disguised vehicle of exploitation, critical engagements with Egypt's newfound prosperity went well beyond an enumeration of winners and losers along lines of nationality. Taking up the occupation's political-economic analysis as such, many writers began instead to interrogate the nature of the wealth that was being created and the kinds of dislocation that it might unleash. Since the 1890s, Egypt's boosters had specifically championed a marriage between financial capital and agricultural production; increased foreign investment, they wagered, would facilitate the reclamation of uncultivated land and raise productivity on existing farms. By the early 1900s, the promise of that virtuous cycle had begun to seem illusory. Some now warned that the financial boom was increasingly unproductive, uneven, and fictitious in character.

The allegation that the boom was unproductive arose from concerns about how the relationship between finance and agriculture had actually played out. Most of the new banks and companies that appeared around the turn of the century named some aspect of agricultural improvement as their main pursuit. The social capital of investors pooled through issues of new stocks and bonds would make possible the reclamation of land, the extension of railway networks, and the construction of new irrigation works.[31] Mortgage loans could facilitate the expansion of landholdings, the purchase of new machinery and livestock, the leveling of fields, or the digging of new canals. But in practice, as the value of both securities and landed property continued to rise, that money could easily flow toward short-term gains from speculation on the continued self-expansion of value. A greater supply of credit might result in the capitalization of agricultural production, but with higher profits to be made elsewhere, it very well might not. Nor were foreign companies alone to blame. *Al-Liwa'* admonished the wealthier classes for leaving the "treasure" of Egypt's farmland "locked away while the keys are in their hands." Rather than invest in bringing more of Egypt's fourteen million feddans under cultivation, "we throng like flies around sweet nectar . . . to buy the shares of foreign companies."[32] At the time, bullish analysts often dismissed such accounts of the boom as hysterical or misleading. While acknowledging the increased incidence of stock market speculation, a two-part exposé in *al-Hilal* entitled "Egypt's Financial Renaissance: Is It Real or Illusory?" ultimately assured readers that "there is no reason to fear for Egypt's recent wealth. Rather, this is still the beginning, because the agricultural lands that are the basis of [that wealth] may still welcome an increase in their price."[33]

Real or illusory, the fortunes of this financial renaissance did not accrue to all Egyptians and all regions in equal measure. Even beyond the privileges conferred by foreign nationality, the unevenness of the boom belied simple pronouncements about Egyptian prosperity. The British had promised that agrarian development would increase the aggregate wealth of the country and alleviate class disparities between pashas and peasants. Achievement of the former goal now appeared to come at the expense of the latter. Among the most persistent issues was the increasing polarization of landholding patterns. Despite its professed desire to improve the lot of peasant smallholders, the government was pursuing policies that yielded just the opposite result. In theory, auctions of state-owned land might have helped poor peasants to acquire property or expand their holdings. But the parcels on auction were so large that only the wealthiest landlords and companies could afford them.[34] Since those buyers enjoyed disproportionate access to credit on preferential terms, the increased availability of mortgage finance only helped to facilitate the consolidation of large landholdings among a privileged few.

Even Lord Cromer acknowledged that government land sales were having this undesirable effect. At one point in his Fayyum address, he thanked the deputy mudir for suggesting that properties should be subdivided and sold on installments to allow "the small peasant" to purchase them. But while approving of the suggestion, an article in *al-Ahram* later that month described a process of social upheaval that extended well beyond government land auctions to the wealthy. The everyday manifestations of prosperity, in this account, were as much the problem as the solution. Echoing familiar concerns about land alienation, the article first denounced the "foreign funds and companies [that] have rained down upon the country and engulfed every bit of it" and warned that they "deprive the peasant day after day of his few bits of land." The danger, however, extended beyond the distribution of property. Boom conditions were creating generalized expectations of affluence that placed even Egypt's poorest cultivators under new pressures to borrow and consume. With the trappings of "urban civilization [*al-madaniyah*] spreading all around him," the lowly peasant found himself "compelled to increase his spending on himself and his family. . . . His son demands an education, and education is not free. His wife asks him for fine clothes, and his daughter demands a dower. The gateway to indebtedness is wide open before him." Rather, than the scheming of the *khawajah* (*foreign*) moneylender, it was the poor peasant's everyday experience of conspicuous consumption that was driving him to borrow beyond his means. The outlook was no less dire. "Day after day, wealth flows from the hands of the many to the hands of the few, and if matters continue in this way," the piece predicted, "the ranks of the destitute will grow numerous and extreme poverty will prevail in the country."[35]

Among the statistics most frequently cited as evidence of peasant prosperity were those concerning the price of land. If property values were rising, so the argument went, then landowners both great and small must be sharing in Egypt's fortunes. In glowing terms, the *Egyptian Gazette* reported that not only had the "value of the best quality of agricultural land in the country . . . increased enormously of late," but "in most cases it is the owners of small holdings that are the purchasers, and speculation does not enter into these transactions. It is with the sole object of cultivation and adding to their property that the fellaheen landowners buy whenever they have accumulated a few hundred pounds."[36] Adding the weight of official statistics, Cromer included a chart comparing figures on the distribution of land between 1900 and 1904 in his annual report for the latter year. There, he reminded his readers that the "policy of the Egyptian Government has been to endeavor to maintain the small proprietors, and, whilst affording all reasonable facilities for the employment of European capital in land development, to do nothing which would tend towards ousting native proprietors and substituting Europeans in their place." While noting that the figures showed some fragmentation of smaller holdings, he judged that "there appears to be nothing inconsistent with the statement that the aims of the land policy adopted in Egypt have been achieved."[37]

Unsurprisingly, the most sustained efforts to rebut such confident proclamations appeared in the pages of *al-Liwa'*. On February 25, 1906, the paper ran a piece entitled "The Rise in Land Prices: Whose Is the Wealth in Egypt?" Taking aim at the British administration's preferred metric for economic progress, the article rejected the claim that "the rise in land prices is a powerful basis for prosperity in this country." On the contrary, the increase in land values had "brought down pain and suffering upon the great majority of the people." In a country where only two million people out of a total of twelve million owned any land at all, the inflation of property prices was hardly a blessing. Since rents tended to rise in step with the purchase price of land, tenant farmers faced higher costs even when the land itself "has not changed or been altered in any way or even loses its fertility due to the abundance of cotton farmed." Those who worked the soil simply forfeited a larger share of their harvest in rent. As land prices continued to shoot upward, the article concluded, "most Egyptians have become like feathers in the gusts of a storm."[38]

Not to be outdone, *al-Mu'ayyad* ran its own piece the very next day under a virtually identical title: "Local Wealth in Egypt or the Rising Value of Land." After rattling off some figures on rising prices, the paper also noted that "the English delight in that [increase] and consider it among the greatest signs of their reform in the country." The occupation had indeed made Egypt an attractive site for investment, but "should these high, expensive prices at which Egyptian properties are now valued be considered local wealth of the people?" Though the anonymous author noted that "all or most areas where values rise . . . are becoming, hour by hour, the property of foreigners," his answer went well beyond the usual tropes about foreign ownership.

What followed instead was a series of vignettes that captured the unsettling contradictions of the recent boom: between the rapid, fluid movements of financial capital and the durable solidity of the landscapes and built environments through which that capital flowed. To his own original question, the author gave an ambiguous answer: both "yes and no." The wealth created by the boom was at once "fixed and permanent [*thabitah mustamirrah*] and ephemeral and mobile [*za'ilah mutanaqqilah*]." On the one hand, new buildings appeared everywhere as evidence of material development on the march. On the other, "trading in land has multiplied to the point where it has become speculation." The physical form of the landscape now seemed to move in time with the Cairo and Alexandria stock markets where the shares of countless land companies were traded. Agricultural fields outside Cairo became building lots overnight. Elaborate villas rose where modest huts had once stood. Wealthy families traded homes in the traditional upscale neighborhoods of Azbakiyah, Isma'iliyah, and Bab al-Luq for small sandy plots in the new suburbs, all in the hope of future payouts. In this constant, churning reconfiguration of space, nothing was quite as it seemed. Not only did the frenzied pace of transactions portend an inevitable crash, but the lines between what was real and fictitious, between what was fixed and fleeting, were growing harder to discern.[39]

The worry that Egypt's boom might not last only became more pronounced when the angle of vision widened to capture the country's place in the world at large. In effect, the fluctuation of values at the scale of individual neighborhoods or rural districts might just as well describe the experience of whole countries. This was the conclusion of a short but remarkable analysis of "The New Financial Movement in Egypt" that appeared in *al-Liwa'* on September 25, 1905. There, the paper set out to explain the "strange leaps" that characterized financial operations in Egypt "to which the laws of the arts of economy [*qawanin fanun al-iqtisad*] hardly apply." The prices of stocks spiked "until one becomes ten and ten becomes hundreds." Plots of land once priced in the double digits now went for two or even three hundred pounds a feddan. Though these local phenomena "cannot enter into the field of rational calculation," there was nevertheless "a wider field within which the source of these strange, exceptional fluctuations may be known."[40]

Doubtless aware of the arguments boosters made to attract European capital, *al-Liwa'* followed the logic of that promotional literature toward a more troubling conclusion. From the vantage of metropolitan investors, Egypt had become "no more than a stopover for the owners of large capitals from all across Europe who demand a wider operation and a more fertile field for their money than they can find in their own countries." Egypt might stand "open to investment in its every aspect," but that state of affairs could only be temporary. The new movements of finance, then, were "without a doubt a blessing for financiers and businessmen" and "a grave danger for the people of the country." In an ominous foreshadowing of the coming crisis, *al-Liwa'* here observed that the flows of capital fueling Egypt's prosperity depended far more on a changing global geography of relative profitability than on any fixed and particular characteristics of the country itself. Once the opportunities for easy profit had ended, the financiers who had "advanced upon us in battalions" would continue their onward march.[41]

In the headiest days of the boom, a rising chorus of critical voices decried the social upheaval and inequality that these armies of capital had wrought and warned that a reversal of some sort was imminent. Undeterred by the diversity and sophistication of such analyses, Lord Cromer went to considerable lengths to allay any concern that "the present prosperity of Egypt is a mushroom growth of the type of which history affords abundant examples, that it is due to temporary and ephemeral causes, and that when these causes cease to exist, a collapse will ensue."[42] Some unease, he explained, was "extremely natural" when understood as a side effect of the occupation's own unusual success. "The change in Egypt from poverty to affluence," he continued, "has been accomplished with a rapidity which is probably without precedent." It was all but inevitable that some observers should be "slow to believe that a country, the Government of which but a few years ago was in a bankrupt condition . . . should suddenly spring into the position of a well-ordered, law-abiding, and thoroughly solvent State, in which money can be invested with no greater risk than is to be incurred in countries whose orderly administration, respect for law, and solvency have been attained more gradually."[43]

To those holding "pessimist views," the consul-general did concede that the "prices of some undertakings may become inflated, and may then suddenly collapse. . . . At times, a monetary crisis of some magnitude may even occur." He also briefly lamented "the extent to which the wealth of the country depends on cotton."[44] But ultimately, he affirmed that "the material prosperity of this country rests on a basis of somewhat exceptional solidity."[45]

POLITICS AND PIGEON HUNTING

The publication of Cromer's report each year was a major event in its own right, and the spring of 1906 was no exception. For readers who had not acquired their own copies from local booksellers, the *Egyptian Gazette* reproduced large sections along with extensive commentary on the contents.[46] Running beside the minutes of board meetings at which Egypt's companies announced yet another year of record profits, this coverage largely echoed the consul-general's triumphal statements. A few dissident voices, however, took the opportunity to question the measure of Britain's success. On May 16, the English poet and essayist Wilfred Scawen Blunt, by this point renowned as Cromer's bête noire and one of the occupation's most outspoken Anglophone detractors, took aim directly at the economistic logic of the document's self-congratulatory analysis. "Lord Cromer's Egyptian Reports," he mused, "always remind me, if I may say it without irreverence, of the first chapters of the Book of Genesis, where we read that 'the Lord saw everything that he had made, and he saw that it was very good.' They are the annual record of a creation of material progress set down with dignified satisfaction by its creator, and as such they have acquired in England an imposing authority." Blunt did not, in this instance, quarrel with "that part of his achievement which is material." Rather, citing his own travel and residence in Egypt, Blunt warned that the "material progress made by the country under English occupation is not associated in the native mind with a need of gratitude, any more than it used to be in Lombardy under Austrian rule, or is in Ireland, if there be any progress, under English rule today."[47]

This of course was the same distinction that Egyptian critics of the occupation had been drawing for years. The problem, at the time, was that the evidence for a weight of public opinion not captured by economic statistics was only ever anecdotal. And even in the Arabic press, assessments of the current moment were anything but unanimous. *Al-Liwa'* and *al-Mu'ayyad* might vie to denounce the boom's unevenness and warn against a coming bust, but rival papers often did just the opposite. Marveling at "the financial policy that Egypt's reformer has devised," *al-Muqattam* informed its readers that Egypt "has become the wealthiest government in the world after the United States."[48] As a means of representing the public appeal of such discordant positions, contending print media seemed hardly more reliable than the occupation's ponderous elaboration of crop yields, revenue figures, and land prices.

Blunt could not have anticipated that less than a month after he published his "Criticism," the terms of the public debate about British rule would be radically and irreversibly altered. But the transformative significance of the famous Dinshaway Incident of June 1906 lay precisely in undermining colonial economism as a mode of political analysis. As Blunt himself would later explain in sensational fashion, the events of that summer exploded the occupation's prior claims about the political effects of "material progress" and thereby forced open new possibilities for representing public opinion.[49] As the single most canonical set piece in the early history of Egyptian nationalism, Dinshaway has already been the subject of extensive scholarly investigation and frequent reinterpretation.[50] That sizable literature is itself a testament to the diversity of meanings Egyptians ascribed to the incident through successive renarrations. But in its immediate aftermath, both the British administration and its nationalist critics understood the importance of Dinshaway specifically in relation to accounts of a colonial regime legitimized through the mutual recognition of improving economic interests.

The earliest official reports described the altercation at Dinshaway on June 13 as the unhappy consequence of several accidents. In his preliminary memorandum to the Minister of the Interior and his British adviser, the mudir of Manufiyah province, Mahmud Shukri Pasha, explained that a group of British officers had accepted the invitation of a local notable to hunt pigeons in the village of Dinshaway. "By an unfortunate coincidence," he continued, "a fire started in a wheat-threshing floor at the moment when these officers were passing at a distance of two or three hundred meters from the grain. Having mistakenly understood that the officers caused the blaze with their firearms, the aggressors wished to strip them of their arms and then set about hitting them with their quarterstaffs. That is what gave way to these unfortunate consequences."[51] The ensuing brawl left two British soldiers badly injured; a third, Captain Bull, died of sunstroke on the road after fleeing to summon reinforcements. Four villagers, including the wife of the local imam, were also wounded by gunfire during the altercation.

Upon receiving word of the incident, G. M. Bullock, the major-general in command of British forces in Egypt, recommended to Cromer that the case be referred to a special tribunal.[52] In February 1895, following an attack on a group of British marines in Alexandria, Cromer had secured the passage of legislation laying out distinct procedures for cases of aggression against the army of occupation.[53] Among the distinguishing features of these exceptional tribunals would be their power to inflict a range of punishments—including the death penalty—much harsher than those sanctioned by Egypt's ordinary criminal code. In justifying the discrepancy, Cromer had suggested that the known threat of such excess violence would render its actual use unnecessary. "I believe and hope," he wrote of the special tribunal, "that its mere creation will go far to obviate the necessity for its action."[54] Elsewhere in his correspondence with London, the consul-general acknowledged that "the permanent influence of the British Government in this country depends in a great degree upon the pressure of the British garrison." But he recognized that the occupation's claims to broad popular support would require that the potential use of violence be contained.[55] When Cromer agreed to Bullock's request and ordered the Council of Ministers to convene a special tribunal, he opened a release on that "pressure" that could not thereafter be shut.[56]

The local papers carried their first major reports on what they variously labeled "The Tala Outrage," "*mu'arakat Dinshaway* [the Dinshaway quarrel]," and "*hadithat Dinshaway* [the Dinshaway incident]" on June 14.[57] The Cairene daily *al-Watan* went to press late enough that day to include news of the special tribunal.[58] That same afternoon, Ahmad Hilmi boarded a train from Cairo to Tanta to begin covering the story on the ground. Although other reporters would soon follow and although Hilmi's own interpretation would change as events unfolded, the editor of *al-Liwa'* thus seized the opportunity to shape the narrative of this "battle between the English officers and a group of the common people." Mindful that conflicting accounts were already circulating, Hilmi was careful to authenticate his lengthy dispatch by leading readers through each step of his journey and each interview he conducted. Even before the trial, this investigative reporting began to mark out an asymmetry between the nature of the encounters in the village and the massive show of force with which the occupation chose to respond.[59]

Al-Liwa' did not directly challenge the idea of an exceptional tribunal or the legal framework that sanctioned its use. Nor did the paper seek to minimize the culpability of the villagers. It simply argued that the circumstances of the confrontation did not qualify as an attack on the army of occupation as such. Hilmi's reporting instead described a long series of contingencies and miscommunications. The 'umdah of Dinshaway happened to be away in the town of Shibin al-Kum that morning; he was therefore unable to mediate between the villagers and the hunting party. The British officers spoke no Arabic, so they could not understand the peasants' warnings against firing their weapons near so much combustible chaff from the grain they were threshing. The soldiers likewise failed to comprehend that the village guards had rushed to the site of the initial affray in the hope of separating the British from the peasants and avoiding further confrontation.[60] As *al-Liwa'* went on to observe on June 17, "*Al-Mu'ayyad, al-Ahram, al-Zahir,* and *al-Sharq* have all affirmed, after research and deliberation, that there was no ill intention between the two parties and that everything that happened was based on mutual misunderstanding."[61] If anyone had so far shown malign intent, it was those who "wish to portray this perfectly clear issue in a distorted manner" and "mention fanaticism and politics in conjunction with this incident."[62]

That same day, however, the British administration circulated its own version of events compiled by Percy W. Machell, adviser to the Ministry of Interior. *Al-Liwa'* ran a translation of Machell's "General Resumé of the Occurrence at Denshawai, June 13, 1906" alongside its own assignment of "Responsibility for the Dinshaway Incident."[63] The contrast was plain to see. In Machell's version, the British soldiers had maintained the utmost professionalism and restraint. The villagers nevertheless insisted on escalating the encounter. Shukri Pasha's original memo had described the grain fire as an "unfortunate coincidence." Ahmad Hilmi's interviews suggested that stray shots from the soldiers' rifles had ignited it. Machell ruled both explanations "utterly impossible" and proposed instead that the fire was "more likely . . . a preconcerted signal for the general attack to take place."[64]

It was in light of these divergent accounts that the incident began to assume a larger significance. Commenting on Machell's report, *al-Mu'ayyad* railed against its "obvious bias toward one of the two clashing parties. . . . The report amplified and exaggerated everything on the side of English interests and cast doubt and suspicion on everything in favor of the native population."[65] *Al-Muqattam* fired back the next day that "the objective of [*al-Mu'ayyad*'s] writer was to transform this narrowly circumscribed incident at Dinshaway between five British soldiers and the inhabitants of a single Egyptian village into a generalized incident between the English and the Egyptians."[66] The daily *al-Zahir,* on the other hand, now warned that the English press itself had raced to blow the incident out of proportion as "a second revolution in the Nile Valley." In a piece entitled "Politics and Pigeon Hunting," the paper—which had long sought to occupy a position of "moderation" between adversarial extremes—implored the British to recognize that "the killing of one or two men should not become a cause for discord between two nations."[67]

The outcome of the special tribunal only reinforced perceptions that the British had deliberately embraced the most alarmist possible interpretation of the incident. The tribunal's final judgment tracked closely with Machell's report, emphasizing the "extreme forbearance and self-restraint" of the British soldiers and the "brutality" of the villagers who perpetrated their assault "in cold blood."[68] In light of these findings, the tribunal meted out sentences for twenty-one of the original fifty-two defendants: "4 of the ringleaders are condemned to death; 2 are condemned to penal servitude for life; 1 to 15 years; 6 to 7 years; 3 to one year and 50 lashes; and 5 to 50 lashes."[69] The hangings and public floggings took place in Dinshaway the following day. A mere two weeks had elapsed since the original altercation.

As was true before the trial, critical responses to the verdict in the press did not seek to portray the Dinshaway villagers as altogether innocent. Instead, they identified in the special tribunal's sentences a degree of violence far in excess of the crimes themselves. Having returned to Cairo after filing his initial reports, Ahmad Hilmi traveled again to Dinshaway to witness the executions. His vivid and deeply disturbing account of what ensued would become an instant classic, remembered by many of his more famous contemporaries as the text that brought home for the first time the magnitude of what had transpired.[70] In chilling detail, he walked his readers minute by minute through the grotesque but methodical public spectacle of lashings and executions. He described the screams and wails of parents, wives, and children forced to watch the killing of loved ones from the rooftops and doorways of the very homes where they had once lived together. The British, he explained, carried out the sentences in situ "so that the people should see how rational, expert power uses its violence and its overwhelming, destructive force. . . . All this so that any who did not know before should know now that the powerful may kill and torture and maim to excess when all just restraint has been removed, and eyes and ears clamp shut at his deeds."[71] In its own "Last Word about the Dinshaway Case and the Ruling," *al-Mu'ayyad* likewise argued that there would be little cause for such an elaborate show of force "if the objective were merely to render judgment upon the offending parties." The occupation, however, was pursuing a different and altogether larger agenda, namely, "that its military aspect should be respected, intimidating, and feared [*muhtaraman, muhiban, wa-marhuban*] among the people."[72]

The choice of language was neither accidental nor unique. In the days that followed, press coverage frequently referred to the executions as an instance of terrorism (*irhab*). By this interpretation, the objective was not to administer justice or even to intimidate a few villagers but rather to secure submission from the Egyptian public as a whole through a calculated display of violence. In the turn toward extreme coercion, many identified a stark contrast with the strategies of rule that the British had for so long emphasized. The pleasant clangor of gilded speech had once drowned out the steady, low rumble of colonial violence, but the shrieks and cries emanating from Dinshaway were now too piercing to be ignored. Questioning this disproportion between consent and coercion, *al-Mu'ayyad* now asked: "The English politicians say that they aim toward one goal, namely to win the hearts of the Egyptian people first of all. Is that end achieved by means of the terror at Dinshaway?"

Following the special tribunal, it was not the mere fact of the occupation's public brutality that its Egyptian critics emphasized. Rather, it was the more specific problem that this rapid escalation of state violence posed for a legitimating discourse of economic improvement. As *al-Mu'ayyad* went on to inquire on July 1, "Does it suffice that the country should progress in the sense that land values rise whereas the bonds of mutual affection have not been fastened between the people and their rulers? Indeed the persistence of antipathy is a reason for delay in the occupation of hearts [*ihtilal al-qulub*], and the English do want to occupy them. So do hearts in Egypt open with a key like the terrorism of Dinshaway?"[73]

The events of June 1906 had torn open a new space in which to interrogate British rule beyond its own criteria of material wealth and reform. Flinging back the tired litany of arguments that British officials and journalists had made for the virtues of their veiled protectorate, an emboldened press chastised those who had dismissed any criticism as petty ingratitude. In its inaugural issue, the newly established paper *al-Minbar* reminded readers that Cromer and his staff claimed to be "the saviors of Egypt from the talons of despotism and decline and from a plunge into the abyss of poverty and bankruptcy." On that basis, they branded Egypt "a nation of ingrates." And yet in Dinshaway, those self-proclaimed saviors had "deepened the chasm they wish to fill and given the Egyptians vindication for protesting against them."[74]

SPECTERS OF FANATICISM

If such authors were quick to interpret Dinshaway as a deliberate performance of British terrorism, that reading of events was only reinforced by the British government's defense of the special tribunal. Both the original incident and the subsequent trial had received detailed coverage in the British press. Wary of negative reporting about the hurried pace of the proceedings, the Foreign Secretary Edward Grey had asked Cairo on June 27 whether "an interval before execution should be allowed, as is always done here, to give time for full consideration."[75] But Charles Findlay, the counsellor at the embassy in Cairo who had been managing the trial in the week since Cromer departed for his summer holiday, replied that under the 1895 decree, "no legal power to interfere in the execution of the decision come to by the Court is possessed either by the Egyptian Government or by His Majesty's Agency."[76] The sentences were carried out as scheduled. As Grey had feared, the Foreign Office soon faced allegations from members of both Parliament and the British public that it had sanctioned a gross perversion of justice.

On July 5, Grey appeared in Parliament to address his critics. "All this year," he announced, "a fanatical feeling in Egypt has been on the increase. It has not been confined to Egypt; it has been stretching along the north of Africa generally."[77] The recent increase of the British garrison and the special tribunal at Dinshaway, he continued, were calculated to nip this fanaticism in the bud. "I doubt," Grey boasted of Cromer's economic achievements, "whether in any generation you will find the lot of the common people has improved so much as that of the Egyptian people has, compared with the original state they were in before we were there." Any show of weakness in the present moment would leave that material progress "to be swept away by a rash of fanatical passion."[78] The only viable course was to crush any threats to the stability of British rule. "If the fanatical feeling in Egypt gets the better of the constituted authority of the Egyptian Government," Grey warned, "you are then face to face with the use of force."[79]

The speech may have dampened the blowback in Parliament, but in Egypt, it only strengthened arguments that had been gaining support since the special tribunal convened. As an explanation for Dinshaway, this effort to conjure the bogey of fanaticism placed the occupation in a bind. By affirming that the spectacle of violence was a response not to a specific crime but to a spectral hostility sweeping the Egyptian population, Grey simultaneously suggested that the improved "lot of the common people" bore no meaningful relation to their attitudes toward British rule. The measures of material progress were not, in other words, functional to public approval. Nor was Grey's the only such endorsement of the Egyptian government's sudden affinity for coercion. In early July, both the *Egyptian Gazette* and *al-Muqattam* ran stories that recast Dinshaway as just one instance of the rampant "lawlessness and savagery" evinced by the fallahin; the best remedy, they suggested, was to normalize extreme forms of punishment and to bring back the *kurbaj* (whip).[80]

While rejecting these latest imputations of fanaticism and criminality, an emboldened opposition seized upon the manifold contradictions of the moment. Mocking the self-congratulation of those who "saved us from the scourge of the old regime and abolished the corvée and kurbaj," *al-Liwa'* asked whether they now envisioned a return to "the Middle Ages, the ages of torture and revenge."[81] To justify such violent impulses, Ahmad Hilmi now observed, the occupation had suddenly contrived a reinterpretation of Egypt's vaunted prosperity: "The English administrators seem to believe that the extraordinary increase in the wealth of the *fallahin* has moved them to greed and inspired in them a strong inclination toward theft and jealousy and mutual hatred." Even if this dubious brand of criminal sociology were correct, it would only confirm what Hilmi and others had been arguing all along. In their singular pursuit of economic development, the British had implemented an impoverished conception of government and its responsibilities, a failure that was signaled most of all by the "paltry sums of money devoted to education."[82] *Al-Mu'ayyad*, meanwhile, leveraged its own earlier analysis of the boom's unevenness to rebut Grey's charge of fanaticism. "These banks have come to establish branches in every district and province," the paper observed, "and they transact with the people . . . at exorbitant interest, interest that is forbidden by Islam and disturbing to their souls." Despite the supposed fanaticism of the Muslim population, however, there were strikingly few incidents of violence against the foreigners who controlled these financial institutions. Any evidence of increased crime in the countryside in fact suggested that Egyptians were mostly harming each other.[83]

In Dinshaway, a rising generation of Egyptian journalists and activists located a new and powerful idiom for narrating the occupation as a political failure, an instance of "dominance without hegemony."[84] But it was not only in the logical and evidentiary basis that it furnished to anticolonial thought that Dinshaway became a watershed in the history of Egyptian nationalism. No less significant for the political struggles that ensued were the new means of representation that Dinshaway helped to make thinkable. Ahmad Hilmi's reporting was only the first in a long series of narrative expositions, spanning multiple genres, through which a wider Egyptian public came to see themselves in the suffering of the peasants at Dinshaway. In one of the earliest examples of this literary memorialization, Hafiz Ibrahim composed his famous poem about the incident on July 2; less than two weeks later, *al-Minbar* began to publish the chapters of Mahmud Tahir Haqqi's serialized novel *'Adhra' Dinshaway* (The Virgin of Dinshaway).[85] By the end of the month, the government's informants were reporting about a new youth organization calling itself the "Rising Generation" in which members gathered to recite poetry about Dinshaway.[86] As Zachary Lockman has argued, the incident thus furnished the basis for an "imaginative linkage" between the peasantry and the literate urban classes who formed the core of the nationalist movement, a linkage now signified by the unifying category *al-sha'b* (the people).[87]

It was not only in these shifting subjective experiences of "imagined community," however, that Dinshaway revealed new possibilities for Egyptian nationalism as a political project.[88] Official discourse had long mobilized the authority of economic statistics to denigrate the occupation's critics as geographically and demographically marginal. The Foreign Office itself now described an alarming breach between the measurable achievement of material progress and the sentiments of the peasants whose interests the occupation claimed to advance. The British could attempt to explain that gap as the expression of a latent fanaticism. But as *al-Mu'ayyad* was quick to note, "the accusation came out of the blue, and to prove it requires more than just charges and allegations."[89] The flimsy evidentiary basis of Cromer's and Grey's fearmongering gave new weight to the rich, on-the-ground reporting of the Arabic press. It also inspired other creative strategies for establishing the spatial extent and numerical magnitude of popular opposition to British rule.

It was in this moment that the National Party pioneered a form of political practice that would later gain renown as one of the signature features of Egypt's 1919 revolution.[90] The British takeover of the Interior in the 1890s had led quickly to the abolition of village elections but left intact the institutional mechanism of petitioning as a necessary source of feedback for administrative discipline. Deprived of other formal channels for collective engagement with state institutions, peasants had continued to develop their own critical analyses of British rule.[91] But the government's own procedures managed this steady flow of paper by sorting the whole into a series of discrete administrative cases pertaining to specific individuals and specific locales. In the aftermath of Dinshaway, Mustafa Kamil's National Party gave this practice a new purpose. Through their journeys to the countryside and their newfound admiration for the peasantry, they identified in the petition a method for aggregating and representing public opinion in the absence of the electoral institutions British officials had sought to constrain or abolish.

By some accounts, it was Ahmad Hilmi himself who first contrived the tactic.[92] On the first anniversary of the Dinshaway trial, supporters of the National Party circulated hundreds of copies of a petition for signatures throughout the country. Addressed to the Khedive, it adopted the conventions of formal address and prose style common to the petitions that peasants often forwarded to the palace. But although a few copies were written out by hand, most had been produced in print; the technologies of the press thus ensured the mass reproduction of a singular message from the people (*al-shaʿb*). The text itself emphasized that "there is no division between great and small in [the experience of] pain and no difference between rich and poor in [their] feelings." To confirm that "every family in Egypt considers the Dinshaway prisoners to be their own children" the signatories listed their towns and villages of residence.[93] In both its form and its content, the document thus proclaimed a convergence between geographies and social constituencies that the British continued to insist on holding apart.

CONCLUSION: COMMERCE AGAINST CONSTITUTIONALISM

These practices were only the most dramatic examples of the mobilization that followed fast upon Dinshaway. The incident rapidly augmented the force and scope of arguments for self-rule on grounds that had little or nothing to do with Egypt's economic condition. At the same time, this energetic expansion of anticolonial activism quickly revealed that the entanglements between the country's material prosperity and the political structures of imperial rule could cut both ways.

As *al-Ahram* noted of Grey's Dinshaway speech, his alarmist claims about fanaticism were especially dangerous because "in the eyes of the other countries" the foreign secretary was "the most knowledgeable about Egypt's secrets, Egypt's affairs, and Egypt's spirit." Whereas Egyptians had once hoped that "the developed countries and civilized peoples and great nations would look upon them and their country with honor and respect after Egypt has gone a long way on the path of progress and . . . achieved the farthest extent of wealth and riches," that one word from Grey's mouth had the potential to cause lasting damage.[94] While *al-Ahram* dealt with this blow to Egypt's global reputation in generic terms, others were quick to calculate

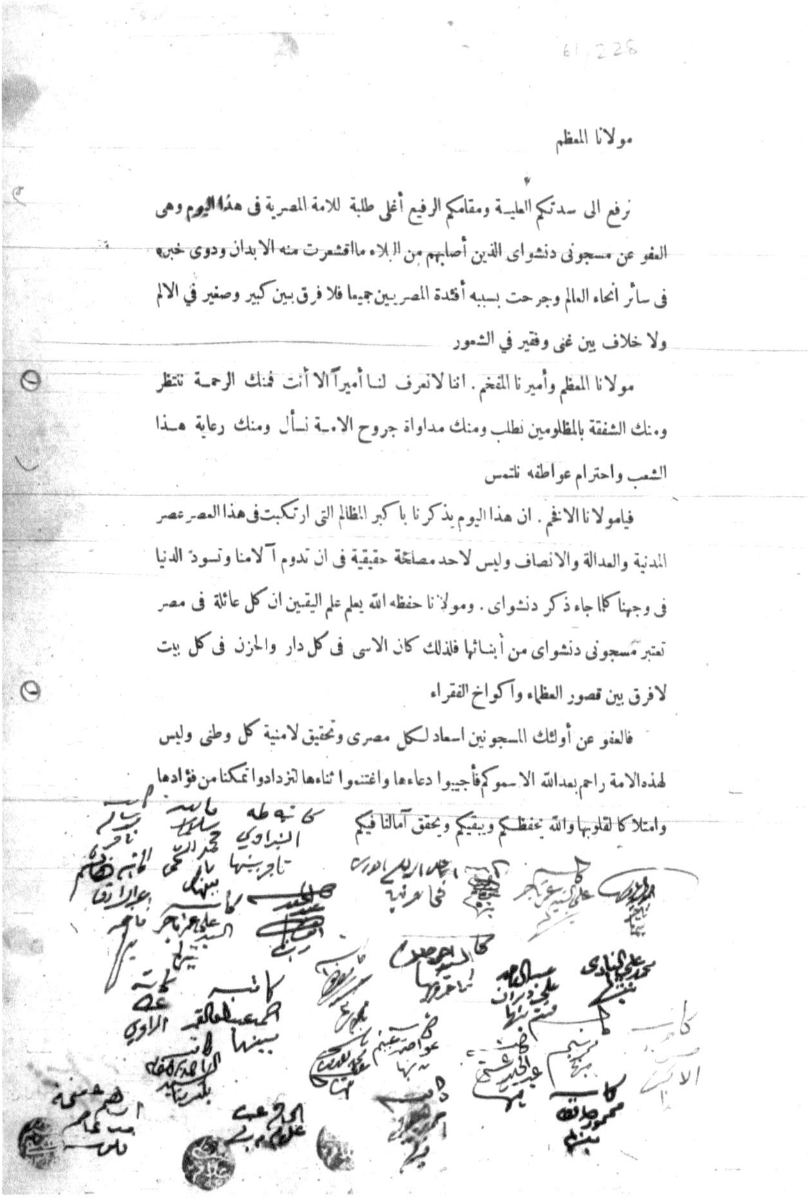
61, 228

مولانا المعظم

نرفع الى سدتكم العليـة ومقامكم الرفيع أغلى طلبة للامة المصرية فى هذا اليوم وهى العفو عن مسجونى دنشواى الذين أصابهم من البلاء مااقشعرت منه الابدان ودوى خبره فى سائر انحاء العالم وجرحت بسببه أفئدة المصريين جميعا فلا فرق بين كبير وصغير في الالم ولا خلاف بين غنى وفقير في الشعور

مولانا المعظم وأميرنا المفخم . اننا لانعرف لنـا أميراً الا أنت فمنك الرحمـة ننتظر ومنك الشفقة بالمظلومين نطلب ومنك مداواة جروح الامـة نسأل ومنك رعاية هـذا الشعب واحترام عواطفه نلتمس

فيامولانا الافخم . ان هذا اليوم يذكرنا باكبر المظالم التى ارتكبت فى هذا العصر عصر المدنية والعدالة والانصاف وليس لاحد مصلحة حقيقية فى ان تدوم آلامنا وتسود الدنيا فى وجهنا كلما جاء ذكر دنشواى . ومولانا حفظه الله يعلم علم اليقين ان كل عائلة فى مصر تعتبر مسجونى دنشواى من أبنائها فلذلك كان الاسى فى كل دار والحزن فى كل بيت لافرق بين قصور العظماء واكواخ الفقراء

فالعفو عن أولئك المسجونين اسعاد لكل مصرى وتحقيق لامنية كل وطنى وليس لهذه الامة راحم بعد الله الا سموكم فأجيبوا دعاءها واغتنموا ثناءها لتزدادوا تمكنا من فؤادها وامتلاكا لقلوبها والله يحفظكم ويبقيكم ويحقق آمالنا فيكم

FIGURE 4: Dinshaway Petition with Signatures from Banha. Source: DUR, HIL 61, 228. Reproduced by kind permission of the Trustees of the Mohamed Ali Foundation and of the University of Durham.

the actual cost of the bad publicity. *Al-Liwa'* published a letter from a foreign cotton merchant residing in Egypt who wished to register his dismay at the foreign secretary's accusation and describe, by contrast, the "hospitality and kindness" he had long experienced in his daily interactions with Egyptian villagers.[95]

In a bitingly sarcastic gloss on such efforts to discredit Grey's speech, Charles Findlay wrote to London at the end of August that the "native press, with the financial acumen of the Egyptian, quickly grasped the fact that it would not pay to be considered fanatical. . . . Many Europeans, deeply interested in financial enterprises, and afraid lest the accusation of fanaticism should affect the flow of foreign capital into the country, found no difficulty in arriving at the same conclusion."[96] In a new twist, however, Findlay went on to suggest that "fanaticism is perhaps more the result than the cause of this unrest." Among causes of the "disease" of which fanaticism was the symptom, he now included "the natural dislike of the Egyptians of all classes to see foreigners amassing large fortunes, which they think might have been theirs, by the rise in the value of land, especially of building sites. It is true that the Egyptian has had his full share of the immense increase of prosperity, but he would like to have it all." In adjusting the established premises of colonial economism, Findlay thus reaffirmed that Egyptians possessed a distinctive "financial acumen." But he went on to interpret the country's economic prosperity not as the solution to anticolonial "unrest" but rather one of its foremost provocations.[97]

By the early months 1907, such unrest and agitation included not only petitions and editorials in the papers but direct calls for a constitution, for more powerful representative bodies, and ultimately for independence. At the beginning of March, these demands culminated in a proposal, adopted by a plenary session of the General Assembly, that "the Egyptians be granted a Constitution, and, as a temporary measure, that the powers of the Provincial Councils, the Legislative Council, and the General Assembly be increased."[98] Long before Dinshaway, boosters like Falconer Larkworthy and Edouard Van Dieren had averred that foreign capital interests would be loath to countenance any alteration of Egypt's political status. Alarmed both by the new intensity of nationalist mobilization and by the support that the nationalist movement now received from Cromer's detractors in the British Parliament, a host of foreign businesses raced to demand reassurance. On March 9, 1907, the British Chamber of Commerce at Alexandria warned Cromer that "any steps that would tend to materially change the existing system of administration of the country would be premature and fatal to the best interests of all classes in Egypt, both native and European, and, while grievously impeding the great and growing commerce of the country, would be a serious blow to her moral and financial prosperity."[99] The Alexandria-based Association du Commerce d'Importation, the Council of Bristol Incorporated Chamber of Commerce and Shipping, and the Birmingham Chamber of Commerce soon transmitted messages expressing identical concerns.[100] Cromer, who was "altogether opposed to the idea of vesting the Legislative Council with an absolute veto upon any proposals made by the Government" forwarded the British Chamber's message to London as evidence of "a very general feeling of anxiety, by no means confined to the special classes represented in this letter."[101] Just a few months earlier, British officials were still insisting that Egypt's new wealth would guarantee the security of their rule and obviate the need for more coercive forms of governance. In the climate of political ferment that succeeded Dinshaway, however, the protection of that wealth itself became another reason to elaborate and extend the repressive tactics the incident had brought to the fore.

Chapter 5

THE MANY AGENTS OF AZMAH

> Perhaps the cause of the crisis in Egypt is the crisis here [in New York], for the ties of commerce that now exist between nations have made the financial world into a net that covers the whole globe so that if one strand is tugged, all the others are pulled along with it, and the movement is felt in every area.[1]
>
> —*al-Jaridah* (August 3, 1907)

ALMOST AS SOON AS IT ARRIVED, the crisis inspired commentaries about the word itself. From the spring of 1907, the "Financial Crisis" and its Arabic cognate *al-azmah al-maliyah* made headlines in Egypt's daily papers. By summer, journalists were reporting that peasant farmers could be heard uttering "the word 'crise' " as they bemoaned a near total absence of credit.[2] The word, it seems, had "passed into Arabic vocabulary as is to designate a period of difficulty and suffering."[3] For some, the disaster marked a kind of arrival: "A country devoid of banks, bourses, or saleable securities would, by force of circumstances, be spared such turmoil."[4] For others, use of the "*grand mot*" was misplaced. While "the true crisis is due to a fortuitous, or even unforeseeable, cause," this event was the "outcome of perfectly known facts."[5] As hopes of a swift rebound faded, others still noted that the meaning of the concept was changing. Both "in the press and in the public, a new sense emerges . . . that the crisis will not end by itself. Doubtless a bit of surprise enters into this sentiment: a crisis is something passing. Everyone knows that!"[6]

Uses of the word *azmah* to name a critical moment were not altogether new to Egypt in 1907. In the 1890s, the press had sometimes described the struggles over ministerial appointments as "political crises."[7] Mustafa Kamil had likewise organized each chapter of his 1898 study on "the Eastern Question" around a major "crisis."[8] In 1907, as in these earlier moments, adopting the language of crisis was a political choice, an "observation that produces meaning."[9] In this respect, reporting on the financial crisis followed well-established patterns. Like the Dinshaway Incident, this latest crisis furnished an opportunity to render judgment on the occupation. Indeed, one reason for the peculiar, historiographical disappearance of an event that received such extensive press coverage may be that British officials went to considerable lengths to minimize the significance of what was happening.[10] The outpouring of journalistic commentary on what different parties to this terminological dispute labeled "the panic," "the crash," or "the crisis" was matched in the correspondence of the British Consulate with little more than silence.

If the adoption of *azmah* to translate *crisis* was not particular to 1907, however, the sudden, ubiquitous reference to "financial crisis" was.[11] For many who employed this category, its significance lay in designating a social phenomenon for which no prior language existed because nothing of the sort had happened before. That many people, in everyday conversation, simply Arabized the French term as the neologism *krizah* is another indication that the concept named a profound disruption of everyday experience that escaped existing vocabulary.[12]

As the upheavals of 1907 unfolded, this new concept served to alter and reorient public debate over the nature and implications of British rule in at least three respects. First, the extensive material hardship that ensued from the initial stock market crash bolstered arguments that the occupation was failing by its own economistic criteria. These were the stakes of the terminological dispute. The more what began as a "crash" for stock speculators rose to the level of a "general crisis" for the population as a whole, the stronger the denunciations grew. Second, as the local press was quick to note, the financial turmoil of 1907 was worldwide in scope. The convulsions that rocked money markets as distant as New York and Alexandria were brought about by economic processes that were both structurally similar and closely interlinked. The world looked different from the City of London than it did from Lancashire. In drawing attention to these distinct, if overlapping, geographies of industrial and financial capital, "crisis" now provided a comparative diagnostic for the peculiar character of Egypt's state under British rule, a state that had demurred in the face of disaster and left the public unnecessarily vulnerable to the fluctuations of modern finance. Finally, as competing accounts tried and failed to pin its causes on particular malefactors, "the financial crisis" induced a troubling reflection on the changing character of social life itself. For many who used it, crisis was becoming a concept for grappling with the "real abstraction" of the problems it named.[13] The events of 1907 revealed that many Egyptians themselves were engaged in the practices of borrowing, lending, and speculation that contributed to the transmutation of a localized crash into a generalized crisis. As a result, it became difficult to identify the particular agents responsible for such diffuse misfortunes. While delivering a new normative basis upon which to claim independence, the crisis thus laid bare the deepening entanglements between forms of political and economic domination that now seemed to distinguish Egypt's colonial condition. The events of 1907 thereby reframed the very question of what it might mean to live differently after British rule.

LEVERAGING THE LAND

Unsurprisingly, contemporary accounts of the upheaval disagreed about when it had begun. Reporting in the *Egyptian Gazette* first referenced "one of the most serious crises" in "the Egyptian market" at the end of March.[14] That "Financial Crisis" made headlines in the *Gazette* by mid-April.[15] Later studies often located the onset in that month.[16] But *al-azmah al-maliyah* became a fixture in the Arabic press only in mid-May. And subsequent reporting sometimes moved the starting point back to January or February.[17] In similar fashion, announcements that the crisis was ending appeared almost weekly from early summer onwards.

If its precise timing remained a matter of some debate, however, most commentators concurred about the underlying mechanism that brought on the disaster. The shifting and uneven global geography of interest rates on different forms of credit was central to this story. When mortgage boosters made their case for Egypt in the

1890s, they were arguing that a pound loaned there would yield a higher and safer return than a similar transaction somewhere else. In the early 1900s, columnists in the nationalist press had turned that case for investment on its head to warn that Egypt's celebrated prosperity was at best relative and temporary. But even among these skeptics, few anticipated the extent of the devastation when boom turned to bust.

When British officials had made their own case for foreign investment, they had conjured a series of interlocking complementarities. Mortgage credit deployed on Egypt's farms would serve the interests of banks and textile mills in tandem, yielding attractive rates of interest for the former and ever-larger supplies of cheap raw cotton for the latter.[18] Central to such optimistic claims was an understanding of Egypt as an "agricultural country" in which foreign capital would naturally flow toward the countryside.[19] At first, the mortgage banks and land development companies had accordingly focused on rural areas, most notably in the Nile Delta. But as the field for agricultural mortgages became more crowded, investors turned elsewhere for higher returns. Capital was redirected from country to town and poured into the development of urban and suburban properties.[20] In a remarkable doctoral dissertation on the Egyptian crisis, the French law student F. Legrand later mused about the role of such building lands as objects of seemingly limitless speculation. Unlike an agricultural field on which "the revenue does not appear susceptible to great variations," for a parcel of land "situated in the environs of Cairo, Melbourne, or Buenos-Aires . . . nothing is more uncertain than its value." In such cases, the prices of urban properties could rise without limit according to "the wealth of these countries and the often-rapid changes in the ways of their inhabitants, all of which are difficult to evaluate."[21] While many of Egypt's banks eagerly contracted mortgages against individual properties in Cairo, Alexandria, and the major provincial towns, the inflation of both urban and rural real estate prices drew its greatest momentum from the capitalization of joint-stock companies in the opening years of the twentieth century. Between 1900 and 1907, no fewer than 160 companies representing an authorized capital of £E 43,335,000 began operations in Egypt.[22] While the earliest of these ventures had dealt mainly with the reclamation and resale of agricultural land, by 1905 there was a marked shift toward urban development schemes and new financial institutions.[23]

FIGURE 5: Stock Certificate of the Cairo Electric Railways and Heliopolis Oases Company, est. March 15, 1906. Source: Collection of the author.

Most of the new companies were financed through the sale of shares and bonds that traded on the bourses of Cairo and Alexandria.[24] And as the value of those shares continued to rise, some lenders began to pursue a more risky line of business. Already in 1899 the officers of the Imperial Ottoman Bank had expressed skepticism about the willingness of their competitors to make advances on margin, not against real estate or commercial goods but against the stock certificates of locally traded companies. In a prescient bit of analysis, E.W.H. Barry of the IOB's London Committee questioned "whether it is good for the country that the Banks should more or less countenance this spirit of speculation by making large advances on the *valeurs publiques*." Since it was unclear "who can eventually purchase these stocks," Barry judged that "the future of these securities now in the Banks' hands is rather a puzzle.[25]

Wary of the risk entailed in this more speculative type of lending, the IOB continued to focus on the annual financing of the cotton crop.[26] The same was not true of its competitors. As rates on conventional mortgages sank to 5.5% or lower,[27] loans on securities typically ranged from 6% to 9% and sometimes carried interest as high as 25%.[28] The temptation proved too great. On the borrowing side, these arrangements allowed the stock speculator "to double and treble his resources, and to indulge in his operations upon a scale twice or three times as great."[29] With share prices rising and many companies offering enormous annual dividends, the banks' interest demands posed little impediment. Eager to maintain their supplies of liquid capital and continue reaping outsize yields, some banks meanwhile expanded their own borrowing on European commercial paper markets, repeatedly rolling over short-term credit from abroad to make long-term loans against Egyptian stocks.

FINANCIAL TECTONICS OF THE BELLE ÉPOQUE

This ramshackle structure of multilayered debts was lashed together with strands of easy credit, and by the autumn of 1906, those ligatures were primed to snap. Egypt's predicament was hardly unique. In his irreverent and virtuosic account of 1907 as a globe-spanning series of crises, the New York–based economist and reporter Alexander Dana Noyes admonished his parochial compatriots for assuming their own "Panic of 1907" was a narrowly American affair. Any serious inquiry, Noyes insisted, "will lead us at once to the foreign markets, or rather, perhaps, to the money markets of the world at large, considered as one financial organism."[30] The global reach and volume of financial transactions had been expanding at a staggering clip since the late 1890s, and the increasingly integrated character of a credit system tethered to the supply of gold coinage helped to ensure that when it arrived "the causes of the entire episode were world-wide in their scope."[31] Noyes's own account suggested that the strain on global credit facilities had been mounting since about the middle of 1905. But the shocks that set in motion a tsunami of crashes, slumps, and panics in countries including Egypt, Chile, Germany, Japan, and the United States arrived the following year.

Ordinarily, the seismic terminology that pervades financial reporting is metaphorical. The tremors that upended financial markets across the globe in 1907, however, began with an actual earthquake. The temblor that rocked the city of San Francisco on April 18, 1906, was devastating. Together, the quake of 8.3 on the Richter scale and the fires that tore through a city built from California redwoods destroyed properties worth somewhere between $350 million and $500 million, sums that represented 1.3 to 1.8% of the gross national product of the US at the time.[32] Stock markets in New York and London tumbled on news of the disaster. Within a week, the

New York Times reported that the New York Stock Exchange had lost close to a billion dollars.[33] Thanks to the international dominance of the British insurance industry, meanwhile, more than half of the fire policies in San Francisco had been issued by firms from London and Lancashire. As an initial wave of relief payments flowed westward from other parts of the US as well as Germany, France, the Netherlands, and Great Britain, most insurers contrived to deny or restrict claims on their policies by arguing that damage caused directly by the earthquake was not covered.[34] Only after several months of litigation and political pressure did the British firms remit payment to policyholders in California. The massive efflux of gold from Britain to the United States thus occurred in two concentrated spurts, first roughly $30 million in April and May and then another $35 million in September and October.[35]

The timing of the latter payout proved disastrous. These transfers represented the single largest outflow of gold from Britain between 1900 and 1913 and resulted in a 14% reduction in the country's stock of hard currency.[36] And by the moment the second wave of shipments was crossing the Atlantic, another unanticipated turn of events was drawing gold from British vaults in the opposite direction. In a darkly ironic twist, the very cotton crop that foreign financial investment was supposed to improve suddenly became another proximate cause of the financial crisis. In 1906, an abnormally bountiful harvest coincided with the highest global cotton prices in four decades to yield the most valuable crop that Egypt had ever seen.[37] Already alarmed by the strain on their reserves, the directors of the Bank of England saw this sudden increase in the seasonal demand for gold to cover the purchase of the £26 million Egyptian crop as reason to act.[38] In the autumn of 1906, eager to replenish their gold reserves, they moved to raise the bank's benchmark interest rate, first from 3.5% to 4%, then to 5%, and then again to 6%. The Germans quickly followed suit.[39] The days of easy credit had ended.

As would soon become clear, the pattern of heavily leveraged financial speculation that some commentators prior to 1907 had derisively chalked up to an Oriental propensity for gambling was not, in fact, particular to Egypt. That the effects of the European rate hikes upon stock markets in Alexandria and New York were so similar, that events in two such distant places could have such powerful reverberations upon each other, and that an anxious Egyptian public could eventually see viable alternatives to their own experience of crisis on the other side of the Atlantic were all consequences of the similar positions the two countries occupied in the financial geographies of the belle époque. Not without reason could one student of the Egyptian crisis remark that "the spirit of speculation and the appearance of crisis occur most of all in what are commonly called 'new countries,' where remunerative enterprises appear numerous." This, he continued, was "a character which the United States seems to have conserved in a permanent fashion."[40] Although it may have dwarfed them in sheer magnitude, the US shared key features with Egypt and the other "emerging markets" of the era, perhaps most significantly the absence of a central bank.[41] In the United States as well, the financial expansion that followed upon the First Great Depression of 1873–1896 had fired a volatile and alchemic combination of easy credit, loose banking regulations, and soaring share valuations. There too, the early 1900s had seen a dramatic increase in lending on margin against stocks and bonds. Unable to counteract the Bank of England's rate hikes, the American banks began to call in their loans and thereby triggered a sell-off of the equities that speculators had pledged as collateral. By March, this "silent crash" or "rich man's panic" had become acute.[42]

Economic reporting in the Egyptian press had been warning about a constriction of the money supply and a new condition of "financial stringency" since at least the end of 1906.[43] In early March 1907, a sharp drop in prices on the Alexandria and Cairo stock markets for the first time raised the specter of "financial crisis."[44] The Egyptian press attributed the turbulence of local stock prices both to the Bank of England's reaction against American demand for gold and to the global reverberations of the slump in New York. Over the following weeks, the local papers closely monitored the unfolding of this short-lived precursor to the more famous American panic that struck in October. In the second half of March, the *Egyptian Gazette* carried several brief reports on what it called the "American Money Panic" or simply "The Financial Crisis." Optimistic in tone, these pieces detailed the efforts of the Roosevelt administration at "allaying the panic" by depositing federal customs revenues with the national banks in order to supply the New York market with additional liquidity.[45] On March 27, the paper pronounced the "Financial Crisis Over," but by that point, the sell-off in New York had raised alarms elsewhere. Unlike the British and the Germans, the French had not altered their benchmark interest rate in the autumn of 1906. But on March 21, the Bank of France decided to raise it for the first time in seven years, from 3% to 3.5%.[46] The *New York Times* complained, "Through all the period of stringency the Bank of France had maintained a serene appearance of dignified calm, and now, when there were some slight symptoms of improvement in the international position, the rise in its bank rate informed the world that in the opinion of its distinguished managers further measures for protection were necessary."[47] Responding to this tightening of credit supplies and to a mounting unease over the speculative fervor of recent years, European banks began to call in loans from their Egyptian counterparts. The renewed strain on the money markets in turn prompted a rush to sell the shares those Egyptian banks had been holding as collateral. Suddenly it seemed that the values of Egyptian equities might be more the effect than the cause of foreign investment.

FROM CRASH TO CRISIS

By late March, the steep decline in shares on the Alexandria and Cairo bourses had won the label of "crisis."[48] But in this opening phase, these developments attracted only intermittent attention. In part, the disaster unfolding in the stock exchanges was eclipsed by more dramatic news. On April 11, 1907, Lord Cromer announced that he would resign and return to England after serving as consul-general since 1883.[49] The decision provoked a flurry of articles about the possible reasons behind it, the implications for British rule, and the character of Cromer's chosen successor, Sir Eldon Gorst. Even as such questions crowded out other stories, coverage of the crisis retained an optimistic tone. Severe as the slump in stock values might be, the damage so far appeared limited to those who owned and traded shares on the local markets. And although the sell-off had depressed stock prices, the underlying business of many Egyptian companies remained sound. This was the assessment of a group of bankers who began meeting in Alexandria in mid-April to coordinate a response to the crash. In the opinion of those present, the "existing crisis had been much exaggerated" and "all serious bankers and capitalists ought to join in discouraging the wild speculation that has of late been encouraged by some brokers and bankers." Some even mooted the opinion that the crash was a welcome corrective that would chasten the speculators and "give a great impetus to rigorous bourse regulations."[50]

A week later, as share prices continued to fall, the stockbrokers' associations of both the Cairo and Alexandria bourses voted to "fix prices below which nobody is to be allowed to sell."[51] This attempt to place a floor on share valuations only intensified the anxieties of investors. By mid-May, a decidedly more bearish *Egyptian Gazette* stressed the urgent "necessity for united action" to surmount "the financial slough of despond in which the Bourses of Alexandria and Cairo are now wallowing." The paper urged the local banks to ease the pressure that was forcing their clients to liquidate shares and recommended that they form a syndicate to facilitate the purchase of Egypt's stronger securities.[52] On May 22, at Eldon Gorst's urging, representatives of the National Bank of Egypt, Bank of Egypt, Bank of Athens, Banco di Roma, Cassa di Sconto e di Risparmio, Comptoir National d'Escompte de Paris, Deutsche Orientbank, Anglo-Egyptian Bank, Crédit Lyonnais, and Imperial Ottoman Bank gathered to discuss the organization of just such a syndicate. The participants voted on a proposal to advance sums totaling half a million pounds to purchase "first class shares" at current prices. This act of collective stimulus, they judged, would restore public confidence, and investors "would thus be induced to buy."[53] The proposal, however, needed ratification by the boards of all the participating banks. Unconvinced that the syndicate would succeed, the Crédit Lyonnais refused to sign on. Because the boards of several other banks had made their own approval contingent upon unanimous ratification, the agreement stalled out.[54] While the syndicate did not dissolve altogether, it failed to mount the kind of decisive action that had inspired a slight recovery in stock prices when its formation was first announced.[55] By mid-June, this failure to "allay the fears of the people" was causing shares to "plummet to depths they had never reached before."[56] At mid-year, the value of all Egyptian stocks in circulation had fallen by 27% from their prices in late February. Shares of banks and credit institutions had lost 22%, and land companies had dropped by a staggering 37%.[57]

THE CULPRITS OF CRISIS

It was in this moment of rising uncertainty that *al-azmah al-maliyah* became a regular fixture on the pages of the Arabic press. Most reports still identified the depressed value of local stocks as the most significant manifestation of the crisis. From this vantage, a sudden withdrawal of investor confidence both in Egypt and abroad was responsible for falling share prices. Even before hopes for coordinated intervention by the banks had evaporated, the crash had prompted questions about other possible determinants of Egypt's global reputation. Most controversial was the allegation that a more assertive nationalist movement had become a repellant to foreign capital. "Is it not possible," asked a letter to the *Egyptian Gazette*, "that owing to the recurrence of disturbing rumours, and the unchecked and mischievous tirades of a spurious

National party, the investing and speculating public has lost confidence?" Between the "misplaced interest" of radicals in Parliament and the "generally recognised weakness of [the Liberal Prime Minister] Sir Henry Campbell-Bannerman," there was a "certain evidence of fear that more power will be given to the natives than they can justifiably claim."[58] The following day, *al-Liwa'* issued a rebuttal. Not only did they "demand nothing more than internal reforms in no way connected to the financial crisis," but "if the words of the nationalist papers had such great influence upon the markets, then we would have seen share prices tumble" in moments of genuine nationalist fervor like the Dinshaway and 'Aqabah incidents of the previous year. Nothing of the sort had taken place. In fact, it was the foreign papers that ought to "lighten their tone so that no harm shall befall their own European compatriots in Egypt whose losses in this crisis are many times greater than those of the native Egyptians." The immediate solution lay not in press reporting but in coordinated action by the government and the business community. The former, *al-Liwa'* suggested, ought to provide the banks with a short-term loan for the purchase of shares and the resumption of the credit that had been so suddenly revoked. The banks, in turn, should "use all means at their disposal to convince those who were previously extending them funds from Europe that the situation in Egypt has not changed and that there is nothing to be feared form this crisis."[59]

In a rare moment of agreement, the Anglophile *al-Muqattam* made a similar call for the government to fulfill its responsibilities to the public. On May 16, the paper chastised the banks that "enticed the people to subscribe for company shares" only to "slam the doors in their faces" when the crash occurred. Many Egyptian companies remained perfectly sound, so the blanket refusal to accept shares as collateral was unwarranted. The directors of the major banks could publish lists of "the companies they find to be reliable" and resume lending against those shares. But the government also bore a responsibility to coordinate with the banks in endorsing those findings. Absent such measures, "the foundations of financial happiness that this land has attained thanks to the [British] reformers will be destroyed in a matter of days, and the suffering of the people from the depression and hardship of crisis will intensify."[60]

Several days later *al-Muqattam* admonished the government more directly for its failure to act. True, public officials had "warned and advised the people" about the dangers of speculation, but that was in the past. Now, when the dire consequences had arrived, the government "stands with its arms crossed and watches the loss of money and the worsening of conditions without extending a hand to alleviate the crisis." Drawing a comparison that would soon gain wide appeal, *al-Muqattam* noted that "ours is not the first country to experience the severity of financial crises due to excessive speculation. In those countries, the United States most recent among them, the governments have taken the initiative to remedy the damage before it becomes uncontrollable." By extending its own funds and pressuring the banks to lend again, the Egyptian government too could avert disaster. Instead, its moralistic condemnation of stock speculators had become an excuse for doing nothing. The losses of those speculators, however predictable and well deserved, would soon spread to property owners, merchants, industrialists, "and others from all the different classes."[61]

News of Gorst's efforts to form the syndicate tempered such criticisms of the government for a time. As the agreement between the banks unraveled in late May, reporting instead revolved around two other possible culprits. The most obvious agents of the crisis were the banks themselves. The underlying sources of the country's wealth, local writers observed, had not changed. None denied that the past few years had seen fortunes amassed through dubious practices of financial manipulation. But the increasing severity of the crisis had long since surpassed any reasonable corrective to the overreach of recent years. On May 27, the daily *al-Zahir*—a paper that had staked out a position of self-conscious "moderation"[62]—launched a broadside against "the stubbornness of the heads of the big banks" who had done "great damage to trade and to Egypt's financial reputation." Analogizing the current situation to a storm at sea in which the life boats arrive too late, the author proclaimed that "the people are the victims of neglect and hesitation more than they are victims of the sea and its waves."[63]

Widespread consensus that the crisis was, first and foremost, financial (*maliyah*) in nature would soon provide the basis for a new and powerful line of argument that identified the institutions controlling the supply of money (*al-mal*) as the foremost threat to the real wealth (*al-tharwah al-haqiqiyah*) of the country. But in these early days, many questions remained unanswered. Why did lenders that had once jockeyed to place their capital in Egypt suddenly lose all confidence? Why had a venerable establishment like the Crédit Lyonnais become so pessimistic about the prospects for a speedy recovery? The answers, some now insisted, lay outside the ordinary workings of financial markets. As the syndicate plan faltered, a second line of commentary revisited the allegation that nationalist politics stood in the way of any improvement.

In this controversy over the chilling effects of nationalist "extremism," *al-Muqattam* took a leading role. Echoing the language Lord Cromer had long employed to dismiss criticism, the paper launched a volley of front-page stories under the title "*Ashab al-masalih al-haqiqiyah* [The Representatives of Real Interests]."[64] The Crédit Lyonnais's withdrawal offered "conclusive proof about the loss of foreign confidence in the Egyptian markets because of turmoil in the political atmosphere of recent times." By "riling those of feeble intellect with false notions of patriotism and love of country," Egypt's soi-disant nationalists were in fact "pursuing their own interests and objectives." With a tone of righteous indignation, *al-Muqattam*'s authors here rehearsed the occupation's own economistic arguments on behalf of British rule. The "real interests" of the Egyptian people lay in the steady improvement of economic fortunes that Britain had overseen. It was for this reason that the nationalist obsession with Egyptian control over political institutions was delusional and dangerous. Like other Egyptians, the supporters of *al-Hizb al-Watani* were pursuing their own self-interest—in this case, as striving opportunists with a smattering of education and an unrealized desire for government employment. The problem, in brief, was that they misrepresented those particular "interests and objectives" as the general interest of the whole country.[65] The "nationalist movement" was not national in extent but "merely personal [*shakhsiyah mahdah*] and limited to a bunch of people consisting of a few leaders and their subordinates."[66] In demanding a premature independence, however, the nationalist press had now upended the economic progress that represented Egypt's "real interests." "This nationalism," the paper warned, "only brings poverty and ruin to the nation and its people."[67]

Casting its own position of support for the occupation as more accurately representative of popular opinion, *al-Muqattam* bolstered its commentary by publishing letters from its readers. On June 1, five authors who described themselves as "esteemed notables" and "representatives of [Egypt's] real interests," wrote in to affirm the paper's analysis of the crisis. "Never before," they noted, "have we composed such a letter or involved ourselves in political affairs, for we concerned ourselves solely with our private interests in agriculture and trade and the improvement of our own material and moral conditions." Only to counteract the malign influence of "those two great calamities, namely *al-Liwa'* and *al-Mu'ayyad*," had these well-meaning Egyptians seen fit to breach the proper separation between politics and the daily pursuit of economic gain. What in "pure literary Arabic" had been dubbed "the financial crisis," the letter concluded, should in fact be called "the result of the stupidity of the fanatical papers and the impertinence of the sowers of discord."[68]

Al-Muqattam's fusillade about the pernicious material effects of nationalist fanaticism (*taʿassub*) soon elicited responses from the country's other leading journals. Lambasting "the papers that call themselves patriotic," *al-Zahir* initially echoed the opinion that by stoking fears of political unrest, "firstly they did not help Egypt or the Egyptians and secondly they increased the worry in the thoughts of Westerners."[69] But assertions about the causal relation between finance and politics could cut both ways. Responding directly to *al-Muqattam*, the new daily *al-Jaridah* condemned what it described as a campaign to "settle the score" with political rivals at public expense.[70] A year prior, British officials had celebrated plans for the *al-Jaridah*'s establishment, under the editorship of the young lawyer and liberal intellectual Ahmad Lutfi al-Sayyid, as an antidote to the unrelenting criticism of the major nationalist organs. They noted in particular that first among the paper's list of founding principles was a determination that "the system of government is to be accepted as it actually exists—that is to say, no question or discussion will be permitted as to past history, as to the advantages or disadvantages of the British occupation, or as to the prospects or desirability of evacuation by His Majesty's army."[71] Under Lutfi al-Sayyid's stewardship, however, the paper's commitments to an expansive liberal universalism and to the welfare of the Egyptian public quickly overwhelmed any a priori reluctance to criticize the occupation. In this regard, the choice to denounce *al-Muʾayyad* and *al-Liwaʾ* with allegations of fanaticism was unacceptable. If the British were actually committed to advancing the material well-being of Egyptians, then surely they could help restore the confidence of European investors. Instead, they did nothing to counteract "the tongues spreading rumors about Egypt that stink with the vile allegation of fanaticism."[72] *Al-Muqattam* had furthermore crossed a line by invoking the fanaticism of its nationalist rivals as grounds to "demand restrictions upon personal freedom." Such opportunistic misrepresentation, *al-Jaridah* responded, belied the Anglophile paper's professed devotion to the "real interests" of the country.[73]

Adopting a more conspiratorial tack, *al-Liwaʾ* explained the relationship between politics and financial markets the other way around. While the "moderate" papers asked why Gorst declined to "reassure Europe with his official reports," the crisis might, in fact, represent an effort to deploy British influence as a cudgel against the opponents of British rule.[74] Having left Egypt humiliated, Lord Cromer—"the stubborn defeated enemy"—was desperate to "exact revenge." He had therefore "used all his power to weaken faith in the Egyptians and labeled them with 'fanaticism' so that no financier should feel that his money was safe."[75]

Over time, even *al-Liwa'* backed away from this most sinister explanation. As *al-Jaridah* noted at the time, the theory that "the financial crisis is a political lesson being delivered to Egypt" held little water. The occupation's representatives had always insisted that "the foremost gift England has bestowed upon Egypt and that Egypt in return acknowledges from the English is material progress, by which they mean economic and financial progress."[76] Why, then, the paper asked, would the British knowingly damage what they understood to be the foundations of their own legitimacy in the country? Moreover, the collapse of financial markets and the devastating interruption of credit were obviously not limited to Britain's veiled protectorate. *Al-Jaridah*'s leading economic reporter Yusuf al-Bustani remarked, "What happened in Egypt is what happened in America, and the similarity between the two is striking." In both countries, the rapid establishment of new companies, driven by an abundance of cheap money, had reached a point where "the market was flooded well beyond the needs of the people." Then "due to a shaken confidence . . . as a result of that condition of recklessness, the supply of money in the hands of the people diminished," and the crash ensued.[77]

Until this point, the local banks had attracted attention chiefly for their role in the fluctuation of stock prices. Public ire over their sudden reluctance to extend credit rested on a presumption that the country's major lending institutions were free to act otherwise. Despite the "abundance of money in [their] vaults," the banks persisted in "the stubbornness that is becoming a cause of all these calamities."[78] By mid-June, however, it had become clear that at least some banks possessed no such hoarded cash. Having drawn down their reserves and leveraged their positions on European money markets, they had replaced the crates of gold that their critics imagined with piles of commercial bills and stock certificates. As local clients scrambled to repay their call loans, some banks faced new troubles with their own creditors. On June 18, the *Egyptian Gazette* reported that the Anglo-Egyptian Bank and the Imperial Ottoman Bank had made an advance to the Cassa di Sconto e di Risparmio to help meet its obligations. While the *Gazette* expressed confidence that "the difficulties of the bank will be surmounted," the news unsurprisingly alarmed local depositors.[79]

Originally founded in 1885, the Cassa di Sconto e di Risparmio had entered into an agreement in 1906 with the Viennese Union Bank whereby the latter extended a credit of four million francs, acquired a growing subset of the bank's shares, and placed three of its own representatives on the board of the directors. Over the course of the next year, the bank's business had swelled. It had raised more capital through a further issue of shares and paid its stockholders a hefty dividend of 14%.[80] But as would soon become clear, the bank had also accrued liabilities roughly 4.5 times its assets and had made extensive loans against bills of exchange and stocks. By June 21, news of its difficulties had provoked a full-blown run on the bank, forcing the Cassa's branches to close their doors and the stock markets of Cairo and Alexandria to suspend trading.[81] Confronted by the possibility that the crisis could menace their own business and cause skittish depositors to withdraw their funds, Egypt's other major banks at last saw reason to coordinate a response. The syndicate that had formed in May agreed to advance £300,000 to meet the Cassa's outstanding liabilities in full. A committee headed by members of the National Bank would thereafter oversee a gradual liquidation of the bank's assets.[82]

THE MOST FAMOUS ECONOMIST

While these measures may have protected the banking sector, the drama of the Cassa's failure raised further questions about the government's refusal to manage the crisis. It was at this moment that the worldwide character of the contemporary financial system and the peculiar synchronicity between events in Egypt and the United States assumed new importance. For an Egyptian public alarmed by the occupation's conspicuous inaction, the American response to the short-lived crisis of March made all the more glaring the shortcomings of Britain's laissez-faire dogma.[83] Suggesting that the financial upheavals in both countries were plausibly commensurable, Egyptian journalists held up the Roosevelt administration as an example of the interventionist approach that British officials refused to adopt. Earlier in June, *al-Mu'ayyad* had reported approvingly on Roosevelt's reputation among financiers and capitalists as "Theodore the Meddler" and described a range of his policy initiatives to promote a more equitable distribution of wealth.[84] Following the run on the Cassa di Sconto, several more papers discussed both the American president's efforts to regulate corporations and trusts and his government's role in alleviating the "rich man's panic." Describing Roosevelt as "the most famous economist known to date," *al-Zahir* praised his efforts to restore the balance between public interest and private gain by constraining the power of American companies and "binding them in chains."[85] *Al-Ahram* noted that even the European papers had begun to criticize Gorst for "leaving this crisis to devour the wealth of the country and to threaten the prosperity of the peasant." While the British permitted local financiers to "strangle the market," the American secretary of the treasury had, by supplying the banks with additional liquidity, ensured that "the American markets are rescued from failure."[86] Even *al-Muqattam* later in the year broke with its usual apologetics. In a direct comparison with the US, the paper criticized the Egyptian government for "its conviction that it should avoid interfering in any matter that only touches upon the outer edge of its domain of competence and not its interior or its very center."[87]

For those who saw a viable alternative in the regulatory reforms of American Progressives, there were many new indications that the crisis was spreading beyond the confines of the Cairo and Alexandria bourses. *Al-Ahram*'s discussion of Secretary Cortelyou's intervention had opened with some alarming figures. Purchase prices for winter crops (which ripened and went to market in early summer) were down as much as 20% from the previous year. Anecdotal reporting suggested that wages for house servants had dropped by a staggering 30%. The money shortage, moreover, presaged serious troubles for peasants who by autumn might have little choice but to sell their cotton crops at bargain rates.[88] The mainstream English press both in Egypt and abroad, meanwhile, insisted that the failure of the Cassa should arouse no new concerns about the extent of the crisis. Offering a positive gloss on the bank's demise, the London-based *Statist* explained, "Of course such a crisis will not pass over without the failure of some of the more reckless speculators. But a serious breakdown is not probable. The country, it will be recollected, is exceedingly prosperous."[89] The *Times* judged that the bank's collapse was the consequence of "wild speculative movement." It would not, however, "permanently injure the economic position of Egypt; the springs of agriculture and commerce are quite uninjured by what has occurred; the peasants and most of the people are prosperous."[90]

Despite its greater proximity to the unfolding disaster, the *Egyptian Gazette* was similarly chipper. When it first reported on the Cassa's troubles, the paper explained that such problems only concerned "the small fraction of the population, European and native, who come within the radius of the Bourse. The voiceless millions of the fellaheen population were never more prosperous, and they have been absolutely untouched by the present depression."[91] A week later, the *Gazette* declared that the "exaggerated gloominess" of the business communities in Cairo and Alexandria "flatters their self-importance for it gives their own misfortunes an air of being only part and parcel of some universal calamity."[92] Over the coming months, the leading paper of Egypt's Anglophone community would hardly waver from this assessment of the class specificity and geographic localization of the crisis. In August, its writers still expressed optimism that "the severe lesson will have had a beneficial effect, confidence will return, and Egypt will continue on her march toward prosperity."[93] While letters to the editor did, on occasion, offer countervailing observations about conditions in the countryside, the October cotton harvest brought with it fresh proclamations of a return to normalcy. "The moral," in this version of things, "is that Egypt must like other countries have its crises, but that its economic situation is based on cotton, the present situation of which is excellent and the future secure—as to production."[94]

The consistency of such reporting—which resonated with the statements emanating from the British Consulate—was just one among a number of elements that coalesced to harden Gorst's position against any direct form of state involvement. In his autobiographical notes for 1907, the new consul-general proudly recorded, "As regards the financial crisis, my object was to let the disaster burn itself out as quickly as possible and to prevent the Government from being hustled into doing something foolish in deference to the universal clamour that 'something must be done.' "[95] Some observers, particularly in the French press, suggested that the government's absenteeism was less the result of any strongly held principle than the consequence of fiscal imprudence. Relieved of oversight by the other foreign powers after the Entente Cordiale of 1904, the British had transferred several million pounds from the Egyptian government's reserve fund to public works projects in the Sudan, thereby drawing down the monies available for any kind of government stimulus.[96] In response to a proposal in January 1908 that the government should advance £2 million to the banks to encourage mortgage lending,[97] Gorst did acknowledge that "the available funds of the Government were already earmarked for public purposes, and the operation suggested could not have been effected without inconvenience to the Treasury."[98] But his comments on the subject also suggest there were other issues at work.

Gorst left no written record of his opinions on the "meddling" of the Roosevelt administration, but on the viability of such policies in Egypt, he was unequivocal. While acknowledging that "the crisis did not materially differ as to its causes and effects from similar phenomena elsewhere," he saw "no sufficient justification . . . for Government interference" and doubted that such measures "would have produced any very material effect on the situation."[99] If, as he proposed, the Egyptian crisis was merely a "natural reaction from a state of over-speculation," then any attempt to soften the blow would impede the market's self-correction. Equally significant was Gorst's public account of the crisis itself. When the nationalist papers called for the government to place public funds at the disposal of private banks, they described this remedy as a check against the contagion of a social malady that threatened the Egyptian public as a whole. The occupation's highest official countered that the "position of the fellah has hardly been affected."[100]

By the time Gorst's annual report for 1907 appeared, that claim amounted to an act of misdirection. The stakes of the disagreement were enormous. For more than two decades, British officials had invoked the quantifiable improvement of peasant livelihoods as the rebuttal to any and all criticism of the occupation. It was on this basis that they dismissed a growing nationalist movement for placing private before public interest. To contemplate the erosion of the economic conditions they had adduced as the "foundation" of their new regime was to throw doubt upon the enterprise of British rule itself. This was a possibility the new consul-general was unprepared to address. Whether wittingly or not, he opted instead for obfuscation.

THE POLITICAL ECONOMY OF INDEPENDENCE

When Gorst published his official account of the crisis in April 1908, evidence to the contrary had been building for almost a year. By June 1907, land values in both urban and rural areas were starting to fall along with stock prices.[101] Many proprietors, it seems, had used their existing holdings and the availability of cheap mortgage credit to purchase more land or to dabble in other forms of investment. When the flow of easy money dried up, they were forced to sell.[102] The mortgage banks watched in dismay as the ranks of their clients in arrears swelled week after week.[103] Urban cloth merchants, suddenly bereft of customers, could no longer pay the installments on the commercial credit advanced by their suppliers in Manchester.[104] Nor, contrary to Gorst's repeated claims, were these difficulties confined to the wealthy elite who had once enjoyed the greatest access to cheap credit. In July, *al-Muqattam*'s provincial correspondents reported that rural merchants were refusing to extend seed loans. Poorer farmers were thereby forced to sell their summer grain crops at discounted prices in order to obtain the money they required to sow cotton and meet their mid-year installments to the Agricultural Bank.[105] Over the next year, the shortfall in payments on those installments swelled to £E 263,758 or 14% of the annual total.[106] By 1908, day wages for both urban and rural laborers had fallen by as much as a third.[107]

Even these alarming figures provide only glimpses of the havoc that the disruption of credit had wreaked. As the French law student F. Legrand would later argue in his meticulous study of the crisis, some of its most devastating effects had appeared in confusing or misleading forms. When asset values began to sink, some prices did not follow. As early as June 1907, correspondents in Egypt's major cities noted that "rents not only keep up, but are rising."[108] Missing no opportunity to bolster its optimistic position, the *Gazette* quipped that "if the rentals were in reality too high for the people to support, they would of necessity cease to exist, and in the meanwhile it is comforting to know, that even in these days of financial depression there is at least one portion of the community which is prospering."[109] Others, however, suggested that the countermovement of purchase and rental prices had more to do with the efforts of real estate speculators to keep up with their loan payments by squeezing tenants.[110]

It was a similar, if more widespread, phenomenon that Legrand set out to untangle in his doctoral dissertation. By the autumn of 1908, prices for a range of agricultural commodities including wheat, barley, fava beans, straw, and clover had spiked to unusual heights even as land prices, wages, and rates of employment continued to fall.[111] This peculiar development was the consequence neither of a decrease in the aggregate yields of animal fodder and foodstuffs nor of a global rise in commodity prices.[112] Instead, the sale and repurchase of these vital commodities had assumed an altogether different role for the peasants British officials continued to describe as prosperous. "During the most severe period of the crisis of speculation in 1907, with the Agricultural Bank and the Crédit Foncier having closed their counters and the National Bank having practically refused all discounting," Legrand explained, "the rate of interest rose in an abnormal fashion in the cities and usury, naturally, reappeared in the villages, much like in the days before the establishment of the Mixed Courts and the founding of the Crédit Foncier, when the farmer could not yet borrow against his land."[113] In effect, the sale and repurchase of the crops those farmers required to feed themselves, their families, and their livestock had become an indirect mechanism for lending at viciously high rates of interest.

Deprived of the credit upon which they ordinarily relied, Egypt's smallholders were forced to sell their winter crops well below the market rate to meet their summer expenses. The shortage of money had a similarly depressing effect on the purchase price of cotton in the provinces. Because poor farmers could not afford to reserve large stocks of grain, rural merchants were able to resell those very commodities back at dramatically increased prices come autumn. For this reason, he concluded, "the difference between the sale and purchase price of cereals for the peasant seems to be the real device according to which one may recognize the depth and gravity of Egyptian crises."[114]

Legrand's study may have made the argument with particular clarity and force for a readership with little or no access to reporting in Arabic, but the basic components of his thesis had been present in the Egyptian press since the first accounts of falling grain prices appeared in June of 1907. *Al-Ahram* read the 20% dip as evidence that "the progress of the damage has quickened pace such that it now affects farmers." The paper, moreover, anticipated that the compulsion to sell cheap to meet short-term obligations would result in a similar depression of cotton prices come September.[115] Sometimes in passing details, at others in more sweeping panoramas, daily reporting from Egypt's provincial towns and villages described a situation far more dire and comprehensive than Gorst's administration was willing to acknowledge. To claims about the limited scope of the damage, *al-Jaridah* fired back, "No! This is a generalized crisis [*azmah ʿammah*] that is felt by all classes of the nation and all the foreign communities residing in Egypt, for the economic process in Egypt, since the not-too-distant past, has become a single chain, formed by links of credit and indebtedness, that begins with the big banks and ends with the lowliest peasant." Noting its mounting toll on "the small peasants, even those who know nothing of the Agricultural Bank," the paper determined that "the evil of the crisis has encircled the people as a whole."[116]

That the "generalized" character of the crisis might pose new challenges to an occupation that had for so long relied on the outward manifestations of economic development was obvious to all who invoked the promise of national independence. But the very extent of the social entanglements that made it possible to name "crisis" as the common experience of "the people as a whole" also raised new complications for the political economy of independence. On a basic level, the reverberations of the crisis among Egypt's producing classes did enable a predictable xenophobic narrative of foreign exploitation. British rule, in this rendition, had opened the country to foreign hucksters, gamblers, and speculators who preyed upon an innocent and hardworking peasantry. But even that most straightforward, Manichean framing offered no easy solution. The banks and companies that had multiplied since 1882 might represent a drain upon the wealth that Egyptians themselves produced. The credit they extended might constitute a social relation of value extraction. But the crisis had also shown that, under current conditions, the country could not function without them. Something of the unease attending that realization is apparent in the serialized exposition of the history of political-economic thought that occupied the front pages of *al-Liwa'* from early August onward. "The science of political economy," the Watanist daily proclaimed, "is the purest of the social sciences. And it is fitting for us after this financial crisis to arm ourselves with it in order to hold at bay from our own monies the predations of the clever European who brings [this science] into the battle of commercial life. We emerge the losers and he the victor, for we are naïve and ignorant while he is cunning and knowledgeable."[117]

While the subsequent exposition of value theory from Quesnay to Smith and Marx did not dwell on the specific implications of this "purest of the social sciences" for the current crisis, *al-Liwa'* did affirm that "agricultural land . . . is the most important among the sources of wealth in our noble country."[118] In identifying agricultural production as the rightful locus of economic activity in Egypt, the anonymous author made recourse to a line of analysis that would figure prominently in nationalist accounts of the crisis in the coming years. Recent events, on this understanding, had exposed a fundamental contradiction between the ephemeral and illusory gains of financial speculation and the dutiful, steady production of "real wealth." Their reliance on an uninterrupted flow of financial capital from abroad not only made the innocent producers of real wealth subservient to their creditors but left the Egyptian public as a whole defenseless against the convulsions of global markets.[119]

It was in response to this particular diagnosis that proposals for the institutional innovations that would captivate the nationalist movement throughout the coming decades first appeared.[120] In July 1907, Ahmad Hilmi advocated for the establishment of a national purchasing syndicate to coordinate the sale of Egypt's cotton crop to European manufacturers. Collective action, he suggested, would eliminate the rapacious intermediaries who deprived farmers of their rightful earnings.[121] Though Muhammad Tal'at Harb would later gain renown as the foremost proponent of the idea, calls for "the establishment of a bank from Egyptian capital" were ubiquitous at the time.[122] And in the spring of 1908, the lawyer ʿUmar Lutfi made an initial case for the agricultural cooperatives he helped to found the following year.[123] What all these ideas shared was an aspiration to devise institutions that would pool the collective capital of the Egyptian public and allow it to grow within the country's borders.

The broad appeal of such arrangements, however, was not limited to their prospective effects on the territorialization of national wealth. Rather, the language of obligation and solidarity that suffused these proposals for a new spatial fix to the unconstrained global movements of finance gestured at a final conundrum. As the captive victims of financial claims emanating from Europe, Egyptians could now identify as crisis a common experience of subjugation that transcended distinctions of class and geography. But the financial wreckage had become general precisely because those same Egyptians were at once the agents and the victims of the crisis. That is, the very same analysis that exposed the breadth of social hardship also pointed toward the implication of Egyptians themselves in the economic practices that had allowed the crisis to affect "the people as a whole."

In an unusually direct articulation of this paradox, *al-Zahir* offered its own gloss on the price inflation that later captivated Legrand. Despite the obvious deterioration in material conditions, the prices of "basic necessities" and property rents had not fallen "in proportion to the severity of the crisis." The root of the problem was that "the Easterner" remained too focused on "his personal interests." This inability to "learn the benefits of collaboration and common endeavor" afflicted both consumers who failed to act together against price-gouging as well as the shopkeepers and landlords who continued to seek private gain at public expense. The everyday manifestations of the crisis now appeared, uncomfortably, as consequences of the narrow economic self-interest that British officials had long decried as an innate impediment to Egyptian self-rule. The proposed solution was for a vanguard of "informed and educated people to practice cooperation and mutual aid [*al-taʿawun wa-l-taʿadud*] in their social affairs." By working together, they would not only resolve Egypt's economic woes but provide "a preamble to the political acts that the country will require in the future." A new ethical project of cooperation would thus revive material fortunes while opening the way toward a different political future.[124]

CONCLUSION: THEY LOWERED THEIR VOICES

As the repercussions of the crisis continued to multiply, the official position of the British administration remained one of muted concern. After contending for several decades with the din of gilded speech, the opponents of British rule heard opportunity in the change of volume. By the closing months of 1907, the economistic discourse of political legitimation that had once defined the occupation had begun to ring hollow. In a speech he delivered in October 1907 at the Zizinia Theater in Alexandria, Mustafa Kamil took stock of the nationalist movement's recent advances. Pausing to consider the grave economic conditions of the moment, Kamil noted wryly, "The English were ever accustomed to claim in our presence as a title to glory the wealth of our country, up to the day when the last crisis arrived; then having wearied us for many long years they lowered their voices."[125]

Kamil's subtle gibe announced the possibility of a major shift in the terms of debate over British rule. As Egypt's once-fabled wealth seemed to vanish, the diverse voices of an emboldened opposition could and did at last turn the occupation's own economistic criteria of progress against it. Public perceptions that British rule served narrowly British interests would only sharpen as Gorst's administration continued to defend what many regarded as an inconsistent and insufficient response to the crisis. Bolstered by the comparative, if fanciful, example of the American government's coordinated interventions, nationalist critics mobilized their own experiences of economic hardship to articulate a forceful claim to political independence. The crisis had furnished a mass of new evidence that only a government run by Egyptians themselves would manage the formidable institutions of the modern state in the interest of the Egyptian people.

But as the effects of that crisis continued to frustrate easy attributions of blame, even the occupation's staunchest critics gave voice to a troubling recognition that the independence they demanded could no longer be construed in narrowly political terms. The crisis had fractured the foundations of a colonial order built on the dubious and deeply racist claim that Egyptians were nothing more than self-interested "ciphers" who would exchange their freedom for money.[126] But this momentous reversal also brought to light constraints upon the freedom nationalists invoked, constraints that Egyptian control of political institutions alone would not remove. And this was not only because European investors had shown themselves susceptible to alarmist fabrications about fanaticism or, worse still, directly opposed to the termination of British rule.

The upheavals of 1907 effected a series of major shifts in the coordinates of nationalist thought and strategy. Perhaps most obviously, the widespread fallout of the credit freeze had shown that the "single chain of the economic process" formed a bond of its own that, like more overt forms of political domination, secured Egypt's subordinate relation to Europe. Not by accident was this the moment in which a coherent discourse of economic nationalism first emerged. For the leading figures of this new current of thought, "crisis" rather than "poverty," "backwardness," or "underdevelopment" named the chief malady that imperialism had bequeathed to the Egyptian public. Many of these thinkers actively affirmed Egypt's economic identity as an "agricultural country."[127] Concerned most of all with protecting the real wealth that Egyptians produced, they advocated for the formation of new institutions—most notably a national bank and a network of agricultural cooperatives—that would mitigate the perilous volatilities of the global financial order.

As new conditions of hardship "encircled the people as a whole," the concept of crisis gained its wide appeal precisely by naming a social experience that was no less real or consequential for defying easy attribution to a specific set of malicious actors. The very extent of a phenomenon that embraced the totality of what *al-Zahir* called "our social life [*hayatuna al-ijtimaʿiyah*]" made visible the peculiar forms of abstract interdependence that now bound millions of anonymous individuals to each other.[128] For several decades, Britain's discourse of colonial economism had described Egypt as a society of narrowly self-interested subjects attuned only to material gain. In the destructive consequences that had followed from the pursuit of boom-time fortunes, the critics of British rule now found reason to fear that colonial economism was remaking Egyptian society in its own image. Subject to global markets and foreign lenders to sustain their everyday lives, Egyptians appeared more and more as the self-interested economic individuals that British officials had once imagined them to be. Nor, it seemed, were they free, under current conditions, to act otherwise. Independence, in that sense, could no longer be treated in narrowly political terms as the mere substitution of Egyptian for British officials. The freedom to which nationalists aspired would require as its preconditions a far more sweeping reconstitution of political-economic subjectivities and the creation of institutions to promote the growth of national capital.

Already by the summer of 1908, the protracted effects of the crisis were giving shape to two interrelated but contradictory impulses. On the one hand, crisis gave a name to forms of privation and uncertainty that seemed, more and more, to have become the common experience of the Egyptian public as a whole. That dramatic upheaval and the new vocabulary to which it lent meaning would inspire unprecedented support for the ideas and practices of a mass popular struggle rooted in collective mobilization against conditions of both political and economic domination. On the other, the specifically financial character of the crisis also helped to prompt an increasingly binary conception of Egypt's economic life that delivered a potent critique of finance as dangerous and illusory, the medium of volatility and value extraction, while at the same time affirming agricultural commodity production for global markets as the virtuous and necessary pursuit of real wealth. On that basis, the country's continued reliance on the cotton crop and the attendant exploitation of peasant labor in the countryside could and did appear to some as the necessary precondition of Egypt's future independence. These conflicting tendencies would come to define the nationalist movement over the coming years.

Chapter 6

UNIONS OF MASS MOBILIZATION

"With all respect, we petition that you grant us a constitution quickly." (7:20 P.M.)

"Our religion is constitutional, your education is constitutional, your Sultan is constitutional, and your people strive for the constitution, so grant us the abrogated constitution." (7:20 P.M.)

"You have the Sultan and the Mikado as a good model, so graciously bestow the constitution." (7:25 P.M.)

"The constitution is the life of nations, so restore it to our nation." (7:45 P.M.)

"May the Khedive live long, and may he grant us the constitution." (7:51 P.M.)

"We welcome our sovereign, and we beg for the constitution." (7:52 P.M.)[1]

THE MESSAGES CONGRATULATED the Khedive on his safe return. But the welcome he received did not offer much reassurance. By his own account, 'Abbas Hilmi II's annual sojourn in the summer of 1908 had left him unnerved. His visit to Istanbul had coincided with the Young Turks' revolt and the restoration of the Ottoman constitution that Sultan Abdulhamid II had suspended three decades prior. As the

Committee for Union and Progress moved to consolidate their stunning victory, the same questions had rankled the Khedive wherever he went. Would he grant Egypt its own constitution, or would he instead provoke his subjects to follow the example of the Ottoman revolutionaries? Alarmed by all he had witnessed, the Khedive set sail for Alexandria with a sense of foreboding.

His anxieties were not misplaced. Calls for an Egyptian constitution and the empowerment of representative institutions had already been building for several years. In February 1908, just six days before his untimely death from tuberculosis, Mustafa Kamil had sent a fiery telegram to the British foreign secretary insisting that "Egypt is as ripe for self-government as many European States."[2] Later that spring, under Kamil's successor, Muhammad Farid, the Egyptian National Party had forwarded petitions to London affirming the Khedive's right to promulgate a constitution without Britain's consent.[3] Earlier in the summer of 1908, prior to the Ottoman revolution, the Khedive had received several written requests to restore the short-lived Egyptian constitution of 1881.[4] But what greeted him on September 17 was at once more dramatic and more insistent. Three days earlier, on the anniversary of the British bombardment of Alexandria, representatives of the Egyptian National Party had cabled the British Foreign Office from points around the country to demand "instant evacuation."[5] Now they deployed that same technique against their own sovereign.

At least a dozen telegrams reached Alexandria on the evening of the 17th, and over two dozen more arrived in the next five days. Nearly half originated from Cairo, but the rest came from smaller cities and towns: Dasuq, Abu Kabir, Tanta, Port Said, Mit Faris, Bilqas, Mahallat Ruh, Zaqaziq, al-Wasta, Abu Qirqas, Quwaysna, al-Zalkun, Matay, Qina, Malwa, Bilbays, and Alexandria itself. Though the wording of the first wave from Cairo varied somewhat, the cables that later arrived from farther afield transmitted a more consistent message, "We congratulate Your Highness on a safe return, and we request the restoration of the constitution for Egypt."[6]

Even before the palace telegraph started buzzing, the Khedive had held an audience with Ronald Graham, then serving as the British chargé d'affaires during Eldon Gorst's summer holiday. Graham could scarcely conceal his amusement at the vice-regent's anxiety. Since his accession, 'Abbas Hilmi II had sought to locate himself at the very center of nationalist opposition to British rule. Now, as that movement's popularity swelled, the Khedive "looked forward to the coming year as likely to prove the most embarrassing, and even dangerous, of his reign."[7] He proposed that "some concession must be granted which would make people imagine 'they were in Paradise.' " In response, Graham "observed that we should indeed be fortunate to find such a panacea, and inquired whether His Highness desired to make a suggestion."[8]

To his superiors in London, Graham noted that while the Khedive's fears might represent an opportunity to shore up his cooperation, the dangers he perceived were "exaggerated." In part, this was the understandable consequence of a long summer absence. But ultimately, such apprehensions rested upon an overestimation of the Egyptian public's capacity for genuine political thought and action. "A national movement, in the sense indicated by the Khedive," Graham explained, "would not be because such a thing as a Constitution is understood or wanted, excepting by a small minority, but because a convenient cry has been found on which to rally the discontented. Any dangers it presents may be no less real on that account, but cannot well be immediate."[9]

Earlier that summer, following the Sultan's capitulation to the revolutionaries' demands, Edward Grey had mused to his ambassador at Istanbul that " 'if Turkey now establishes a Parliament and improves her government, the demand for a constitution in Egypt will gain great force.' "[10] Wary of that possibility, Graham had been monitoring the situation closely. Though he acknowledged the sudden ubiquity of "a convenient cry," he continued to rehearse the occupation's well-worn tropes about the class specificity, finite urban geography, and racial limitations of Egyptian political consciousness. In August, he reassured London that "the mass of the peasant population, to whom at this period of the year the progress of the Nile flood is the one matter of absorbing importance, appears to view a political change which has no immediate effect on its welfare with complete indifference."[11] After his audience with the Khedive, he judged that the novel phenomenon of urban crowds chanting " '*Aizine el-Destour*' ('We want a Constitution')" marked no fundamental shift.[12] Most Egyptians, Graham averred, could not understand what they were shouting for. The "small minority" who claimed to represent the nation were, as usual, casting outsize shadows by manipulating the credulous masses. That the majority possessed no genuine comprehension of political affairs was evinced by their own understanding of this latest demand. When asked to explain "constitution," Graham reported, a group marching through the streets of Alexandria had replied, " 'Certainly, it means a rise of wages all around.' "[13]

For Graham, the anecdote seemed to confirm that what sometimes masqueraded as politics in Egypt was only ever an expression of base economic interests. That the urban rabble could confuse electoral representation with their wages was, in other words, grounds to dismiss their demands as muddled and insubstantial. Nor was Graham alone in that assessment. In a confidential memorandum to Grey that summer, Harry Boyle had declared, "In character, the Egyptian is eminently materialist, and he is little inclined to take a strong interest in any matter which does not appear likely in some way to affect his own direct concerns."[14]

As a political assessment, this crisp distillation of colonial economism would soon prove wildly inaccurate. The months that followed the restoration of the Ottoman constitution saw a rapid and extraordinary expansion of Egyptian nationalism from an intellectually rigorous but socially constrained project of anticolonial critique into a mass movement capable of attracting significant popular support both in the country's major cities and, at least potentially, in the countryside. By May of 1910, Ronald Graham himself was convinced that revolution might be imminent.[15]

Occurring in the midst of a deepening financial crisis, what Gorst later described as a "wave of insubordination to constituted authority" might appear to buttress official accounts of popular politics as the mere effect of underlying economic causes.[16] On this reading, Graham and Boyle simply misjudged the gravity of the reversal to which an "eminently materialist" population was reacting. Unsurprisingly, once the extent of popular mobilization had grown harder to dismiss, such an economistic reading of recent events would figure prominently in British efforts to devise a counterinsurgent strategy.[17] The few extant histories that identify the stunning multiplication of new political associations, student organizations, labor unions, strikes, and mass demonstrations as a significant development in this period have tended to pursue a similar line of analysis. Both the sudden proliferation of political parties in the latter half of 1907 and the intensification of Egyptian labor militancy in 1908 are thus explained as the political effects of deeper economic causes emanating from the crisis of 1907.[18]

The severe upheaval that growing numbers of Egyptians apprehended as crisis was indeed pivotal for the explosive emergence of mass politics. But on their own, such arguments provide an incomplete and misleading explanation for this remarkable surge of popular activism. Howsoever unintentionally, they also resonate with the very mode of economistic reasoning that British officials themselves employed to discount what was taking place. Neither a mechanistic response to economic hardship nor a derivative appropriation of foreign ideas, this eventful conjuncture witnessed the consolidation of a range of novel concepts and organizations that threatened to upend the occupation's insistent separation between properly political claims and mere economic grievances. In asserting new rights to represent themselves, a diverse cohort of workers, students, lawyers, and teachers seized upon the Ottoman revolutionary language of "union," "progress," and "freedom."[19] And having once expressed ambivalence toward "the people" in whose name they claimed to speak, the leaders of Egypt's foremost nationalist parties likewise identified in these new popular energies the rudiments of a movement capable of mounting a genuine challenge to Britain's veiled protectorate.

As they tracked the unfolding of the financial crisis from the spring of 1907 onwards, the occupation's critics in the Egyptian press had begun to develop a line of analysis that challenged the conceptual separation between the economic and the political as profoundly misleading. Over the course of the three years that followed, this insistence on the dense entanglements between forms of economic and political domination became a central feature not only of anticolonial thought but of political practice on the ground as well. Drawing inspiration and momentum from the wave of revolutionary movements they saw unfolding across the globe, the growing constituencies of an increasingly radical nationalist movement began to imagine for themselves what it might mean to live differently after British rule.

THE YEAR OF THE PARTIES

The earliest of Egypt's formal political parties were established not to extend the nationalist movement's claims to representation but rather, as Hussein Omar has shown, "to stymie the wave of anti-imperialist sentiment overwhelming the country."[20] Before 1907, the Arabic word *hizb* often connoted loose coalitions or affiliations. The Khedive's spies had referred to collaborators as *hizb al-Ingliz*, "partisans of the English."[21] Supporters of an organized opposition affiliated with the "patriotic" dailies *al-Mu'ayyad* and *al-Liwa'* had called themselves *al-Hizb al-Watani* or "the National Party."[22] At the same time, particularly for those who sought to convey a unified front against the occupation, the very existence of such "parties" betokened a fractious social malady of *tahazzub* (partisanship) that could bolster the case for British rule. Proposals for formal political parties, moreover, begged an obvious question: what use would they serve so long as Egypt lacked real electoral institutions?

About this sudden "host of parties," the *Egyptian Gazette* observed wryly in the autumn of 1907 that until recently "we were informed that for all practical purposes only one party existed in the country—to wit the party which owns Mustapha Pasha Kamel as its chief and demands the instant withdrawal of the 'occupying nation' horse and foot, bag and baggage."[23] It was exactly those monopolistic claims that the young Egyptian journalist Hafiz Afandi 'Awad sought to rebut when in the summer of 1907 he announced the formation of Egypt's first official party, *al-Minbar* (*the Pulpit*).[24] Likewise, when Muhammad Wahid Bey began organizing *al-Hizb al-Watani al-Hurr* (the Free National Party) in late July, the name he chose made clear his intentions. Though often rendered in English as the "Egyptian Liberal Party," the Arabic deprived Kamil's organization of its singularity as *the* National Party.[25]

Until that moment, the leadership of Kamil's party had relied upon its numerous publications and its creative deployment of telegrams and petitions to convey the magnitude of popular support. To be sure, the diversity of opinions on display in the Arabic press already belied strong claims to national unanimity. For just that reason, the British had encouraged the publication of Ahmad Lufti al-Sayyid's *al-Jaridah* earlier in 1907 as a moderate alternative to the supposed extremism of *al-Liwa'*. But the disagreements that played out on the pages of those journals were, by definition, confined to a limited reading public. In the formation of parties lay the potential to mobilize much larger constituencies and to represent "the people" as an active political force. Responding to the Egyptian Liberal Party's provocation, the political cliques that had formed around the country's leading dailies moved by autumn to launch parties of their own. On September 20, 1907, the shareholders of *al-Jaridah* held the first official meeting of *Hizb al-Ummah* (the People's Party), and in late October Kamil's National Party followed suit.[26] Shaykh 'Ali Yusuf and his supporters published the charter of their "Party of Reform According to Constitutional Principles" in December.[27]

The financial crisis, then, did not trigger this sudden multiplication of parties, but it did figure into the new development in several significant ways. First, like other companies, many Egyptian dailies had raised money through the sale of shares. The crash had shown how erratically stock values could fluctuate and, it seems, alerted the boards of these papers to the possibility that hostile investors could purchase a controlling majority. Making a paper the official organ of a party became one means of insulating the written expression of political ideas from the vicissitudes of the market.[28] Moreover, the subscription of members for each new party itself bore a formal resemblance to the subscription of the companies that had multiplied during the boom. Sounding a cautionary note in December 1907, *al-Muqattam* mused that if "the year that will soon come to an end has been known as the 'year of the companies,' . . . we fear that the coming year will be 'the year of the parties.' . . . And it is quite possible that it too will end in financial loss for those subscribing to them."[29] *Al-Muqattam* drew the comparison in order to condemn its rivals. Party members might not expect financial reward, but this use of their money could be every bit as disastrous if their main objective was to "deprive us of the confidence [of European countries] and to weaken the stature of the local government."[30] In this thinly veiled denunciation of *al-Hizb al-Watani*, the Anglophile daily raised the possibility that money itself could represent political will. As the National Party worked to attract broader support, its own leaders would remain wary of gauging popularity by the size of the party's coffers. But in another sense, all of Egypt's new parties seized upon the connection that *al-Muqattam* made explicit. The crisis had revealed that stock speculation was a dubious means of advancing the real interests of the country. In that moment of disillusionment, a party subscription could appeal as an alternative investment in Egypt's future.

Efforts to subscribe members and collect dues also had more straightforward material implications for the character of political sociability. Clubs, societies, and associations had existed for decades, and the Watanists had been working for some time to establish more spaces for the promotion of nationalist ideas.[31] But the existence of parties with dedicated operating budgets brought opportunities to engage new sectors of the population through meetings, speeches, classes, and plays. The governing committees were generally filled by men of considerable means, and for an annual membership of £E 8 in Cairo and £E 4 in the provinces, even the National Party's clubs remained well beyond the reach of most Egyptians.[32] But as they competed to attract supporters, Egypt's new political organizations sponsored a busy calendar of public events. And as the gulf between official accounts of a short-lived crash and everyday experiences of protracted hardship continued to widen, talk of "the crisis" and "the economic situation" featured prominently in these gatherings.

The publication of Eldon Gorst's annual report in May 1908 furnished an important occasion for the parties to clarify their positions.[33] On the evening of May 14, 'Ali Fahmi Kamil took the stage at Alexandria's Zizinia Theater, where his brother

Mustafa had delivered the platform of the National Party just seven months prior. Seizing upon Gorst's assertion that "this crisis did not materially differ as to its causes and effects from similar phenomena elsewhere," Kamil railed against those who had once laid the blame on the nationalist movement.[34] What really distinguished Egypt from other countries was the presence of an occupying force that had failed to manage the "chaos" of financial markets or protect its taxpaying subjects. Gorst's refusal to extend the kind of government assistance that France, the United States, and Britain had provided for their own people under comparable circumstances was only the latest evidence that the occupation must end. This malign neglect had moreover revealed a "greater responsibility that falls directly upon the nation, particularly after it has learned this useful lesson in economy despite itself." The establishment of a national bank funded by Egyptians themselves would not only hasten the end of the crisis. It would also mark a practical step toward overcoming a servile dependence on officials who had proven themselves indifferent to the real suffering of the people.[35]

Ahmad Lutfi al-Sayyid issued a strikingly similar call to national self-reliance at the Club of the People's Party in Cairo three days later. *Al-Liwa'* in fact praised Lutfi al-Sayyid for an address so replete with "fierce attacks on the politics of the occupation" that the audience might be forgiven for "imagining that it was one of the speeches of the National Party." When the speech ended, the crowd first "cheered for the speaker, *al-Jaridah*, and *Hizb al-Ummah*," and then went on to "raise their voices in a loud cry for the National Party, its eminent leader, and *al-Liwa'*."[36] If the objective of Egypt's earliest parties had been to undermine any appearance of a unified front, Lutfi al-Sayyid's remarks suggested that the distance between the country's two most important nationalist organizations was already narrowing.

Like Kamil, the editor of *al-Jaridah* presented his comments as a rebuttal of Gorst's report. For too long, he announced, Egypt's people had placed the burden of achieving independence on the shoulders of others. In an oblique reference to Mustafa Kamil, he described the failure of diplomatic efforts in Paris and Istanbul. But he also distanced himself from his own paper's occasional optimism about the benign intentions of Britain's new Liberal government and the man they had sent to replace Lord Cromer. The only discernible difference was the "reconciliation [*al-wifaq*]" that Gorst had reached with the Khedive. That improved relationship posed "a greater danger to us than Lord Cromer's disagreements with him, for upon whom may we now rely to attain our independence?" The answer was obvious. It was "Egyptians who must undertake to educate themselves and to achieve social, political, and economic progress so that then it will only remain for Europe to recognize their independence."[37] In preaching for national self-reliance, Lutfi al-Sayyid too delivered a scathing indictment of Gorst's approach to the financial crisis. Not only had Britain's political fearmongering exacerbated Egypt's problems, but appeals to the doctrine of laissez-faire were plainly unconvincing. The same government that saw fit to plaster the walls of railway stations with signs warning tourists against giving "bakhshish" to the poor "lest it habituate them to laziness" had "published not a single word of caution for the shareholders of the companies that it refused to supervise." In both the minute regulations it enforced and in those it refused to undertake, the occupation had shown that "the hand of politics" would touch upon economic affairs only insofar as it served the interests of the British themselves.[38]

FROM STRIKES TO UNION

By the time Lutfi al-Sayyid delivered this indictment of the occupation's hypocrisy, a rising wave of strikes and protests had begun to target a similar pattern of regulatory inconsistencies. From one direction, the advent of the financial crisis had forced Egypt's two leading nationalist parties to consider the many linkages between the politics of imperial rule and the new manifestations of economic subordination. From another, growing numbers of working-class Egyptians had, by the summer of 1908, begun to see the economic grievances that had commonly provided the impetus for collective action as closely bound up with the priorities and practices of a government in which they had no say.

On its own, the practice of striking was not new to Egypt in the early 1900s. In April 1882, the coal heavers of Port Said had famously organized the first large-scale act of labor militancy by Egyptian workers to demand a doubling of their pay. In that moment of revolutionary upheaval, they succeeded in enlisting ʿUrabi's government to pressure the foreign-owned coaling companies into granting the raise. Following the British invasion, however, the companies coordinated a lock-out and forced a reversion to the pre-strike rate.[39] If Egypt's working classes in 1908 were quick to associate constitutionalism with "a rise of wages all around," there were good historical reasons for them to do so.

During the early years of the occupation, British labor policy was closely directed at severing, or even inverting, the relationship between material gains and political representation. In a move that closely paralleled its treatment of the village headman, Khedive Ismaʿil's government had, in the 1860s, granted Egypt's various craft guilds (*tawa'if*) the right to elect the shaykhs who served as intermediaries of the government's revenue demands. And beginning in the early 1890s, as they were moving to abolish village elections, the British imposed what John Chalcraft has aptly described as "the regressive bargain: 'no representation without taxation.' " By reducing and then eliminating the professional taxes and license fees that had once served as the state's primary revenue source among the urban trades, the occupation effectively eliminated the guild's reason for existence. The result, for a time, was a relative demobilization and atomization of Egyptian workers who had been "freed" from these old institutions of collective deliberation and action.[40]

Over the next decade or so, it was mainly immigrant laborers who staged the most conspicuous strikes and protests. Attracted to Egypt by the economic opportunities of the boom, foreign-born workers from around the Mediterranean rim brought with them other traditions of militancy along with knowledge of radical, socialist, and syndicalist ideas.[41] In many cases, these skilled or semiskilled laborers established craft-based organizations for which they commonly used the designations "league" or "association."[42] On a few notable occasions, they launched strikes that attracted coverage in the local press. In 1899, the largely Greek and Syrian workforce at Cairo's cigarette factories succeeded in pressuring owners to negotiate a wage increase. Their victory furnished a well-publicized demonstration of the power of collective action.[43]

By the early 1900s, smaller walkouts and protests in Cairo and Alexandria were becoming more common, even among Egyptian laborers.[44] In mid-February 1906, the cab drivers of Alexandria coordinated a citywide stoppage and won from the Municipal Commission an increase on their hourly rates.[45] Later that same month, an unexpected event presaged several significant shifts in the character of subsequent strikes and mass protests. On February 26, students at the Khedivial Law School went on strike to challenge the new regulations that the Ministry of Education had issued at the behest of its British adviser Douglas Dunlop.[46] As conditions for returning to their classes, they stipulated that students be permitted to sit for exams regardless of their attendance records, that those who failed be permitted to retake exams in subsequent years, that they be granted a review period before exams, that the doors of the school be left open during lectures so that students could come and go, and that no courses be held in the afternoon.[47]

Some of these demands, particularly the last, did express basic material grievances: following a recent tuition hike, poorer students were finding it harder to cover the costs of commuting to and from home twice a day. But in at least three key respects, this latest strike was different. First, because law students were not conventional workers, their choice of tactics suggested that the strike did not belong to any one class. As the Watanist daily *Misr al-Fatah* would later explain, "The other classes of the Egyptian nation continued to look upon striking with disdain and to allege that it was not appropriate for those of their status, until the law students rose up and blazed a trail for the educated and the well-to-do with their strike from classes when the Ministry of Education imposed its tyrannical law."[48] Second, the strike pitted the students directly against the government and its British advisers. In that respect, what they demanded was a voice in the process by which the law of their school was decided. It was this distinctly political aspect of their protest that the *Egyptian Gazette* recognized when referring sarcastically to their "Bill of Rights."[49] Finally, the strike was contagious. Almost as soon as the law students announced their decision to walk out, their peers at the medical, polytechnic, and agricultural schools issued statements of solidarity and, in the latter two cases, went on strike themselves.[50]

On its own terms, this surge of youthful activism brought no great victory. By expelling the ringleaders, threatening to end the school year prematurely, and promising to consider their grievances, the Ministry of Education cowed the students into submission. But in widening both the spectrum of social groups for whom striking might serve as a legitimate practice and the range of demands that this practice might leverage, the student strike revealed the potential for a new convergence between what had been class-specific repertoires of contention on the one hand and the representational strategies of the nationalist movement on the other. A decade earlier, that affinity had seemed improbable. The leadership of the National Party had once regarded labor militancy with great apprehension.[51] It was one thing to speak for the people and quite another to encourage them to speak for themselves. In the aftermath of Dinshaway, nationalist writers and strategists clearly became more eager to locate and publicize authentic expressions of popular opposition to British rule. But it would be a mistake to interpret this tentative rapprochement between nationalism and mass politics simply as an opportunistic appropriation of the latter by the former.

By the spring of 1907, when the frequency and intensity of strikes started to increase, it was not just wages and compensation that Egyptian workers were protesting. If the occupation had managed, for a time, to contain the energies of popular politics, it had done so by restricting the pathways of both individual and collective engagement with the state and by minimizing the causes for such engagement. But the longevity of British rule had opened the way to new ambitions and with them a host of minute interventions enacted under the capacious banner of reform. Ahmad Lutfi al-Sayyid was not alone in identifying the uneven and arbitrary character of these regulations. Nor did Cairo's laborers and craftsmen need the example of striking law students to recognize their own conditions of disenfranchisement. At the same time, the increasing prevalence of both nationalist discourse about self-rule and expressions of nationalist sympathy for the daily struggles of "the people" likely bolstered their confidence that such actions might now garner broad support. The risks of striking seemed more worth taking when those taking the risks saw that they were not alone.

By far the most dramatic of these popular protests was the cab strike that brought Cairo to a standstill in April 1907. The main target of their protest was the government's health and safety regulations for the livestock that drew the cabs.[52] As a result of the new rules, Cairo's cabbies had been forced to bear the costs of both legally sanctioned fines and illicit extortion by the local police. In that sense, the relief they sought would mean higher compensation. But here once again, the cab drivers were specifically protesting a pattern of regulation that had been imposed with no input from those affected and that showcased the disproportionate influence of a resident British community that had lobbied for strict enforcement to protect the welfare of the animals. The strike thus became a mechanism for asserting a kind of political participation that the government had withheld. And thanks both to the magnitude of the disruption and the support they garnered from the nationalist press, the cabbies were able to exact several major concessions.[53] Their remarkable victory soon inspired petitions, demonstrations, and strikes from workers in a host of other trades. Some, like the silk weavers and mat makers, demanded a simple wage increase. But others, like the butchers of Cairo and the fishermen of Matariyah, now sought redress from what they too understood to be patterns of government intervention in which they enjoyed no say.[54]

In using the strike to press their claims to representation, these diverse groups of workers and students prepared the way for a new convergence of political and social forces. The changing forms and constituencies of collective protest moreover delivered a practical challenge to the occupation's strict demarcation of the political. When Ronald Graham mocked the conflation of a constitution with rising wages, he was suggesting both that Egyptians could not conceive of aspirations beyond the *merely* economic and that *properly* political demands must be distinct from any pursuit of economic gain. The groups that launched this surge of activism made little attempt to downplay their material demands. Instead, by their actions, they suggested that the criteria British officials had invoked to circumscribe political participation were doubly misleading. On the one hand, the occupation showed little concern to police the boundary between economics and politics so long as the interests served were British. On the other, if the scope of the strikers' demands did not exclude bread and butter issues, neither was it limited to them. In contesting what they experienced as legislation by fiat, those who took to the streets now asserted a right to negotiate for themselves over the terms and objectives of government policy.

Though this remarkable expansion in both the incidence and meaning of strikes was well underway before 1907, the financial crisis did help to consolidate several important shifts in the wider landscape of political contention. Certainly, the double squeeze of falling wages and price inflation gave many Egyptians new reasons to protest.[55] But the fact of economic hardship explains little about the forms those protests assumed or the ideas they articulated. More significant than the basic occurrence of strikes was their growing mutual affinity with a nationalist movement that now spoke in a language of independence and freedom. This was a rapprochement from two sides. If workers had already taken to using strike tactics to force open new avenues of political participation, the deepening effects of the crisis impelled Egypt's two leading nationalist parties to regard the tribulations of workers and peasants as effects of imperial rule that would need to be addressed along with the transformation of political institutions. Not only did columns in *al-Liwa'*, *Misr al-Fatah*, and *al-Jaridah* now include frequent meditations on the entangled global structures of political and economic domination. The broad appeal of an analysis that refigured imperialism as an instance of class exploitation on a worldwide scale opened up the radical possibility that the union and the strike could become techniques for mobilizing the claims of the nation as a whole.

FIGURE 6: "Egypt in the Talons of the Foreigners." Source: *al-Siyāsah al-Muṣawwarah* (*Cairo Punch*) (April 3, 1908).

REVERBERATIONS OF REVOLUTION

It was this possibility that gave the events of July 1908 their particular resonance in Egypt. Across the Ottoman Empire, the restoration of the constitution and the Declaration of Freedoms roused new expectations about the changes that might ensue from this moment of revolution. In mass rallies, residents of the Empire's provincial cities explored new spaces of public expression. After decades of censorship and surveillance, a reinvigorated press broached topics that only months before had been taboo.[56] In huge numbers, workers dared to insist that a constitution could and should mean "a rise of wages all around." By some estimates, upwards of 100,000 individuals went on strike in the course of 1908, a figure that represented nearly half of all wage laborers in the Empire.[57]

Wary of this surge in worker militancy, the Committee for Union and Progress moved swiftly to contain it. By October 1908, they had promulgated a law banning strikes in public enterprises.[58] At issue in this early display of the CUP's more authoritarian tendencies was a contest over the meaning of *union* itself. Strong adherents of scientific positivism and social Darwinism, many among the CUP leadership harbored a deep suspicion toward popular representation. For them, the constitution was a necessary component of Ottoman modernization and a check against Sultan Abdulhamid II's retrograde tyranny. The "union" in the name they gave to their secret society was a substitution for "order" in the French positivist philosopher Auguste Comte's motto "Order and Progress."[59] In this version, union named the total coherence that a rightly governed social organism could achieve. But by 1908, *union*—*ittihad* in both Arabic and Ottoman Turkish—had acquired other associations, most notably with the practices of labor struggle. The term was still uncommon as a name for workers' organizations; the French-derived *association* (*jam'iyah*) and *syndicat* (*niqabah*) were more typical.[60] But for those who invoked *ittihad*, the category already signified something more than unity plain and simple. More often, it referenced both the principle and the practice of solidary, collective actions through which subordinate classes might challenge the powerful. And whereas the CUP in Istanbul struggled mightily to hold these two meanings of union apart, to endorse the former while squelching the latter, a growing coalition of political forces across the Mediterranean was eager to weld them together.

When the ripples of the Ottoman strike wave reached Egypt's shores in October 1908, the government responded with its own show of force. On the morning of October 18, roughly 1,600 workers from the Société des Tramways du Caire surrounded the company's depots and laid down on the tracks to block the company's trams.[61] The demands they had presented to the company and forwarded to local papers in the days beforehand included an eight-hour workday, a wage increase, an annual vacation, and paid sick leave. But here once again, the workers also pressed for new kinds of representation and self-governance, in this case the establishment of a committee, including equal numbers of workers and managers, to investigate complaints and oversee disciplinary procedures.[62] Siding with the company, the governorate of Cairo dispatched the police under British Commandant Mansfield Pasha to clear the workers from the tracks and arrest them.[63] Though the Société des Tramways did grant a wage increase, it refused to consider the workers' other proposals. Unsurprisingly, these minimal gains did little to dissipate the popular energies that the strike had channeled. Reflecting on this charged atmosphere, *al-Ahram* proclaimed, "The era of subjugation has ended, for the nation now has a will that cannot be defeated."[64]

THE POLICY OF CONCILIATION

The man who had replaced Lord Cromer may have questioned the authenticity of that will and the coherence of the nation that expressed it. But since becoming consul-general, Eldon Gorst had held that the "general Anglophobe feeling" spreading through the country would require a new approach. Privately, Gorst acknowledged that in Cromer's later years "a rein was given to racial antipathy and caste prejudice." The result was an "English invasion" that saw Egyptians "ousted from the posts which had still remained to them in the government service." The potential for resentment was only increased by the "strained relations which the whole world knew to exist between the Khedive and Lord Cromer."[65] What Gorst referred to as his "policy of conciliation" and "experiment in local self-government" was thus calculated to "render our rule more sympathetic to the Egyptians, and to the Mohammedans in particular."[66]

On the face of it, this new policy represented a significant departure. Gorst announced that the occupation would attempt to "meet the desire which exists among certain sections of the population for a larger participation in public affairs."[67] He likewise pressed for more Egyptians to be hired in government positions and reduced the staff of British inspectors in the ministries.[68] Having enjoyed cordial relations with the Khedive during his years as financial adviser between 1898 and 1904, the consul-general granted the palace greater leeway to pursue its own projects.[69] His staff also began drafting legislation to expand the powers of the Provincial Councils.[70]

Offering public support to his successor, Cromer affirmed that the occupation had entered a new phase. Speaking before the Eighty Club at the Savoy Hotel in London on December 15, 1908, he invoked a favorite metaphor to explain the pedagogical function of Gorst's experiment. He reminded the audience of Egypt's extraordinary prosperity and mused that the country had "now arrived at the stage of development when a moral and intellectual superstructure had to be imposed gradually on those material foundations."[71] Alarmed by even so mild a concession to Egyptian demands, hard-line champions of the British Empire lambasted the new consul-general over the next two years for going soft and rewarding Egyptian defiance. But as Gorst made clear in both private correspondence and public statements, his objective was not to promote Egyptian independence but precisely to blunt opposition to the occupation in England and Egypt alike.

By opening some limited avenues for Egyptian involvement in the routine work of government, these latest "experiments" would "from the House of Commons point of view" have "the desirable result of pushing the Egyptian question well into the background."[72] Within Egypt, Gorst's response to the changing character of the nationalist movement remained consistent with the logic of colonial economism. If what called itself nationalism was just an expression of middle-class frustrations over the influence and employment opportunities afforded to foreigners, then a few simple concessions would dampen that ire. Self-interested as their political pretensions might be, however, Egypt's new nationalist parties and their papers continued to wield the threat of "stirring up the ignorant masses to bloodshed." Peasants and the working poor might be unable to reason beyond their material circumstances, but they were nevertheless susceptible to the fanaticism and xenophobia that Cromer and Gorst alike maligned as inherent defects of Islam. Abusing the liberties that British rule afforded, the consul-general now alleged, opportunistic "extremists" played upon these crude sensitivities to conjure the specter of a popular movement. That was a danger the occupation could no longer countenance.[73]

Alongside his plans to "give the Egyptians more opportunities of showing their aptitude for taking part in public affairs," Gorst directed a sweeping expansion of the state's coercive powers.[74] In September 1908, he proposed to revive the 1881 Press Law, unused since the 1890s. The law empowered the Ministry of Interior to issue warnings and fines "in the interest of public order, of religion, or of morality" and, upon repeated warnings or with the approval of the Council of Ministers, to suspend or suppress an offending periodical. Since the law was already on the books, he assumed, its reactivation would require less political wrangling than new legislation. Although the Interior might lack the power to punish offenders with heavier fines or imprisonment, Gorst judged that the Press Law's "administrative methods" would prove "efficacious" while "avoiding the risk of aggravating the evil by the advertisement of an unsuccessful prosecution."[75] Convinced that the National Courts had been infiltrated by Watanist ideologues, the consul-general heralded the Interior's administrative procedures as the best means to prevent "the extreme nationalist party" from "stirring up the ignorant masses to bloodshed."[76] A similar argument led to the promulgation of a new law subjecting "dangerous characters" to police supervision and administrative banishment.[77] As Gorst explained, such measures might be "to a certain extent restrictive of liberty," but they provided the only "effectual remedy" for "the most notorious malefactors [who] frequently escape punishment and are encouraged by this immunity to persevere in their criminal practices."[78]

Controversial as these extrajudicial procedures may have been, they were at least well publicized. Both measures required months of negotiation, and both provoked heated debates in the local press.[79] The same could not be said for the staggering intensification of domestic surveillance that took place in this same period. The Interior had run a Secret Police division before the British takeover in 1894; the few extant records of its operations suggest that its main function was to investigate government officials for professional misconduct.[80] Though this Secret Police had been disbanded prior to Gorst's appointment to the Interior, Shimi Bey claimed that several of its agents had been reassigned to other departments, where they began to collect intelligence for their new British masters.[81] The Khedive's informants had moreover suggested that their work was hampered periodically by the counterespionage of the government's own spies.[82]

Fifteen years later, the Khedive was no longer forced to compete with the clandestine services of the Interior. The ministry's agents were now working on his behalf. The surviving records of this vast intelligence operation contain only fleeting clues about how it was expanded and at whose behest. Gorst's correspondence with London provides little indication that the British were directing this domestic surveillance or even fully aware of it. Only later did British officials begin to demand more comprehensive briefings from what they referred to as the "Secret Service."[83] In all likelihood, the spread of political surveillance ensued from the "policy of conciliation" in two respects at once. First, in cultivating ʿAbbas Hilmi II as an ally, Gorst granted him a freedom of action that Cromer had long withheld. The daily memoranda the Khedive was receiving from the Interior by 1909 suggest that he had seized upon this new latitude to monitor organizations that might now challenge his authority.[84] Second, public awareness about the Khedive's rapprochement with the British exposed him to new levels of popular disapproval. The Interior's growing web of informants reflected this heightened polarization of political energies, as parties, societies, unions, and student associations seemed to multiply day by day.

AN UNLIKELY UNION

In early 1909, a new exemplar of that upsurge in political activism emerged from what many at the time described as the unlikeliest point of origin. On January 21, roughly 1,400 students marched from the gates of the Azhar, the Islamic world's oldest and most prestigious institution of higher learning, to the Jazirah Gardens in the middle of the Nile. There they planned to halt all lessons until the rectorship of the Azhar met their demands.[85] Repeating the tactic that had crushed the law students' strike two years prior, the university administration announced its intention to punish any Azharis who continued to demonstrate. This time, the deterrent failed. Two days later, students and 'ulama' again rallied near the old mosque and marched together through the broad thoroughfares of downtown Cairo. By the time they reached the Jazirah Gardens, their numbers had swelled to several thousands.[86]

Like the informants who infiltrated the crowd and recorded its proceedings, the new regulations that motivated the Azharis to strike were a result of the widened discretion that Gorst had afforded the palace. For centuries, the great mosque-university had trained the 'ulama' who served as jurists, clerks, bureaucrats, teachers, and local imams. Calls to reorganize the Azhar, to update its curriculum, and to prepare its graduates better for the demands of modern life had been a recurrent feature of public discourse in Egypt since at least the early nineteenth century. Perhaps most famously, Shaykh Muhammad 'Abduh had spent the later years of his life advocating, unsuccessfully, for reform. Judging 'Abduh complicit in British plans to curtail his influence over religious institutions, 'Abbas Hilmi II had once helped to scuttle his efforts. But as relations with the nationalist movement grew more tenuous, the Khedive sought to burnish his public reputation by assuming the mantle of reform. In December 1907, he tasked his palace secretary Ahmad Shafiq Pasha to draft a new law governing both the curriculum and administration of the university.[87] Those regulations, known as the New Order, were finalized in March 1908 and enacted the following October. The reforms included the expulsion of nonenrolled individuals from the grounds of the Azhar, the progression of students through a systematized curriculum, the implementation of standardized annual exams, and the inclusion of "modern" subjects in the course of study.[88] The New Order also established a Higher Council—headed by the Rector of the Azhar and comprising the Mufti of Egypt, the Shaykhs of the Maliki, Shafa'i, and Hanbali madhahib, and two government employees (both handpicked by the Khedive)—which would thereafter administer the Azhar and the other major religious institutes in Alexandria and Tanta.

Critics of the Azhar strike at the time attempted to dismiss it as at best an expression of institutional conservatism and religious suspicion toward science.[89] Lampooning the seminarians who had adopted the language and practices of militant labor, the *Egyptian Gazette* described their movement as "wanton idiocy" that might nevertheless "engulf the country in a kindergarten revolution."[90] From the beginning, however, the Azharis made clear their enthusiasm for the new curriculum. In the lists of demands they sent to the papers, they stipulated that the university hire instructors qualified to teach the new courses; that it cover the cost of books and scientific instruments; that exams be introduced gradually so that students in upper years would not be held accountable for material they had never studied; that a degree from the Azhar guarantee basic employment; that student stipends and faculty salaries be increased; and finally, that the members of the administration be elected by the ʿulama' of the Azhar itself. As had been true of other recent strikes, the Azharis thus combined basic material demands with pressure for forms of political participation that had been withheld, or even actively removed, in the drafting of the New Order.[91]

From the start, the strikers presented their situation within the university as a microcosm of Egypt's collective struggle for self-rule. At the demonstration on January 23, the organizers invoked the concept of union to make those connections explicit. According to a report compiled by the Ministry of Interior, one speaker "set about urging union upon his brethren so that they might be like the Japanese." Another reminded them of "the duty of union and of agreeing upon what might be best for the students." He then recited "a *qasidah* against the Westerners who reside in Egypt to sap its resources and deprive the people of them." A third "goaded the students toward union" and "encouraged them to persevere in their demands without fear of the government's attacks." While avoiding direct criticism of the Khedive himself, the Azharis staked out a clear position in Egypt's divided political field. Denouncing Shaykh ʿAli Yusuf's pro-palace journal with shouts of "Down with *al-Mu'ayyad*," the crowd cheered for the papers that supported their cause, and they passed by the offices of *al-Liwa'* as they processed back to the Azhar at dusk.[92]

The confrontation between the striking Azharis and the palace escalated rapidly over the coming days. The Khedive established a government committee to investigate their grievances. The Azharis in turn formed an official body, the Azhar Union Society (*jamʿiyat ittihad al-Azhar*) and elected ten delegates to represent them in negotiations with the committee.[93] But rather than acquiesce to the government's suggestion that they return to class, they prolonged the strike. Enraged by this show of defiance, the Khedive and his supporters took more draconian measures. *Al-Mu'ayyad* launched a smear campaign, alleging that the impressionable students were being manipulated by the National Party's politicos.[94] On February 1, the

Khedive then announced that all students above the first and second years would be expelled and stripped of their stipends and bread rations.[95] Several days later, the Higher Council offered to readmit any students who signed a special petition begging the Khedive's forgiveness and repudiating the strike.[96] At an emergency meeting, the leadership of the Azhar Union Society urged its members to "tear [this petition] up and slap anyone who carries it with your sandal."[97]

Hoping to avert a confrontation, the Rector of al-Azhar, Shaykh Hassunah al-Nawawi, pushed back against the Higher Council's divisive ultimatum, pledging to resign if the government did not readmit the students in return for ending their demonstrations.[98] The Khedive was unmoved, so al-Nawawi stepped down. On February 17, the day appointed for the penitent students to return, a large crowd continued to picket outside the university gates. The Higher Council had deputized the Director of Religious Endowments, Khalil Hamadah Pasha, to oversee the proceedings. When an altercation broke out between the strikers and the university guards, Hamadah Pasha summoned the police. In the violent skirmish that followed, witnesses claimed to have seen the pasha himself beating students with a club. The government's recourse to "terrorism [*irhab*]" against the Azharis proved scandalous.[99] Some even described the event as "a new Denshawai."[100] Responding to the public outcry, a large delegation of notables and representatives from both the National Party and the People's Party marched to ʿAbdin Palace and petitioned the Khedive to resolve the impasse. The following morning, ʿAbbas Hilmi II relented; he announced that all the students would be pardoned and readmitted and that the New Order would be suspended while a committee deliberated over amendments.[101]

Even before the Azharis scored this stunning victory, the mere fact of their staging a strike had inspired extensive commentary about its possible implications. The apparent incongruity that their detractors cast as a symptom of muddled thinking and political immaturity, others described as a deliberate challenge to the categorical distinctions that defined the terrain of political participation under British rule. "How is it," *al-Liwa'* asked, "that those we considered the group least likely to act have risen to hold the authorities to account and to square off against them, confident in themselves and certain of victory?"[102] If the Azharis could so thoroughly disrupt expectations, why not other segments of the population whom the ruling order had similarly deemed unfit to represent themselves? In a similar vein, *Misr al-Fatah* narrated the progressive adoption of strike tactics as a measure for "the development of a love for freedom and independence in an oppressed people." Noting that prevailing norms had once confined uses of the strike to "the working class," the paper proclaimed that the Azharis had surpassed the important precedent set by the law students in 1906. By gathering "twelve million Egyptians around a single opinion and a single demand," they had "ripped away from the faces of the nation the stigma with which their enemies and the pessimists among them had once disgraced them, the stigma of mutual discord."[103] Mindful that some might dismiss support for the Azharis as "a mere act of religious solidarity," Ahmad Lutfi al-Sayyid emphasized that enthusiasm for the strike had come from Muslims and Christians alike. That this unusual movement had so captivated Egyptians from all walks of life, he insisted, had given it "the stamp of nationalism" and revealed a widespread "love for the defense of freedom and the law."[104]

SPECTERS OF MASS POLITICS

On their own, such journalistic efforts to resituate the Azhar strike within a broader narrative about the consolidation of public opinion or the progress of a unified movement for self-rule were hardly surprising. But by the spring of 1909, these ideas were no longer confined to the pages of the nationalist press. When Lutfi al-Sayyid urged his readers in May of that year to "train yourselves for freedom" by adopting practices of collective self-representation, growing numbers of his compatriots had for months been doing just that.[105] As they scrambled to keep pace with the quickening tempo of events, the Interior's spies tracked the meetings and rallies of a list of new organizations that had sprung up almost overnight: the Life Society, the Society for Modern Youth, the Society of Fraternal Solidarity, the Union Society, the Society for Strong Eastern Union, the Egyptian Union Society, the Society for Islamic Progress, and the Society for Youth Progress.[106] At these gatherings, a motley assortment of Azharis, students from other schools and professional institutes, workers, and luminaries from al-Hizb al-Watani and Hizb al-Ummah organized elections and drafted constitutions in miniature to govern their internal procedures.[107] They staged didactic plays in the city's poorer quarters; in one such performance, a cast of recognizable social types lamented the country's financial despoliation and sang, "Oh Egypt, your children are naked, the foreigner gathers money, and there is a mounting crisis in the country."[108] Drawing clear inspiration from recent events, these groups continued to invoke "the merits of union . . . by which nations gain their rights."[109]

Within weeks of the Khedive's capitulation to the striking Azharis, these hopeful appeals to the promise of union were also translating into new forms of collective action. Groups of workers held their own meetings to establish formal associations and devise representative structures for making decisions.[110] Members of the National Party, meanwhile, offered guidance and logistical support. As part of their "effort to gather all classes of the people into syndicates [*niqabat*] under their leadership," the Watanists had by early June convinced nearly a thousand individuals to join a new Manual Trade Workers Association (*jam'iyat al-sana'i' al-yadawiyah*).[111] Nor were these cross-class solidarities restricted to conventional modes of labor organizing. Under the guidance of Shaykh 'Abd al-'Aziz Jawish, who had taken over the editorship of *al-Liwa'* after Mustafa Kamil's death and quickly distinguished himself as their most influential and effective political strategist, the National Party established "People's Night Schools" for the urban poor.[112] And in a practical rejoinder to the occupation's long-standing claims about the bounded urban geography of opposition to British rule, a number of groups began to make inroads beyond Egypt's major cities. With the encouragement of the National Party, the student members of the Life Society agreed to spend their summer holidays in the countryside "serving the nation by delivering lectures among the people to guide them and inform them about the conditions of their country."[113] In similar fashion, the Azhar Union Society instructed its members to form associations in their home villages that would "instruct the people in reading and writing, religion, and love of the nation."[114]

After the Azhar strike, Lutfi al-Sayyid, Jawish, and others had praised the coalitions that succeeded in forcing the government's hand. By raising cheers for both *al-Jaridah* and *al-Liwa'*, the Azharis themselves called upon Egypt's two largest nationalist organizations to overcome their divisions.[115] By this point, speakers and columnists for al-Hizb al-Watani and Hizb al-Ummah had acknowledged that the substantive disagreements between them were dwindling. Confronted with Gorst's repressive tactics, their leaderships began to collaborate more directly. At the end of March, after the revival of the Press Law, huge crowds again took to the streets. Following the very same routes they had used two months prior, large numbers of Azharis helped to replicate the orderly processions that had distinguished the opening gambit of their strike.[116] The police responded by turning fire hoses on the crowds and staging mass arrests.[117] Incensed by this escalation of state violence, members of the National Party and the People's Party held a joint meeting in mid-April. There they agreed to raise money together and send delegations to the capitals of Europe to publicize the recent crackdown on press freedoms and the government's refusal to promulgate a constitution.[118]

Well aware that the British might read each new confrontation as evidence of fanaticism, both parties urged discipline upon their supporters. Even as al-Hizb al-Watani welcomed the arrival of new popular constituencies, they issued reminders that public demonstrations would be most effective as a "peaceful weapon" and that representing Egypt's collective readiness for self-rule in the streets would require a calm and orderly appearance.[119] By mid-summer, as the government carried out more fines, publishing suspensions, and arrests, at least some among the nationalist leadership began to grow more skittish. In August, the British charged 'Abd al-'Aziz Jawish with libel for an article condemning the roles that several prominent Egyptians, including the current Prime Minister Butrus Ghali Pasha, had played in helping the British to prosecute their sham trial against the villagers of Dinshaway; Jawish was convicted and sentenced to three months in prison.[120] Wary of meeting with similar consequences, some members of the National Party became more reticent about endorsing the popular protests that erupted to support the firebrand editor of *al-Liwa'*.[121] For many others, however, the occupation's recourse to such overt acts of repression only strengthened their resolve.

In the immediate aftermath of the Ottoman revolution, Jawish himself had written about "the rot of espionage" and the "intense surveillance of the press" that characterized Sultan Abdulhamid II's paranoid reign.[122] By the summer of 1909, those very same defects seemed, in the eyes of its detractors, to have tainted an Egyptian state that refused to embrace the constitutional spirit of its times. With little apparent sense of irony, the Interior's informants now transcribed speeches in which the targets of their surveillance denounced the spies in their midst.[123] Bucking the campaign of intimidation, some named these new symptoms of tyranny as grounds to escalate their struggles. At the end of November, the Deputy Rector of al-Azhar, Shaykh Muhammad Shakir, announced that he would deprive students who participated in political demonstrations of their stipends. In response, the former leaders of the strike reactivated what they now called *al-Ittihad al-Azhari* (the Azhari Union).[124] Lambasting Shaykh Shakir as a British collaborator, the union leadership reminded the students that together they were "as one hand, for there are in the Azhar people from every village in the country."[125] Members of the Life Society and the Society for

Modern Youth, meanwhile, pursued that notion of a wider union toward its most radical implications. Citing the constitutional movements in Iran and the Ottoman Empire as well as the ongoing anticolonial struggles in India and Ireland, they looked forward to the imminent arrival of "revolution [*thawrah*]" in Egypt as well.[126]

CONCLUSION: ASSASSINATION AND THE END OF THE EXPERIMENT

That more thoroughgoing challenge to the existing order did not arrive, at least not in this moment. On February 21, 1910, a young pharmacist named Ibrahim Nasif al-Wardani decided to take matters into his own hands and assassinate Prime Minister Butrus Ghali Pasha. As the subsequent investigation would reveal, al-Wardani had been active in several of Egypt's more militant political organizations. His public testimony about his motivations echoed—albeit in a far more violent register—many of the statements that the Interior's spies had recently recorded. To the young assassin, Butrus Ghali's had been a long career of contemptible subservience, exemplified by his role in the Dinshaway trial and his more recent defiance of public opposition to a British plan to extend the Suez Canal concession by fifty years.[127]

However typical al-Wardani's stated concerns may have been, his recourse to violence was profoundly divisive. The extraordinary mobilizations of the previous eighteen months had built upon a fragile merger of class factions and political parties that had found common cause in an expansive ideal of union. The controversy that ensued from al-Wardani's crime drove them apart. He may have insisted otherwise, but the fact of a Muslim man killing Egypt's most prominent Coptic Christian raised questions about sectarian motives. The assassination revived old allegations that the popular appeal of nationalism was really fueled by religious chauvinism. Many of Egypt's more well-to-do nationalist luminaries had already shown discomfort with the unruly and self-directed character of mass politics. Facing the wave of repression that followed al-Wardani's crime, their enthusiasm for dramatic acts of public defiance continued to soften.[128]

For the British too, the assassination forced a reckoning with the momentum of recent events. In the summer of 1908, Ronald Graham had judged the Khedive's anxieties to be "exaggerated." Two years later, his estimation of the political forces ranged against the occupation had changed. Writing to London, Graham now warned that under "the plea of advocating self-government for Egypt" the nationalists had been pursuing a "campaign of misrepresentation and intimidation." Already the "semi-educated classes" and the "impressionable youth of the country" had become "thoroughly permeated with a spirit of unreasoning hostility and suspicion towards the authorities, whether British or Egyptian." More worrisome still were their recent attempts to "spread this spirit among the working classes and the fellaheen, who have not hitherto shown an interest in politics." Unless the government could devise "some more effectual check," he feared that these efforts to "render any form of government impossible" would "prove successful at no distant date."[129]

As Graham's report indicated, this new "interest in politics" did not lead British officials to reassess the political capacities of those they had long dismissed as unable to think and act for themselves. Instead, those insurgent aspirations became the bad results of what Gorst now deemed a failed experiment. The consul-general explained the recent "manifestations of Anglophobia stirred up by the Nationalist party" not as expressions of public opinion or political consciousness but rather as the malign effects of Britain's recent "concessions" toward the demand for self-government. "The time has come," he advised London, "to cry a halt." Citing his "many years of experience of the Egyptians," Gorst offered the chilling assertion that "if they can be made clearly to understand that they have nothing to hope from a continuance of the agitation, they will yield to the inevitable."[130]

Less than a month later, Edward Grey rose before Parliament to assert that "if all that we can do in that direction of stimulating greater interest on the part of the people in their own Government, and in allowing them to criticize the action of the Government or its merits is simply going to increase the agitation against the British occupation, we can go no further in that direction." Echoing Gorst's bloodless request for clarity, the foreign secretary explained, "I have spoken strongly on this point because I think it is essential that there should be no misunderstanding about it. If ever there is misunderstanding it will encourage agitation and undermine the confidence which is essential for the prosperity of the country."[131] The experiment with self-governing institutions had ended.

Chapter 7

PUNJAB ON THE NILE

ON JANUARY 31, 1914, the lead column in the *Egyptian Gazette* opined after "The Financial Future of the Egyptian Fellah." Lamenting that he was "too ignorant to argue out for himself the advantages and disadvantages of a given line of action" and that "no amount of laws and regulations will change this state of things," the semiofficial organ of the local Anglophone community found little reason for optimism. The evidence of recent years had shown this "unreformable creature" to be a menace not only to himself but to the overall prosperity of his country. "When a bank is founded to enable him to break away from the usurer's clutches," the paper continued, "he borrows from the bank, and, when the time comes round to pay the annual installment, is unprovided with the requisite funds, and has to resort to the very man from whom the Government wishes to protect him, to procure the necessary money." In similar fashion, when provided "an abundant supply of water for his crops, he turns a deaf ear to advice and promptly proceeds to water-log his land by irrigating it whether water is required or not. His shortsightedness leads him to over-crop his land and so treat with contempt the well-worn advantage of the goose and the golden eggs." Worst of all was "his extreme improvidence in money matters." Despite having been "raised to comparative independence and liberty" and "blessed by nature with a fertile soil and the most generous climatic conditions," the *Gazette* judged, he "does everything he possibly can to retard his own progress by encumbering himself with debt and living ahead of his income."[1]

In attributing these behaviors to limited education, "climatic conditions," and "*malesh*, a sort of irresponsible resignation with respect to everyday affairs of life," the *Gazette* offered a dismal portrait of the fallah as a discrete racial type. On their own, claims about the anomalous and unchanging nature of the peasant were nothing new.[2] The specific content of those claims, however, was.[3] When Harry Boyle had insisted, six years beforehand, that "the Egyptian is eminently materialist," the resident Orientalist at the British Agency was also describing an immutable racial character. Boyle's pronouncement about "the Egyptians properly so-called" was a shorthand for the twin postulates that had long underpinned the discourse of colonial economism.[4] To say that "the Egyptian is eminently materialist" was most obviously to posit a human subject narrowly attuned to the "direct concerns" of economic interest. And to invoke that "materialism" as a bulwark against opposition to British rule was also to insist that "the Egyptian" could recognize and act upon those interests. Implicit in the *Gazette*'s litany of policies for which the fallah had shown himself both inadequate and ungrateful was a recognition that the British had once anticipated different outcomes. In that regard, the paper's insistence that it was "impossible for him to conduct his affairs in a rational fashion" marked a significant departure.[5]

Even in its heyday, colonial economism had represented something of an outlier position within the wider currents of imperial thought. At the very moment when a rising cohort of British officials began to draw inspiration from the ideas of Henry Sumner Maine, the occupation had championed an array of policies that were plainly at odds with that "conservative turn."[6] If Cromer's relentless opposition to Egyptian self-rule put him in line with the leading proponents of colonial conservatism—many of them close personal friends and confidants—the program of agrarian development that gained his administration global renown bucked that trend.[7] But as was also true of their conservative contemporaries, the proponents of colonial economism were generally pessimistic about the kind of "governmental" subject formation that liberal administrators had once championed.[8] Their program of economic development would succeed or fail on the basis of what the peasant already was, not what he might become.

Since its earliest days, the occupation had described its most controversial policies as experiments. At times, this choice of language did suggest that the colonial laboratory would yield results worthy of wider application. Eldon Gorst's "experiment in local self-government" might offer a model for political pedagogy in other colonial settings. The Agricultural Bank of Egypt might represent an institutional solution to problems of peasant indebtedness everywhere. But even before the data started pouring in, this language of experiment implied another mode of reasoning and making sense of the world.

On this understanding, the independent variable of the occupation's experiments was the racialized population of colonial subjects upon whom each new policy was tested. Here, the crude pseudoscience of racial taxonomy provided a ready-made schema for managing the spatial and temporal unevenness of imperial rule across disparate regions of the globe, or even within colonies.[9] This was so in several respects at once. First, divergent policies in different locales could easily betray substantive disagreements between officials occupying different positions within a world-spanning imperial order. Attributing those discrepancies instead to the innate particularities of raced human subjects offered a capacious means of accommodating otherwise obvious contradictions.[10] Second, racial experiment became a dominant—though certainly not exclusive—idiom for debating the transmissibility and comparability of policies across and between colonial contexts. When the Agricultural Bank of Egypt gained global renown, discussions about its adaptation did in some instances concern technical details like the servicing of its loans.[11] But just as often, they turned on assessments of the human subjects who would receive the bank's mortgages. As news of the bank's formation first reached the United States, for example, the *Louisiana Courier-Journal* thus mused, "If such a plan succeeds in developing the agricultural resources of Turkey and Egypt, and there is sufficient sense of financial responsibility among these people to prevent serious losses, it is possible that similar benefits could be obtained in the Philippines."[12] Finally, this way of framing the experiment offered a racially determined subjectivity—the peasant's "sense of personal financial responsibility" or its absence—as the primary explanation for a range of possible outcomes.

In this way, as the anthropologist Fernando Coronil argued several decades ago, the essentialist categories of colonial discourse performed a "necessary mystification" that closely paralleled, or even replicated, the fetishized character of social relations under capitalism. The taxonomies of colonial thought, in other words, systematically misrecognized complex relations between people as inherent features of fixed and "thinglike" human types.[13] By this mode of reasoning, the failures and unexpected consequences of successive policies could be reinterpreted as yet more experimental data revealing the precise contours of racial anomaly.

It was a closely punctuated succession of such apparent failures that precipitated the British occupation's turn toward the manifestly conservative position echoed in the *Egyptian Gazette*'s gloomy assessment of the fallah's financial future. By the time the Foreign Secretary Edward Grey announced that "the maintenance of good Government and order" must preempt any further "talk . . . about self-governing institutions," it was not only Eldon Gorst's political experiments that were generating bad results.[14] Having once maintained that the market convulsions of 1907 had left the country's peasant majority unscathed, the occupation was forced by 1910 to reckon with a body of new statistics about the alarming rate of smallholder defaults. Nor were these reverberations of the financial crisis the only threat to Egypt's once-vaunted material prosperity. The ecological stresses of intensive monocrop cultivation had been mounting for some time. In the very moment when paper fortunes had vanished and cotton exports appeared once again as the primary source of Egypt's "real wealth," those accumulated problems threw crop yields into decline. Whereas once the peasant smallholder had stood as the ideal subject of imperial rule and the worthy beneficiary of British reform, that same figure now became the presumed culprit behind the country's newly precarious position. Greedy and shortsighted, he overcropped his land, exhausted the soil, and refused to heed scientific advice about how best to protect his crops. Borrowing well beyond his means, he was unable, or perhaps just unwilling, to pay his debts. And having reaped the bounty of economic development for close to three decades, he had proven himself no less susceptible to the xenophobic appeal of fanaticism.

That there was a pattern to these behaviors was no accident. But that pattern had nothing to do with the alleged racial defects of peasant farmers and a great deal to do with the peculiar "ecology of interest" that decades of British policy had helped to produce.[15] During the boom years, Egypt's new lending institutions had developed their own class designations as a means of calculating the risk on loans of different sizes and types. The sharp striations of the credit market translated into very different pressures on different classes of proprietors. Those pressures grew more, not less, intense when the flow of easy money stopped in 1907. At least some commentators at the time discerned the dense tangle of socioecological relations that had together shaped this crisis-prone agrarian landscape. But for others, that same patterning lent credence to assertions that the real problem was the innate character of the Egyptian smallholder. Around that line of argument, an array of powerful groups—not least among them the banks themselves—began to agitate for new forms of state intervention against a peasant subject they now judged unable to "conduct his affairs in a rational fashion." The case for this revised position was only bolstered by concerns that the social dislocation of recent years had left the peasantry more susceptible to the machinations of an emboldened nationalist movement. Looking back to India for a model of colonial conservatism that they had once abjured, British officials in Egypt set about implementing an array of paternalist measures that aimed to insulate the fallah from market transactions and modern institutions that he was now deemed unable to navigate on his own.

CHILD CONSCRIPTS AND HUNGRY CATERPILLARS

Although the clustering of phenomena that drove this conservative turn occurred only in 1910, the earliest indications of the shift had taken place several years prior. The occupation's reassessment of the peasant as a human subject began with its struggle to combat a tiny, nonhuman enemy. The cotton-leaf worm (*prodenia littoralis*) or *dudat al-qutn* had made its first appearance as a menace to Egyptian cotton as early as 1877.[16] The caterpillar's popular moniker was, in the most literal sense, a misnomer. It had subsisted for millennia on the clover (*birsim*) that farmers used as animal fodder. With the spread of cotton farming, however, a new source of food became available, and its population began to grow. In this sense, the subsequent association between bug and crop was testament to the produced nature of the agrarian landscape. Almost as soon as the caterpillar had won the status of a pest, those concerned to check its spread began to attribute its presence in the cotton fields to specific social problems. In his reporting for the Dufferin Commission, Villiers Stuart had described the caterpillar infestations of 1882 as symptomatic of rural upheaval during the ʿUrabi revolt.[17] A decade later, the Khedive's spies had explained

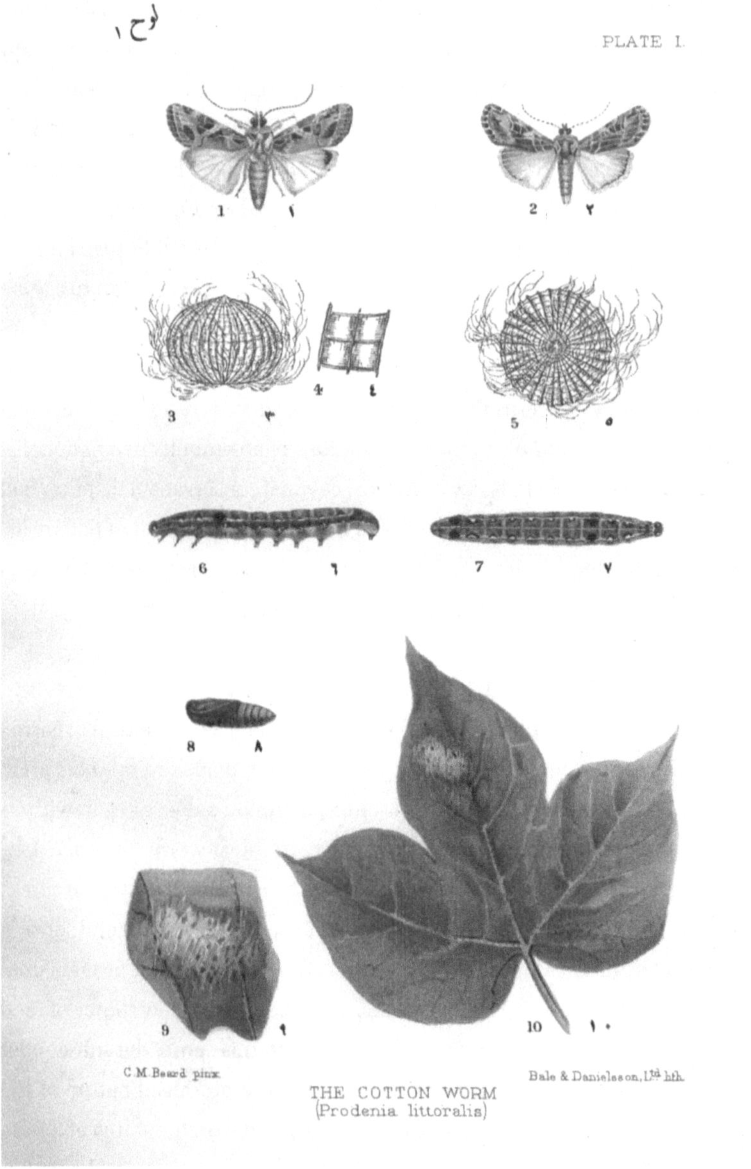

FIGURE 7: The Cotton-Leaf Worm. Source: *Yearbook of the Khedivial Agricultural Society* (Cairo: National Printing Press, 1906).

the bug's attacks as evidence that provincial officials under British supervision were neglecting their responsibilities.[18]

In the early days of the occupation, the Council of Ministers had formed a commission to study the cotton worm and propose a remedy. Having determined that the most effective method was to cut and burn any leaves on which its eggs were found, they advised that the Ministry of Interior should "urge [farmers] to inspect every plant with the utmost concentration" and follow their recommended procedures.[19] The government thereafter issued annual reminders to the village shaykhs, instructing them to ensure that the peasantry remain vigilant in protecting their crops. Though written in strong, even militaristic, language, these early directives merely provided guidance and left their enforcement to the discretion of provincial officials.[20]

In 1895, another severe infestation occasioned the establishment of a new government commission along with a flurry of articles, opinion pieces, and private studies published in the local press.[21] No longer concerned simply to understand the life cycle of the insect in isolation, a number of amateur entomologists now sought to account for the overall occurrence of exploding caterpillar populations. Several studies identified the adoption of a two-year rather than a three-year rotation for the cotton crop as a significant contributing factor. It was at this moment that a new explanation for Egypt's insect problem began to gain traction. In this rendition, the ravages of the cotton-leaf worm could be pinned upon a specific social actor: the greedy and shortsighted peasant farmer. Writing in the scientific journal *al-Muqtataf*, Major-General Mukhtar Pasha, a former overseer of the Khedive's private estates, warned that poorer farmers "took to farming half their land in cotton rather than a third of it, and not just that, but moreover they crowded their land with cotton plants until the number per feddan was five thousand or more."[22]

Mukhtar Pasha was not alone in identifying the more intensive crop rotation with the farming practices of Egypt's smallholders. For more than a decade, British officials had been doing the same, but they had once judged the practice as a virtue. Decrying the khedivial regime's mismanagement of water resources, Villiers Stuart had noted that "as a general rule cotton is grown only every third year on the same land; it could be grown every alternate year, provided sufficient water were available."[23] In the productivist drive of the occupation's early years, the engineers of the Public Works Department had taken the aggregate yield of the cotton crop as their primary metric of progress. Heralding the equitable distribution of irrigation water as a materialization of "British justice" on the land, they readily attributed this rising output to the class of smallholders whose economic potential a despotic order had once held in check.[24]

In both their older positive and their newer negative variants, assessments of peasant productivity assumed the form of claims about human nature. In the former case, the fallah was an industrious creature whose sole concern was to tease riches from the soil; in the latter, he was a grasping spendthrift whose assault upon the land would destroy Egypt's God-given patrimony. As the agrarian historian Alan Richards demonstrated long ago, such accounts consistently ignored the social conditions that made adoption of the two-year rotation far more likely for smallholders than for wealthier proprietors. Claims about their ignorance and aversion to science notwithstanding, most farmers were likely aware of the ecological risks entailed.[25] Cotton required more cash and labor than other crops, and more land under cotton meant that less food could be grown for family subsistence. It moreover increased exposure to global price fluctuations.[26] On their own, these considerations might have made smallholders less, rather than more, inclined to grow more cotton. What impelled them to do so anyway was "their position in the credit market."[27] Having been forced to borrow at exorbitant rates throughout the 1860s and 1870s, poorer peasants adopted the more intensive rotation as the lesser of two evils: overcropping their land was better than losing it to foreclosure. Once new irrigation infrastructures made more water available, it was mainly for this reason that poorer peasants opted, in disproportionate numbers, to grow more cotton. They thereby appeared to confirm British claims about their economistic character and simultaneously prepared the way for later allegations of ecological myopia.

After the establishment of the Agricultural Bank in 1902, lower interest rates may have attenuated these pressures somewhat. But as Alfred Eid's calculations (discussed in Chapter 3) made clear, even those improved rates, which ranged between 8% and 9% per annum, were high enough to require rising productivity if the borrower was to gain anything from the loan. The same was not true of the country's wealthier proprietors, for whom borrowing costs fell steadily throughout the boom years.[28] As a publicly traded company beholden to its shareholders, the Agricultural Bank was also far more stringent in the enforcement of its loans than the village moneylenders, many of whom had to maintain relationships in the communities with whom they conducted their business.[29]

If claims about the improvident, unscientific character of the smallholder had been circulating for some time, they took on a new significance when they received endorsement from the British experts tasked with vanquishing the insect menace. In 1898, a group of Egypt's wealthiest landowners, along with representatives of several foreign companies involved in fertilizer production and land reclamation, had founded the Khedivial Agricultural Society.[30] Over the next decade, this "parastatal" organization provided direction on the government's agricultural policies through its own staff of resident British scientists.[31] In the summer of 1904, the cotton crop suffered its worst caterpillar attack to date. The bug destroyed as much as half the crop in some districts. The damage was particularly severe in the western Delta province of Buhayrah, where much of the land was held in large estates by wealthy proprietors and foreign companies.[32] Acting through the Agricultural Society and its staff entomologist F. C. Willcocks, a coalition of these large landed interests successfully lobbied the government to take more aggressive action against future infestations. The supposed improvidence of the smallholder would now provide justification for a raft of direct and coercive interventions inside the formerly private domain of the farm.[33]

At the beginning of February 1905, Lord Cromer announced that the government was deliberating over criminal penalties for farmers who failed to implement the prescribed eradication procedures for the cotton worm. Pushing back against such "legislation of compulsion and force," a columnist for *al-Mu'ayyad* asked, "Who is the stupid peasant that sees the worm devouring the fruits of his labor hither and yon . . . and then leaves it be?" The irrational peasant, in this view, was a convenient fiction concocted to validate "an assault upon the personal freedom that is the most special distinction of humankind and the holiest of its rights."[34] As this line of argument suggested, the government's proposed penalties seemed directly at odds with the liberal guarantees of private property that the occupation had once championed.

The contradictions only became more glaring when the government circulated a full draft of the regulations for public comment and debate in the press.[35] Not only did the new legislation mandate fines and prison time for farmers who neglected to inform the provincial authorities about caterpillars on their land. It also empowered the provincial administration to conscript all able-bodied children to serve in gangs, under the supervision of the village headmen, to pick, transport, and burn infested cotton leaves. Though the children would be compensated at a standard wage determined by the ma'mur of their home district, participation in these "cotton-worm campaigns" would be compulsory. Farmers who refused to provide the labor of their children would be subject to imprisonment for up to one month or a fine of up to two Egyptian pounds. Children found negligent in their work for the eradication campaigns or refusing to appear would likewise face imprisonment for up to one week or a fine of one pound.[36]

For well over a decade, Lord Cromer had listed the abolition of corvée among the occupation's proudest achievements. It was in the enjoyment of rights to dispose of their own labor, he had argued, that peasants would most easily recognize the difference between "khedivial despotism" and "British justice." The dissonance of a government campaign to conscript thousands of peasant children was nowise resolved by the fact that those boys and girls would receive nominal payment for work they were not at liberty to withhold.

Conscious of the problem, Cromer attempted in his annual report for 1905 to explain it away. His case hinged on a four-part argument that obligatory, state-mandated child labor was, in fact, distinct from corvée. First, he suggested, "it was shown that, by careful supervision, the evils generally supposed to be a necessary incident of the forced-labour system might be averted."[37] Here, as elsewhere, British managerial prowess would provide the antidote to the flaws of Oriental misrule. Second, despite the "theoretical objections to forced labour, of which no one is more fully aware than myself," few measures had "met with such universal approval in Egypt as that now under discussion."[38] Though Cromer was famously disdainful of Egyptian public opinion, in this case it would provide cover for an otherwise problematic decision. In this appeal to "universal approval," then, lay the explanation for the government's rare willingness to circulate the draft legislation in the press and convene the General Assembly to ratify it.[39] Third, quoting from Percy W. Machell's report as adviser to the Interior, he noted that " 'European and wealthier proprietors' " had been cleaning their crops of caterpillar eggs for years. Machell had admitted that, thanks to the complexities of the Egyptian judicial system, the new regulations applied only to the native Egyptian population.[40] Understandably, some critics in the Arabic press had objected to this unequal and inconsistent application as another flaw of the new decree.[41] In Cromer's report, however, the terms of that critique were inverted. European exemption from the law's strictures was not a problem because Europeans did not need to be compelled to act.

Finally, Cromer insisted, "there is an immense difference between organizing labour to deal with an agricultural crisis, such as that occasioned by the presence of the cotton worm, and obliging people to labour on ordinary works undertaken for the general development of the country."[42] With this concluding flourish, the consul-general attempted to square the details of the campaigns with the claim that had been foundational to the occupation's program of economic development until that point. In the present case, "those employed readily understand that it is in their own immediate interest to work," whereas with the old regime of corvée, "the interest, if any, is more remote, and is certainly, in their eyes less comprehensible."[43] In a convoluted pretzel of reasoning, Cromer asserted that this instance of forced labor was not corvée because peasants could appreciate their own "immediate interest" in emergency measures that the government had justified precisely by asserting that those same peasants could not recognize and act upon their own interests—in protecting their crops—without the direct threat of coercion.

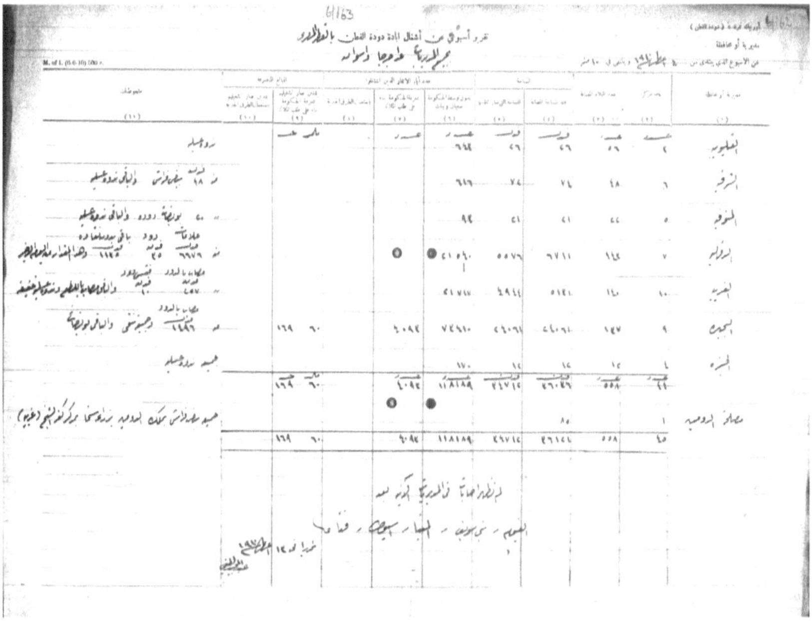

FIGURE 8: Report of the Work of the Cotton-Worm Campaigns for the Week of August 4, 1910. Source: DUR, HIL 6, 162–63. Reproduced by kind permission of the Trustees of the Mohamed Ali Foundation and of the University of Durham.

It is doubtful, of course, that either the peasant proprietors who lost reliable access to family labor or the children pressed into service by the agents of the Interior regarded these new acts of compulsion as "little more than persuasion."[44] Machell's report noted that in several locales where the demand for labor outstripped the available supply, children had to be transported from one province to another.[45] By proposing that future revisions to the cotton-worm decree should include some provision for a bread ration whenever "it is found necessary to move parties of boys out of their own district," he insinuated that many of these children may have gone without food in the summer of 1905. And because wages were fixed at the discretion of local officials, the rates Machell quoted in passing were both strikingly varied and consistently minimal.[46] An addendum to his report acknowledged, "Pay was in many cases too low, and this, besides the injustice, is an inducement to farmers to apply to the Government for labour which they could procure themselves, but which would cost them more."[47]

DECLINING YIELDS AND THE ADVENT OF AGRICULTURAL REGULATION

The cotton-worm campaigns resumed over the next two summers, but despite these exceptional measures, the average yield of the cotton crop continued to fall, from a peak of 5.8 cantars per feddan in 1898 to 3.85 cantars in 1906.[48] In March of 1908, the Khedivial Agricultural Society established a new commission to investigate the causes of the decline. In the report they submitted on May 29, the commission listed seven likely factors: deterioration of the soil, irrigation and rotations, drainage, climate, deterioration of the plant, insects, and seed stock.[49] With the possible exception of climate, all of these proved to merit new worries. In increasing the available supply of irrigation, it seems, the British engineers had been less attentive to ensuring that water flowing onto the fields could eventually pass on to the sea. As subsequent studies also indicated, the water table in the Delta had begun to rise, leading to problems of increased soil salinity and asphyxiation of crop roots.[50] In addition to providing fodder for swarms of insects, the prevalence of the two-year crop rotation was hastening the depletion of vital nutrients in the soil. Inconsistencies in the seeds that farmers employed meant wide variations in the length and quality of the fibers that Egyptian cotton plants produced. And just months after the commission submitted this first report, an infestation of cotton-hungry caterpillars once again wreaked havoc on the crop.

In the aftermath of the 1908 attack, the cotton-worm earned yet another interpretation as the effect in nature of a distinctly human problem. The Agricultural Society sent a letter to the Council of Ministers complaining that after three successful years, "in 1908 the government was slow to take the necessary steps." The resulting damage to the harvest, they cautioned, was all the more serious "in a year when farmers, and the people in general, are suffering from the financial situation."[51] To this line of criticism, Gorst had a ready response. As the consul-general explained, removing British oversight from the provincial administration had been a significant feature of his experiment in local self-government. The unchecked spread of the cotton worm thus became evidence that in the absence of British inspectors, "the local authorities failed to infuse the required energy, with the result that the measures were far from being as efficacious as under the old system."[52] A full year before the wholesale abandonment of his experiment, in other words, the consul-general was reading the caterpillar infestations as data about the enduring necessity of colonial tutelage.

The case for concerted intervention only grew stronger the following year when a new species, the pink bollworm, caused even greater harm to the cotton crop. Unlike the cotton-leaf worm, this new menace would only reveal itself when farmers went to harvest the cotton fibers and found the bolls devoured from the inside.[53] Echoing the Agricultural Society's earlier warnings, Gorst admitted that another poor harvest had thwarted hopes that a bumper crop "might clear away the financial stagnation from which the country has been suffering ever since the crisis of 1907."[54] Nor, by 1910, were diminished yields the only serious problem facing Egypt's cotton farmers. Several years of strained supply had driven the price of Egyptian cotton high enough to threaten the market segmentation that had once furnished some protection from global competition. This was the dire prognosis offered by John A. Todd, professor of political economy at the Khedivial Law School, in an article he published with the *Cairo Scientific Journal* in January 1910.[55]

Egyptian cotton had once enjoyed a premium on the world market because its fine long staple was uniquely suited to a range of high-end industrial applications. Since the 1890s, when H. A. Lowe had perfected the process of mercerization to produce strong cotton thread with a lustrous shine, manufacturers in both England and the US had relied on Egyptian fiber to meet the growing demand for cotton fabrics that mimicked the look and feel of silk. By driving up the price of Egyptian cotton,

Todd argued, reduced yields had incentivized the spinning factories to retool their machines and accommodate American fiber. Though somewhat lower in quality, the resulting textiles were less expensive and therefore more appealing to middle-class consumers who had been unable to pay a premium for Egyptian cotton. The ironic outcome was that "the high price of Egyptian cotton is driving it out of the very trade which it originally made for itself by its low price as compared with silk."[56] Egypt would never regain its command of that particular market. The best alternative, Todd now argued, would be to focus on a range of ultra-high-end applications: typewriter ribbons, webbing for automobile tires, mail bags, sail cloth, and the like. But while "the future demand for these goods is almost unlimited," Egypt's ability to dominate that niche market was anything but assured.[57] "The great aim of the Egyptian cotton grower," Todd concluded, "must therefore be not only to restore and, if possible, improve the former yield, but above all things to maintain the quality of the crop upon which alone its special market now depends."[58]

The argument that Egypt faced a double threat of declining yields and inconsistent quality would gain ground rapidly in the months that followed. The result was a concerted expansion of the regulatory apparatus that the cotton-worm campaigns had first established.[59] In 1910, the government hired a new staff of five British "agricultural inspectors" to oversee the management of the cotton-worm campaigns and also announced plans for a new Department of Agriculture.[60] Housed within the Ministry of Public Works and headed by Gerald Dudgeon, formerly Inspector of Agriculture in British West Africa, the department served, from the beginning, as a new site from which to realize the Foreign Secretary Edward Grey's call for "more assertion of our authority."[61] Within months of his arrival, Dudgeon was coordinating the formulation of agricultural policy directly with the British advisers to the Ministries of Public Works and the Interior.[62] In his private correspondence with the Khedive, Prime Minister Muhammad Saʿid complained that the British advisers and inspectors were now circumventing their Egyptian counterparts from the ministerial level on down to the provinces.[63]

What ensued from this increased visibility of British officials was a rapid multiplication of new rules and procedures that touched on nearly every aspect of farming practice. In the name of protecting Egyptian cotton, government circulars instructed farmers about when they could irrigate their land, when they could plant and harvest their crops, how they should clear their fields after the cotton harvest, and even where they could store manure.[64] All of these regulations now carried the threat of fines and imprisonment not only for offending landowners but also for local officials found negligent in their surveillance of the farms in their villages.[65]

Building on earlier criticisms of the two-year cotton rotation, many of these measures targeted practices that held particular importance for farmers working small plots on very narrow margins. Beginning in 1909, on the recommendation of the Agricultural Society, the government imposed severe penalties for watering *birsim* (clover) after early May. The objective was to reduce waterlogging and starve the insect population before cotton plants began to ripen. But the rule also deprived farmers of the animal fodder that subsequent cuttings would have provided and, in the long run, the nitrogen that this clover would have fixed in the soil. Those who chose to buck the law rather than purchase substitute feed and fertilizer now became obstacles to scientific farming and enemies of the public good.[66] In similar fashion, the government's entomologists could contrive no other way to combat the pink bollworm than to mandate that farmers uproot and burn all the stalks of their cotton plants immediately after the harvest.[67] By eliminating a competing supply of firewood and fuel for irrigation pumps, these measures empowered rural coal merchants to ratchet up their prices in times of shortage.[68] Here again, farmers who could not afford to buy what they had once acquired from the land for free assumed the status of traitors in a national war against insects.

The Department of Agriculture's staff of British inspectors stressed that the provincial authorities should "pass as severe sentences as possible in order that they may have the desired effect."[69] Gone was the ambivalence that had led Cromer to gloss the original cotton-worm campaigns as a form of "persuasion." Agricultural regulations now assumed a peasant subject who could not intuit a path toward his own improvement without the constant fear of punishment. Nor did this approach admit of much possibility for change. Indeed, what limited efforts the new Department of Agriculture undertook to educate the rural population appealed not to their putative materialism but rather to their religious faith as Muslims. While the village headmen were tasked with monitoring farms and enforcing rules, it was the imams of rural mosques who now received orders to conduct lessons about combating insect pests after Friday prayers.[70] This appeal to the putative fanaticism of the peasantry also distinguished the new genre of instructional primers and booklets that the Department of Agriculture began to produce for rural schoolchildren.

The first such publication consisted of a series of instructional dialogues between a student from the Khedivial Agricultural School named Hussayn and the child of a farmer named Muhammad. Hussayn concludes their exchange with a stern admonition: "Duty obligates every individual to work day and night to save his agriculture. Anyone who violates that [duty], violates God's will. . . . Failure to pick the cotton worm is a violation against the sovereign, and God will punish this on the day of judgment."[71]

PEASANT DEFAULTS AND THE CLASS EFFECTS OF CRISIS

By 1912, when the Department of Agriculture made this first clumsy attempt at a children's literature of applied entomology, the intractable longevity of what Cromer had once deemed a passing agricultural crisis was hardly the only problem for which a retreat from the axioms of colonial economism seemed to offer a solution. In 1905, the consul-general's awkward rationalizations had been necessary because the underlying argument for reviving peasant conscription was so plainly at odds with prevailing theories of Egypt's economic regeneration. Cromer continued at the very same time to tout the success of a financial experiment that attributed to the Egyptian peasant the rudiments of a liberal economic rationality.[72] Throughout the boom years, the balance sheets of the Agricultural Bank had served as a key piece of evidence for claims about the newfound prosperity of Egypt's smallholders. And for a full two years after 1907, British officials continued to insist that the crisis had not spread to the countryside. When the bank's own figures made that position untenable, it was their own earlier optimism about the peasant's capacity to treat a mortgage as capital that they blamed for the discrepancy.

In the spring of 1910, the Agricultural Bank made the shocking announcement that fully 40,000 of its roughly 238,000 loans were in default.[73] By the following year, that figure had risen to 49,000.[74] As was true of farming patterns, the genesis of these alarming figures was closely bound up with the class inequalities of the credit market. In the climate of easy lending and rising asset values prior to 1907, landowners both great and small had chosen to leverage their holdings, borrowing against existing properties to buy more land. When that flow of credit dried up, many were unable to meet their installments. Now, the very conditions that had favored Egypt's wealthier proprietors when times were good also worked to their advantage when the loans started to go bad.

The weekly minutes of the Gresham Life Insurance Company's local committee offer a rare glimpse at how these dynamics played out. Lending practices that had targeted Egypt's wealthiest landowners at the height of the boom put the banks in a delicate a position when the crisis began. In November 1905, as an added enticement to borrowers who might prefer to make payment after the autumn cotton harvest, the Gresham had decided that all new loan contracts should allow postponement of the June installment until December of the same year for a small additional fee.[75] The local committee received its first request to exercise that provision in June of 1907. Anticipating more such notifications as the crisis continued, they decided to extend the accommodation even to clients whose mortgage contracts did not include it.[76] The number of loans in arrears continued to rise throughout the summer, and by winter, delinquent borrowers began to request a new round of postponements, this time moving their December installments to the following June.[77]

Over the next two years, the Gresham went to considerable lengths to avoid court proceedings against their well-to-do borrowers. Beyond the postponements they granted, they scheduled meetings to cajole their clients into paying. Sometimes, they sent threatening letters through their lawyers.[78] The few occasions on which they did foreclosure only heightened their overall reluctance to do so. Having contracted ever-larger mortgages against ever-larger properties at ever-higher valuations, lenders like the Gresham now had little choice but to let their clients stall for time. By 1909, land prices in some parts of the country had fallen by as much as 25%. Taking title to a large estate under those conditions would leave the bank with few good options. If they could find a buyer, they would risk selling at a loss or, at best, forego the future profits that the loan was scheduled to yield. But with credit everywhere in short supply, there was no guarantee that a buyer could be found. Failure to resell a foreclosed property could saddle the bank with the burden of managing an actual farm, a task that they were ill-equipped to bear.[79] In effect, lenders like the Gresham discovered that their largest mortgages might be too big to fail.

The Agricultural Bank, meanwhile, offered no such leniency. The tiny plots of land against which it made most of its loans were still easy to sell. The bank had neither the motivation nor the resources to manage relationships with its smallholder clientele. When the arrears on a given mortgage surpassed a threshold of 40%, the bank initiated legal proceedings. Seizing upon the magnitude of the figures the bank had released, its critics condemned such mechanistic enforcement. Demanding "the intervention of the public authorities," *La Bourse Égyptienne* railed, "They are ruining the country, and what is shameful is that they are ruining it stupidly. . . . All land transactions are stalled, and they destroy all agricultural credit in order to throw a hundred thousand feddans onto the market by fractions of a feddan."[80] In this rush to the courts, however, some peasant debtors located an opportunity to seize for themselves the kind of reprieve that both the government and the Agricultural Bank had so far withheld. Even before the onset of the crisis, Egypt's Mixed Courts had scrambled to process a growing caseload.[81] When litigation for bad debts flooded the dockets after 1907, the courts fell further and further behind. Short on other viable options and confident that foreclosure proceedings could take months or even years to work their way to a ruling, a growing number of the Agricultural Bank's clients opted simply to stop paying.[82]

When he reported on the extent of the Agricultural Bank's arrears, Gorst noted that "there is evidence . . . of a considerable amount of borrowing from the village money-lenders during the less favourable seasons of 1908 and 1909. When a fellah owes money both to the Agricultural Bank and to the money-lender, there is no doubt that the latter recovers his loans before the Bank."[83] Yet alongside this account of both structural conditions and contingent events that might explain the sudden rise in peasant insolvency, Gorst advanced a second, contrasting narrative. In this version, the bank's smallholder clients had "begun to realize the obstacles in the way of enforcing prompt payment" and chosen to "take advantage of them to postpone the fulfillment of their obligations even when they are in a position to pay." Criticism of efforts to recover bad debts in the courts was "very unreasonable." The Agricultural Bank, after all, had a "duty to the shareholders to maintain amongst its debtors a sense of respect for their obligations."[84] Peasant borrowers had shown little such respect. The best way to slow the pace of defaults, then, was to render the operation of the courts more efficient by "facilitating the sales of land, and reducing the cost of legal proceedings."[85]

Responding at first to the public outcry over its refusal to intervene on behalf of the peasantry, the government did briefly negotiate a delay in the bank's legal proceedings "in the hope that cases might be settled without expropriation." But when this modest reprieve failed to yield swift results, the bank took the opposite tack and began to widen the scope of its legal action against delinquent borrowers.[86] By this point, the Agricultural Bank had radically curtailed the form of lending for which it was originally created. It placed a moratorium on all new loans in Upper Egypt, where rates of default were highest, and it contracted few new mortgages even in the Delta.[87] Invoking responsibility to their shareholders, the bank's directors, moreover, began lobbying the British administration for added assistance. They sought government authorization to invest in larger mortgages. And to accelerate enforcement of bad debts, they pressed for a revision to the foreclosure proceedings of the Mixed Courts. Channeling the bank's own arguments in the spring of 1911, Gorst now observed, "There appears to be little doubt that the fellah has accustomed himself during the past few years to a higher scale of living—aided thereto by the increase in value of his crops and by the loans of the Agricultural Bank—and that it is only by the severest pressure of circumstances that he can been brought to recognize the necessity of fulfilling his obligations at the sacrifice of comfort."[88] Reinterpreting the decision to halt payment as evidence of a unique character deficit, the consul-general cast efficient foreclosure as a necessary corrective. In making its case for such draconian procedures, the Agricultural Bank effectively rejected the very premise on which it had been founded. A decade prior, its promoters had insisted that, whatever their other limitations, Egyptian peasants were thrifty and responsible economic actors. The bank itself now implied that the opposite was more likely true.

FRIEND OF THE FELLAH

Gorst had requested an early leave in April 1911 to seek medical attention in England. In June he was diagnosed with cancer of the pancreas and liver, and a month later, on July 12, he passed away.[89] If a shift in the occupation's conception of agrarian society had been gaining force for some time, the man that the Foreign Office selected as Gorst's replacement oversaw the consolidation of a new order modeled more directly on the conservatism of Henry Maine and the "Punjab school" of Indian administration. Two decades prior, Herbert Kitchener had supervised the reorganization of the army and served as inspector-general of the police before commanding Egyptian forces in the reconquest of the Sudan.[90] To many observers, the choice of a soldier, rather than a civilian, confirmed that the liberal experiments of Gorst's tenure would not resume.[91] Fond of grand pageantry, the new consul-general made frequent appearances in towns and villages under a banner, written in both Arabic and English, that read "Welcome to Lord Kitchener, the Friend of the Fellah."[92]

Like his predecessors, Kitchener held that the fallah whose friendship he professed was the natural ally of British rule; it was in the countryside that the occupation would be secured. Holding that the peasant was motivated, above all, by his material interests, the signature policies of Cromer's tenure had sought to secure political quiescence by involving the rural population more directly in the transactions of agrarian capitalism. As Gorst had reminded his readers, the "main end" for which the Agricultural Bank had been founded was to "maintain, and if possible, increase, the peasant proprietary class, and thus create a conservative element in the country which would make for stability."[93] Following through on the reversals of the past few years, Kitchener now sought to reach that same "main end" by different means.

For the colonial conservatives who had risen to prominence in India after 1857, the consequence of a misplaced liberal universalism had been the social dislocation that culminated in rural insurgency. Leaning variously on notions of custom and race, they championed new methods of rule that would investigate and codify the established practices of the village community and thereby hold the disruptive forces of modern society at bay. Convinced that the failed experiments of recent years had confirmed the wisdom of that approach, Kitchener drew upon conservative models for a number of significant new initiatives. Holding that free and unsupervised commerce was leaving peasant cultivators exposed to fraud and deception at the hands of inland merchants, the government now assumed direct responsibility for the market itself. Beginning in 1912, a network of village markets or *halaqat* would bring the cotton trade under the supervision of state officials and ensure that current prices at Alexandria were transmitted across the countryside. As the government continued to extend its regulatory influence over cultivation, these halaqat also provided an infrastructure for the distribution of standardized seed strains and nitrate fertilizers.[94] The Ministry of Justice, meanwhile, announced plans to develop a new system of "cantonal courts" in the countryside. Like earlier measures that had conferred jurisdiction upon the village headman, these new institutions would ease the burden of low-level cases on the dockets of the National Courts. But in at least one crucial respect, the cantonal courts—which effectively relieved the ʿumdah of his judicial responsibilities—were different: a ministry-selected tribunal of three local notables would render decisions not on the basis of codified laws but rather according to "local usage."[95] In a lengthy memorandum explaining the new court system to the Council of Ministers, the Minister of Justice Hussayn Rushdi made repeated reference to the ethnographic neologism "*al-qurawiyin* [villagefolk]."[96] For three decades, the occupation had marked the distance between "British justice" and its khedivial antecedents by proclaiming that positive law would constitute the inclusive domain of what Samera Esmeir has called "juridical humanity."[97] Now, in the name of preserving and respecting "established local customs," the reorganization of the court system would exclude vast segments of the rural population from the operations of that legal universalism.[98]

The third and most famous of Kitchener's signature, conservative policies was what came to be known as the "Five Feddan Law." In this instance, the reliance on precedent from the Punjab was most obvious and explicit. At the time he published it in the 1880s, Septimus Thorburn's *Muslmans and Money-Lenders in the Punjab* was more than a mere theoretical indictment of Britain's liberal agrarian policy. Staking out a clear position in the debates about peasant indebtedness, the tract was a carefully crafted piece of political advocacy. Building upon his assessment of the dangerously unequal capacities of Muslim peasants and Hindu moneylenders, Thorburn had proposed to "make it illegal for any person deriving profits from a shop or from money-lending, to acquire any interest in arable or pasture land, other than land in the immediate vicinity of a town or large village."[99] Copies of Thorburn's text circulated widely, sparking more than a decade of deliberation about the merits of such paternalistic restrictions against the right to buy, sell, and mortgage land.[100] By the turn of the century, Thorburn's ideas had provided the basis for the piece of legislation sometimes referred to as the Magna Carta of Punjab's peasantry.[101] Drawing upon the novel taxonomies of colonial ethnography, the Punjab Alienation of Land Bill of 1900 prohibited the transfer of land from "agriculturist" to "non-agriculturist" groups.[102]

Though its legal protections would differ, Kitchener referred to "the Punjab Land Alienation Act" as the inspiration for the most famous and consequential measure of his brief stint as consul-general. Echoing the racial typologies and clichés of Thorburn's text, Kitchener explained:

> The Egyptian peasant has had from time immemorial an ingrained habit of spending more money than he can afford on ceremonies, such as marriage, &c., and moreover he willingly ruins himself in litigation rather than make terms with his adversary. These defects of character make him an easy prey to the usurer, who is always on the spot, ready to advance money on his land. The fellah,

> though I hope learning, has not yet acquired habits of thrift, and had, up to the establishment of savings banks in the villages, no secure place to keep his money. It will no doubt take a long time to change the habits of centuries. Meanwhile, the security of the cultivator's tenure required safeguarding.[103]

Although the introduction of legal protections against the usurer seems to have been Kitchener's own idea—and something of a surprise to his fellow officials at that—his pessimistic description of the spendthrift peasant was, by this point, commonplace.[104] It closely echoed the line of argument that mortgage lenders like the Agricultural Bank had been making for several years. In fact, it was the government's capitulation to those financial interests that prompted Kitchener to introduce the restriction on future loans.

Though often described as a stand-alone act, the Five Feddan Law was just one of several amendments to the procedures of the Mixed Courts passed by the Alexandria Mixed Court of Appeals. In the summer of 1912, the Alexandria Court (which exercised legislative authority over the legal codes of the Mixed Courts) altered the foreclosure rules to "render the process of seizure for debt more rapid and efficient."[105] As Kitchener described it, the Five Feddan Law was "a complement to this extension of facilities to creditors."[106] The safeguard in this instance banned the expropriation of properties of five feddans or fewer for debt. The Mixed Courts would help the banks to accelerate foreclosures on their existing loans, but court procedure would now bar the peasant's "defects of character" from making him "an easy prey to the usurer."[107] Pointing to the "conspicuous success" of its Punjabi precedent, the Judicial Adviser Malcolm McIlwraith noted that this restriction was the "corollary and complement" of the new regulations simplifying "the seizure and sale of land in general." The measure, moreover, figured into the government's "general scheme of preservation and assistance" to protect the peasantry "against the abuses of usurers and the financial oppression, at the hands of powerful creditors, to which, by reason of their ignorance and helplessness, they are continually exposed."[108]

CRISIS PROFITEERING AND THE DEMISE OF THE AGRICULTURAL BANK

Kitchener's surprise modification was not well received. An outpouring of columns in the press and letters to the Foreign Office protested that far from protecting smallholders, the Five Feddan Law would force them into the clutches of village moneylenders.

Because land that could not be seized was useless as collateral, the new restrictions would effectively bar peasants from contracting mortgages with all possible lenders whose nationality placed them under the jurisdiction of the Mixed Courts. But since the new law in no way obviated the farmer's need for credit, its critics argued, it would simply move the market for this class of loans off the books. And in contracting unregistered loans against other forms of security, those willing to conduct such business would now be free to charge interest well above the legal limit of 9%.

The Agricultural Bank made just these arguments in its correspondence with both the British Consulate in Cairo and the Foreign Office in London as its directors complained that the Five Feddan Law would force an abrupt cessation of its loans to smallholders.[109] Existing histories of the Five Feddan Law have taken the bank's protestations at face value.[110] But as should by now be clear, there is reason to suggest that the bank's directors made such claims in bad faith. The bank had already placed its own restrictions on the very sort of lending it predicted that the Five Feddan Law would render impossible. As Milne Cheetham, then counsellor of the British Consulate, put it, "with 30 per cent of its capital unemployed . . . I am accordingly inclined to think that it may be taken for granted that the detrimental effect of the new law on the interests of the Agricultural Bank has been very largely overestimated."[111]

In all likelihood, the bank's directors were perfectly aware of their own current business practices. Their complaints against the proposed legislation may have been as much an attempt to extract further concessions from the government as to defend an area of lending they had already all but abandoned. Cheetham himself signaled the Egyptian government's willingness to "consider, and, if possible, adopt or support, any practical measures" which might "assist the Agricultural Bank in putting its business on a sounder footing."[112] By March of the following year, the bank's director F. T. Rowlatt was able to report that they had reached an agreement over several such concessions aimed at "averting injury to the interest of the shareholders." The bank would receive first consideration as financier of any government programs to create new systems of agricultural credit. The government raised the upper limits on loans the bank could make, though the village tax collectors would continue to service those loans free of charge. Finally, the bank won permission to employ its surplus funds in "approved securities, or in the manner which approaches nearest to the original object of the bank, vis: in loans on first mortgage of land in Egypt."[113]

The Agricultural Bank's directors wasted little time in turning this last point to their advantage. The earliest phases of the 1907 crisis had frozen access to credit across the country. In that climate of extreme caution, several enterprising businesses had seen a rare opportunity. Recognizing that the sudden contraction of supply had driven up the price of money, the French Crédit Foncier was the first to act and thereby won accolades as a valiant savior of Egypt's financial markets in the face of government inertia.[114] Inspired by the Crédit Foncier's discovery that they could now contract mortgages at much higher rates of interest, a group of British financiers and veteran officials from the occupation launched their own new venture in October 1908, the Mortgage Company of Egypt. Viscount Milner served as chair, and the board included William Garstin, Cromer's brother Everard Baring, and several other former British advisers to the Egyptian Ministry of Public Works. Lord Cromer himself offered the strength of his own reputation to the new company by serving as one of two trustees for successive issues of debentures.[115] By Milner's description, the company adopted a "very cautious policy," investing only in first mortgages against large estates deemed "first-rate security." Credit was in such sort supply that the company had little difficulty placing its first million pounds. Following on this initial success, they raised another million pounds through preference shares in 1909, a third million in mortgage debentures in 1910, and an additional £750,000 in 1911.[116]

Only by the most peculiar convolutions of language could this company lending at inflated rates of interest to Egypt's wealthiest landlords be described as functioning in a manner that "approaches nearest to the original object" of the Agricultural Bank. Nevertheless, it was to the Mortgage Company of Egypt that the Agricultural Bank turned upon securing the right to reinvest its surplus capital. In July 1913, the Agricultural Bank advanced the company £380,000 against a bundle of existing mortgages bearing interest at 6%.[117] In an added ironic twist, it was the foremost champion of the Agricultural Bank, Lord Cromer himself, who had to approve this final step away from the business of lending to smallholders.[118] As one of the two trustees of the Mortgage Company's debentures, Cromer authorized the first of what became a series of major capital investments by the Agricultural Bank. Later that same year, the two businesses cemented their new relationship when the Agricultural Bank, with approval from the Egyptian government, purchased 97% of the Mortgage Company's ordinary shares for just over £400,800.[119] The following March, the Agricultural Bank made yet another loan of £140,000.[120] A company established and managed by former officials of the British occupation thereby oversaw the dismantling of an institution those same figures had once promoted as the most distinctive achievement of the veiled protectorate's agrarian reforms.

CONCLUSION

Colonial economism was, at its core, a discourse of and for Egyptian smallholders. While it glossed over finer gradations of class among Egypt's poorest landowners and largely overlooked the growing population of peasants who possessed no land at all, the occupation's program of economic development before 1910 was aimed specifically at advancing the position of "small proprietors."[121] To be sure, the British never contemplated policies of state-led redistribution. At its most ambitious, this colonial development regime would render peasants prosperous by drawing them into legal institutions and commercial practices—complete freedom to allocate their own labor and that of their families, improved rights to landed property, civil litigation under standardized legal codes, mortgage credit from corporate banks—to which their wealthier counterparts already had access. In the early years of the occupation, British officials were, moreover, quite explicit about the ways in which the landed elite, as the prime beneficiaries of so-called Oriental despotism, might represent not the allies but the foremost adversaries of agrarian reform. That British rule served to exacerbate forms of inequality it was supposed to correct was, in this period, not just the effect of colonial designs but also of a failure to recognize the myriad ways in which class distinctions figured into the very mundane transactions of the free market that the occupation aimed to promote. Nowhere was this more true than for Egypt's burgeoning financial sector, within which both the availability and the cost of credit were calibrated according to the lenders' own designations of class.

When the outcomes of their development schemes began to diverge more and more catastrophically from the future their own political-economic dogma had conjured, British officials made recourse to a supplementary theory of racial anomaly to account for the discrepancies. It was at this point, amidst a multiform crisis of financial contraction and agro-ecological degradation, that the occupation abandoned its earlier confidence in the economic potential of the smallholding peasantry and began to adopt policies that more actively favored wealthy landlords as the social agents capable of reviving agricultural production. This colonial restatement would have at least three important implications for the political struggles of the years leading up to the outbreak of World War I. First, although it entailed a renunciation of earlier hypotheses about the peasant's ability to recognize and act upon his own material interests, the occupation's conservative turn did not represent a total break with the economism of that earlier moment. It is better understood as a kind of colonial economism in a minor key. That is, the political quiescence of Egyptian peasants might not be a reliable function of economic prosperity, but material deprivation would still render them more susceptible to all manner of fanaticism and demagoguery. In this respect, the occupation's new conservatism was every bit as antipolitical as the theory of colonial society that it replaced. Second, at least according to its own self-description, the new conservative strategy of rule renounced any serious effort to reform or educate a peasantry it deemed unequipped to navigate the hazards and vicissitudes of a modern capitalist society. The state's increasingly minute interventions into the everyday practices of the farm were thus explained as exceptional correctives to a deficient human subject who could not reliably internalize habits of self-discipline.[122] From this perspective, the growing preoccupation of prewar nationalists with new technologies and institutions of mass subject formation might be understood less as a derivative replication of colonial practices than an appeal to forms of governmentality that were conspicuous by their absence and that, howsoever problematically, appeared to represent viable alternatives to the colonial state's own coercive excess. Finally, although these altered conditions may have favored the large landholding class in objective terms, the forms of foreign profiteering that accompanied the government's belated response to the crisis were no secret. Public awareness of the ways in which even the country's wealthiest proprietors were themselves the objects of exploitation left available the plausibility of arguments that foregrounded class relations between countries rather than within them. That tension would loom ever-larger in the competing imaginaries of economic nationalism that distinguished the years immediately prior to the outbreak of war.

Chapter 8

THE MATERIAL OCCUPATION

"IF THAT MEMORABLE DAY should arrive when the English and their soldiers depart from this country, they will leave behind their appendages in the form of the companies that own the land." Writing for *Misr al-Fatah* in September 1909, the columnist Abu Bakr Lutfi offered his compatriots a grave warning: Egypt had been occupied not once but twice. After imposing "the political occupation" by superior force of arms, the British had prepared the way for a second and more insidious "material occupation." If Egyptians might be forgiven the former calamity, because "the weak will necessarily fall before the powerful," they could make no such excuse for the latter. In the dire exigencies of the current moment, Lutfi saw both reason and possibility for action.[1]

Gone from this account was any pretense that British rule had made the country prosper. Lutfi now described Egypt's condition as an illness that might "become chronic so that no treatment or remedy will help." The British had opened the country to foreign interests that acted "like leeches upon the bodies of the Egyptians, taking without giving anything back."[2] No institution had fulfilled that role more faithfully than the Agricultural Bank. Alerting his readers to the 26,000 foreclosure cases it had recently brought before Mixed Courts, Lutfi denounced the bank as an instrument of national dispossession. Having enticed Egypt's smallholders to borrow beyond their means, the Agricultural Bank was empowered to seize their land and sell it off to other foreign companies. The country's wealthier proprietors had hardly fared better. The day would thus soon arrive when "the people become, like the inhabitants of Ireland, mere laborers on their own land, which is owned by the wealthy of England." Were that process to run its course, the achievement of political independence would do little to counteract the country's subordination to foreign capital.[3]

Against this grim assessment, Lutfi held out the promise of an alternative future. The power to combat the material occupation remained in the hands of Egyptians themselves. At the moment he was writing, other supporters of the National Party continued to hold rallies, to plan for anticolonial solidarity with the peoples of other nations, and to call for mass struggle against British rule.[4] Lutfi's proposal was comparatively modest and hardly revolutionary. Indeed, he listed among the potential dangers of the material occupation the spread of "socialism [*al-ishtirakiyah*]," which might "become a local disease so long as the wealth of the country accumulates in the hands of [a few] individuals when once it was in the hands of the many." To forestall that eventuality, he offered two practical suggestions. First, he urged "the wealthy of each province" to establish a company for purchasing lands that the banks were putting up for auction. They could thereby block the transfer of property to foreign owners. Second, he called upon those same wealthy Egyptians to implement 'Umar Bey Lutfi's proposal for a national bank. By establishing an alternative source of credit, they would "preserve the wealth of the country inside the country [*tharwat al-bilad fi al-bilad*]."[5]

In its very simplicity, this call to defend "the wealth of the country inside the country" exemplified both the critical force and the looming contradictions of the economic program that became the foremost priority of the Egyptian nationalist movement by the early 1910s. In the opening pages of his immensely influential essay *Imagined Communities*, Benedict Anderson once suggested that it would be "easier" to treat nationalism "as if it belonged with 'kinship' and 'religion' rather than with 'liberalism' or 'fascism.' "[6] In building the case for the nationally scaled institutions they envisioned, Abu Bakr Lutfi and his contemporaries argued just the reverse. As opposition to British rule in Egypt continued to coalesce around a more specific demand for national independence, its leading proponents sought to locate—or rather triangulate—their nationalism in relation to the other major ideological currents of their times. In the years immediately prior to World War I, writers such as ʿUmar Bey Lutfi, Yusuf Nahhas, Muhammad Talʿat Harb, Muhammad Zaki ʿAli, and ʿAbd al-Rahman al-Rafiʿi articulated a position that was antifinancial, antiliberal, and anti-imperialist but not anticapitalist.

Through their articles, speeches, and book-length studies, these thinkers developed a robust and nuanced critique of the occupation that drew widely on ideas and insights that the nationalist movement, in all its diversity, had nurtured through the long aftermath of 1907. In three crucial respects, this corpus of nationalist thought offered a powerful rejoinder to the discourse of colonial economism. First, as Abu Bakr Lutfi's title begins to indicate, these figures rejected as profoundly misleading the notion that the economic and the political existed in practice as insular and separate domains. The history of British rule as they narrated it was an object lesson in the power of political institutions to organize economic practice in particular ways and in service of particular interests. In the nation–state they saw the vehicle not for enforcing a separation they deemed illusory but for rearranging the entanglements between the economic and the political toward different ends.

Second, they rejected the "synchronic essentialism" that was so glaring and persistent a feature of the occupation's assertions about Egyptian society.[7] As many other studies have noted, Egyptian nationalists in this moment were captivated by questions of subject formation.[8] But their desire to shift the coordinates of selfhood was not simply a "derivative" effort to lay claim to the disciplinary apparatus of a colonized state.[9] When nationalists insisted that Egyptians, like all other people, were malleable subjects, they were responding to decades of British statements that attributed problems in the historical present to timeless defects of fixed racial types. From this perspective, the narrowly self-interested individual around whom the British had crafted their policies was not who Egyptians had been in the past or needed to be in the future so much as what the occupation had caused them to become.[10]

Third, building on arguments that had first gained prominence during the financial crisis, these thinkers directly challenged liberal notions of the economic as the primary locus of freedom. Previous studies of what is sometimes called economic nationalism have approached its leading advocates as the historical progenitors of a developmentalist agenda that would only come to fruition decades later, in the 1950s and 1960s. On this understanding, their main grievance was Egypt's status as an "agricultural country," and their chief objective was to rectify an uneven global division of labor by promoting industrial enterprise.[11] It is certainly true that Muhammad Tal'at Harb and others advocated for economic diversification and the establishment of new industries on Egyptian soil. But this focus on industrialization misconstrues the fundamental problem that they sought to address. By the early 1910s, growing numbers of Egyptians had come to see the occupation not simply as a problem of control over government institutions but rather as a more complex condition in which forms of political and economic domination had become densely interwoven. Not by accident did many Egyptian authors in these years refer to the country's status as one of slavery or servitude. Training their sights on the malign imbrication between foreign finance and foreign rule, they skewered the occupation's response to the ravages of crisis as both inadequate and self-serving. Whether at the level of the individual or the country as a whole, they identified the existing mechanisms of foreign lending as both structurally necessary and necessarily destructive. On the first count, a long history of imperial exploitation had ensured that most Egyptians could no longer sustain their own livelihoods without regular access to credit. On the second, so long as those debts continued to accrue, they would leave Egypt's producing classes both poorer and more susceptible to forms of global volatility they could not control.

As the radical energies of the protest movement just a few years prior had shown, this critical diagnosis of the country's condition could point in more than one direction. Those who had taken part in the marches, demonstrations, and strikes had also spoken in a language of self-government and national independence. That the leaders of Egypt's major nationalist organizations now signaled a shift in priorities was, in part, the result of changing circumstances. To some degree, their emphasis on the establishment of financial institutions funded with Egyptian capital reflected a narrowing of horizons for direct political mobilization after the British crackdown of 1910. But those new strictures, on their own, explain little about the signature proposals that animated the nationalist movement in these years or the aspirations that attached to them.

In assessing their present predicament, nationalist thinkers suggested, often through metaphors of servitude, that economism had become something more than a problem of thought and discourse. Many observed that Egyptians really did seem to have become grasping individuals bent on personal gain. But they also argued that these behaviors were the consequence neither of racial defects nor of limited capacity to imagine other ways of living together. If they acted like the "eminently materialist" subjects British officials had long accused them of being, it was because the social relations that the occupation had introduced left them less and less free to do otherwise. At times, this line of analysis approached a critique of capitalism as a form of life in which the generalized practices and transactions that allowed ordinary people to sustain their everyday existence contributed to their own conditions of domination. It was this peculiar kind of unfreedom that Marx famously referred to as "the fetishism of the commodity." His concern was not simply that people lacked a clear understanding of how their society really worked but that arriving at such an understanding would, on its own, make little difference.[12] The problem was precisely that of a "society that does not require its own truth to be known."[13]

The figures covered in this final chapter were not reading Marx, nor would they have been sympathetic to his political project if they had been. On the contrary, they were frequently explicit about their desire to avoid the revolutionary future that socialists elsewhere hoped to bring about. At their most incisive, however, they were grappling with a version of the problem that this much-debated section of *Capital* raises. In the vicissitudes of commodity markets and financial flows, they too discerned a form of social power that now operated "independently of the will, foreknowledge, and actions" of specific individuals or political institutions.[14] Economistic behavior, so understood, was neither a universal feature of all societies nor the innate defect of discrete races or peoples. It was a symptom of historically specific ways of organizing social life.

The object of their economic nationalism, in this sense, was not development or growth but freedom, freedom from the hazard, uncertainty, and exploitation they now associated with their colonial condition. But whereas the socialists from whom they distanced themselves identified such abstract forms of social domination with capital in general, these Egyptian nationalists located the source of the problems they sought to address in the particular distortions of British rule. The result was not a critique of capitalism as such so much as an effort to rescale capital accumulation inside the territory of the nation–state. This was the other side of the coin, so to speak. The trajectory of national independence that many of these figures envisioned would preserve existing hierarchies—of class, gender, and religious affiliation—and assign managerial authority to a small, self-described elite. The case for the nation–state, as they argued it, all too often became a means of denigrating struggles over other structures of power as inimical to the needs of the Egyptian public as a whole. And in linking their current predicament mainly to the disruptive and disempowering effects of foreign finance, they actively endorsed the continued production of cotton for sale on the world market as a necessary precondition for any greater program of economic sovereignty. The upshot was a persistent, almost willful, confidence in the power of national capital and national institutions to resolve the devastating contradictions they themselves so forcefully denounced in their own current situation.

PEACEFUL WARS

By the autumn of 1909, when *Misr al-Fatah* published "The Material Occupation," the article's take on Egypt's economic malady was widely shared among those who identified with the nationalist movement. But the strategic agenda Abu Bakr Lutfi laid out was not. Earlier that spring a member of the Society for Islamic Progress had dismissed the current fixation with political independence and constitutionalism as mere "talk and tumult," insisting that only greater economic autonomy would prepare the way for an end to British rule. To thunderous applause, a series of other speakers at that gathering had shouted him down. They pointed out that British control of the government had so far scuttled nationalist efforts to found independent institutions, be they schools or factories. They urged the crowd to "shut your ears" against anyone who sought to minimize the urgency of direct political action.[15]

By the following spring, however, the British crackdown was beginning to take its toll. A more aggressive police presence made protests and demonstrations harder to sustain. Application of the revived press law had led to suspensions for several papers. And the threat of prison time or exile had caused even the most outspoken nationalist leaders to adopt a more circumspect tone.[16] Nor was the sense of caution misplaced. Throughout the month of May 1910, Eldon Gorst maintained an almost obsessive correspondence with the Foreign Office about the possibility of seizing and deporting ʿAbd al-ʿAziz Jawish.[17] Although the Watanist editor and organizer was likely unaware of these plans, he had already served time in prison for writings the occupation judged incendiary, and he had become a frequent target of public broadsides in the *Egyptian Gazette*.[18]

The question of a nationalist strategy appropriate to this new climate of repression loomed large in the pages of the daily *al-ʿAlam* throughout the summer of 1910. The paper itself was a testament to those more challenging times. A rift within the National Party following Mustafa Kamil's death had widened until, in March of 1910, Muhammad Farid and Jawish had decided to abandon *al-Liwaʾ* as their official organ and open a new paper.[19] Within days of publishing its first issue, *al-ʿAlam* earned its first suspension under the revived press law.[20] On May 26, a week after publication resumed, Jawish ran a sprawling front-page editorial under the oxymoronic title, "Peaceful Wars [*al-hurub al-silmiyah*]."[21] A note scrawled in English across the translation that reached the Foreign Office read simply: "Suggests boycott of British goods as way to Independence."[22] The vertiginous survey of an eventful global present that Jawish laid out was considerably more ambitious than that summary might suggest.

As the British continued to brandish their coercive tactics, Jawish counseled his readers that "their being deprived of military forces does not prevent [the Egyptians] from gaining all that they desire by peaceful means without requiring the destruction of lives and the tainting of the earth with human blood." He conceded that the occupation enjoyed a superior force of arms. The task he set himself was to demonstrate that such existing asymmetries could still be overturned and that Egyptians might draw hope and inspiration from the new solidarities that were forming all around them. Throughout his long career, Jawish would develop an interpretation of Islam that emphasized its potential to guide a radical egalitarian politics.[23] Gesturing at that larger thesis, he opened by noting that Islam had delivered a message that all people are equal "in their earthly human rights and their other-worldly obligations" centuries before the oppressed (*al-mustadaʿfun*) of Europe started to see that they could become "a formidable force." The struggles waged by "the peasant, the servant, the cook, the worker" against the wealthy and the powerful, he suggested, had no uniquely European provenance. It was only much more recently that the working classes of "the Western countries" had recognized "that they are a force not to be trifled with." Their accomplishments, however, could now furnish an example for others. By "strengthening the bond of union [*ʿaqd al-ittihad*] among the masses and establishing economic syndicates and savings funds so that they might have something to rely upon on the day the capitalists wage war against them," the workers of Europe had "won a victory that raised their status from humiliation and . . . allowed them to combat the wealthy."[24]

Jawish at this point made a familiar transposition. He observed that the "peaceful wars" waged by workers against capitalists had become a model for the struggles of "weak or oppressed nations [*al-umam al-daʿifah aww al-mustadaʿfah*]" against the empires that ruled them. As countless others had done in recent years, he thus suggested that class relations within countries and colonial relations between them represented meaningfully comparable forms of inequality. His choice of language here was significant. While Jawish mentioned numerous instances of economic exploitation, the operative binary that organized his survey of recent events was not that between the rich and the poor but rather between the powerful and the weak. He thus implied that "economic affairs" were at once an expression of and a mechanism for a more general distribution of social power. In the aftermath of the 1907 crisis, nationalist critics had frequently detailed how the British instrumentalized political control to secure the extraction of Egyptian wealth. Jawish now swung that analysis around to show how the entanglements between political and economic occupation might be deployed against "the party of the colonizers like Lord Cromer and Sir Grey."[25]

After briefly enumerating various tactics by which weaker groups had discovered new strength by banding together, Jawish turned his attention to the boycott movements that had taken on the great imperial powers of the moment. "We still hear the reverberations," he declared, "of that war the peoples of China launched against American merchants, for it put a stop to the profits of their trade and brought many of their financial houses to bankruptcy."[26] He likewise praised the Ottoman boycott of Austrian goods following the annexation of Bosnia-Herzegovina in October 1908.[27] But it was India's Swadeshi movement that Jawish held up as the finest and most significant exemplar of this new phenomenon. "Does a day ever pass," he asked, "when we do not hear about that faithful determination and pure, true patriotism that has compelled the Hindus to stand resolute in their intention to boycott English commerce?"[28]

Although at least some of its practitioners understood Swadeshi as a movement for native industries, it was not this developmentalist agenda that drew Jawish's attention. Instead, he emphasized two other features of the Indian experience. First, a boycott on such a large scale, he claimed, had already contributed to the closure of "a number of important factories in Manchester."[29] If the boycott were to continue, he averred, it would bring the die-hard proponents of colonial rule into conflict with both "the English nation itself" and "the masters of great financial interests among the English." The latter, in turn, would see Indian independence as commensurate with their own material well-being. That day of victory might be near or distant, but in either case, the movement's success would hang on the ability of the Indian people to maintain "a fixed will and a powerful heart" against the pressures and temptations of the market. It was precisely the way the boycott had come to permeate everyday thought and practice that Jawish identified as the second reason for his admiration. He observed with amazement, "We see the great philosophers, doctors, and holders of high degrees wearing rough Indian fabric, believing that beautification lies in the total avoidance of anything such as fine silk garments or pretty robes made in England."[30]

In alighting upon what Manu Goswami has described as the "broad socioaesthetic complex" of the Swadeshi movement, Jawish located concrete evidence for what was fast becoming a central contention of nationalist thought in these years: namely, that the monadic, self-interested individual posited by classical political economy was not a fixed and natural fact of human existence but a product of specific sociohistorical conditions.[31] By the summer of 1910, British officials were beating a hasty retreat from their own earlier claims about Egyptians as economic subjects. But as Jawish and others were well aware, their revised outlook still rested on the attribution of an immutable racial essence. What the mass adoption of Swadeshi practice offered, by contrast, was confirmation that the characteristics of selfhood organizing the most basic transactions of social existence were historically mutable.[32]

A consummate organizer and an unrelenting strategist, Jawish delivered these comparisons as an optimistic testament to the possibilities of an uncertain moment. By one reading, the capacious binary division between the weak and the strong pointed toward the most radical implications of the "peaceful wars" he advocated. In discovering the sources of their own power, the "oppressed [*mustadaʿfun*]"—or more literally "deemed weak"—might forge new bonds of solidarity and gain the strength to fashion a more equal world. True to his earlier support for mass mobilization, Jawish continued to stress the horizontalist character of tactics that relied on the collective efforts of ordinary people. But even here, in his eagerness to recover the energies of a popular militancy he had long encouraged, Jawish left unresolved several fundamental ambiguities that could describe a rather different mode of anticolonial politics. First, although he cast the practice of boycott as a continuation of earlier struggles, his text could be read as a retreat from direct demands for independence and political representation to a more mild adoption of economic pressure tactics. Second, notwithstanding Jawish's prominent role in the labor movement, his article was vague at best about how anticolonial struggles between nations might relate, in practice, to class struggles within them. His excitement about the role of Indian elites in the Swadeshi movement might suggest a kind of wishful confidence in the power of national unity to transcend other divisions of status and class. Third, Jawish's refusal of the occupation's racial typologies and essentialist claims rested on an insistently historical sensibility; what British officials attributed to an unchanging and defective human nature, he recast as the pernicious consequences of colonial rule. But the very intensity of that anticolonial critique could easily lead toward a uni-causal understanding of social and political conflicts. Not only did that outlook leave him ambivalent about the future of class-based solidarities. It could also spur a dismissal of other differences and struggles within the imagined national public as the mere effects of colonial divide-and-rule strategies.[33]

THE MEANS OF INDEPENDENCE

If these tensions remained unresolved in Jawish's own writings, by the summer of 1910 the National Party's commitments to practices of mass protest and popular self-representation were giving way, even in the pages of *al-'Alam*, to a new center of gravity. The government's repressive measures, the dire condition of the cotton crop, and the ongoing effects of the financial crisis all provided fodder for the case against British rule. Day after day, columnists in *al-'Alam* lambasted the occupation as a form of government that had ruined the land and impoverished its people. In the heady fervor of the protest movement, Jawish and others had leveraged a similar critique of imperial rule from the standpoint of Egypt's producing classes to open new avenues for political participation by the people themselves. Now, as they continued to refine a systematic rebuttal to the occupation's analysis of Egypt's deepening woes, these authors advanced a vision of national improvement that was decidedly more managerial and elitist in character.

At a moment when the occupation's regulatory ambitions still remained uncertain, one prominent line of argument continued to develop the association between self-rule and a strong interventionist state that had earlier motivated the nationalists' peculiar, and ultimately misguided, adulation for Theodore Roosevelt.[34] What tentative steps the occupation had taken to address the disruption of credit or the decline in cotton yields were, from this perspective, both insufficient and self-serving. Although the government had announced plans to establish the new Department of Agriculture in April 1910, some described that choice as a half measure. In a series of full-page articles on "The Works of the Occupiers in Egypt," the unnamed financial correspondent for *al-'Alam* laid blame for the deterioration of the cotton crop at the hands of the government's British advisers.[35] Far from helping Egypt to advance "the quality and abundance of its crops," they had watched yields fall and "taken no measures to stop this sickness from leading to ruin." Although "mortgage debts have risen on most properties to an alarming degree," they had likewise done nothing to reverse that trend.[36] The papers of the National Party had "always devoted several pages each week to financial and economic questions" and "paid great attention to the condition of the *fallah*." Their warnings about the coming danger had been met with "dereliction, ignorance, and waste" by a colonial regime bent on "driving the peasant toward danger, poverty, and insolvency."[37] Here, then, was the answer to the occupation's rhetorical question, "What does a constitution matter to the *fallah*?"[38] The issue, so framed, was not simply one of direct political participation. Rather, in forcing the transition from "absolute and irresponsible government to an orderly government that assumes the burden of every decision it makes," the constitution that Egyptians demanded would empower them at last to use state institutions to rectify Britain's disastrous attitude of malign neglect.[39]

Delineating the material promise of the nation-state was one thing, however, and arriving at that desideratum was another. In the same weeks as *al-'Alam* published "The Works of the Occupiers," the paper ran a second serialized column by the lawyer Muhammad Zaki 'Ali entitled "The Means of Independence: Men and Money."[40] Zaki 'Ali described his articles as pieces of a map, guiding his compatriots along "the routes they must follow to reach that ultimate goal."[41] In his opening installment, he explained that "the occupation from which we suffer is not [only] those soldiers who reside in the barracks and strut about in the streets. Rather, the occupation is that mental force that oppresses the minds of Egyptians such that ignorance or cowardice causes them to forget their true status and their natural rights."[42] Unsurprisingly, this interpretation of colonial rule as a subjective condition led toward some familiar arguments about the importance of educating a national public. But this critique of the country's colonized mentality also figured prominently in a subsequent analysis of economic affairs.

Like the author of "The Material Occupation," Zaki ʿAli warned against the steady transfer of landed property such that "the independence of the country has become threatened at all times by the danger of foreign interests." The root cause of this problem, however, was neither poverty nor inequality, "for the country is rich by its nature and its wealth is distributed among nearly all its children." The issue instead was an attitude of miserliness, "a love for money and a tendency to hoard it in the ground and a fear about using it for purposes of investment [*al-istithmar*] that require some courage and trust and hope in the future."[43] What followed was an idiosyncratic plea for the productive employment of Egypt's idle riches as national capital. Addressing himself to "the wealthy [*al-aghniya'*]," Zaki ʿAli stressed a contrast between charitable contributions through the Islamic institution of *waqf* and investment in businesses and enterprises that would increase and protect the wealth of the country. It was by educating the poor for work and creating opportunities for their employment, not by wasting their money on unproductive endowments, he argued, that those of means would realize God's will. The highest service they could render would be to "work in commerce and industry" so that "according to the laws of economy the wealth of the nation might derive from multiple sources."[44]

While Zaki ʿAli seemed here to propose a kind of voluntaristic moralism as an adequate solution to the problem of economic development, his very next article in the series provided a rather different explanation for the country's current condition. Surveying the decades prior to 1882, he saw ample evidence of thriving commerce and rising industries. In this recent past, the miserly hoarding of money was nowhere to be found. That his own present looked so utterly different was a result of the occupation's concerted efforts to "obstruct and destroy" the progress prior generations had achieved. It was in light of that "colonial objective [*gharad istiʿmari*]" that the past thirty years should be understood. "All that the English do under the pretext of enriching and benefiting the country," he explained, "in truth they do to confine the Egyptians to agriculture so that trade should be in the hands of others, and the English in particular."[45]

Most basic to this assessment was an identification of British rule with narrowly British interests, interests that now appeared to diverge from those of the Egyptian public. By pursuing that agenda, the "colonial" government was responsible for "undermining Egypt's independence through foreign financial interests" and "rendering the wealth of the country dependent upon a single source."[46] Given the recent tribulations of Egyptian agriculture, "that narrow domain surrounded by danger and destruction," the only sensible solution was a process of diversification "meaning that Egyptians should work in trade and industry."[47] He went so far as to suggest that Egypt might adopt a system of tariffs to protect fledgling industrial ventures. The point, he noted, was not that Egyptians should work in commerce and industry and "neglect agriculture." Rather, he proposed the return of a balanced economy in which "division of the power of productive labor" might better protect Egyptians against the kinds of losses that a single "plague [*afah*]" would currently bring. In time, the promotion of commerce and industry might address the wild economic distortions of a country in which "attention is limited to agriculture alone and . . . people flock to purchase agricultural land even if its price has become ten times what it was in prior times."[48]

Rather than an end in itself, the diversification of productive activity represented just one component of a larger program to rectify both the manifest precariousness of everyday life and the powers of foreign finance that now seemed to constrain Egyptians at every turn. The problem, as he explained it, was that in their mundane reliance on existing sources of credit, ordinary Egyptians reinforced their own conditions of dependency and domination. "Do you not see," Zaki 'Ali asked, "that if there were a national bank [*masraf watani*] in this country to provide for the wants of the needy, then the properties of Egyptians would not slip into the hands of foreigners, and the independence of the country would not be threatened always by the danger of foreign interests?"[49] Whereas the occupation's pessimistic verdict on its recent experiments now attributed both the ravages of the cotton worm and the high incidence of smallholder defaults to the innate defects of peasant mentality, Zaki 'Ali interpreted these repeated shocks as symptomatic of the structural deformations that British rule had imposed. He did not deny that the routine practices of Egyptian farmers might be contributing to these problems. But his insistence that the occupation had become as much a subjective as an objective condition was plainly at odds with the colonial regime's ahistorical racial typologies. For Egyptians concerned to achieve a lasting independence, their challenge lay in establishing a complex of new institutions that might counteract the historical effects of British rule upon men and money alike.

FROM GILDED SPEECH TO GILDED RIVER

As several leading figures of the nationalist movement acknowledged at the time, the decision to emphasize a new program of economic ventures was, in part, a matter of self-conscious strategy. In a letter to the enthusiastic young lawyer and journalist ʿAbd al-Rahman al-Rafiʿi, Muhammd Farid conceded, " 'If fear of those in power has come to restrain many from demonstrating their patriotic feelings, then what is stopping them from directing their attention toward economic projects?' "[50] But the authors and promoters of those "economic projects" did more than simply reorder the steps that the nation would need to follow on its journey toward independence. They articulated a distinctive vision of what that independent future would look like. As they continued to refine a critique of Egypt's relation to foreign finance as a form of collective slavery, they simultaneously advanced the formation of national capital as the overarching mission to which all Egyptians would need to contribute.

The contradictory implications of that shift were fully on display at the Egyptian Conference held in the new Cairo suburb of Heliopolis between April 29 and May 3, 1911. The gathering was originally conceived in response to the Coptic Congress held two months earlier in the Upper-Egyptian city of Asyut. Citing their increasing marginalization within the nationalist movement and Egyptian society more broadly, the participants in the congress advocated a range of platforms to address their position as a minority community in Egypt. These included separate representation for Copts on the provincial councils, government funding for Coptic schools, strict meritocracy in civil service appointments, and the closure of government offices and schools on Sundays.[51] In response, the opening sessions of the Egyptian Conference entailed a thoroughgoing, and often unabashedly chauvinistic, rejection of those proposals. In his report on the proceedings at Heliopolis, Milne Cheetham noted, "The views expressed were on the whole distinctly moderate in tone, though, as was to be expected, uncompromisingly antagonistic to real or supposed Coptic claims."[52] In this context, the choice to devote much of the latter of half of the conference to speeches and reports concerning economic conditions took on a rather ambivalent meaning. Following repeated denunciations of the Coptic Conference as, at best, a naïve embrace of divisive, foreign ideas and, at worst, a sign of collaboration with the British, the nationalist luminaries who rose to speak in the later sessions of the gathering insinuated—and in a few cases asserted directly—that an objective analysis of their economic interests would reveal the common plight of all Egyptians regardless of sect or creed. They thereby suggested that the existing social divisions that the delegates of the Coptic Congress, among others, wished to enshrine in new legal protections were superficial effects of a more foundational colonial condition that their economic programs would rectify.

This was the nub of the commentary with which Yusuf Nahhas began his "Report on Egypt's Economic and Financial Situation" for the conference. "It saddens me," he remarked, "to see so many of our efforts wasted on matters of little importance or on controversies that, if they were not wholly barren, produced dissension and estrangement among the children of a single nation [*abna' al-watan al-wahid*]."[53] Himself the son of a Syrian Christian immigrant who had amassed considerable landholdings in the Delta, Nahhas was the first Egyptian to receive a doctorate in economics.[54] The body of his report combined a withering indictment of colonial wealth extraction with a characteristic assurance in the power of national economic institutions to overcome the social cleavages that marred Egyptian society in the present.

Where Ahmad Hilmi had once decried the occupation's "gilded speech," Nahhas now pointed to "the gilded river [*al-nahr al-dhahabi*] that flows without interruption from Egypt to Europe."[55] In place of the famed prosperity that had once posed such a formidable obstacle to critics of the occupation, Nahhas now elaborated his own drain of wealth thesis. The primary mechanism of that drain, in his account, was the interest on both Egypt's private mortgage loans and the government's public debt, an annual financial burden the he placed at £E 4 million in the former case and £E 3.5 million in the latter. This "huge sum that annually exits our pockets, crosses the sea, and finds its way into the clutches of the creditors" was all the more striking given that "the system of mortgage credit did not exist in Egypt until thirty years ago and did not begin to play a significant role until a mere ten years ago."[56] Decrying a general failure to stanch the outward flow of capital, he asked, "Is this atrocious neglect of ours what will lead us to freedom and independence?"[57]

The debt default of 1876 ought to have delivered a clear lesson, but "shockingly, that experience ran its course, and we took no warning from it." Instead, he continued, "we have become dependents [*tabi'in*] upon Europe, which has placed its money among us at rates that are very pleasing to it and has assigned to itself the fixed right over us that every creditor has over the security of his loan." Those financial obligations had become "a means to our subjugation [*wasilatan li-ikhda'ina*], a subjugation that contradicts our national dignity."[58] Like Zaki 'Ali, he recognized the cost and danger of the country's reliance on a single export crop and advocated for diversification, but his chief concern was the overall burden of financial claims upon the value of the goods Egyptians produced. In the independent nation he envisioned, agricultural exports would likely remain the primary source of Egypt's wealth. The aim of a national economic policy, in these terms, was to promote the expanded production of commodities for export and ensure that the money they earned would remain within the country.

For Nahhas, "the latest crisis" had thrown the country's subservience to foreign creditors into sharp relief. As the crisis intensified, "we raged against England because she did not send us much gold, and we strung garlands of praise for France because she provided the Crédit Foncier with four million pounds."[59] Berating his compatriots for their credulity, Nahhas drew a rather different lesson from the French bank's decision to recommence its mortgage lending operations in 1908. "All those who came knocking at the Crédit Foncier," he continued, "were forced to accept the higher rate of interest inasmuch as no loans were given below 7%."[60] What others mistook for foreign assistance, he explained, was little more than a strategy to make Egyptians pay more dearly for their own misfortunes.

If this "subjugation" could not be rectified overnight, Egyptians could still take concrete steps toward the country's political-economic liberation. Nahhas here added the imprimatur of his economic expertise to the paired proposals that nationalists had been championing for some time. First, he advocated "our abstention from the misuse of credit" through the promotion of financial cooperation and the establishment of agricultural syndicates. Second, to avert "the general danger of extending our hand for foreign monies with no reflection or foresight," he called for the creation of "national banks for lending [*masarif wataniyah li-l-taslif*]."[61] Cooperative credit would do more than provide an alternative to the heavy burden of interest payments. Village syndicates would "engender strong solidarity among farmers, elevate their ambitions, and advance their condition both morally and materially."[62] As for the new bank, its "capital should be purely national [*wataniyan sirfan*], and its upper administration should be exclusively Egyptian." Only in this way, by freeing "the price of money" from its status as "a slavish dependent servant

[*ʿabdan tabiʿan raqiqan*] to the bank rate in Paris and London," could capital serve "the advancement of Egypt's economic condition."[63]

Nahhas was circumspect in his criticism of the British occupation, often resorting to a vague language of "us" and "them."[64] He nevertheless commented throughout the report on how a mere three decades had altered the very character of the Egyptian people. He judged "the decay of the morals of the mass of the nation" as the "most dangerous" of the many afflictions that a new "habit of mortgaging our properties" had visited upon the country. This new kind of credit had rendered the fallah "agitated, inclined towards disputes."[65] He moreover chastised "the elite of the nation [*safwat al-qawm*]," among whom he included himself, for "paving the way to the latest crisis, which has spread misery and ruin upon the throngs of the weak." The peasants who had "fallen prey to the ravenous usurers" would have every right to "scream in the faces of the wealthy" for leaving them helpless against the onslaught of rapacious lenders.[66]

At both ends of a social hierarchy he seemed disinclined to challenge, Nahhas saw the generalized pursuit of self-interest as threatening to Egypt's independence, social cohesion, and material advancement. Far from idealizing the atomistic individual of classical political economy, he expressed hope that the paired institutions of agricultural syndicates and a national bank would contribute to "the quality of union and solidarity" that the country seemed currently to lack.[67] The position he took up, however, was decidedly less egalitarian or revolutionary than the conceptions of "union and solidarity" that had animated the wave of strikes and protests just two years beforehand. For Nahhas, like many other delegates at the conference, the nation–state seemed to represent a moderate third way between the corrosive, individualism that British rule had so disastrously promoted and the specter of socialism that loomed ever larger as the ravages of foreign exploitation continued unchecked.

That kind of political triangulation was all the more direct in the writings and speeches of the man widely credited as the founder of Egypt's cooperative movement. Immediately following the reading of Nahhas's report, ʿUmar Bey Lutfi rose to address the Egyptian Conference on "Financial Cooperation and Agricultural Syndicates." Having traveled to Italy in 1908 to study its systems of agricultural credit and cooperation, Lutfi offered glowing praise for the Italian-Jewish politician Luigi Luzzatti, who had played a leading role in founding that country's agricultural syndicates.[68] Luzzatti himself held that "rural cooperation implies the transformation and crystallization of the choicest labor into the most legitimate kind of capital, a capital which is fruitful and should be inviolable, inasmuch as both the heart and mind of the least of the producers contribute to its formation." While fostering "a condition of general and equitable prosperity," cooperation would simultaneously function as "the surest antidote to, the safest buttress against, Socialism."[69] Having met with Luzzatti during his travels, Lutfi praised the Italian for showing that "the improvement of the condition of the lowly worker and the small farmer . . . promotes the increase of general wealth [*izdiyad al-tharwah al-ʿumumiyah*]."[70]

Drawing a familiar distinction between "the development of the sources of real wealth" and the speculative activities that had caused "the present financial crisis," ʿUmar Lutfi stressed that "the basis for freedom and independence in every nation is economic independence."[71] At present, he reminded the audience, the main source of "real wealth" in Egypt was the production of agricultural commodities for export. Any future diversification of those sources would therefore depend upon securing a greater share of the value that Egyptians themselves currently produced. The cooperative, as he described it, was less an organizational form for leveling inequalities and projecting "union" into the countryside than a technology for transforming the labor of countless peasants into a pool of national capital. The sharing of resources and collective liability would allow small farmers to secure loans at far more reasonable rates, thereby "liberating the country step by step from servitude to the creditors." At the same time, the cooperative would also serve as a new locus for the regulatory and disciplinary measures required to protect Egypt's cotton crop from the dangers of declining quality and falling yields. Perhaps most striking was Lutfi's confidence that the co-op should aid in "combatting the cotton worm by uniting all the farmers in the village and coordinating their efforts to root out the germ of this mortal foe." With a flourish of military metaphors, he thus refigured the occupation's revival of peasant conscription as a contribution to the nation's collective struggle for freedom.[72] Far from advocating the abolition of the coercive labor practices that had long characterized the production of Egypt's most valuable crop, the "father of cooperation" here affirmed their continuation as necessary for the defense of national capital.

EGYPT'S ECONOMIC CURE

The platforms laid out by the delegates to the Egyptian Conference were unabashedly elitist. Many of the speeches were punctuated by formulaic pronouncements about the backward mentality and unscientific farming habits of the peasantry.[73]

Although vernacular forms of communal lending, co-ownership, and cooperative labor were already essential to the routines of village life, the leading voices of economic nationalism showed little interest in investigating such practices.[74] Nor did they contemplate measures to reverse the class stratification of rural society through redistribution of land or regulation of wages. In all likelihood, their optimism about the redemptive potential of agrarian capitalism was augmented by the status and privilege that many of these men enjoyed. Yet their shared understanding of the world they inhabited was not so easily reducible to the class position they occupied. For one thing, individuals from the same class background, even those who self-identified with the nationalist movement, had frequently disagreed on a whole host of other issues germane to the cause of Egyptian independence. The ubiquitous, almost droning endorsement of proposals for cooperatives and a national bank described a kind of consensus outlook that was unusual even by contemporary standards. For another, their shared description of the problems they sought to address was remarkably different from those of their patriotic predecessors in earlier decades. The Khedive's spy Muhammad Rushdi was no more critical, in the 1890s, toward the hierarchies of Egypt's existing social order. But having watched firsthand the rural dislocation that ensued from the fluctuation of global cotton prices, Rushdi had identified Egypt's colonial predicament chiefly with its deepening reliance on the production of that global commodity.[75] While the economic nationalists of the 1910s, like Rushdi before them, did consistently mention the importance of diversification, they now interpreted the absence of Egyptian industrial and commercial enterprises as symptoms of a deeper cause.

It was that underlying illness that Muhammad Tal'at Harb sought to diagnose in his study *'Ilaj Misr al-Iqtisadi* (Egypt's Economic Cure). No figure has received more attention as a prophetic pioneer of national industrialization than Harb, who went on to found one of Egypt's most powerful business conglomerates of the interwar era and whose statue still adorns one of Cairo's central squares.[76] However much Harb may or may not have merited that reputation in his later years, his writings suggest that the global division of labor between agriculture and industry was not his primary concern in 1912. As had been true since he began publishing columns for *al-Jaridah* in the autumn of 1907, Harb's chief preoccupation remained the relationship between political and economic independence. In continuing to develop the case for a national bank, Harb did list among its benefits the promotion of commerce and industry.[77] But in his lengthy survey of recent economic history, those secondary objectives quickly faded from view. For Harb, it was the government's selective and inconsistent responses to the two-pronged ills of agricultural decline and financial crisis that revealed the real costs of the occupation.[78]

Quoting at length from Gorst's annual reports, Harb endorsed the government's efforts to revive crop yields and continue the cultivation of a distinctly agricultural wealth. His chief concerns were with the occupation's failure to address glaring problems of agricultural credit provision and the role that existing financial institutions had played in undermining Egypt's former prosperity. Harb was careful to note that foreign banks had made positive contributions to the country's economic development. The problem was that the well-being of the Egyptian people could not be their main objective. Such companies, he explained, were bound to pursue "the interests of their shareholders with no regard for the interests of the country except when those agree with their own interests."[79] Armed with the latest statistics on its foreclosure rate, Harb once again singled out the Agricultural Bank as a prime example of this tension. Although the financial crisis had been devastating for its smallholder clients, "the Agricultural Bank, which was founded for their benefit, did not save them."[80] The country's ailing economic condition thus revealed a fundamental injustice: "All of these problems did not come from the Egyptians, but it is [Egyptians] who must taste their bitterness and bear their burden."[81] A new bank funded wholly by Egyptians themselves, by contrast, would bring the interests of borrowers and lenders into alignment and allow for a process of development less subject to the crisis tendencies of the present.

In places, Harb's comments echoed the language of his British sources in their newly skeptical observations about the economic backwardness of the rural masses who "have not become accustomed, until now, to planning, economy, and the investment of their surplus monies."[82] At the same time, his analysis marked a subtle but significant departure from the occupation's own verdict on recent events. Far from claiming to adopt or surpass a colonial project of agrarian governmentality and rural subject formation, Harb, like many of his contemporaries, suggested that these were tasks that the British had failed utterly to undertake. In the occupation's feckless and inconsistent responses to the financial crisis, Harb saw a near-total neglect for the developmental agenda that independent governments the world around were pursuing on behalf of their own populations. Whereas the British were content, by

1912, to ascribe the condition of the peasantry to immutable defects of mentality, Harb stressed their isolation from institutions that might guide and educate them to act otherwise. The country's existing banks, he explained, "limit their dealings to prominent merchants and large landowners, abandoning the class of the smallholders among the Egyptians" to the machinations of "the usurers."[83]

NATIONS OF COOPERATION

Anchoring the confident, even utopian, character of such writings on the transformative qualities of national capital was a shared comparative imaginary of the contemporary world. Jawish, Nahhas, Lutfi, and Harb all drew freely on models and examples from abroad. In so doing, however, they were not simply reproducing the stagist logic of colonial developmentalism. Instead, what made these comparisons meaningful and instructive was an insistence that Egypt inhabited the same historical present as France, Belgium, India, Japan, or the United States. The taxonomic category they most often employed to describe Egypt—an agricultural country—was specific neither to colonies alone nor to one side of a global division between East and West. Other agricultural countries encountered similar practical challenges around problems of credit supply, productive diversification, and rural education. When viewed in this way, the disparate conditions prevailing in countries of the same type could be understood not as expressions of unchanging cultural, racial, or geographic difference but rather as consequences of the ideas and institutions they had adopted, or been forced to adopt, to address those common problems. If ʿUmar Lutfi believed that Egypt could enjoy a form of capitalism devoid of the crises and social conflicts that so marred its recent past, it was in no small measure because he also believed that this was exactly what Italy was achieving. And if, conversely, Egyptians of all classes experienced the accumulation of capital as a process of collective enslavement and immiseration, it was because the British had imposed a set of arrangements that amplified those same problems.[84]

Although this variety of pragmatic comparativism had been an increasingly common feature of nationalist thought since at least 1907, it received its most systematic treatment in the encyclopedic study that the young ʿAbd al-Rahman al-Rafiʿi published in 1914, on the eve of World War I. Al-Rafiʿi would later gain renown as the official historian of the Egyptian nationalist movement. His accounts of Egypt's modern history would become canonical for generations of Egyptian schoolchildren.[85] But in the 1910s, he was working as a lawyer in the city of Mansurah and writing for the National Party on the side.[86] 'Umar Lutfi had passed away in 1911, and at the urging of Muhammad Farid, who had by that point fled the country under fear of incarceration, al-Rafi'i volunteered to document and extend the project of Egypt's "father of cooperation." The result of his efforts was a substantial tome entitled *Niqabat al-ta'awun al-zira'iyah: nizamuha wa-tarikhuha wa-thamaratuha fi Misr wa-Uruba* (*Agricultural Cooperative Syndicates: Their Organization, History, and Benefits in Egypt and Europe*).

Like other authors in this genre, al-Rafi'i was relatively cautious in tone. His few direct comments on the British occupation were buried in the book's closing chapters. But his study left little doubt as to the reasons behind Egypt's current troubles. And the overarching purpose of his sweeping comparative investigation was announced in the striking preface it received from Ahmad Lutfi, brother of the deceased founder of Egypt's first cooperative. In recent years, he explained, the Egyptian had come to recognize "the truth about the progress of modern countries and about the causes of his own backwardness and stagnation." He had discovered, in brief, that "selfishness and love of the self [*al-atharah wa-hubb al-dhat*] and the work of people as individuals for their own private interests" were "among the most important factors behind his remaining in his current state of backwardness."[87]

For decades, British officials had proclaimed that organizing Egyptian society around the unfettered pursuit of economic self-interest was a necessary step in a universal journey toward the realization of the prosperity and freedom that other more modern countries had already attained. Cooperation, John Stuart Mill had once argued, was the particular endowment of "civilized" peoples that qualified them to engage in politics and govern themselves. It was because they lacked a capacity to overcome their self-interest that "savage communities" required the "vigorous despotism" of colonial rule.[88] While he made no direct reference to Mill, Ahmad Lutfi now identified such arguments as an invidious form of colonial exceptionalism, one that represented the very antithesis of the path that countries all across Europe had actually followed. If there was a universal ideal in the world Lutfi surveyed, it was cooperation, not "selfishness and love of the self." The very organization of al-Rafi'i's study mirrored that vision of a world in which Britain was at best an anomaly and at worst the violent enforcer of a misleading ideology that held colonial societies in their "current state of backwardness." Along with Germany, France, Italy, Austro-Hungary, Denmark, Switzerland, Russia, Poland, and Finland, the book did contain a chapter on England and Ireland. But it was the latter that earned his attention and praise. In the realm of agricultural cooperation, al-Rafiʿi pronounced England to be "backward." Although in recent years "some agricultural cooperative societies have been founded on the Irish model," these had made "no progress to speak of."[89]

It was "thanks to cooperation," Ahmad Lutfi proclaimed in his preface, that all across Europe "agriculture has enjoyed a great renaissance." On the basis of that overwhelming success, he continued, "it is hoped that cooperation in Egypt might become one of the factors that saves the country from the perils of the dismal economic condition into which it has fallen, that condition that is like shackles around our legs that prevent us from movement or work, or like an iron collar around our necks that bars us from inhaling the sweet breath of life."[90] Drawing from the writings and speeches of ʿUmar Lutfi, al-Rafiʿi opened the second half of the book with a detailed accounting of that "dismal economic condition." While "leaving the people to prostrate themselves before the foreign banks," the British had done little to alleviate the many "faces of deprivation and fragility in the economic life of the peasant."[91] Describing the same veiled credit mechanisms that had figured so prominently in Legrand's thesis on the crisis, he noted that the small farmer's want of capital placed him always at the mercy of local merchants who controlled the purchase and resale of each harvest.[92] Even the most judicious and thrifty of peasants, moreover, had only limited access to information about the market price of their crops.[93] As al-Rafiʿi explained matters, the behaviors that seemed to distinguish smallholders from wealthier proprietors were largely the consequence of unequal relationships that the government had willfully overlooked or even encouraged. Acting alone as an individual consumer, borrower, and seller of agricultural commodities, the peasant stood little chance of profiting from the produce of his land.

These problems had only become more glaring since the onset of the financial crisis. Far from working to rectify them, the British had made matters worse. Writing of the Agricultural Bank, al-Rafiʿi warned that "the old system is still in place after the experiment failed." In a scathing indictment of the Five Feddan Law, he observed that "the lawmakers" had neither addressed the peasantry's need for loans "to make their small properties produce" nor afforded genuine protection against the worst abuses of existing credit arrangements. On the contrary, village usurers had seized the opportunity to raise interest rates or pressure farmers into selling their crops at a discount.[94]

Against this bleak tableau of foreign exploitation and peasant dispossession, al-Rafiʿi held out the promise of the agricultural syndicate as the ideal solution to each of the many problems he listed. Yet the story of the Egyptian movement, as he told it, seemed to be headed for tragedy. Upon his return from Italy, ʿUmar Lutfi had convinced first the Khedivial Agricultural Society and then the Council of Ministers to study the applicability of various cooperative models to Egypt.[95] Both committees had recommended a combination of cooperative credit funds and agricultural syndicates for group purchases and sales. The former would facilitate collective borrowing at much lower rates than any individual smallholder could find. Thanks to the joint liability of the co-op members, it would also provide a disciplinary mechanism to ensure that farmers put their loans to productive use. The latter would help them to secure better prices for necessary farm inputs like seed, livestock, and fertilizer and to market their crops on more advantageous terms.

Unfortunately, the country's existing corporations laws made no provision for cooperative organizations of either sort.[96] So rather than wait on new legislation, ʿUmar Lutfi had decided in January 1910 to establish a number of trial syndicates that would work within the confines of existing laws.[97] By al-Rafiʿi's account, these experiments went well beyond the limited scope of the Agricultural Society's proposals. In addition to facilitating collective purchases and sales and functioning as both a source of credit and a local savings bank, these village societies had begun to organize lectures and demonstrations on the latest farming techniques. They had also built local gins and storehouses for their cotton crops. Writing for *al-ʿAlam* in May 1910 to report on the "The First Agricultural Syndicate in Egypt," Lutfi had described this new institution as a promising mechanism of agricultural improvement and moral uplift that would "help us to proceed along this path so that slowly but surely the country will be liberated from the enslavement of creditors [*ʿabudiyat al-daʾinin*]."[98]

It was here that a project to advance Egypt's economic autonomy had ultimately collided with the occupation's heavy-handed tactics. Responding to the popularity of these independent endeavors and the support they received from the National Party, the government finally set about drafting a new set of laws and regulations in the spring of 1913. In a report he prepared for Kitchener, Gerald Dudgeon had endorsed, in theory, the spread of village cooperatives. But the director-general of agriculture's proposals introduced several deliberate modifications to existing arrangements. Two in particular attracted al-Rafiʿi's attention. First, Dudgeon recommended that the Department of Agriculture should appoint a Registrar of Cooperatives with the authority to inspect and audit existing societies, control the sources from which they could borrow, and void the registration of "any Society misusing its powers for objects other than those defined in the statues (such as political purposes, etc. . . .)." Second, he had proposed that the Agricultural Bank should become the sole source of loans to government-registered cooperatives. By this arrangement, the bank would "be saved the necessity of having to write off debts which they cannot recover, the cost of collecting, legal expenses, and running expenses to a large extent."[99] Both recommendations had found their way into the government's new draft legislation.

Having devoted nearly three hundred pages to documenting the transformative potential of the cooperative principle, al-Rafiʿi judged that the new law, as drafted, would reproduce the very conditions that it should have overturned. Without mentioning directly the National Party's aspirations to mobilize political support in the countryside, he identified the plan for centralized registration as an attempt to "confine and restrict the syndicates within a narrow range of activities and goals."[100] This rather predictable political maneuver, however, was nothing when compared to the government's financing scheme.[101] Reiterating that Egypt's heavy reliance on foreign capital had left the country "exposed to the financial, social, and political upheavals [*taqallubat*] that happen in Europe," al-Rafiʿi predicted that the sweetheart arrangement with the Agricultural Bank would invert the very purpose of cooperation itself. Whereas "the concern of the advocates of cooperation in Europe is directed toward making the societies stand on their own, dispensing, by means of their own funds, with financing from conventional banks," this decision suggested that the government "wants the syndicates to live as a dependent [*ʿalah*] upon those banks, bound to them by a bond of subjection and need."[102]

Al-Rafiʿi thus concluded on a rather bleak note, conceding that "the matter is settled, and the hope has been dashed that agricultural cooperation in Egypt might have a law that stands upon the methods and principles that European legislation established."[103] He correctly anticipated that the new law would soon be ratified.[104] In this tone of limited expectations, he returned to familiar themes of voluntarism and self-reliance. At present, the best that those committed to the principles and objectives of cooperation could do was to establish independent syndicates free from "the tutelage of administrative authority." Noting that "the deposits of Egyptians in foreign banks are sufficient, as experts have shown, to found a large Egyptian bank," he implored "the enlightened class of the nation and the wealthy" to fund undertakings that might "gradually relieve the burden of debt that weighs upon the shoulders of the Egyptians."[105] With their leadership, the spirit of the movement might still "gather under its banner all the classes of the nation so that mutual solidarity and collaborative work might become the guiding principle of one and all."[106]

CONCLUSION: WORLDS OF FINANCE AND ANTICOLONIAL COMPARISON

On the eve of World War I, that vision of a transformed Egyptian society appeared all too distant. Three decades prior, Egypt's new advisers had announced that their program of economic development, aided by ample flows of foreign capital, would hasten Egypt's eventual return to prosperity and self-rule. By the second decade of the twentieth century, that promise had gone unrealized. For al-Rafiʿi and his contemporaries, foreign rule and foreign capital worked in tandem to reinforce the country's continuous subjection and immiseration. But if his tentative exhortations to the independent initiative of the wealthy and enlightened classes betrayed the deeper sense of an impasse that beset the nationalist movement in these years, the comparative ambition of al-Rafiʿi's study helps to explain the growing appeal of that movement and the program of political-economic transformation that it aspired to implement.

Al-Rafiʿi's was a resolutely anti-imperialist text, written in service of national autonomy. At the same time, he presented that struggle for autonomy in plainly and affirmatively comparative terms. If Dufferin and Cromer had once described the occupation as the agency of a universal justice that would correct and replace the deviant particularities of "Oriental despotism," al-Rafiʿi now staged an elaborate argument that the institutions and ideologies of colonial rule were, in fact, the anomalous obstacles to a universal process of national development and self-rule. Like many others who espoused similar ideas, al-Rafiʿi was troubled neither by characterizations of the Egyptian peasant as ignorant, shortsighted, and backward nor by the elitist notion that the country's wealthier classes would play a leading role in any future project of nationalism. Though their pitiable condition played a central role in the indictment of British rule, the oppressed and exploited peasantry suffered in silence throughout such texts. At the same time, al-Rafiʿi's own methodical, repetitive mode of presentation, proceeding from one country to the next, together with his detailed counternarrative of Egypt's own recent history, implied that the colonial regime's aggressive recourse to essentialist tropes about the immutable and defective subjectivity of the fallah was profoundly misleading. What rendered a comparison between Egypt and Italy, Belgium, France, Germany, or Ireland plausible and compelling, for al-Rafiʿi, was a shared experience of the world as it currently existed. And from that perspective, what distinguished the figure of the long-suffering, indebted Egyptian peasant from his counterparts in these other countries was chiefly the colonial government's determination to undermine the policies and institutions that might gradually contribute to meaningful conditions of freedom and prosperity. It was in permitting Egyptians to draw freely from the ideas, practices, and institutional forms shared across this common global field, nationalists like al-Rafiʿi now argued, that an independent nation–state would achieve its own break with the colonial past.

Conclusion

ECONOMISM MILITARIZED

FOR MORE THAN THREE DECADES, British officials had alleged that what destined Egyptians for colonial tutelage as a "subject race" was their single-minded pursuit of economic gain. It was this defect that had led the khedives to enrich themselves and bankrupt the country. It was their experience of material duress that had left Egypt's lower classes susceptible to the demagogue revolutionary Ahmad 'Urabi. It was their sensitivity to personal profit and loss that would allow an illiterate but industrious peasantry to recognize their own interests in the continuation of British rule. And it was this limitation of an "eminently materialist" population that rendered them unqualified to govern themselves. By the early 1910s, the occupation had all but abandoned the more optimistic iterations of these claims. The 1907 crisis had provided grounds to question the rural population's readiness to navigate the complexities of agrarian finance, and the ensuing vigor of nationalist mobilization had raised new doubts about the correspondence between economic development and political consent. But even the occupation's conservative turn in the 1910s represented less an abandonment of colonial economism than a narrowing of its ambit: Egyptians might lack the capacity to associate material benefit with the virtues of British rule; but an aversion to economic hardship was still the strongest motivator of their discontent.

The occupation's critics had often observed that these ideas about Egyptian society entailed a kind of hostile projection: it was the British themselves, they responded, whose judgments and actions most closely tracked the dictates of economic interest. But they also noted that the occupation's claims were no less dangerous for their falsehood. Behind the retrospective moralism of the Khedive's spies lurked an awareness that British discourse might be more prescriptive than diagnostic. Cromer may have questioned whether Egypt's "national character" was likely ever to change. But in the occupation's ambitions to reorganize the institutions and routines of government, its opponents saw a possibility that imperial rule might be remaking Egyptians into the narrowly self-interested subjects the British imagined them to be. That concern had taken on new resonance when boom turned to bust in 1907. Nationalist accounts of the crisis located Egypt within a global geography of uneven financial flows that exposed the distinctive vulnerabilities of their colonial condition. While they denounced the British for withholding the kinds of intervention that independent polities had provided under comparable circumstances, these same figures were forced to reckon with the deepening involvement of their own compatriots in Egypt's subordination to foreign finance. In a race to secure easy profits, they had ensnared themselves in a tangle of credit relations that left them not only less wealthy but also less free. If growing numbers of Egyptians now seemed driven by the imperatives of economic interest, it was not because they lacked the agency, will, or imagination to pursue other ways of living. Rather, it was because their reliance, both individually and collectively, on the circulation of foreign capital to maintain their everyday existence made it increasingly difficult and perilous to do otherwise.[1] For growing numbers of Egyptian nationalists, the redemptive potential of new institutions like national banks and cooperatives lay in breaking that cycle of domination and forging a new population of national subjects. On this understanding, the expansion of the money supply circulating within Egypt's borders would be the necessary point of departure for any meaningful process of both political and economic liberation.

In ways that figures like Harb and Nahhas could not anticipate, World War I delivered that very precondition of their emancipatory aspirations. With the advent of war, the quantity of money inside the country grew at an unprecedented rate, reaching a total of £E 67 million by 1919. But what ensued was a realization of nationalist calls for financial autonomy in travestied and inverted form. The war years proceeded as a vicious reprise of colonial economism in its more limited, conservative register. Having declared that the varied manifestations of popular politics were only ever instinctive responses to economic privation, the British subjected the country to five years of brutal expropriation and then explained the arrival of a mass rural insurgency as confirmation that Egypt's fallahin could do little more than react against material duress.

Familiar assumptions about the political effects of economic hardship figured prominently in Britain's treatment of Egypt at the start of the war. As soon as it became clear that the Ottoman Empire would join the Central Powers, British authorities cut Egypt's residual ties to Istanbul. In December 1914, the veiled protectorate became a British protectorate plain and simple.[2] Concerned that the economic strain of wartime might cause "widespread distress leading to ill-feeling and unrest," the British immediately took steps to reassure the Egyptian public. The army issued a proclamation that "Great Britain takes upon herself the solemn burden of the present war without calling upon the Egyptian people for aid therein."[3] To ensure that there was enough money in the country to purchase the autumn cotton crop, the protectorate also designated the banknotes of the National Bank of Egypt as legal tender and allowed the bank to print up to double the value of its gold reserves.[4] As the reasoning went, Egyptians could hardly object to a war that cost them nothing.

But cost them it did. In practice, both of these early measures served not to diminish the hardship of the war but to make the full extent of Britain's exactions harder to discern. Technically, the British military could not impose direct claims upon the Egyptian government's budget. So instead, the protectorate authorized the army to make charges against a "suspense account," a running tally of IOUs to be settled later on. Wary of reinstituting the corvée, the military met its growing need for Egyptian labor through paid recruitment.[5] The wages of this new Labor Corps, however, were billed to the suspense account. In effect, Egyptian taxpayers were lending Britain the costs of their own labor. And any real suspense about repayment was resolved by 1917 when, under pressure from the military, the Council of Ministers voted to waive the full £E 3 million of the suspense account "as a token of gratitude to Great Britain for protection from the risk of invasion."[6]

Egypt's new paper money supply quickly became a mechanism for a similar kind of covert borrowing on a much larger scale. Because the various military applications of Egyptian long-staple cotton led to a spike in global demand while the disruption of Mediterranean shipping caused imports to fall, Egypt ran a substantial trade surplus through most of the war. As a result, the quantity of money circulating within Egypt's borders continued to grow. Ostensibly, this was the very scenario that nationalists before the war had hoped to achieve. But thanks to an act of monetary subterfuge, the war did not, in fact, help to retain "the wealth of the country inside the country." Initially, the National Bank's paper notes were backed by gold, stored partly in its own vaults and partly at the Bank of England. But in 1916, the British Treasury refused to earmark any more gold to cover Egypt's new paper currency. So under instructions from its British financial adviser, the Egyptian government authorized the National Bank to substitute British treasury bonds for gold.[7] The change had two momentous implications. First, because British bonds were denominated in British pounds, it had the practical effect of pegging Egypt's new paper currency to sterling.[8] Since Britain had effectively abandoned the gold standard in 1914 while Egypt had not, the decision to replace gold with British treasury notes forced the Egyptian public to endure rampant inflation while at the same time making Egyptian goods more affordable for British consumers.[9] Second, it meant that each new Egyptian pound represented not an equivalent quantity of gold but a British pound's worth of debt. The expansion of the paper money supply thus became a means of lending the value of all goods and services produced within Egypt directly to the British war effort.[10] Altogether, as at least one British official acknowledged, this monetary policy placed Egypt "in the position of having a very powerful partner able at any moment to dip into her pocket."[11]

By the war's end, the sheer rapaciousness of Britain's forced requisition of Egyptian money, crops, livestock, and labor had brought the self-serving character of colonial economism more sharply into focus than ever. But in a final twist, equal parts tragedy and farce, British officials adduced the devastation wrought by their own war-time demands to claim, yet again, that Egyptians could do little more than react to economic circumstance.

For colonial subjects in many other parts of the world, the end of the war brought with it expectations that peace would lead toward the denouement of imperial rule. Anticolonial nationalists around the globe had developed their own arguments for self-determination long before Woodrow Wilson delivered his famous Fourteen Points. But having struggled for decades to bend the contradictions of colonial discourse to their own advantage, some saw opportunity in taking the American president at his word.[12] When a group of Egyptian politicians, led by the former Minister of Education and Justice Saʿd Zaghlul, requested to form an Egyptian delegation (*wafd*) to the Paris Peace Conference, however, the Foreign Office quickly refused. The British were disinclined to relinquish their new protectorate.

The popular protests that followed that initial setback drew upon repertoires of political practice that Egyptians had tested and refined throughout the years of the occupation. In both the strategies they employed and the solidarities that they activated, the events of 1919 revived forms of contention that the nationalist movement had practiced in the long crescendo of mass mobilization a decade prior. The group that orchestrated the original request first sought to formalize their representative status by establishing a new political party named for their purpose: the Wafd. Adapting the techniques Ahmad Hilmi had devised in the aftermath of Dinshaway, they bombarded the British High Commission and the Foreign Office with univocal telegrams and petitions. To convey the full measure of public support for the Wafd, they circulated copies of a form granting them the "proxy [*tawkil*]" to represent Egypt at Versailles. Within weeks, these *tawkilat* had garnered thousands of signatures.[13] In response, the British too followed established routines. Like Cromer and Gorst before him, the High Commissioner Reginald Wingate alleged that "this patriotism was artificially engineered" by a handful of "extremists."[14] Availing themselves of extrajudicial procedures that the occupation had pioneered and the protectorate had only extended, British forces arrested the leaders of the Wafd and on the morning of March 9, 1919, deported them to Malta.[15]

When the demonstrations commenced, it was the very same groups who had led the protest movement a decade beforehand who first took to the streets. Students from Cairo's high schools and colleges staged the earliest rallies on March 8 and 9.[16] By the morning of March 10, the Azharis had organized their first march from the precincts around the university. Reactivating solidarities they had forged in 1909, they processed to the railway yards and summoned the workers there to join them.[17]

Under encouragement from this old vanguard of the labor movement, government employees from the Ministries of Public Works and Education walked off the job on March 11.[18] This new strike wave quickly gained momentum. Next, the fear that had long haunted the occupation and prompted the crackdown in 1910 was finally realized.[19] By the end of the first week, protests had spread to provincial cities and towns and into rural districts as well. There, the crowds not only staged marches and demonstrations of their own but targeted the infrastructures and institutions most closely associated with British rule in the countryside. They burned police stations, banks, and ʿizab. They blocked and sabotaged agricultural roads. They tore up train tracks and severed telegraph wires. In a few remarkable cases, rural communities announced the establishment of independent, self-governing republics.[20]

To each other, British officials admitted that "the extent and violence of the movement" had "come as a complete surprise."[21] That the Egyptian peasantry was incapable of genuine political thought or action had been the single most enduring axiom of their rule since its inception. Holding fast to that assumption, British authorities deemed the uprising a chaotic eruption of raw violence and responded with a terrifying spectacle of force. They deployed troops to quash the protests. They tried the protesters under swift military tribunals.[22] And where damage to transport infrastructures hampered movement on the ground, they used the new technology of "air power" to bomb rural communities into submission.[23]

On April 7, in a move calculated to undercut the urban politicians whom he believed to be pulling all the strings, the new High Commissioner Edmund Allenby permitted the Wafd leadership to travel to Paris.[24] The British officials at Versailles had no intention of meeting with them or allowing the Peace Conference to decide the country's fate.[25] They nevertheless recognized that the uprising had utterly defied expectations, that they lacked a clear understanding of why it had occurred, and that this postwar moment would require some adjustment to Egypt's status. It was for those reasons that they dispatched a mission, led by the old veteran of the occupation Alfred Milner, to " 'enquire into the causes of the late disorders in Egypt' " and to ascertain " 'the form of constitution which, under the Protectorate, will be best calculated to promote its peace and prosperity, the progressive development of self-governing institutions and the protection of foreign interests.' "[26]

A detailed history of the ideas and political imaginaries that emerged through the Egyptian Revolution of 1919 has yet to be written.[27] Compiling the raw materials for such a history, however, was not the task that the Milner Mission set out to perform. The animating question behind the inquiry presupposed its own answer. For Milner, the man who had once proclaimed that "our interests in Egypt are absolutely identical with those of the Egyptian people," there was little possibility that the events of 1919 might upend established tropes about the peasant's aberrant subjective capacities.[28] How then to explain the involvement, in huge numbers, of the very people the occupation had judged incapable of properly political thought and action?

The answer to that question was, by this point, entirely predictable. But it did require some concessions to a changing reality. For Milner, who had served as chairman of the company that oversaw the dismantling of the Agricultural Bank, there might remain little hope that the fallah could become the thriving yeoman capitalist of the occupation's earlier fantasies. He nevertheless retained the conviction that rural protest could only ever express a response to the peasant's base economic circumstances. By acknowledging some wrongdoing on the part of the British military, Milner produced an account that overwhelmingly attributed the agrarian insurgency to recent material hardship and thereby sustained that durable antipolitical conceit.

Following an old line of reasoning, Milner reminded his readers that support for a nationalist movement, in whatever form, was restricted to "the educated and semi-educated classes, who constitute less than 10 per cent. of the fourteen million inhabitants of Egypt." Echoing almost to the word Ronald Graham's dismissal of popular demands for a constitution eleven years earlier, he continued, "The turbulent crowds of the great towns may indeed be easily worked up to excitement by political catchwords, which they vociferate without understanding. But the fellahin, as a body, are normally very indifferent to politics." Their "whole interest in life" remained fixed on "those wonderful crops which are the bed-rock of Egyptian prosperity." Though British rule had not altered this state of affairs, it had made the peasantry "far more tenacious of their rights than in the old days of despotism." Far from an indictment of Britain's presence, then, Milner here suggested that the revolt provided evidence of its long-term achievements. By this interpretation, the events of 1919 confirmed the political theory upon which the occupation had for so long rested. The material ravages of the war "shook for a time their confidence in our justice and good-will, and were predisposing causes of the savage outbreak of anti-British feeling. . . . But these excesses were abnormal and short-lived."[29]

The point here is not to suggest that the British military's practices of conscription, requisition, and outright theft were not severe or that unconscionable experiences of hunger, disease, and violence did not figure among the rural population's motives to revolt. Instead, it is to draw attention to the work that Milner's narrative performed in attempting to explain 1919 away as a predictable response to "short-lived" conditions of economic devastation by a people who could not be expected to act otherwise. The revolt, in other words, was merely the consequence of British mismanagement, not the expression of any more serious aspirations and grievances on the part of its protagonists. In this sense, the very predaciousness of Britain's war effort in Egypt was made to serve as justification to continue the Empire's dominion under different guises.

Egypt's new postwar order was closely tailored to this latest reprise of colonial economism. To satisfy and dissipate the demands of the small minority for whom nationalism might be a meaningful project, Egypt would gain a qualified independence. But the political system of that pseudo-independent state would continue to limit and obstruct the avenues of popular political participation. In its unilateral declaration of independence in 1922, Britain stipulated four "reserved points" on which its government would retain the authority to intervene: the security of imperial communications (including the Suez Canal), the interests and safety of foreigners on Egyptian soil, the threat of foreign invasion, and the status of Egypt's relationship with the Sudan. Egypt would at last receive the constitution for which generations of nationalists had clamored, but here again, British oversight helped to ensure that old arrangements would remain intact. The new bicameral parliament would enjoy broad legislative authority, but its indirect electoral procedures were specifically designed to insulate representatives from the whims of the rural populace. The newly invented monarchy was granted sweeping authority to dissolve the elected government by sovereign fiat, an option the palace exercised throughout the interwar years.[30] And in the final phases of the drafting process, the British judicial adviser to the constitutional committee inserted broad powers not only for the government to declare a state of emergency but also to legislate restrictions on the rights and freedoms that Egyptian citizens would enjoy under ordinary circumstances.[31]

In Egypt, as in many parts of the world, the war had exploded, at least for a moment, the bounds that once allowed the economic and the political to appear as separate. For better and for worse, the sheer scope of efforts to plan and regulate supplies of labor, goods, and capital through direct state oversight threw open the possibility that the production and distribution of social wealth, and with them social life itself, could be organized differently in peacetime as well. It was through the rapid foreclosure of those alternatives, as he witnessed them in Italy, that Antonio Gramsci came to see economism not simply as a way of describing the world but of remaking it toward particular ends. Well before they had experienced the worst privations of the war, large numbers of Egyptians had reached the same conclusion. Whereas the occupation had claimed to free the domain of the economic from the distorting impositions of Oriental despotism, its critics too saw this colonial variant of liberalism as "a deliberate policy, conscious of its own ends, and not the spontaneous, automatic expression of economic facts."[32]

That basic critique of economism, in both its metropolitan and colonial variants, had always pointed in more than one direction. In 1919, as in the protest movement a decade before, the radical energies of the uprising had briefly disclosed the promise of a future in which ordinary people might claim for themselves the right to imagine and build together their own conditions of life. The terms of Egypt's new, qualified independence after 1922 foreclosed, or at least postponed, the realization of that more revolutionary future. In its place, the leading proponents of economic nationalism would again make the case that their managerial program of national capital formation represented the country's best available route toward more durable conditions of collective freedom.[33] The exclusionary arrangements forged in the heyday of the occupation would thus continue to cast a dark shadow over Egyptian politics for decades to come.

NOTES

INTRODUCTION

1. Lord Cromer (1841–1917) was born Evelyn Baring. For the sake of clarity and consistency, I refer to him throughout the whole of this book as Lord Cromer, the title he received when he was raised to the peerage in 1892. In citations, however, I use the name by which he signed at the time each document was written.

2. Owen, *Lord Cromer*, 344.

3. Willcocks, *Sixty Years in the East*, 116–18.

4. MEC, Harry Boyle Papers, GB 165-0035, Box C, File 4: Harry Boyle to Nellie Boyle (August 20, 1909).

5. Lord Cromer, *Abbas II*, xx.

6. Ibid., xxi.

7. Ibid., xxii.

8. Martial law was imposed on November 2, 1914, and the protectorate was declared on December 18, 1914. See, TNA, FO 371/1970: Milne Cheetham to Edward Grey (November 3, 1914); McIlwraith, "Declaration of a Protectorate."

9. Lord Cromer, *Abbas II*, xvii.

10. See "The Government of Subject Races" in Cromer, *Political and Literary Essays*, 3–53.

11. Lord Cromer, *Abbas II*, xi. Sometimes, as in this instance, Cromer referred to it as "the machinery of the Government," but elsewhere in his writings, "the machinery of government" was more common. See, for example, Lord Cromer, *Modern Egypt*, 260. On Cromer's fondness for mechanical metaphors, see Barak, *On Time*, 3.

12. On the political *and* economic virtues of Cromer's "fiscal moderation, fiscal security, and fiscal equity," see also Colvin, *Making of Modern Egypt*, 211.

13. Lord Cromer, *Abbas II*, xiv.

14. One notable departure from this trend is Elizabeth Holt's brilliant study of the dense interrelations between this process of financialization and both the content and (serialized) form of the early Arabic novel. See Holt, *Fictitious Capital*.

15. The clearest and most influential articulation of this continuity thesis appeared in Owen, "Egypt and Europe." See also, ʿAbbās, *al-Niẓām al-ijtimāʿī fī Miṣr*; Abbas and El-Dessouky, *Large Landowning Class*; Beckert, *Empire of Cotton*; Dasūqī, *Kibār mullāk al-arāḍī al-zirāʿīyah*; Owen, *Cotton and the Egyptian Economy*; Richards, *Egypt's Agricultural Development*; Tignor, *Modernization and British Rule*; Zayn al-Dīn, *al-Zirāʿah al-Miṣrīyah*.

16. Rothstein, *Egypt's Ruin*, 305.

17. Lord Cromer, *Modern Egypt*, 451–52.

18. Tignor, *Modernization and British Rule*, 367.

19. On this process of financial expansion, see Arrighi, *Long Twentieth Century*, 172; Cain and Hopkins, *British Imperialism*, 309; Harvey, *Limits to Capital*, 319; Jessop, *State Theory*, 200; Hobsbawm, *Age of Empire*, 52. Arrighi's more developed analysis of the relationship between financialization and imperialism in *The Long Twentieth Century* expanded on an earlier critique of the "theory of imperialism" expounded by Owen and the other organizers of the 1969 conference that gave rise to the volume *Studies in the Theory of Imperialism*. See, Arrighi, *Geometry of Imperialism*, 9–10, 158–59.

20. London School of Economics Archive (LSE): Ionian Bank Papers 10/18: Mr. F. Larkworthy, "Report on Egypt as a Field for Banking Business" (Alexandria: March 24, 1905).

21. In a characteristically evocative aside, James C. Scott once referred to 1907 as a worldwide "dress rehearsal" for the Great Depression. Scott, *Moral Economy of the Peasant*, 85. A truly global history of these events has yet to be written.

22. Aḥmad Ḥilmī, "al-Kalām al-dhahabī: al-ḥālah al-mālīyah fi Miṣr (al-taqaddum al-sarīʿ)," *al-Liwāʾ* (December 28, 1905).

23. My efforts to showcase the range and sophistication of political-economic thought in the Arabic press, in this regard, complement and build upon Hussein Omar's crucial insight about the error of mistaking an absence of specific genres of writing for an absence of political thought itself. See Omar, "Liberal Cage," 18.

24. In their sensitive and richly ethnographic accounts of urban life in Alexandria, for example, both Shane Minkin and Will Hanley offer useful reminders that a great many British subjects in Egypt, like the members of other foreign communities, had experiences and perspectives on the country quite distant from those of Cromer's circle in the Agency. See, Hanley, *Identifying with Nationality*; Minkin, *Imperial Bodies*; Minkin, "Documenting Death."

25. Guha, *Rule of Property*; Said, *Orientalism*, 149; Seigel, "Beyond Compare"; Stoler, "Tense and Tender Ties"; Zimmerman, "Counterinsurgency and the Science Effect." On the particular relevance of comparisons with India, see Owen, "Lord Cromer's Indian Experience"; Tignor, " 'Indianization' of Egyptian Administration"; Derr, *Lived Nile*, 23–25, 37.

26. Deutscher, *Stalin*, 31–32; Bottomore, *Dictionary of Marxist Thought*, 168–69.

27. Lenin, *Essential Works*, 112.

28. Kwak, *Economism*; Slobodian, *Globalists*, 269.

29. Fraser and Jaeggi, *Capitalism*, 7–8.

30. See, for example, Owen, *Cotton and the Egyptian Economy*; Owen, "Studying Islamic History"; Owen, "Middle East in the Eighteenth Century"; Islamoğlu and Keyder, "Agenda for Ottoman History." For a detailed account of this critique of Orientalism before *Orientalism*, see Lockman, *Contending Visions*, 162–71. A similar impulse underpins the comparative framework of Pomeranz, *Great Divergence*.

31. For a compelling critique of this approach, see Karl, *Magic of Concepts*, 22–25.

32. Fraser, "Behind Marx's Hidden Abode"; Fraser and Jaeggi, *Capitalism*; Fraser, "Legitimation Crisis?"

33. The work of denaturalizing "the free market" has taken on a particular urgency and critical valence in recent decades as a response to the widespread normalization of neoliberal discourse. See, for example, Beckert, *Empire of Cotton*; Jessop, *State Theory*; Çaliskan, *Market Threads*; Callon, "Embeddedness of Economic Markets."

34. Coronil, *Magical State*; Harvey, *Justice, Nature, and the Geography of Difference*; Moore, *Capitalism in the Web of Life*; Moore, "Ecology, Capital, and the Nature of Our Times"; Moore, "Transcending the Metabolic Rift"; Moore, "Wall Street Is a Way of Organizing Nature"; Malm, *Fossil Capital*; Smith, *Uneven Development*.

35. The so-called free gifts of nature are rarely, if ever, actually free. See Jakes, "Boom, Bugs, Bust."

36. For the outlines of an approach to racialization and capital accumulation as "articulated systems of domination," see Dawson and Katzenstein, "Articulated Darkness."

37. Scott, "Women in the Making of the English Working Class"; Vogel, *Marxism and the Oppression of Women*; Federici, *Wages Against Housework*; Fraser, *Fortunes of Feminism*. For a particularly incisive and innovative exploration of this argument as it pertains to the organization of agricultural labor in Egypt, see Tucker, *Women in Nineteenth-Century Egypt*.

38. See, for example, Dawson, "Hidden in Plain Sight"; Robinson, *Black Marxism*; Ralph, *Forensics of Capital*; Hudson, *Bankers and Empire*.

39. Mies, *Patriarchy and Accumulation*, 77.

40. As the political scientist Richard Ashley made this point more than three decades ago, "I hope it is clear that economism is not just an inconsequential mistake that intellectuals sometimes make when they too hastily objectify the society they study. Economism is a social pathology of advanced capitalist society." See, Ashley, "Three Modes of Economism," 492.

41. Marx, *Contribution to the Critique of Political Economy*, 20. Like much of Marx's work, this passage has been the subject of intense and ongoing debate. There is ample reason to suggest that Marx's own understanding of this controversial passage and its notorious metaphor was quite different from the meanings others soon assigned to it. Engels, for example, advanced an overtly determinist and developmentalist reading of the metaphor in Engels, "Speech at the Graveside of Karl Marx." For alternative interpretations more consistent with Marx's dialectical method, see Ollman, *Alienation*; Sayer, *Violence of Abstraction*; Williams, "Base and Superstructure"; Elson, "Value Theory of Labour."

42. Gramsci, *Prison Notebooks*, 159.

43. Ibid., 159–60.

44. Mitchell, *Rule of Experts*, 4. Earlier versions of the argument appeared in Mitchell, "Fixing the Economy"; Mitchell, "Society, Economy, and the State Effect." A subsequent revision, emphasizing the conceptual and material relations between the fluid circulation of petroleum and new practices of national income accounting, appears in Mitchell, *Carbon Democracy*, 134–43.

45. Mitchell, *Rule of Experts*, 6.

46. Ibid., 7.

47. For examples of recent works that, despite other significant differences and disagreements, take Mitchell's thesis about the invention of the economy as a point of departure, see Çaliskan, *Market Threads*; Chhabria, *Making the Modern Slum*; Mathew, *Margins of the Market*; Seikaly, *Men of Capital*; Shafiee, *Machineries of Oil*; Shamir, *Current Flow*. The remarkable variety of arguments these works make and theoretical frameworks they employ in responding to Mitchell, whether critically or approvingly, is its own testament to the catalytic quality of his intervention.

48. See, for example, Goswami, *Producing India*, 335–36; Slobodian, "How to See the World Economy," 308.

49. Mitchell, "Fixing the Economy," 91–92; Mitchell, *Rule of Experts*, 82.

50. Mitchell, *Rule of Experts*, 4, 82. As Mitchell explains in the introduction, his gloss on classical political economy draws directly from Foucault's famous lecture on governmentality. See, Foucault, *Security, Territory, Population*, 105–7.

51. This, as I understand it, is the point of Susan Buck-Morss's contention that "the economy, when it was discovered, was already capitalist, so the description of the one entailed the description of the other." As Mitchell is quick to note, Buck-Morss's use of the definite article is anachronistic, but that terminological imprecision might also be addressed by reading her arguments in relation to the emergence of "the economic" rather than as a pretext to dismiss the arguments in toto. Buck-Morss, "Envisioning Capital," 439; Mitchell, *Rule of Experts*, 81.

52. For a lucid and characteristically capacious account of the processes and struggles by which such surplus wealth came to be produced in the first place, see Scott, *Against the Grain*.

53. Polanyi, *Great Transformation*; Schumpeter, "Crisis of the Tax State," 108–12; Marx, *Capital, Vol. 1*, 170.

54. Wood, "Separation of the Economic and Political," 81. Wood's article is notably absent from Mitchell's various critical engagements with prior efforts to historicize "the economy." It is significant in that regard that while her arguments resonate closely with those of other accounts that Mitchell does mention, Wood quite consistently names the objects of her inquiry "the economic" and "the political" rather than "the economy."

55. Sartori, "History of Political Economy," 111; Sartori, *Bengal in Global Concept History*, 48–49; Sartori, *Liberalism in Empire*, 9.

56. Sartori, "History of Political Economy," 113.

57. Smith, *Wealth of Nations*, 15.

58. Milgate and Stimson, *After Adam Smith*, 46.

59. Foucault, *Birth of Biopolitics*, 16; Elden, *Foucault's Last Decade*, 104.

60. Gramsci, *Prison Notebooks*, 159.

61. Wood, "Separation of the Economic and Political," 82.

62. Ricardo, *Principles of Political Economy and Taxation*, 95.

63. Smith, *Wealth of Nations*, 747–875.

64. Ibid., 875. As Buck-Morss observes, "Smith called upon traditional notions of civic virtue to compensate for the moral inadequacies of the laws of political economy. This is a weakness in his thought because the civic society he desires is founded on principles inimical to the economic society he describes." See, Buck-Morss, "Envisioning Capital," 456.

65. Elyachar, *Markets of Dispossession*, 17–20; Hont, *Jealousy of Trade*.

66. Bentham, *Principles of Morals and Legislation*, 31.

67. Ibid., 24–25.

68. Ricardo, *Principles of Political Economy and Taxation*, 16.

69. Smith, *Wealth of Nations*, 14. See also, Foucault, *Birth of Biopolitics*, 270–76.

70. Pincus, "Neither Machiavellian Moment nor Possessive Individualism"; Hont, *Jealousy of Trade*.

71. Sartori, "History of Political Economy," 115; Sartori, *Liberalism in Empire*, 10–11.

72. Milgate and Stimson, *After Adam Smith*, 82–83.

73. Marx, *Capital, Vol. 1*, 280; Marx, *Grundrisse*, 239–45.

74. Elyachar, *Markets of Dispossession*, 19.

75. Smith, *Wealth of Nations*, 840.

76. Bell, *Reordering the World*; Guha, *Rule of Property*; Mehta, *Liberalism and Empire*; Pitts, A *Turn to Empire*; Sartori, "Liberal Mission"; Sartori, *Liberalism in Empire*; Scott, "Colonial Governmentality"; Stokes, *English Utilitarians and India*.

77. Mill, "Considerations on Representative Government (1861)," 567. See also, Sullivan, "Liberalism and Imperialism"; Mehta, *Liberalism and Empire*, 106. Curiously, Mehta attributes the quoted passage to Mill's *On Liberty*.

78. Bell, *Reordering the World*, 225; Ball, "Formation of Character," 41; Leary, "Mill's Proposed Science of Ethology."

79. On Mill's "contingent racism," see Goldberg, *Racial State*, 63–72.

80. Pitts, A *Turn to Empire*, 124–25.

81. Mill, *Principles of Political Economy*, 962–67; Goswami, *Producing India*, 43–44. Mill's ideas about colonization drew directly on the work of Edward Wakefield. See Semmel, *Rise of Free Trade Imperialism*.

82. Mill, "Considerations on Representative Government," 567.

83. Mill, "Civilization," 131.

84. Goldberg, *Racial State*, 65.

85. Mill, "Unsettled Questions of Political Economy," 323.

86. Ibid., 321.

87. Ibid.

88. Brown, *Undoing the Demos*, 70, 97.

89. Ibid., 85, 95.

90. Mill, "Civilization," 134.

91. Ibid., 136; Mill, *Principles of Political Economy*, 706–9.

92. Mill, "Civilization," 144.

93. Ibid., 143.

94. "On Bentham" in Mill and Bentham, *Utilitarianism and Other Essays*, 164.

95. "Utilitarianism" in ibid., 304.

96. Mill, "Considerations on Representative Government," 401.

97. Dewey, "Influence of Sir Henry Maine"; Mamdani, *Citizen and Subject*; Mantena, "Crisis of Liberal Imperialism," 128–31; Mantena, *Alibis of Empire*; Metcalf, *Aftermath of Revolt*, 289–327; Sartori, *Liberalism in Empire*, 37.

98. Maine, *Village-Communities*, 223.

99. Ibid., 191.

100. Maine, *Ancient Law*, 22.

101. Maine, *Popular Government*, 25.

102. Mantena, *Alibis of Empire*.

103. On the antipathy of all but a "relatively small portion of the human race" toward this "age of reform," see Maine, *Popular Government*, 143. On the Government of India's efforts after 1857 to reconcile "the utilitarian call to economic progress on the one hand, and the paternalist imperative of cultural preservation on the other," see Birla, *Stages of Capital*, 3–4.

104. Lugard, *Dual Mandate*; Mamdani, *Define and Rule*.

105. Mitchell, *Rule of Experts*, 52–56; Mantena, *Alibis of Empire*, 7.

106. On the influence of utilitarian thought on the British occupation, see Robinson and Gallagher, *Africa and the Victorians*, 275; Marlowe, *Cromer in Egypt*, 282–83; Esmeir, *Juridical Humanity*, 120–21.

107. Milner, *England in Egypt*, 214.

108. Ibid., 215.

109. Colvin, *Making of Modern Egypt*, 212; Tignor, "Lord Cromer: Practitioner and Philosopher of Imperialism," 147.

110. Lord Cromer, *Abbas II*, xxiii.

111. Omar, "Minority as Microbe."

112. For an early example of this treatment of Egypt's role as a cotton producer as historical "background," see Mitchell, *Colonising Egypt*, 16.

113. Anderson, *Imagined Communities*, 5.

114. Gershoni and Jankowski, *Egypt, Islam, and the Arabs*; Gershoni and Jankowski, *Redefining the Egyptian Nation*.

115. Baron, "Making and Breaking of Marital Bonds"; Baron, *Egypt as a Woman*; Kholoussy, *For Better, For Worse*; Pollard, *Nurturing the Nation*.

116. Gasper, *Power of Representation*.

117. El Shakry, *Great Social Laboratory*.

118. Jacob, *Working Out Egypt*; Ryzova, *Age of Efendiyya*.

119. Hanley, *Identifying with Nationality*.

120. Armbrust, *Mass Culture and Modernism in Egypt*; Fahmy, *Ordinary Egyptians*.

121. Anderson, *Imagined Communities*, 5.

122. A recent and notable exception to this trend is the work of Hussein Omar. See, Omar, "Liberal Cage"; Omar, "Rule of Strangers."

123. Lockman, "Social Roots of Nationalism"; Amin, "Gandhi as Mahatma."

124. Brown, *Peasant Politics*; Khuri-Makdisi, *Making of Global Radicalism*; Abul-Magd, *Imagined Empires*.

125. Beinin, *Workers and Peasants*, 70; Davis, *Challenging Colonialism*, 54; Saul, *La France et l'Égypte*, 695.

126. I take this kind of generalized social transformation to be the point of Andrew Sartori's observation that "we cannot limit critical engagement to the role of colonial state agency in the constitution, regulation, and maintenance of economic relations as if the colonial story were only a perpetually arrested moment of 'primitive accumulation.' " See, Sartori, "History of Political Economy," 123; Sartori, *Liberalism in Empire*, 27.

CHAPTER 1

1. Al-Iskandārī, *Dalīl al-Manūfīyah*, 13.

2. Ibid., 11–12.

3. Berque, *Egypt: Imperialism and Revolution*, 148.

4. On Cromer's mechanical metaphors, see Barak, *On Time*, 70–71.

5. Higher Committee for Agrarian Reform, *Silent Struggle*, 10.

6. 'Abbās, *al-Niẓām al-ijtimāʿī fī Miṣr*; 'Abd al-Fattāḥ, *al-Qaryah al-Miṣrīyah*; Abbas and El-Dessouky, *Large Landowning Class*; Barakāt, *Taṭawwur al-milkīyah al-zirāʿīyah*; Dasūqī, *Kibār mullāk al-arāḍī al-zirāʿīyah*; Zayn al-Dīn, *al-Zirāʿah al-Miṣrīyah*. On the contributions and influence of this " 'Ayn Shams School" of Egyptian social history, see Gran, "Egyptian Historiography"; Gorman, *Historians, State, and Politics*, 124–26; Di-Capua, *Gatekeepers of the Arab Past*, 327–35.

7. Owen, *Middle East in the World Economy*, 224.

8. A *feddan*, the standard unit of land in Egypt, is equal to 1.038 acres. A *qirat* is 1/24 of a feddan.

9. For an emblematic treatment of smallholding peasantries as the enduring other to the creeping forces of capitalist modernity see, in particular, Scott, *Weapons of the Weak*;

Scott, *Art of Not Being Governed.* For a critical response to this transhistorical ideal type of the smallholding peasant, see Zimmerman, *Alabama in Africa*, 16, 259.

10. Beckert, *Empire of Cotton*. Though Beckert's title offers an immensely useful shorthand for situating individual sites of cotton production within a comparative global field, his own analysis in the latter half of the book tends in places to reproduce this normative idealization of the smallholding.

11. Jakes and Shokr, "Finding Value."

12. Mill, *Principles of Political Economy*, 295–96.

13. Writing in 1916, for example, Egypt's leading British botanist and expert on the cotton crop laid special emphasis on the merits of the small family farm. "In the first place," he explained, "there is an ample supply of hand-labour at a reasonable price; cotton can be grown with the use of horse-hoes and similar appliances, but it cannot be grown to its highest productivity . . . ; further, the harvest of cotton has to be picked from the open fruits by hand, and where labour is scarce and dear this item may cost half as much as the cotton is worth; the small-holding fellah, incredibly industrious in his patient way, and with a numerous progeny, solves both of these labour difficulties automatically." See Balls, *Egypt of the Egyptians*, 193.

14. To the extent that this study hews closely to the discursive content of the occupation's sources, it runs an obvious risk in places of reproducing that erasure. This is a limitation of the research that I prefer to acknowledge as an indication of how much work remains to be done. For exemplars of Egyptian social history that employ the archives in creative ways to counteract the gendered omissions of official discourse, see Tucker, *Women in Nineteenth-Century Egypt*; Hammad, *Industrial Sexuality*; Derr, *Lived Nile*.

15. Fahmy, *All the Pasha's Men*.

16. Owen, *Cotton and the Egyptian Economy*; Rivlin, *Agricultural Policy of Muḥammad ʿAlī*.

17. On the attractions of "hooking up to the British entrepôt" in this era, see Arrighi, *Adam Smith in Beijing*, 244.

18. ʿAbbās, *al-Niẓām al-ijtimāʿī fī Miṣr*; Abbas and El-Dessouky, *Large Landowning Class*; Baer, *History of Landownership*; Barakāt, *Taṭawwur al-milkīyah al-zirāʿīyah*.

19. Owen, *Middle East in the World Economy*, 123; Toledano, "Social and Economic Change," 261.

20. Crouchley, *Investment of Foreign Capital*, 12–13.

21. Luxemburg, *Accumulation of Capital*, 410–13.

22. Harvey, *Paris*; Merrifield, *New Urban Question*, 35-39.

23. Ahuja, *Pathways of Empire*; Davis, *Late Victorian Holocausts*; Goswami, *Producing India*, Chapter 1; Harvey, *Limits to Capital*, Chapters 12 and 13; Karabell, *Parting the Desert*; White, *Railroaded*.

24. Beckert, "Emancipation and Empire."

25. Mestyan, *Arab Patriotism*, 50–83; Fahmy, *In Quest of Justice*, 132–78.

26. Landes, *Bankers and Pashas*.

27. Cole, *Colonialism and Revolution*, 110–26; Berque, *Egypt: Imperialism and Revolution*, 112–26; Schölch, *Egypt for the Egyptians*; EzzelArab, "Fiscal and Constitutional Program."

28. Cain and Hopkins, *British Imperialism*, 312–17; Hopkins, "Victorians and Africa."

29. On Dufferin's career as a diplomat in the Ottoman Empire, see Genell, "Empire by Law," Chapter 2.

30. TNA, FO 78/3565: Earl of Dufferin, "General Report by the Earl of Dufferin Respecting Reorganization in Egypt" (February 6, 1883).

31. Al-Sayyid, *Egypt and Cromer*, 33.

32. Dufferin, "General Report," 3.

33. Ibid.

34. Ibid., 10.

35. For an illuminating excavation of the role of the Organic Law in the emergence of a new "science of politics," see Omar, "Rule of Strangers," Chapter 2.

36. Dufferin, "General Report," 10.

37. Ibid., 1.

38. Ibid., 43.

39. Ibid., 22.

40. Ibid.

41. Ibid., 16.

42. Ibid., 13.

43. Ibid., 15.

44. Ibid., 13.

45. Ibid., 22.

46. Ibid., 23.

47. Ibid., 20.

48. Ibid., 21.

49. Ibid, 43.

50. Ibid, 43–44.

51. Owen, *Lord Cromer*, 176–79.

52. Dufferin, "General Report," 8.

53. Lord Cromer, *Political and Literary Essays*, 24–25.

54. Dufferin, "General Report," 21. Dufferin alluded directly to the movement for such protective legislation in India.

55. Lord Cromer, *Political and Literary Essays*, 44.

56. Lord Cromer, *Modern Egypt*, 451–52.

57. "Lord Cromer on Egypt," *London Times* (December 16, 1908): 12.

58. These policies figure centrally in Chapters 2 and 3 respectively.

59. For an overview of British education policy and the struggles it provoked, see Tignor, *Modernization and British Rule*, 319–46.

60. Milner, *England in Egypt*, 210.

61. Dufferin, "General Report," 15. See also, Beinart and Hughes, *Environment and Empire*, 130–47.

62. See Mikhail, *Nature and Empire*, Chapter 1.

63. Barak, *On Time*, Chapter 1; Hunter, *Egypt Under the Khedives*, 61–62; Rivlin, *Agricultural Policy of Muḥammad ʿAlī*; Derr, *Lived Nile*. Roger Owen puts the sum expended between 1863 and 1875 on works relating to the agricultural sector alone at £E 30,000,000. Owen, *Cotton and the Egyptian Economy*, 140.

64. See Fahmy, *In Quest of Justice*; Mestyan, *Arab Patriotism*.

65. Kemmerer, "Fiscal System of Egypt."

66. Brown, *History of the Barrage*, 18.

67. Ibid., 20–21.

68. Tignor, "Hydraulic Policy," 65.

69. 1885 was also the year of a major currency reform whereby the relative values of the Egyptian pound (£E) and the British pound (£) would be fixed at £E 0.975 to £1. The Egyptian pound was subdivided in 100 piasters or 1000 milliemes per £E 1. In practice, very few Egyptian pounds were struck, so the pound sterling was the main gold coin in circulation. This arrangement would remain in place until World War I. See, Owen, *Cotton and the Egyptian Economy*, 384–85. Throughout this book, I have retained the original currency designations as they appear in the sources.

70. Colin Scott-Moncrieff, "Report for 1885," excerpted in Willcocks and Craig, *Egyptian Irrigation*, I, 376.

71. Scott-Moncrieff, "Report for 1886," excerpted in ibid., 378.

72. Ibid.

73. Egypt. No. 3 (1891), *Report*, 5.

74. Ibid.

75. Owen, *Cotton and the Egyptian Economy*, 124, 238; Ministère de l'Intérieur, *Essai de Statistique Générale*.

76. The *qinṭār*, usually rendered in English as *kantar* was the largest unit of weight in Egypt at the time and the standard measure for cotton yield. As Owen notes, its measure relative to other units varied somewhat across the nineteenth century, but the *Statistique de l'Égypte, 1873* set it as the equivalent of 44.5458 kilograms. See Owen, *Cotton and the Egyptian Economy*, 382–83.

77. Egypt. No. 3 (1891), *Report*, 5.

78. Ibid., 13.

79. Scott-Moncrieff, *Aʿmāl al-rayy (1885–1886)*.

80. Derr, *Lived Nile*, 4, 39–40. On the longer history of this uneven relationship between the Delta and the Ṣaʿīd, see Abul-Magd, *Imagined Empires*.

81. Egypt. No. 3 (1891), *Report*, 14.

82. Jakes, "Scales of Public Utility."

83. Egypt. No. 6 (1888), *Condition of the Agricultural Population*, 15. Clarke was one of several British diplomats working at the Agency in Cairo at the time. Hunter, *Power and Passion*, 35.

84. TNA, FO 78/4310: Undated report by "Mr. Evans" in Evelyn Baring to Lord Salisbury (May 24, 1890).

85. Ibid.

86. DWQ, MNW 0075-034152: Scott Moncrieff to Council of Ministers (February 8, 1886).

87. DWQ, MNW 0075-034156: Majlis al-Nuẓẓār to Niẓārat al-Ashghāl al-ʿUmūmīyah (July 11, 1888).

88. R. Hanbury Brown, "Administration Report of the Irrigation Department in Lower Egypt for 1899," in Public Works Ministry, *Report (1899)*, 140.

89. TNA, FO 78/4145: E.W.P. Foster to Evelyn Baring (March 21, 1888).

90. Ibid.

91. Brown, "Corvée," 118.

92. Brown's main interlocutor seems to be Safran, *Egypt in Search of Political Community*.

93. Brown, "Corvée," 135. As Samera Esmeir has recently noted, Brown's argument relies on a problematic separation between liberalism and political economy. See Esmeir, *Juridical Humanity*, 90.

94. DWQ, MNW 0075-036383: Colin Scott-Moncrieff, *Note sur la Corvée en Égypte* (Le Caire: Imprimerie Nationale, 1886).

95. Egypt. No. 6 (1888), *Condition of the Agricultural Population*, 6.

96. DWQ, MNW 0075-036270: ʿAlī Mubārak, "Ṣūrat taqrīr muqaddam li-l-ḥaḍrah al-fakhīmah al-khidīwīyah min saʿadat nāẓir al-ashghāl al-ʿumūmīyah," (January 24, 1881).

97. Egypt. No. 1 (1895), *Report*, 50.

98. Lord Cromer, *Modern Egypt*, 410.

99. Ibid., 397.

100. Scott-Moncrieff to Nubar Pasha (January 31, 1885) in Egypt. No. 15 (1885), *Reports on the State of Egypt*, 50.

101. Hunter, *Egypt Under the Khedives*, 206; Karam, ed. *al-Niẓārāt wa-l-wizārāt al-miṣrīyah*, 78.

102. Brown, "Corvée," 126; Jallād, *Qāmūs al-idārah*, 3, 284–85.

103. Esmeir, *Juridical Humanity*, 115; Jallād, *Qāmūs al-idārah*, 3, 225.

104. DWQ, MNW 0075-034208: Scott-Moncrieff to Council of Ministers (November 15, 1887).

105. Scott-Moncrieff, "Note sur la Corvée."

106. In a frank explanation of this dynamic, Charles Roux observed, "[France] had the right to think that England had so decided not due to the urgency of reform but to the moral profit that [the English] would thereby gain and the consolidation of their dominion in Egypt that would result." See Roux, *Le Coton en Égypte*, 241.

107. "The Egyptian Preference Debt," *The Economist* (April 21, 1888): 497–98; "France and the Egyptian Debt Conversion," *The Economist* (June 29, 1889): 829; "The Egyptian Debt Conversion," *The Economist* (May 24, 1890): 657; TNA, FO 141/275: Lord Lytton to Salisbury (July 6, 1890); FO 78/4383: Evelyn Baring to Marquis of Salisbury (January 12, 1891); Milner, *England in Egypt*, 242; Tignor, *Modernization and British Rule*, 122.

108. Lord Cromer, *Modern Egypt*, 414–15. Rather than follow through, the British government ultimately assented to release its share of the Suez Canal revenues to cover the contested £250,000.

109. Egypt. No. 2 (1890), *Further Correspondence*, 77–78.

110. TNA, FO 78/4311: Gerald Portal to Marquis of Salisbury (July 9, 1890); Milner, *England in Egypt*, 242.

111. TNA, FO 78/4449: Raphael Borg to Marquis of Salisbury (January 22, 1892); "Décret," *Journal Officiel*, No. 16 (January 30, 1892).

112. TNA, FO 78/4388: Scott-Moncrieff to Baring (December 4, 1891). For statistics on the number of individuals called up for the "Nile corvée," see TNA 78/4385: Baring to Salisbury (May 24, 1891).

113. TNA, FO 78/4388: Ibid.

114. TNA, FO 78/4514: William Garstin, "Note on Payment of the Nile Corvée" (May 24, 1893).

115. TNA, FO 78/4452: Arthur Hardinge to Earl of Rosebery (October 2, 1892). In a subsequent letter, Hardinge noted that the timing of the Nile corvée coincided with the cotton harvest when demand for agricultural labor was particularly intense. Ibid.: Hardinge to Rosebery (October 10, 1892).

116. Garstin, "Note on Payment of the Nile Corvée."

117. Egypt. No. 1 (1906), *Reports by His Majesty's Agent (1905)*, 22.

118. The full text of the decree can be found in Hanīn, *al-Aṭyān wa-l-ḍarā'ib*, 240–41.

119. Baer, *History of Landownership*, 10–12.

120. ʿAbbās, *al-Niẓām al-ijtimāʿī fī Miṣr*, 22–23; ʿAbd al-Fattāḥ, *al-Qaryah al-Miṣrīyah*, 59–63; Abbas and El-Dessouky, *Large Landowning Class*, 212; Barakāt, *Taṭawwur al-milkīyah al-zirāʿīyah*; Shalabī, *al-Rīf al-Miṣrī*.

121. Mitchell, *Rule of Experts*, Chapter 2. See also, Guha, *Rule of Property*; Mehta, *Liberalism and Empire*; Esmeir, "Work of Law."

122. This process of financialization is the central topic of Chapter 3. For an analysis of landed property's role under capitalism as "a pure financial asset," see Harvey, *Urban Experience*, 96.

123. Egypt. No. 3 (1892), *Report*.

124. Cuno, *Pasha's Peasants*.

125. Hanīn, *al-Aṭyān wa-l-ḍarā'ib*, 502.

126. Al-Wakīl, *Milkīyat al-arāḍī fī Miṣr*, 622–23; Mitchell, *Rule of Experts*, 67.

127. TNA, FO 78/4384: Baring to Salisbury (April 19, 1891); Hanīn, *al-Aṭyān wa-l-ḍarā'ib*, 502.

128. DWQ, MNW 0075-036454: Niẓārat al-Ashghāl al-'Umūmīyah to Majlis al-Nuẓẓār (April 6, 1891).

129. Hanīn, *al-Aṭyān wa-l-ḍarā'ib*, 503. A draft of the new law had been completed in 1893, but it required the approval of the Mixed Courts in order to apply to foreign proprietors as well as Egyptians. After three years of delay, the Ministry of Public Works moved to promulgate the law for application under the National Court system rather than continue to delay. See DWQ, MNW 0075-036463; 0075-036468.

130. Ibid.

131. TNA, FO 78/4384: Baring to Salisbury (April 19, 1891).

132. TNA, FO 78/4243: Baring to Khedive Tawfiq (December 11, 1889).

133. TNA, FO 78/4042: Baring to Salisbury (March 31, 1887).

134. Egypt. No. 15 (1885), *Reports on the State of Egypt*, 50.

135. DWQ, DAU 4003-010856: William Garstin, "Note on Proposed Country Roads Suitable for Wheeled Traffic" (January 1889).

136. DWQ, MNW 0075-036456: 'Alī Pasha Mubārak, "Note sur le Project Conçernant les Routes Agricoles" (March 11, 1889).

137. Ibid. On the longer history of reformist discourses about "public utility" and "public interest" in Egypt and the Ottoman Empire at large, see Hamzah, "From 'Ilm to Ṣiḥāfa"; Khuri-Makdisi, *Making of Global Radicalism*, 63; Gasper, *Power of Representation*, 50.

CHAPTER 2

1. Durham University Library (DUR), Abbas Hilmi II Collection HIL 16, 66–76: Muḥammad Rushdī to Muḥammad Sa'īd Shīmī Bey (November 17, 1894).

2. Ibid., 68–69.

3. Brown, "Brigands and State Building."

4. For an illuminating treatment of "territoriality" in the era of the occupation, see Ellis, *Desert Borderland.*

5. Abul-Magd, *Imagined Empires*, 17–40; Mitchell, *Rule of Experts*, 61.

6. Cuno, *Pasha's Peasants*, 85–86.

7. 'Azabāwī, *'Umad wa-mashāyikh al-qurá*, 10; Cuno, *Pasha's Peasants*, 94–96.

8. Baer, *Studies in Social History*, 53–54; Cuno, *Pasha's Peasants*, 161.

9. Baer, *Studies in Social History*, 40; Fahmy, *All the Pasha's Men*, 70.

10. For an account that casts Ismā'īl's reign as "a gentle revolution" by focusing on the patronage of cultural institutions, see Mestyan, *Arab Patriotism*, Chapter 4. It is worth noting that Paul Draneht Pasha, whom Mestyan credits with overseeing Ismā'īl's "cultural system," was also intimately involved in the management of the Khedive's sugar plantations, on which much of the labor was performed by conscripts and slaves. See, Derr, *Lived Nile*, 78; Luxemburg, *Accumulation of Capital*, 412.

11. Mitchell, *Rule of Experts*, 60.

12. Abul-Magd, *Imagined Empires*, 92. The term for these bandits, *falatīyah,* also retained connotations of freedom or escape.

13. Ibid., 92–94, 109–14; Mitchell, *Rule of Experts*, 62–66; Rieker, "Sa'id and City," Chapter 5.

14. Mitchell, *Rule of Experts*, 61.

15. Esmeir, "Work of Law," 302; Esmeir, *Juridical Humanity*, 202. Working through a collection of murder cases from these large estates, Esmeir's extraordinary dissertation documents in vivid detail the forms of violence in the agricultural production process that proliferated within these de facto sovereign enclaves.

16. On the diversity of these arrangements for "subcontracting" the state outside the areas where cotton was grown, see Derr, *Lived Nile*, 98; Ellis, *Desert Borderland*, 13–39.

17. On the role of petitions as sites of hegemonic articulation, see Chalcraft, "Counterhegemonic Effects," 187. For a rich account of the role of peasant petitions within the wider Ottoman imperial formation, see Mikhail, *Nature and Empire*, Chapter 1.

18. Chalcraft, "Counterhegemonic Effects," 187.

19. Hunter, *Egypt Under the Khedives*, 52.

20. On the institution of elections for guild shaykhs, see Chalcraft, "Coal Heavers of Port Sa'id."

21. Chalcraft, "Engaging the State," 316.

22. Cuno's study provides a table on "the continuity of village families holding the position of village shaykh or 'umda, 1743–1988." Thirty-two of the fifty-two families listed held these positions for over a century In nine of these fifty-two cases, however, the long tenure of a single family ended in 1867, the year the new election statutes went into effect. Cuno, *Pasha's Peasants*, 174–75. See also, Davis, *Challenging Colonialism*, 29–41.

23. Chalcraft, "Engaging the State."

24. TNA, FO 78/3565: Earl of Dufferin, "General Report," 8.

25. In this regard, Mestyan's emphasis on the persistently elite and elitist character of the khedivate is clarifying. Mestyan, *Arab Patriotism*; Mestyan, "Domestic Sovereignty, A'yan Developmentalism."

26. Coles, *Recollections and Reflections*, 23.

27. Tollefson, *Policing Islam*, 16–18.

28. Colvin, *Making of Modern Egypt*, 193–98.

29. Cromer, *Modern Egypt*, 189.

30. Ibid., 397.

31. TNA, FO 78/4307: William Garstin to Evelyn Baring (May 14, 1888).

32. Colvin, *Making of Modern Egypt*, 197–98.

33. Brown, "Brigands and State Building," 268–74.

34. The Arabic root *'azaba* literally means "to be far or distant; to escape." In official terminology, *'izbah* (pl. *'izab*) often appeared interchangeably with the term *kafr* (pl. *kufūr*),

which also describes a small, remote hamlet. See also, Berque, *Egypt: Imperialism and Revolution*, 54.

35. DWQ, MNW 0075-006539: "Ṣurat mā nushira min niẓārat al-dakhilīyah fī ghāyat rabīʿ al-awwal 1297."

36. DWQ, MNW 0075-006539: "Ṣūrat al-maddah al-sādisah min mulḥaq qānūn al-ghafar al-ṣādir fī 10 nūfambar 1884."; Jallād, *Qāmūs al-idārah wa-l-qaḍḍā'* (*1889 Edition*), 2, 477–79.

37. DWQ, MNW 0075-006556: Petition from ʿIzbat al-Shaykh Ibrāhīm ʿAbdullah in Manūfīyah Province (1887).

38. DWQ, MNW 0075-006557.

39. Though most of the files date from the period immediately following the promulgation of the new *ghafīr* law, the vast collection of formal requests to destroy ʿizab runs into the 1910s. The bulk of this collection is housed in one continuous series in the papers of the Council of Ministers. See DWQ, MNW 0075-006536 to 006656.

40. Brown, "Brigands and State Building," 276–78; Esmeir, *Juridical Humanity*, 274–75; Tollefson, "1894 British Takeover," 548.

41. TNA, FO 78/4239: Report by Charles Legrelle to Ministry of Interior (April 6, 1889).

42. Ibid.: Baring to Salisbury (April 30, 1889).

43. Ibid.

44. Ibid.

45. TNA, FO 78/4312: Baring to Salisbury (November 6, 1890); FO 78/4383: Baring to Salisbury (February 18, 1891). The Khedivial Decree appointing Scott as Judicial Adviser was issued on February 16, 1891.

46. TNA, FO 78/4312: Baring to Salisbury (December 23, 1890).

47. Muṣṭafá Kāmil, the leader of the Egyptian National Party, would later call the takeover of the Interior "the most fatal blow to our autonomy." Kamel Pasha, *Égyptiens et Anglais*, 61; Tollefson, "1894 British Takeover," 547.

48. As was the convention at the time, Muṣṭafá Fahmī Pasha was both Minister of Interior and Prime Minister. Tollefson, "1894 British Takeover," 549.

49. TNA, FO 78/4513: Cromer to Lord Rosebery (January 9, 1893).

50. Blunt, *My Diaries*, Vol. 1, 86.

51. TNA, FO 78/4513: Cromer to Rosebery (January 25, 1893).

52. Ibid.: Cromer to Rosebery (January 27, 1893); translations of articles from "El Ustaz."

53. Ibid.: Mr. S. Felice [Vice Consul at Zagazig] to Mr. Borg [Consul at Cairo] (February 11, 1893).

54. TNA, FO 78/4515: Arthur Hardinge to Rosebery (July 23, 1893).

55. Ibid.: Hardinge to Rosebery (August 5, 1893).

56. Colvin, *Making of Modern Egypt*, 234; Tollefson, "1894 British Takeover," 553.

57. MEC: Gorst GB 165-0122, Box 1: Gorst Diary, 1894. Nūbār's reappointment was announced on April 16. See Karam, ed. *al-Niẓārāt wa-l-wizārāt al-miṣrīyah*, 153.

58. TNA, FO 141/303: Eldon Gorst, "Confidential Memorandum on the Reorganization of the Administration of the Interior" (August 24, 1894). See also, Gorst Diary, 1894, entries for August 9, 12, 16, and 19.

59. DWQ, MNW 0075-003426: "Lā'iḥat al-ʿumad wa-l-mashāyikh," (March 16, 1895). The minimum age for both positions was twenty-five. An ʿumdah would need to own at least ten feddans of land and a shaykh at least five. Preference would be given to candidates for these positions who could read and write.

60. Tollefson, *Policing Islam*, 102.

61. Egypt. No. 1 (1896), *Report on the Finances, Administration, and Condition*, 16.

62. Ibid., 17.

63. DUR, HIL 15, 27: Shīmī Bey to AHII (June 11, 1894).

64. Ibid., 26b; HIL 15, 61: Shīmī Bey to AHII (July 29, 1894).

65. DUR, HIL 16, 47: Muḥammad Rushdī to Shīmī Bey (July 21, 1894).

66. DUR, HIL 15, 26–28: Shīmī Bey to AHII (June 11, 1894).

67. DUR, HIL 15, 116–123: Shīmī Bey to AHII (October 28, 1894).

68. Cromer, *Abbas II*, xiii.

69. Blunt, *My Diaries*, 1, 86.

70. In his excellent study of Egypt's western desert region, Matthew Ellis has shown that this spy network was just one among a number of efforts to mobilize resources and institutions connected to the palace in order to carve out new enclaves of influence beyond British control. Ellis, *Desert Borderland*, 62–64.

71. DUR, HIL 15, 285: Shīmī Bey to AHII (August 4, 1895).

72. See, for example, DUR HIL 15, 65: Shīmī Bey to AHII (August 3, 1894).

73. DUR, HIL 15, 116–23: Shīmī Bey to AHII (October 28, 1894).

74. For a rich and lucid history of the category of the *futūwah* from its genesis in the Middle Ages through its resignification as the Other to the normative masculine subject of interwar Egypt, see Jacob, *Working Out Egypt*, Chapter 8.

75. DUR, HIL 15, 63–67: Shīmī Bey to AHII (August 3, 1894).

76. DUR, HIL 15, 34: Shīmī Bey to AHII (June 15, 1894).

77. DUR, HIL 16, 69: Muḥammad Rushdī to Shīmī Bey (November 17, 1894).

78. Ibid.

79. DUR, HIL 15, 137: Shīmī Bey to AHII (November 22, 1894).

80. DUR, HIL 16, 89: Muḥammad Rushdī to Shīmī Bey (January 27, 1895); HIL 16, 93: Muḥammad Rushdī to Shīmī Bey (January 30, 1895).

81. Ibid., 86. Throughout their correspondence, the spies made occasional reference to the intelligence networks that Ministry of Interior itself controlled.

82. Ibid., 93.

83. Ibid., 86.

84. Egypt. No. 1 (1896), *Report on the Finances, Administration, and Condition*, 16.

85. DUR, HIL 260, 132–4: Ismāʿīl Jawdat to Shīmī Bey (April 30, 1895).

86. DUR, HIL 260, 106–8: Ḥussayn Naṣṣār to Shīmī Bey (May 19, 1895).

87. Ibid.

88. DUR, HIL 260, 132.

89. DUR, HIL 260, 106.

90. DUR, HIL 260, 132–34.

91. "Rasāʾil Dākhilīyah," *al-Ahrām* (April 25, 1895).

92. DUR, HIL 260, 132.

93. Tollefson, *Policing Islam*, 62.

94. "Maṣāʾib qawm ʿanda fawāʾid qawm," *al-Fallāḥ* (January 15, 1895).

95. DWQ, MNW0075-003434: "Mudhakkarah ʿan mashrūʿ al-amr al-ʿālī alladhi yukhawwil li-l-ʿumad haqq ikhtiṣāṣ juzʾī fī al-qaḍāyā al-madanīyah" (1898).

96. Al-Barūdī, *Dalīl al-ʿumdah*, 5. See also, Rifʿat, *Wājibāt al-ʿumdah*; Ṣabrī, *Ḥadīth al-ʿumad.*

97. Rifʿat, *Wājibāt al-ʿumdah*, 4.

98. DWQ, DD 2001-026178: *Al-Nashrah al-idārīyah* (November-December 1897).

99. Scott, *Seeing Like a State.*

100. Egypt. No. 1 (1896), *Report on the Finances, Administration, and Condition*, 16.

101. In this respect, Gabriel Baer's influential study of "the village shaykhs" unwittingly reproduces both the language and the empirical claims of its colonial sources. See Baer, *Studies in Social History*, 30–61.

102. Rifʿat, *Wājibāt al-ʿumdah*, 7.

103. DWQ, WA 0069-024179: "Sijil ʿArḍḥalāt Dīwān Khidīwī," No. 870, Fātimah Bint Sālim ʿAbdullah (May 6, 1903).

104. Ibid., No. 946, Dasūqī Ḥamādah (May 23, 1903).

105. Ibid., No. 947, Ismāʿīl Muḥammad (May 23, 1903).

106. The certificate was a printed form, "Government Form 157," the body of which contained a questionnaire to be completed by the ʿumdah, followed by his signature affirming that the bearer of the certificate was "poor and unable to undertake the fees in the case he wishes to bring against [the defendant]." I located a copy of the form in DWQ, Mudīrīyat Manūfīyah, 2016-002839: "Tarikat Ḥussayn al-Hādī," (August 14, 1899).

107. DWQ, WA, 0069-024181: "Sijil ʿArḍḍḥālat bi-l-Dīwān al-Khidīwī 1904" (May 19, 1904).

108. On the colonial-era regulation of prostitution and the persistence of unlicensed sex work, especially among poor women in the provinces, see Hammad, " 'National Purity' and 'Local Flexibility' "; Kholoussy, "Monitoring and Medicalising Male Sexuality."

109. The account of al-ʿAshrī's troubles is compiled from numerous petitions recorded in the registers of the Khedive's diwan between 1904 and 1907. DWQ, WA, 0069-024181, 013657, 013658, 013659: Petitions from al-Sibāʿī al-ʿAshrī to ʿAbbās Ḥilmī II (June 2, 1904; October 26, 1907; November 24, 1907; December 2, 1907).

110. Ibid.

111. Poulantzas, *State, Power, Socialism.*

112. On the "state effect" as the unstable outcome of projects to impose order and coherence on the inherently diverse and divided institutions of government, see Jessop, *State Theory*; Jessop, *State Power*; Mitchell, "Society, Economy, and the State Effect."

CHAPTER 3

1. LSE: Ionian Bank Papers 10/18: Mr. F. Larkworthy, "Report on Egypt as a Field for Banking Business" (Alexandria: March 24, 1905).

2. LSE: Ionian Bank Papers 10/17: G. J. Marshall to J. Skelton Esq. (November 25, 1904).

3. Larkworthy, "Report on Egypt," 39–40.

4. Ibid., 51.

5. Exod. 16:3: "And the children of Israel said unto them, Would to God we had died by the hand of the Lord in the land of Egypt, when we sat by the flesh pots, and when we did eat bread to the full; for ye have brought us forth into this wilderness, to kill this whole assembly with hunger."

6. Arminjon, *La Situation Economique*, 590–91.

7. "Al-Sharikāt wa-l-muḍāribah fī Miṣr," *al-Jarīdah* (March 20, 1907).

8. Crouchley, *Investment of Foreign Capital*, 53.

9. Working with a slightly longer time frame, Bent Hansen puts foreign capital investment in Egypt at £E 96.9 million in 1884, as compared to £E 156.9 in 1914. See Hansen, "Interest Rates and Foreign Capital." On the concentration of foreign investment in banks, mortgage companies, and land development schemes, see also Tignor, *State, Private Enterprise, and Economic Change*, 18, 40.

10. Sir R. Hamilton Lang, "The Egyptian Boom," *Financial Review of Reviews* (July 1907): 120–21.

11. Ibid., 117.

12. "Egypt's Progress: Review of the Situation," *Egyptian Gazette* (EG) (February 6, 1907).

13. The term *spatial fix* first appeared in David Harvey's 1981 *Antipode* article, "The Spatial Fix: Hegel, Von Thünen and Marx," republished in Harvey, *Spaces of Capital*, Chapter 14. He published a more thorough and systematic elaboration of the concept the following year in Harvey, *Limits to Capital.* See also, Jessop, "Spatial Fixes."

14. On this suggestive treatment of "Haussmannization" as a global process, see Merrifield, *New Urban Question*; Harvey, *Paris.*

15. Davis, *Late Victorian Holocausts*; Goswami, *Producing India*; Toledano, "Social and Economic Change"; Strachey and Strachey, *Finances and Public Works of India.*

16. Harvey, *Limits to Capital*, 319; Hilferding, *Finance Capital*; Lenin, "Imperialism: The Highest Stage of Capitalism."

17. Arrighi, *Long Twentieth Century*, 164. In characterizing the depression as a crisis of overproduction, Arrighi rebuts the thesis of S. B. Saul that the depression was a "myth," noting

that Saul's analysis fails to distinguish between productivity and profitability. See Saul, *Myth of the Great Depression.* Arrighi's analysis of the crisis-induced tension between British industry and the City is echoed in Cain and Hopkins, *British Imperialism*, 309; Harvey, *Limits to Capital*, 319; Jessop, *State Theory*, 200.

18. Arrighi, *Long Twentieth Century*, 166.

19. Hobsbawm, *Age of Empire*, 52.

20. Arrighi, *Long Twentieth Century.* The precise magnitude and geographic distribution of this wave of capital transfers from Europe abroad have been the topic of more than a century of debate among economic historians. All accounts agree, however, that the scale of foreign investment dramatically outstripped that of the preceding decades and that the United States was the leading recipient of European capital. See Feis, *Europe, the World's Banker*; Cottrell, *British Overseas Investment*; Platt, *Britain's Investment Overseas*; Tiberi, *Accounts of the British Empire*; Hall, ed. *Export of Capital from Britain.*

21. ʿAbbās, *al-Niẓām al-ijtimāʿī fī Miṣr*; Dasūqī, *Kibār mullāk al-arāḍī al-zirāʿīyah.* Despite a very different theoretical point of departure, Mitchell arrives at a similar analysis of landed property in *Rule of Experts*, 54–79. In an innovative variant, drawing on the work of Giorgio Agamben, Samera Esmeir argues that property law effectively formed a juridical barrier around the "hidden abode of production" that placed violence in the agricultural labor process beyond the reach of the new legal order's "humane" protections. Esmeir, *Juridical Humanity.*

22. Harvey, *Limits to Capital*, 348.

23. Stuart, *Reports*, 8.

24. Ibid., 2; Chaudhuri, "Measure of Value"; Postel, *Populist Vision*; Iyer, "Paradox of Poverty and Plenty."

25. Charlesworth, "Deccan Riots," 418–21.

26. Catanach, *Rural Credit in Western India*, 10–11; Hardiman, *Feeding the Baniya*, 218.

27. Catanach, *Rural Credit in Western India*, 11.

28. East India (Deccan Riots Commission), *Report of the Commission.*

29. See Henderson, "Nature and Fictitious Capital"; Henderson, *California and the Fictions of Capital.*

30. Henderson, *California and the Fictions of Capital*, 113–14.

31. Ali, *Punjab Under Imperialism*; Banerjee, *Agrarian Society of the Punjab*; Ludden, *Agricultural Production*, Preface to the Second Edition; Gilmartin, *Blood and Water.*

32. Thorburn, *Musalmans and Money-Lenders*, 10, 1.

33. Ibid., 37.

34. Amin, *Sugarcane and Sugar in Gorakhpur*; Banaji, "Capitalist Domination and the Small Peasantry"; Bose, *Peasant Labour and Colonial Capital*; Bose, *Credit, Markets, and the Agrarian Economy.*

35. Barrier, "Punjab Alienation of Land Bill"; Washbrook, "Law, State, and Agrarian Society."

36. TNA, FO 78/3565: Dufferin, "General Report," 22.

37. See Chapter 7.

38. Catanach, *Rural Credit in Western India*, 28.

39. Charlesworth, *Peasants and Imperial Rule*, 96; Ratcliffe, *Wedderburn*, 30–32.

40. Wedderburn, "Agricultural Banks for India," 7.

41. Ibid., 29.

42. Wedderburn, "Paper to Be Read at a Meeting of the Manchester Chamber of Commerce," 14.

43. Ibid.

44. Berque, *Egypt: Imperialism and Revolution*, 183; Crouchley, *Investment of Foreign Capital*, 34.

45. Catanach, *Rural Credit in Western India*, 27; Wedderburn, "Agricultural Banks for India," 30–31.

46. On the role of these bond guarantees in infrastructural projects, see Goswami, *Producing India*, Chapter 1.

47. BL, Add. MS. 43, 596 (Lord Ripon Papers): Baring to Ripon (September 6, 1881).

48. Catanach, *Rural Credit in Western India*, 20–30; Ratcliffe, *Wedderburn*, 41.

49. Cromer, *Modern Egypt*, II, 249–50.

50. Ibid., 251.

51. TNA, PRO 30/57/42: Lord Cromer to Lord Kitchener, July 25, 1912.

52. Derr, *Lived Nile*, 47; Egypt. No. 3 (1891), *Report*, 5.

53. DUR, HIL 16, 66–76: Muḥammad Rushdī to Shīmī Bey (November 17, 1894)

54. Egypt. No. 1 (1895), *Report on the Finances, Administration, and Condition*, 5.

55. Baer, *History of Landownership*, 13–31.

56. Abbas and El-Dessouky, *Large Landowning Class*, 11.

57. Willcocks and Craig, *Egyptian Irrigation*, II, 804. A piaster was one one-hundredth of a pound.

58. Cromer, *Political and Literary Essays*, 45.

59. Egypt. No. 1 (1895), *Report on the Finances, Administration, and Condition*, 5.

60. Colvin, *Making of Modern Egypt*, 233.

61. Egypt. No. 1 (1895), *Report on the Finances, Administration, and Condition*; Owen, *Cotton and the Egyptian Economy*, 246–47.

62. DWQ, MNW 0075-022260: *Rapport sur les Opérations de la Péréquation de l'Impôt Foncier en 1895–1896*. On the intellectual origins of the Permanent Settlement, see Guha, *Rule of Property*.

63. The findings of the commission were published immediately after its conclusion in a directory with tables of rental values by village. See Ministry of Finance (Egypt), *Projet de Péréquation de l'Impôt Foncier*.

64. Willcocks and Craig, *Egyptian Irrigation*, II, 803.

65. Lyons, *Cadastral Survey of Egypt*, 4; Mitchell, *Rule of Experts*, 84–93.

66. Hanīn, *al-Aṭyān wa-l-ḍarā'ib*, 274–75.

67. DUR, HIL 16, 132–1: Muḥammad Rushdī to Shīmī Bey (October 8, 1895); HIL 260, 3–5; 21–28; 60–82.

68. "Shirkah Musāhamah Basandīlah," *al-Mu'ayyad* (September 8, 1896).

69. Egypt. No. 1 (1895), *Report on the Finances, Administration, and Condition*, 29.

70. DWQ, MNW 0075-0222991: Elwin Palmer, "Note au Conseil des Ministres" (January 24, 1895).

71. Ibid.

72. Egypt. No. 1 (1895), *Report on the Finances, Administration, and Condition*, 29. See also, TNA, FO 141/309: Lord Cromer to Earl of Kimberley (January 31, 1895).

73. As part of his effort to garner support for his "Five Feddan Law," Lord Kitchener commissioned a national survey of debts on properties of five feddans or less in 1913. The findings of the survey were collated and published in his annual report for that year. Egypt. No. 1 (1914), *Reports by His Majesty's Agent (1913)*, 12. See also TNA, FO 141/763/2, "Usury"; FO 141/620.

74. I was fortunate enough to locate and read through a collection of several hundred such inventories from a few districts of Manūfīyah and Gharbīyah provinces between 1899 and 1901: DWQ, Mudīrīat al-Manūfīyah (MM): 2016-002322 to 2016-003003 and Mudīrīat al-Gharbīyah (MG): 2017-006512 to 2017-006600.

75. The borrower would take a sum of money in exchange for a piece of land over which the lender would enjoy usufruct until the original sum was repaid. The produce of the land or the rent the creditor received for it would take the place of interest on the loan.

76. It is often suggested that after the creation of the Mixed Courts and National Courts in 1876 and 1883 respectively, Egypt's Sharī'ah Courts were left to handle matters of personal status alone. In fact, they continued to serve as another forum for a range of other cases and transactions, including those pertaining to land and credit. See, for example, DWQ, Maḥkamat al-Gharbīyah al-Shar'īyah (MGS) 1033-001688: "Maḥkamat mudīrīyat al-Gharbīyah al-shar'īyah bi-Ṭanṭā: sijill al-'uqūd wa-l-aḥkām wa-l-ruhūn al-wārid li-l-maḥakim al-shar'īyah (1901)."

77. Muḥammad Ḥasanayn Sharaf al-Dīn, for example, owned just over 2.5 feddans of land at the time of his death. He owed money to his brother Ibrahim, his children, and a Ḥurmah Hasan bint 'Alī 'Īd. DWQ, MM 2016-002457: "Tarakat Muḥammad Ḥasanayn Sharaf al-Dīn" (September 16, 1900). The debt census from 1913 also revealed that, even after the effects of the financial boom and the considerable expansion of foreign lending institutions, "the fellaheen were much more indebted to each other—especially to the women-folk—and much less to Greeks, Syrians, and foreign mortgage institutions than was imagined at that time." FO 141/763/2: Westropp to Martin (June 7, 1931).

78. DWQ, MM 2016-002465: "Tarakat al-marḥūm Ḥasan Aḥmad al-'Īsawī," (October 11, 1900).

79. Coles, *Recollections and Reflections*, 171.

80. Kemmerer, *Report on the Agricultural Bank*, 5. See also, "*Taslīf al-nuqūd li-l-fallāhīn bi-fawā'id qalīlah*," *al-Waṭan* (January 24, 1896).

81. Ibid.; "*Mashrūʿ al-taslīf li-l-ahālī*," *al-Ahālī* (January 27, 1896).

82. Egypt. No. 1 (1896), *Report on the Finances, Administration, and Condition*, 9.

83. National Bank of Egypt, *National Bank of Egypt, 1898–1948*, 16–19.

84. Colvin, *Making of Modern Egypt*, 279–80. See also Mabrūk, "al-Bank al-ahlī."

85. Kemmerer, *Report on the Agricultural Bank*, 6.

86. Colvin, *Making of Modern Egypt*, 280; Kemmerer, *Report on the Agricultural Bank*.

87. TNA, FO 78/5226: Lord Cromer to Marquess of Lansdowne (March 25, 1902).

88. Agricultural Bank of Egypt, *Decret, Acte Préliminaire D'Association, Statuts* (Le Caire: Imprimerie Centrale, 1902). Subsequent issues raised the guaranteed rate to 3.5%. Barclays Bank Archive (BBA), Anglo-Egyptian Bank Papers, 0080-3250: "The Agricultural Bank of Egypt."

89. Kemmerer, *Report on the Agricultural Bank*, 11; Egypt. No. 1 (1903), *Reports by His Majesty's Agent (1902)*, 16–17; Egypt. No. 1 (1904), *Reports by His Majesty's Agent (1903)*, 13–14; Egypt. No. 1 (1905), *Reports by His Majesty's Agent (1904)*, 29; Egypt. No. 1 (1906), *Reports by His Majesty's Agent (1905)*, 35; Egypt. No. 1 (1907), *Reports by His Majesty's Agent (1906)*, 52. See also, "Agricultural Bank of Egypt," *The Economist* (April 6, 1907), 598. In 1907, the bank lowered the maximum rate on its loans from 9 to 8%.

90. DWQ, MM 2016-002767: "Tarakat Ramaḍān Aḥmad Fūla min Kafr al-Shaykh Ibrāhīm" (March 1902).

91. DWQ, WA 0069-009061, "Iltimāsāt wa-shakāwa huqaddamah ilá dīwān khidīwī Miṣr min baʿḍ al-ahālī, sannat 1911," undated petition from the villagers of al-Ḥasānāt in Qena Province. The petitioners complained that they had "been deceived that if we resorted to dealing with the bank it would unify our debts, and we would see a beneficial result, but it turned out that its conduct was very harsh, to such a terrible degree that we now expose it to justice, begging for mercy."

92. Kemmerer, *Report on the Agricultural Bank*, 11–12.

93. BL, IOR P/7558, Government of the Punjab, Department of Revenue and Agriculture Proceedings, October to December 1907: Sir Frederick Nicholson, "Memorandum on the Egyptian Agricultural Bank" (February 5, 1904).

94. Uttar Pradesh State Archives, Revenue Department, 671/1907: "Establishment of Agricultural Banks."

95. Kemmerer, *Report on the Agricultural Bank*.

96. "Farmers' Bank Pays: Egypt's Lending Institution Is Proving Successful. Takes Place of Usurers," *Washington Post* (January 7, 1907).

97. Rosenberg, *Financial Missionaries to the World*, 53.

98. Nagano, "Agricultural Bank of the Philippine Government," 314.

99. Even Cromer's pronouncements on the subject were rather subdued. In 1904, for example, he observed, "So far as can be judged, the peasant proprietary class is not only

holding its own, but is also possibly showing a slight tendency to increase. It is, however, difficult to furnish absolutely conclusive proof of the truth of this statement." See Egypt. No. 1 (1904), *Reports by His Majesty's Agent (1903)*, 15.

100. Van Dieren, *Les avantages . . . des placements hypothécaires.*

101. Hobson, *Imperialism*; Hilferding, *Finance Capital*; Lenin, "Imperialism"; Luxemburg, *Accumulation of Capital.*

102. Van Dieren, *Les avantages . . . des placements hypothécaires*, 3.

103. Ibid., 4.

104. Ibid., 5.

105. Ibid., 8.

106. Ibid., 9.

107. "Lord Cromer on Egypt's Finances," *The Economist* (April 22, 1905), 670.

108. Derr, *Lived Nile*, Chapter 2.

109. Larkworthy, "Report on Egypt," 49.

110. Ibid., 53.

111. Ibid., 31.

112. Ibid., 27.

113. London Metropolitan Archives (LMA), MS 241005/1, Imperial Ottoman Bank (IOB): R. Harding Milward to John Reeves (January 26, 1899).

114. The first foreign-financed bank in the country was the Bank of Egypt in 1856, followed by the Anglo-Egyptian Banking Company in 1864. See Crouchley, *Investment of Foreign Capital*, 29–30.

115. LMA, MS 241005/1, IOB: E.W.H. Barry to Lord Hillingdon (February 20, 1899).

116. Ibid.: Reeves to Barry, February 20, 1899.

117. Alger, *Report to His Excellency Herbert H. Lehman, Governor of the State of New York*, 8.

118. Levy, *Freaks of Fortune*, 164.

119. LMA, MS 241005/1, IOB: John Reeves to E.W.H. Barry (March 8, 1899).

120. LMA, MS 24008, Imperial Ottoman Bank, Cairo 1899–1904: Moxley to Barry (August 15, 1902).

121. LMA, MS 17908/1, Minutes of Local Committee for Egypt No. 1 (Gresham Life Assurance Society Papers): "Minutes of a Meeting of the Local Board held on the 11th February 1904."

122. Ibid. The Crédit Foncier remained the largest mortgage lender throughout this period. See also, Saul, *La France et l'Égypte*, 295–361.

123. Colvin, *Making of Modern Egypt*, 272.

124. DWQ, MNW 0075-017234: Survey Department, "Report on the Progress of Survey and Publication of Maps, 1912"; Cunningham, *To-Day in Egypt*, 144.

125. ING Bank, Baring Brothers Papers, MC 15.2.3, Behera Company: Lord Cromer to Windham Baring (June 23, 1904). The Behera Company, which undertook land reclamation projects, was headed by E.W.P. Foster, a former irrigation inspector.

126. Willis and Barrett, eds., *Anglo-African Who's Who*, 134–35; British Chamber of Commerce of Egypt, *List of Companies*.

127. Van Dieren also noted the importance of finding an expert to assess the worth of mortgaged property. Van Dieren, *Les avantages . . . des placements hypothécaires*, 15.

128. LMA, MS 17908/1: "Minutes of a Meeting . . . on the 8th March, 1904."

129. LMA, MS 17908/1: "Minutes of a Meeting . . . on the 11th February 1904."

130. Van Dieren, *Les avantages . . . des placements hypothécaires*, 11.

131. LMA, MS 17908/1, Part 2: "Minutes of a Meeting . . . on the 11th January 1905."

132. LMA, MS 17908/1, Part 2: "Minutes of a Meeting . . . on the 11th January 1905."

133. LMA, MS 17908/1 Part 1: "Minutes of a Meeting . . . on the 11th February 1904"; "Minutes of a Meeting . . . on the 2nd June 1904"; 17908/1 Part 2: "Minutes of a Meeting . . . on the 29th March 1905."

134. LMA, MS 241005/1, Imperial Ottoman Bank: Mr. Barry to Lord Hillingdon (February 20, 1899).

135. Arminjon, *Present Financial Crisis*.

136. Eid, *La fortune immobilière*; Eid, *Al-tharwah al-ʿaqārīyah*. Eid's study first appeared as part of the annual report of the Belgian Consulate for 1906. The *Egyptian Gazette* ran a four-part series detailing his findings. See "Mortgages in Egypt," *EG* (January 24, 1907; January 28, 1907; February 1, 1907; February 4, 1907). On Eid's career, see Davis, *Challenging Colonialism*, 73–74.

137. Eid, *La fortune immobilière*, 143.

138. Ibid., 145.

139. Ibid., 131–33.

140. Lang, "The Egyptian Boom," *Blackwood's Magazine* (July 1907), 124.

141. Goswami, *Producing India*; Sarkar, *Swadeshi Movement*.

142. Muḥammad Ibrāhīm, "Al-Khaṭar al-muntaẓir ʿalā tharwat al-bilād", *al-Liwāʾ* (February 8, 1905).

143. "Al-Nahdah al-mālīyah al-Miṣrīyah: wahamīyah hiya am ḥaqīqīyah," *al-Hilāl* Vol. 14, No. 8 (May 1, 1906): 443.

CHAPTER 4

1. "Al-Miṣrīyūn wa-l-Inklīz," *al-Muʾayyad* (February 7, 1905).

2. "Khuṭbat al-Lūrd Krūmar," *al-Muʾayyad* (February 5, 1905).

3. "Lord Cromer's Trip," *Egyptian Gazette* (February 4, 1905). The paper's title is hereafter abbreviated as *EG*.

4. "English and Egyptians," ibid.

5. "Al-Khiṭṭah al-jadīdah li-l-iḥtilāl, al-Lūrd Krūmar, wa-l-ahālī," *al-Muʾayyad* (February 6, 1905).

6. "Khuṭbat al-Lūrd Krūmar," *al-Ẓāhir* (February 6, 1905).

7. "Al-Lūrd Krūmar khaṭīban," *al-Baṣīr* (February 8, 1905).

8. This recourse to new modes of statistical representation for the "progress" of government policy was by no means unique to Egypt in this period. Indeed, part of the power of the story the occupation's annual reports told lay in the availability of a growing array of similar documents from other countries to which these measures could be compared. See also, Frankel, *States of Inquiry*; Cook, *Pricing of Progress*.

9. Arminjon, "Les enseignements de la crise financière égyptienne," 265.

10. For the most comprehensive extant list of periodicals, see https://www.zmo.de/jaraid/index.html. See also, Abū 'Arjah, *Al-Muqaṭṭam*; Khan, *Egyptian-Indian Collaboration*, 23–25; Mīkhā'īl, *al-Ṣaḥāfah al-Miṣrīyah*.

11. "Aqwāl al-jarā'id wa-khuṭbat al-Lūrd Krūmar," *al-Liwā'* (February 6, 1905).

12. Aḥmad Ḥilmī, "Al-Kalām al-dhahabī: al-ḥālah al-mālīyah fī Miṣr (al-taqaddum al-sarī')," *al-Liwā'* (December 28, 1905).

13. Mestyan, *Arab Patriotism*, 292–95.

14. Goldschmidt, "Egyptian Nationalist Party," 318–19. This personal animus was exacerbated by Shaykh 'Alī Yūsuf's controversial decision to marry Ṣafīyah al-Sādāt against her father's will. *Al-Liwā'* joined the public outcry while the Khedive offered his unwavering support. See Kholoussy, *For Better, For Worse*, 112–13.

15. See, for example, "Maṣā'ib qawm 'anda qawm fawā'id," *al-Fallāḥ* (January 15, 1895).

16. The name *al-Hizb al-Waṭanī* (the National Party) was thus commonly used to refer to Kāmil, his associates, and their paper well before they announced the formal establishment of a political party on October 22, 1907.

17. Muṣṭafá Kāmil, "al-Miṣrīyūn wa-l-muḥtillūn wa-kāyfa ya'īshūna ma'an," *al-Liwā'* (January 6, 1905).

18. Ibid.

19. "Miṣr wa-abnā'uhā," *Miṣr* (February 1, 1897).

20. DUR, HIL 16, 66–76: Muḥammad Rushdi to Shīmī Bey (November 17, 1894).

21. "Hal yastaqill al-Miṣrī wa-kayfa yastaqill," *al-Rā'id al-Miṣrī* (April 22, 1897).

22. Musallamī, *Aḥmad Ḥilmī*, 15–19; Badawī, *Aḥmad Ḥilmī*, 31–33.

23. In the French education system, political economy was a subdiscipline of the law.

24. Aḥmad Ḥilmī, "Bī' al-maḥṣūlāt wa-ra'ī al-Lūrd Krūmar," *al-Liwā'* (February 7, 1905).

25. MEC, GB 165-0035, Harry Boyle Papers: Box B, File 3: Harry Boyle to Nellie Boyle (April 12, 1900).

26. Egypt. No. 1 (1907), *Reports by His Majesty's Agent (1906)*, 45.

27. ING Bank, Baring Brothers Papers, MC 15.2.6: Cromer to Lord Revelstoke (October 22, 1905).

28. "Egypt's Amazing Prosperity," *EG* (January 28, 1905).

29. Ḥilmī, "Al-Kalām al-dhahabī."

30. "Al-Sharikāt al-ajnabīyah fī al-diyār al-Miṣrīyah," *al-Liwā'* (May 6, 1905).

31. Examples include the Anglo-Egyptian Land Allotment Company, the Delta Light Railway Company, and the Société Anonyme du Béhéra.

32. "Al-Araḍī al-zira'īyah fī Miṣr," *al-Liwā'* (May 18, 1905).

33. "Al-Nahḍah al-mālīyah al-Miṣrīyah: wahamīyah hīya amm ḥaqīqīyah?," *al-Hilāl* Vol. 14, No. 9 (June 1, 1906), 542. The monthly journal *al-Hilāl* was founded in 1892 by Jurjī Zaydān, who emigrated from Mount Lebanon to Egypt in the 1880s. For a brilliant account of the relationship between the financial boom and the rise of the Arabic novel, in which Zaydān and his journal played a pivotal role, see Holt, *Fictitious Capital.*

34. Abbas and El-Dessouky, *Large Landowning Class*, 46–53.

35. "Al-Lūrd Krūmar fī khidmat al-bilād," *al-Ahrām* (February 23, 1905).

36. "Land Values in Egypt. Upward Tendency in Prices," *EG* (August 26, 1905).

37. Egypt. No. 1 (1905), *Reports by His Majesty's Agent (1904)*, 30–31.

38. "Irtifā' athmān al-arāḍī wa-li-man al-tharwah fī Miṣr?" *al-Liwā'* (February 25, 1906).

39. "Al-Tharwah al-maḥallīyah fī Miṣr aww irtifā' qīmat al-arāḍī," *al-Mu'ayyad* (February 26, 1906).

40. "Al-Ḥarakāt al-mālīyah al-jadīdah fī Miṣr," *al-Liwā'* (September 25, 1905).

41. Ibid.

42. Egypt. No. 1 (1906), *Reports by His Majesty's Agent (1905)*, 17.

43. Ibid.

44. Ibid., 18.

45. Ibid., 21.

46. The paper announced the publication of the report on April 27 and carried analysis of its various sections over the next month. Beginning on May 16, the bookseller Borman & Co. began advertising that copies of the report could be purchased for 7 piasters.

47. Wilfred Scawen Blunt, "Lord Cromer's Report. A Criticism," *EG* (May 16, 1906).

48. "Al-Ḥukūmah al-ghanīyah," *al-Muqaṭṭam* (March 5, 1906).

49. Blunt, *Atrocities of Justice.*

50. al-Masaddī, *Dinshawāy*; Clément, "Fallāḥīn on Trial"; Esmeir, *Juridical Humanity*; Fahmy, *Ordinary Egyptians*; Gasper, *Power of Representation*; Lockman, "Imagining the Working Class"; Selim, *Novel and Rural Imaginary*; Sharīf, *Ḥādithat Dinshawāy.*

51. DWQ, MNW 0075-027330, "Taqrīr min Shukrī Bāshā mudīr al-Manūfīya 'ammā ḥadatha fī 6/13/1906." The enclosed report is written in French.

52. TNA, FO 371/66: Major-General Bullock to Cromer (June 14, 1906).

53. TNA, FO 78/4668: Cromer to the Earl of Kimberley (February 14, 1895).

54. TNA, FO 78/4668: Cromer to Kimberley (February 24, 1895).

55. TNA, FO 78/4237: Baring to Salisbury (February 23, 1889).

56. TNA, FO 371/66: Cromer to Boutros Pasha Ghali (June 14, 1906).

57. "Ḥādith muhimm," *al-Mu'ayyad* (June 14, 1906); "Mu'rakah hā'ilah," *Miṣr* (June 14, 1906); "Mu'rakah," *al-Liwā'* (June 14, 1906); *Al-Jawā'ib al-Miṣrīyah* (June 14, 1906); "Ḥādithat

Dinshawāy," *al-Ahrām* (June 15, 1906); "News from Tala," *EG* (June 14, 1906); "Tragedy Near Tala. Grave Outrage on British Officers," *EG* (June 15, 1906); "The Tala Outrage," *EG* (June 16, 1906). Talā is the seat of the district of Manūfīyah province in which the village of Dinshawāy is located.

58. "Maḥkamah makhṣūṣah," *al-Waṭan* (June 14, 1906).

59. "Mu'rakat Dinshawāy," *al-Liwā'* (June 16, 1906).

60. Ibid.

61. "Al-Mas'ūlīyah fī ḥādithat Dinshawāy," *al-Liwā'* (June 17, 1906).

62. Ibid.

63. "Balāgh al-ḥukūmah fī qaḍīyat Dinshawāy," *al-Liwā'* (June 17, 1906). The full English text of Machell's "General Resumé" can be found in TNA, FO 371/66: Cromer to Sir Edward Grey: June 17, 1906. In his letter, Cromer informs Grey that "the present dispatch has been communicated to the press."

64. Ibid.

65. "Ḥādithat Dinshawāy," *al-Mu'ayyad* (June 18, 1906).

66. "Al-Ḥādithah al-mushawwamah," *al-Muqaṭṭam* (June 19, 1906).

67. "Al-Siyāsah wa-ṣayd al-ḥamām," *al-Ẓāhir* (June 19, 1906).

68. TNA, FO 371/66: Charles Findlay to Grey (June 27, 1906).

69. Ibid.

70. Al-Musallamī, *Aḥmad Ḥilmī*, 34–38; Badawī, *Aḥmad Ḥilmī*, 47–49.

71. Aḥmad Ḥilmī, "Yā dāfi' al-balā': al-i'dām wa-l-ta'dhīb fī Dinshawāy," *al-Liwā'* (June 29, 1906), reprinted in *Majallat al-majallāt*, Vol. 8 (February 1, 1908): 304–313.

72. "Al-Kalimah al-akhīrah fī qaḍīyat Dinshawāy wa-l-ḥukm fīhā," *al-Mu'ayyad* (June 28, 1906).

73. "Ba'da Dinshawāy mādhā," *al-Mu'ayyad* (July 1, 1906).

74. "Ḥādith Dinshawāy wa-natā'ijuhu," *al-Minbar* (July 1, 1906) *Al-Minbar* was established by Muḥammad Afandī Mas'ūd and Aḥmad Ḥāfiẓ 'Awaḍ, both of whom had previously written for *al-Mu'ayyad*. "New Papers for Egypt," *EG* (June 14, 1906); "New Arabic Daily," *EG* (June 26, 1906).

75. TNA, FO 371/66: Grey to Findlay (June 27, 1906).

76. Ibid.: Findlay to Grey (June 28, 1906). Findlay had been corresponding with London in Cromer's stead since June 21.

77. "Foreign Office Vote, Egypt and the Congo," *London Times* (July 6, 1906) clipped in TNA, FO 371/67.

78. Ibid.

79. Ibid.

80. "Corporal Punishment. Plea for Its Revival," *EG* (July 2, 1906); "Dinshawāy wa-dhuyūluhā," *al-Muqaṭṭam* (July 4, 1906).

81. "Mādhā aṣābakum ayyuhā al-muḥarriḍūn?" *al-Liwā'* (July 8, 1906).

82. "Aḥmad Ḥilmī, "Anẓurū li-l-amn al-ʿāmm," *al-Liwāʾ* (July 9, 1906).

83. "Lā taʿaṣṣub fī Miṣr," *al-Muʾayyad* (July 11, 1906).

84. Guha, *Dominance Without Hegemony*.

85. Fahmy, *Ordinary Egyptians*, 93–4.

86. TNA, FO 371/67: Findlay to Grey, July 30, 1906.

87. Lockman, "Imagining the Working Class," 179–81. See also, Gasper, *Power of Representation*, 207–11.

88. Scholarship on the mediation of Dinshawāy through print genres has commonly taken Benedict Anderson's immensely generative essay as its point of departure. See Anderson, *Imagined Communities*.

89. "Lā taʿaṣṣub."

90. Gershoni and Jankowski, *Empire, Islam, and the Arabs*, 44; Manela, *Wilsonian Moment*, 70.

91. For more on this process, see Chapter 2.

92. Sladen, *Egypt and the English*, 148.

93. In the Abbas Ḥilmī II collection at Durham University, the hundreds of copies of this petition constitute an entire archival unit. See DUL, HIL 61.

94. "Al-Taʿaṣṣub," *al-Ahrām* (July 9, 1906).

95. "Lā taʿaṣṣub ʿandakum," *al-Liwāʾ* (July 9, 1906).

96. TNA, FO 371/67: Findlay to Grey (August 26, 1906).

97. Ibid.

98. TNA, FO 371/245: Cromer to Grey (March 16, 1907). The General Assembly convened for four days from March 2 to March 5 to discuss eighty-five different proposals, of which this was by far the most significant from the perspective of the British administration. For the minutes of the Assembly see Ismaʿīl, ed. *Maḥādir jalisāt al-jamʿīyah al-ʿumūmīyah*, 363–455.

99. TNA, FO 371/245: British Chamber of Commerce, Egypt to Cromer (March 9, 1907).

100. Ibid.: (March 15, 1907; March 21, 1907; May 23, 1907, respectively).

101. Ibid.: Cromer to Grey (March 16, 1907); Cromer to Grey (March 10, 1907).

CHAPTER 5

1. "Al-Azmah al-mālīyah al-Amīrikīyah" *al-Jarīdah* (August 3, 1907).

2. "Al-Azmah al-mālīyah," *al-Ẓāhir* (July 22, 1907).

3. Legrand, *Les crises de 1907 et 1908*, iii.

4. Arminjon, *Present Financial Crisis*, 4.

5. Lévy, "Les événements de 1907," 506.

6. Granduillot, *Étude sur la crise Égyptienne*, 3.

7. TNA, FO 78/4515: Arthur Hardinge to Earl of Rosebery (August 5, 1893); "Al-Azmah al-siyāsīyah al-Inklīzīyah," *al-Muʾayyad* (January 24, 1895); "Taʿahuddāt Inkiltarā bi-l-iḥtilāl wa-l-wizārah al-Miṣrīyah," *al-Muʾayyad* (March 21, 1895).

8. Kāmil, *Al-mas'alah al-sharqīyah.*

9. Roitman, *Anti-Crisis*. See also, Hay, "Crisis and the Structural Transformation of the State"; Goldberg, "Historiography of Crisis."

10. Among older studies of the period, Owen relied on other published materials to produce one of the better extant accounts of the crisis and its implications for the cotton economy. Robert Tignor's study employs the occupation's annual reports for 1907 and 1908 to offer a brief narrative that, like its sources, treats the crisis mainly as a recession on local stock markets. Peter Mansfield delivers that same version of events in a single paragraph. John Marlowe does not mention the crisis at all. Mansfield, *British in Egypt*, 181; Owen, *Cotton and the Egyptian Economy*, 283–87; Tignor, *Modernization and British Rule*, 370–72; Marlowe, *Cromer in Egypt*.

More recent scholarship, attentive to Arabic sources, has touched in places on the possible implications of the crisis for the formation of nationalist political parties (Davis), the eruption of new forms of labor militancy (Beinin and Lockman; Chalcraft), the growing appeal of socialism (Khuri-Makdisi), and the consolidation of a new ideal of companionate marriage (Baron; Kholoussy). Mitchell's brief treatment of the crisis attributes its occurrence implausibly to an increased circulation in banknotes and locates its onset in 1911, rather than 1907 when it occurred. Baron, "Making and Breaking of Marital Bonds," 279; Beinin and Lockman, *Workers on the Nile*, 57; Chalcraft, *Striking Cabbies*, 125, 29; Davis, *Challenging Colonialism*, 50–55; Kholoussy, *For Better, For Worse*, 23–25; Khuri-Makdisi, *Making of Global Radicalism*, 127; Mitchell, *Rule of Experts*, 107.

Far less reliant on official British sources, Samir Saul's massive study offers a more detailed and accurate account of how the crisis unfolded and accords considerably more importance to its prolonged effects. Saul, *La France et l'Égypte*, 684–696.

The most extensive study of the crisis to date is provided in Isaac Miller's superb MA thesis from American University in Cairo. See, Miller, "Egyptian Financial Crisis."

11. Notably, the language of *azmah mālīyah* was not used to describe the fiscal difficulties of the khedivate in the 1870s.

12. In his history of the concept in European thought, Reinhart Koselleck briefly describes a similar process in the mid-nineteenth century whereby "crisis" began to name an economic "experience increasingly common in daily life." Koselleck, "Crisis," 389.

13. On "real abstraction" see the Introduction to this book and Sartori, "History of Political Economy," 111; Sartori, *Bengal in Global Concept History*, 46–47; Postone, *Time, Labor, and Social Domination*; Sohn-Rethel, *Intellectual and Manual Labor*.

14. "Chronique Financière," *The Egyptian Gazette* (*EG*) (March 30, 1907).

15. "Financial Crisis: A Possible Remedy," *EG* (April 16, 1907).

16. Noyes, *Forty Years of American Finance*, 360; Granduillot, *Étude sur la crise Égyptienne*, 24.

17. "The Financial Crisis," *EG* (May 22, 1907); "The Financial Crisis," *EG* (June 25, 1907).

18. Wedderburn, "Paper to Be Read at a Meeting of the Manchester Chamber of Commerce," 14.

19. On the history of British commercial geography and its taxonomies of "comparative advantage," see Smith, *Uneven Development*, Chapter 4.

20. Chalcraft, *Striking Cabbies*, 124; Owen, "Building Boom."

21. Legrand, *Les crises de 1907 et 1908*, 6–7.

22. Crouchley, *Investment of Foreign Capital*, 53; *Annuaire de la Finance Égyptienne*.

23. Crouchley, *Investment of Foreign Capital*, 53.

24. Cotton futures trading had taken place in Alexandria since the 1860s. A new Alexandria Bourse was established in 1883, and its Cairo counterpart was founded in 1903. See Çaliskan, *Market Threads*, 106–07; Taymūr, *al-Būrṣah wa-tijārat al-quṭn*, 47.

25. LMA, MS 24006/1, Imperial Ottoman Bank: E.W.H. Barry to Hewett Moxley (December 5, 1899).

26. See also, Rifaat, *Monetary System of Egypt*, 91.

27. The Gresham's largest loans to high profile clients carried 5.5% interest by 1906. LMA, MS 17908/2 (Part 1).

28. "The Egyptian Slump," *EG* (July 3, 1907); Arminjon, *Present Financial Crisis*, 11.

29. Ibid.

30. Noyes, "A Year After the Panic," 193.

31. Ibid., 206.

32. Odell and Weidenmier, "Real Shock, Monetary Aftershock," 1003.

33. Ibid., 1011.

34. Ibid., 1012.

35. Ibid., 1016. At the time, the exchange rate was roughly $4.80 to £1.

36. Bruner and Carr, *Panic of 1907*, 14.

37. Owen, *Cotton and the Egyptian Economy*, 197.

38. Rodgers and Payne, "How the Bank of France Changed U.S. Equity Expectations," 422. Rodgers and Payne note the abnormal outflow of gold to Egypt but admit that this development is "less well-understood." The value of the cotton crop in the autumn of 1906 is the piece of information they are missing. See also, Bank of England, C13/1: "Record of Outstanding Events"; "Five Per Cent," *The Economist* (October 13, 1906); "Six Per Cent," *The Economist* (October 20, 1906).

39. Bruner and Carr, *Panic of 1907*, 15; Clapham, *Bank of England*, II, 384–86; Sayers, *Bank of England*, 1, 54–56.

40. Legrand, *Les crises de 1907 et 1908*, 2–3.

41. Bruner and Carr, *Panic of 1907*, 8.

42. Arminjon, *Present Financial Crisis*, 13; Bruner and Carr, *Panic of 1907*, 19–20; Noyes, *Forty Years of American Finance*, 359–60; Odell and Weidenmier, "Real Shock, Monetary Aftershock," 1021.

43. "The Financial Stringency in Egypt," *EG* (January 14, 1907); Miller, "Egyptian Financial Crisis," 42.

44. "Chronique Financière," *EG* (March 9, 1907); "Nashrah usbūʿīyah mālīyah," *al-Jarīdah* (March 12, 1907).

45. "American Money Panic," *EG* (March 16, 1907); "American Share Market," *EG* (March 18, 1907); Bruner and Carr, *Panic of 1907*, 21.

46. "Bank of France Raises Its Rate," *New York Times* (March 22, 1907).

47. "A Chain of Absurdities," *New York Times* (March 25, 1907).

48. "Chronique Financière," *EG* (March 30, 1907).

49. "Lord Cromer's Resignation," *EG* (April 12, 1907). Most texts attribute Cromer's departure to the backlash against the Dinshawāy Incident. In private correspondence Harry Boyle suggested a more mundane but embarrassing cause, namely that the consul-general was suffering from gastric ailments so severe that he had lost the ability to digest solid food. See MEC, Harry Boyle Papers GB 165-0035, Box C, File 3: Harry Boyle to Nellie Boyle (March 27, 1907).

50. "The Financial Crisis: Representative Meeting," *EG* (April 18, 1907).

51. "The Financial Crisis. Extraordinary Measures," *EG* (April 24, 1907).

52. "The Financial Crisis. Need of Cooperation. Causes and Remedies," *EG* (May 22, 1907).

53. "The Financial Crisis. Important Meeting of Bankers. A Syndicate to Be Formed," *EG* (May 23, 1907); "Al-Azmah al-mālīyah," *al-Ẓāhir* (May 22, 1907).

54. "The Financial Crisis. The Meeting of the Banks," *EG* (May 27, 1907). See also, Saul, *La France et l'Égypte*, 689.

55. "Al-Ḥālah al-mālīyah," *al-Muqaṭṭam* (May 24, 1907).

56. "Al-Azmah al-mālīyah," *al-Muqaṭṭam* (June 11, 1907).

57. *Annuaire de la Finance Égyptienne*, 37.

58. "To the Editor of the 'Egyptian Gazette,' " *EG* (May 22, 1907).

59. "Al-Azmah al-mālīyah al-ḥālīyah," *al-Liwā'* (May 23, 1907).

60. "Al-Ḥālah al-mālīyah," *al-Muqaṭṭam* (May 16, 1907).

61. "Al-Azmah al-mālīyah," *al-Muqaṭṭam* (May 21, 1907).

62. See "Al-Iʿtidāl," *al-Ẓāhir* (December 24, 25, and 27, 1906).

63. "Al-Azmah al-mālīyah," *al-Ẓāhir* (May 27, 1907).

64. "Aṣḥāb al-maṣāliḥ al-ḥaqīqīyah," *al-Muqaṭṭam* (May 29, May 30, June 1, June 4, June 5, June 6, June 8, June 10, June 12, June 14, June 18, 1907).

65. Ibid. (May 30, 1907).

66. "Al-Ḥālah al-mālīyah," *al-Muqaṭṭam* (May 24, 1907).

67. "Aṣḥāb al-maṣāliḥ al-ḥaqīqīyah," *al-Muqaṭṭam* (May 30, 1907).

68. "Aṣḥāb al-maṣāliḥ al-ḥaqīqīyah," *al-Muqaṭṭam* (June 1, 1907).

69. "Al-Azmah al-mālīyah," *al-Ẓāhir* (June 16, 1907).

70. "Man hum aṣḥāb al-maṣāliḥ al-ḥaqīqīyah?" *al-Jarīdah* (June 2, 1907)

71. TNA, FO 371/67: Charles Findlay to Edward Grey (August 5, 1906). The first meeting to establish the paper was held at the home of Maḥmūd Sulaymān on June 23, 1906, and the first issue of the paper appeared on March 9, 1907. See Kazziha, "Jarīdah-Ummah Group," 379–80.

72. Yūsuf al-Bustānī, "Al-Asbāb wa-l-natā'ij li-l-azmah al-ḥādirah," *al-Jarīdah* (June 2, 1907).

73. "Man hum aṣḥāb al-maṣāliḥ al-ḥaqīqīyah?," *al-Jarīdah* (June 2, 1907).

74. "Al-Azmah al-mālīyah: iqfāl bunūk, taḍaʿḍaʿ wa-irtibāk," *al-Zāhir* (June 22, 1907).

75. Aḥmad Ḥilmī, "A lā yanbaghī ann nuʿidd min alʾān ʿudditanā?" *al-Liwāʾ* (July 20, 1907).

76. "Kalimah fī al-ḥālah al-ḥāḍirah," *al-Jarīdah* (June 16, 1907).

77. Yūsuf al-Bustānī, "Naẓrah shāmilah fī al-azmah al-ḥādirah," *al-Jarīdah* (June 23, 1907).

78. "Al-Azmah al-mālīyah," *al-Ẓāhir* (May 27, 1907).

79. "The Financial Crisis," *EG* (June 18, 1907).

80. "The Financial Crisis: Cassa Di Sconto," *EG* (June 26, 1907).

81. "The Financial Crisis: Cassa Suspends Payment," *EG* (June 21, 1907);

82. "Cassa Di Sconto: Yesterday's Meeting," *EG* (July 3, 1907). Thanks to the special concessions it enjoyed from the government, the National Bank of Egypt here assumed the role of an "unofficial lender of last resort." See Miller, "Egyptian Financial Crisis," 89–96; National Bank of Egypt, *National Bank of Egypt, 1898–1948*, 30–34.

83. Al-Bustānī, "Naẓrah shāmilah."

84. "Rūzifalt al-faḍūlī," *al-Muʾayyad* (June 6, 1907). On the nickname, see James Creelman, "Theodore the Meddler," *Pearson's Magazine* XVII, no. 1 (January 1907), 3–28.

85. "Al-Sharikāt," *al-Ẓāhir* (June 26, 1907).

86. "Al-Sīr Aldun Ghurst wa-l-azmah al-mālīyah," *al-Ahrām* (June 27, 1907).

87. "Al-ḥukūmah wa-l-azmah," *al-Muqaṭṭam* (November 21, 1907).

88. "Al-Sīr Aldun Ghurst wa-l-azmah al-mālīyah."

89. "Egypt," *Statist* (June 22, 1907).

90. "The Alexandria Crisis," *Times of London* (June 24, 1907).

91. "The Financial Crisis: Effect on Land," *EG* (June 18, 1907); "Financial Crisis in Egypt is Kept within Small Limits," *Financial News* (June 26, 1907).

92. "The Financial Crisis: Bourse and Banking Co.," *EG* (June 25, 1907).

93. Arthur S. Delany, "Egypt and Finance: Dangers of Credit," *EG* (August 3, 1907).

94. "Egypt's Prospects," *EG* (October 5, 1907).

95. MEC, Eldon Gorst Papers, GB 165-0122, Box 10, No. 3: "Autobiography from 1886," 117.

96. "Lettre d'Égypte: La Crise et la Situation Financière," *Le Figaro* (March 13, 1908). In his autobiographical notes, Gorst did comment on the spending down of the reserve fund in the years prior to his arrival, but he drew no connection between the state of the reserves and his own reaction to the crisis. On the depletion of the reserve fund, see also Rothstein, *Egypt's Ruin*, 356–57; Saul, *La France et l'Égypte*, 691.

97. "The Financial Crisis: The Government and the Loan," *EG* (January 29, 1908), 6.

98. Egypt. No. 1 (1908), *Reports by His Majesty's Agent (1907)*, 6.

99. Ibid., 4, 6.

100. Ibid., 5–6.

101. Al-Bustānī, "Al-Asbāb wa-l-natā'ij."

102. "Al-Azmah al-mālīyah fī al-qurā," *al-Ẓāhir* (July 16, 1907).

103. For more on this pattern of bad debts and foreclosures, see Chapter 7.

104. "Al-Azmah al-mālīyah wa-'ajz al-tujjār 'an al-tasdīd," *al-Ẓāhir* (July 7, 1907).

105. "Al-Azmah al-mālīyah fī al-Ṣa'īd," *al-Muqaṭṭam* (July 27, 1907).

106. Egypt. No. 1 (1910), *Reports by His Majesty's Agent (1909)*, 13.

107. Legrand, *Les crises de 1907 et 1908*, 29.

108. "Deputation to Sir Eldon Gorst Expresses Its Views on the Situation," *Financial News* (June 26, 1907).

109. "Rents in Cairo: Continued Increase," *EG* (October 3, 1907).

110. Lévy, "Les événements de 1907," 517.

111. Legrand, *Les crises de 1907 et 1908*, 29–30.

112. Ibid., 42.

113. Ibid., 103.

114. Ibid., 83–94.

115. "Al-Azmah al-mālīyah wa-'awāqibuhā," *al-Ahrām* (June 26, 1907).

116. "Kalimah fī al-ḥālah al-ḥādirah," *al-Jarīdah* (June 16, 1907).

117. "Al-'ulūm al-ijtimā'īyah: 'ilm al-iqtiṣād al-siyāsī," *al-Liwā'* (August 3, 1907).

118. "Al-iqtiṣād al-siyāsī," *al-Liwā'* (August 17; August 26, 1907).

119. See, for example, "Al-Azmah al-mālīyah: iqfāl bunūk, taḍa'ḍa', wa-irtibāk," *al-Ẓāhir* (June 22, 1907).

120. On efforts to implement these plans in the interwar era, see Shokr, "Beyond the Fields."

121. Aḥmad Ḥilmī, "A lā yanbaghī ann nu'idd min al'ān 'udditanā?" *al-Liwā'* (July 21, 1907).

122. "Kalimah fī al-ḥālah al-ḥāḍirah," *al-Jarīdah* (June 13, 1907).

123. 'Umar Luṭfī, "Wājib al-ahālī naḥwa tafrīj al-azmah," *al-Liwā'* (April 9, 1908).

124. "Ḥayātunā al-ijtimā'īyah," *al-Ẓāhir* (August 14, 1907).

125. Moustafa Kamel Pasha, "What the National Party Wants," 25.

126. Lord Cromer, *Modern Egypt*, II, 132, 94.

127. See, for example, Muḥammad Ṭal'at Ḥarb, "Haqīqah Murrah," *al-Jarīdah* (October 1, 1907).

128. "Ḥayātunā al-ijtimā'īyah," *al-Ẓāhir* (August 14, 1907).

CHAPTER 6

1. DWQ, WA 0069-012272: "Talaghrāfāt wa-iltimāsāt 'ilá khidīwī Miṣr li-l-muṭālibah bi-l-dustūr."

2. TNA, FO 371/449: Moustapha Kamel Pasha to Sir Edward Grey (February 4, 1908). Kāmil died on February 10, 1908.

3. TNA, FO 371/449: Mohamed Farid Bey to Grey (April 12, 1908).

4. DWQ, WA 0069-012273: Petition from Muṣṭafá Ḥusnī al-Shamāsharjī (March 1, 1908) and Petition from Ḥassan Rasmāḥa, Maḥmūd ʻAlī, Fahmī Ḥussayn, Muḥammad Ḥussayn, Ḥassan Aḥmad Ḥabīb, and Maḥmūd Bayūmī (May 18, 1908).

5. TNA, FO 371/452: Petitions from subcommittees of the Egyptian National Party and F. A. Campbell to Ronald Graham (September 18, 1908).

6. DWQ, WA 0069-12272.

7. TNA, FO 371/452: Graham to Grey (September 18, 1908).

8. Ibid.

9. Ibid.

10. TNA, FO 800/78: Grey to Gerald Lowther (July 31, 1908), quoted in Ahmad, "Great Britain's Relations with the Young Turks," 303.

11. TNA, FO 371/449: Graham to Grey (August 12, 1908).

12. TNA, FO 371/452: Graham to Grey (September 18, 1908).

13. Ibid.

14. MEC, GB 165-0035, Harry Boyle Papers, Box C, File 5: Boyle to Grey (August 16, 1908).

15. TNA, FO 371/892: Graham to Gorst (May 3, 1910).

16. TNA, FO 800/47: Gorst to Grey (February 21, 1909).

17. See Chapter 7.

18. On the first count, Eric Davis argues that it was "no coincidence that the formation of political parties, which represented the institutionalization of cliques, occurred in 1907." See Davis, *Challenging Colonialism*, 54. On the crisis as the main cause of renewed labor militancy among Egyptian, as opposed to foreign, workers, see Beinin, *Workers and Peasants*, 81; Beinin and Lockman, *Workers on the Nile*, 57.

19. I thank Benoit Challand for drawing my attention to this double meaning of *representation* and its particular significance in (post)colonial contexts.

20. Omar, "Rule of Strangers," 219.

21. See, for example, DUR, HIL 260, 106–8: Ḥussayn Naṣṣār to Shīmī Bey (May 19, 1895).

22. See Goldschmidt, "Egyptian Nationalist Party."

23. "Egyptian Politics: Cliques and Divisions," *Egyptian Gazette* (*EG*) (October 4, 1907).

24. Omar, "Rule of Strangers," 220.

25. "Al-Ḥizb al-Waṭanī al-Ḥurr," *al-Muqaṭṭam* (July 25, 1907). The official establishment of the party, with a public announcement of its platforms, occurred on September 12, 1907. See ibid., 222.

26. Kamel Pasha, "What the National Party Wants"; Omar, "Rule of Strangers," 227.

27. "Ḥizb al-Iṣlāḥ ʻalá al-Mabādiʼ al-Dustūrīyah," *al-Muʼayyad* (December 9, 1907).

28. Raḍwān ʻAbd al-Wahāb, "Siyāsat al-Inklīz fī Miṣr," *al-Quṭr al-Miṣrī* (November 12, 1909); Omar, "Rule of Strangers," 237.

29. "ʻĀm al-aḥzāb," *al-Muqaṭṭam* (December 13, 1907).

30. Ibid.

31. On the early history of the *jam'īyah*, see Pollard, "Egyptian by Association," 241. On the National Party's encouragement of "front organizations" like the Higher Schools Club, see Lockman, "Exploring the Field," 146–47.

32. "Egyptian Politics: Kamel's Party," *EG* (December 30, 1907).

33. "Sir Eldon Gorst's Report," *EG* (May 4, 1908).

34. Egypt. No. 1 (1908), *Reports by His Majesty's Agent (1907)*, 4.

35. "Al-Khuṭbah al-waṭanīyah al-kubrá," *al-Liwā'* (May 15, 1908).

36. "Al-Ḥālah al-ḥādirah," *al-Liwā'* (May 18, 1908).

37. Aḥmad Luṭfī al-Sayyid, "al-Ḥālah al-ḥādirah," *al-Jarīdah* (May 18, 1908), republished in Luṭfī al-Sayyid, *Turāth Aḥmad Luṭfī al-Sayyid*, 533–50.

38. Ibid., 549.

39. Beinin and Lockman, *Workers on the Nile*, 29–30.

40. Chalcraft, *Striking Cabbies*, 160.

41. Ibid.; Khuri-Makdisi, *Making of Global Radicalism*.

42. Beinin and Lockman, *Workers on the Nile*, 53.

43. Ibid., 51–52; Chalcraft, *Striking Cabbies*, 171; Shechter, *Smoking, Culture, and Economy*, 43–44.

44. Beinin and Lockman, *Workers on the Nile*, 56; Khuri-Makdisi, *Making of Global Radicalism*, 133.

45. "Cab Strike at Alexandria," *EG* (February 10, 1906); "The Cab Strike. Latest Phases. Carters' Strike Probable," *EG* (February 12, 1906); "The Cab Strike," *EG* (February 14, 1906); "The Cab Strike and Tariff," *EG* (February 20, 1906).

46. "Cairo School Strikes," *EG* (February 26, 1906); Lockman, "Exploring the Field," 147; al-Rāfi'ī, *Mudhakkirātī*, 18–19.

47. "The School Strike. Absurd Claims. Other Schools Come Out," *EG* (February 28, 1906).

48. "Al-I'tiṣābāt fī Miṣr," *Miṣr al-Fatāh* (February 9, 1909).

49. "The School Strike," *EG* (March 1, 1906).

50. "Cairo School Strikes," *EG* (February 26, 1906); "The School Strike," *EG* (March 2, 1906).

51. Lockman, "Imagining the Working Class," 171.

52. Chalcraft, *Striking Cabbies*, 165. British revisions to the Penal Code in 1895 had, for the first time, mandated imprisonment and hard labor for those found guilty of deliberately killing or injuring animals used for riding, carriage, or hauling. New provisions in 1902 criminalized cruelty to animals itself. See Esmeir, *Juridical Humanity*, 127–28.

53. Chalcraft, *Striking Cabbies*, 174.

54. Ibid., 178–83.

55. Legrand, *Les crises de 1907 et 1908*, 29.

56. Campos, *Ottoman Brothers*; Sohrabi, *Revolution and Constitutionalism*; Kayali, *Arabs and Young Turks*; Der Matossian, *Shattered Dreams of Revolution*.

57. Beinin, *Workers and Peasants*, 78; Karakişla, "1908 Strike Wave," 155. See also, Quataert, *Social Disintegration and Popular Resistance.*

58. Beinin, *Workers and Peasants*, 80.

59. Hanioglu, *Young Turks in Opposition*, 74.

60. Beinin and Lockman, *Workers on the Nile*, 55, 68.

61. "I'tiṣāb al-tarāmway," *al-Ahrām* (October 18, 1908).

62. "'Ummāl al-tarāmway," *al-Ahrām* (October 15, 1908); Beinin and Lockman, *Workers on the Nile*, 59.

63. "I'tiṣāb al-tarāmway," *al-Ahrām* (October 21, 1908).

64. Ibid.

65. MEC, GB 165-0122: "Gorst Autobiography," 112–14.

66. Ibid., 119–20.

67. Egypt. No. 1 (1909), *Reports by His Majesty's Agent (1908)*, 6.

68. The change was most pronounced in the Ministry of Interior, where "Englishmen were compelled to keep in the background and the executive authority of the mudirs of the provinces became more obvious." See MEC, GB 165-0148, Andrew Holden Papers: "Some Reflections on the Growth of Egyptian Nationalism," 2.

69. Marlowe, *Cromer in Egypt*, 272.

70. TNA, FO 371/450: Gorst to Grey (July 2, 1908).

71. "Lord Cromer on Egypt," *The Times of London* (December 16, 1908).

72. MEC, "Gorst Autobiography," 124.

73. Ibid., 124–136; TNA, FO 371/451: Gorst, "The Press in Egypt" (October 1908).

74. "Egypt and England. Sir Eldon Gorst's Declarations," *EG* (October 23, 1908).

75. TNA, FO 371/451: Gorst, "The Press in Egypt."

76. MEC, "Gorst Autobiography," 134.

77. Egypt. No. 1 (1910), *Reports by His Majesty's Agent (1909)*, 24; Ministry of Justice, *Report (1909)*, 11–12.

78. Egypt. No. 1 (1910), *Reports by His Majesty's Agent (1909)*, 24.

79. Contrary to Gorst's expectations, the revival of the Press Law also touched off a months-long diplomatic scramble to secure the cooperation of the other foreign powers. Germany in particular refused to sanction the application of the Press Law to its own subjects. By orchestrating a transfer of ownership to a German subject shortly after the reactivation of the Press Law, *Miṣr al-Fatāh* thereby succeeded in evading censorship. See TNA, FO 371/660.

80. DWQ, DD 2001-02394: "Mukātibāt min mudīrīyat al-amn al-'āmm: ba'ḍ al-malaffāt al-sirrīyah al-khāṣṣah bi-l-amn al-'āmm" (May 31, 1891).

81. DUR, HIL 15, 44–5 (July 1894).

82. See, for example, DUR, HIL 16, 86: Muhammad Rushdī to Shīmī Bey (January 27, 1895).

83. On August 13, 1910, for example, Milne Cheetham wrote to Eldon Gorst, "Harvey Pasha told me the other day that his Secret Service, though still in the stage of early

growth, is progressing satisfactorily." See MEC, GB 165-0055, Sir Milne Cheetham Collection, File 1.

84. It is notable, in this regard, that Saʿīd's intelligence briefings cover an extraordinary range of activities from meetings of *al-Ḥizb al-Waṭanī* and *Ḥizb al-Ummah* to informal gatherings by groups of cab drivers, but the palace-funded organizations connected to Shaykh ʿAlī Yūsuf and his Constitutional Reform Party are conspicuous by their absence.

85. "Muẓāhirat ṭalabat al-Azhar," *al-Jarīdah* (January 23, 1909).

86. "Ṭalabat al-Azhar al-sharīf," *al-Muqaṭṭam* (January 25, 1909).

87. Gesink, *Islamic Reform and Conservatism*, Chapter 9.

88. Shafīq, *Mudhakkirātī*, 3, 137.

89. See, for example, Alexander, *Truth About Egypt*, 223. The very limited historiography of the strike has sometimes reproduced this interpretation. See, for example, Crecelius, "Nonideological Responses of the Egyptian Ulama to Modernization," 193. Gesink offers an important corrective by examining the strike's actual demands, but in relying chiefly on *al-Mu'ayyad*, her account inadvertently replicates that paper's pro-palace line about the "degeneration" of the strike under the influence of nationalist politics. See, Gesink, *Islamic Reform and Conservatism*, 198.

90. "The Azhar Strike," *EG* (February 1, 1909).

91. "Iʿtiṣāb ṭullāb al-Azhar wa-ṭalabātuhum," *al-Jarīdah* (January 24, 1909); "Mas'alat al-Azhar: ʿuyub al-niẓām al-jadīd," *al-Liwā'* (January 24, 1909); "Al-Azharīyūn wa-maṭālibuhum," *al-Mu'ayyad* (January 25, 1909); "The Al Azhar Strike: Demands of the Students," *EG* (January 27, 1909); "Maṭālib al-Azharīyīn," *al-Ahrām* (January 28, 1909). The final demand, concerning faculty self-governance, was not included in the earliest lists.

92. DUR, HIL 52, 171: January 24, 1909.

93. "Iʿtiṣāb al-Azharīyīn: al-Azharīyīn yaqsimūna ʿalá al-Qur'ān bi-l-ittiḥād," *Miṣr al-Fatāh* (January 26, 1909); "Ittiḥād al-Azharīyīn: sabaʿūn junayhan iʿānah li-l-ṭalabah," *Miṣr al-Fatāh* (January 28, 1909).

94. "Al-Azharīyūn wa-maṭālibuhum," *al-Mu'ayyad* (January 25, 1909).

95. "Al-Shiddah fī mawḍiʿ al-līn," *Miṣr al-Fatāh* (February 2, 1909).

96. *Al-Liwā'* published the full text of the petition in "Mas'alat al-Azhar," *al-Liwā'* (February 15, 1909).

97. DUR, HIL 6, 34: February 14, 1909. Unless otherwise noted, all files from this unit, HIL 6, are intelligence memoranda signed by Muḥammad Saʿīd.

98. DUR, HIL 6, 34: February 17, 1909.

99. Aḥmad Luṭfī al-Sayyid, "Min ajl dhalik naṭlub al-dustūr," *al-Jarīdah* (February 18, 1909).

100. "Al-Azhar Strike: Flogging the Theologians," *EG* (February 18, 1909). In March, Ḥassan Marʿī, who had written one of the earliest dramatizations of Dinshaway, published a play about the altercation. See Marʿī, *Riwāyat al-Azhar*.

101. The full text of the Azhar Rectorship's decree announcing the resolution was published in *al-Mu'ayyad* (February 22, 1909). See also, "'Afū al-Janāb al-'Ālī al-Khidīwī," *Miṣr al-Fatāh* (February 20, 1909).

102. "Mas'alat al-Azhar," *al-Liwā'* (February 7, 1909).

103. "Al-I'tiṣābāt fī Miṣr," *Miṣr al-Fatāh* (February 9, 1909).

104. Aḥmad Luṭfī al-Sayyid, "al-Ra'ī al-'āmm," *al-Jarīdah* (February 22, 1909).

105. Aḥmad Luṭfī al-Sayyid, "Rawwaḍū anfusakum 'alá al-ḥurrīyah," *al-Jarīdah* (May 30, 1909).

106. DUR, HIL 6, 38–9: March 8, 1909; FO 371/1114: "Report respecting Secret Societies" (June 22, 1911).

107. DUR, HIL 6, 32–33: February 8, 1909; HIL 6, 37: March 7, 1909; HIL 6, 38: March 8, 1909.

108. DUR, HIL 6, 83: May 1, 1909.

109. DUR, HIL 6, 39: March 8, 1909.

110. Ibid.

111. DUR, HIL 6, 117: June 2, 1909. For a breakdown of membership in this new association, see Beinin and Lockman, *Workers on the Nile*, 69.

112. DUR, HIL 6, 63: April 18, 1909; HIL 6, 82: April 29, 1909. See also, Lockman, "Social Roots of Nationalism," 450.

113. DUR, HIL 6, 58: April 13, 1909; HIL 6, 66: April 22, 1909; HIL 6, 98: May 10, 1909; HIL 6, 156: August 1, 1909.

114. DUR, HIL 6, 103: May 10, 1909.

115. DUR, HIL 6, 36: February 23, 1909.

116. DUR, HIL 6, 53: March 31, 1909. The Interior's informants estimated the size of the crowd at 2,000 people. *Miṣr al-Fatāh* claimed it was closer to 5,000. See, "Muẓāhirat al-ams al-kubrá fī sabīl ḥurrīyat al-ṣiḥafah," *Miṣr al-Fatāh* (April 1, 1909).

117. TNA, FO 371/660: Graham to Grey (April 4, 1909).

118. DUR, HIL 6, 62: April 17, 1909.

119. "Muẓāhirat al-ams al-kubrá."

120. TNA, FO 371/664: Graham to Grey (August 8, 1909; August 30, 1909). Graham noted that the crackdown "has filled the extreme Nationalists with dejection, and should exercise a moderating influence on the tone of their press organs."

121. DUR, HIL 6, 301: November 21, 1909.

122. Quoted in Qunaybir, *'Abd al-'Azīz Jāwīsh*, 160–61.

123. DUR, HIL 6, 181: August 19, 1909.

124. British sources subsequently referred to the organization as "the Azharian Union." TNA, FO 141/530/3: "The Azharians" (December 22, 1912).

125. DUR, HIL 6, 312: November 28, 1909.

126. DUR, HIL 6, 159: August 4, 1909; HIL 6, 195–96: September 4, 1909; HIL 315: November 29, 1909

127. Badrawi, *Political Violence in Egypt*, 32; Khan, *Egyptian-Indian Collaboration*, 43–44.

128. By the summer of 1910, Graham had tasked George Harvey, then commandant of the Cairo police, with organizing a "secret service bureau for political work" that would intensify surveillance of political organizations and societies. See, MEC, GB 165-0055, Sir Milne Cheetham, File 1: Cheetham to Gorst (August 13, 1910).

129. TNA, FO 371/892: Graham to Gorst (May 3, 1910).

130. TNA, CAB 37/102/19: Gorst, "Memorandum Respecting Self-Government in Egypt" (May 22, 1910).

131. TNA, FO 371/393: Parliamentary Debates, Sir Edward Grey (June 13, 1910).

CHAPTER 7

1. "The Financial Future of the Egyptian Fellah," *Egyptian Gazette* (*EG*) (January 31, 1914).

2. Brown, *Peasant Politics*, 59–82; Said, *Orientalism*.

3. On the historical specificity of the ahistorical claims that often distinguished Orientalist discourse, see Ludden, "Orientalist Empiricism."

4. MEC, GB 165-0035, Harry Boyle, Box C, File 5: "Draft of a Confidential Despatch," Boyle to Grey (August 16, 1908).

5. "The Financial Future of the Fellah."

6. Dewey, "Influence of Sir Henry Maine."

7. Mamdani, *Citizen and Subject*; Mantena, *Alibis of Empire*; Owen, "Imperial Policy and Theories of Social Change"; Owen, *Lord Cromer*.

8. Scott, "Colonial Governmentality." On the tendency in some Foucauldian readings of colonial rule to flatten significant differences between competing political theories, see Sartori, *Liberalism in Empire*, 86.

9. As Étienne Balibar has noted, "Theories of academic racism mimic scientific discursivity by basing themselves upon visible 'evidence.' " Balibar, "Neo-Racism," 19. See also, Zimmerman, *Alabama in Africa*, 14.

10. On the internal differentiation of British policy in India, particularly after 1857, see Ludden, *Agricultural Production*.

11. See, for example, BL, IOR P/7558, Government of the Punjab, Department of Revenue and Agriculture Proceedings, October to December 1907: "Proposed Establishment of an Agricultural Bank in the Punjab."

12. "Mortgage Banks Suggested for Benefit of Philippine Farmers. Turkey and Egypt Given as Examples, but Sense of Personal Financial Responsibility Needful," Louisiana *Courier-Journal* (August 18, 1902).

13. Coronil, "Beyond Occidentalism," 77.

14. TNA, FO 371/393: Parliamentary Debates, Sir Edward Grey (June 13, 1910).

15. Jakes, "Boom, Bugs, Bust." In reading both the racial type of the improvident peasant and the insect-infested landscape upon which he labored as features of a social ecology

"produced" by the spatial and temporal unevenness of the credit market, my arguments in this chapter build on a rich tradition of theory about the capitalist "production of nature." See, in particular, Harvey, *Justice, Nature, and the Geography of Difference*; Lefebvre, *Production of Space*; Moore, *Capitalism in the Web of Life*; Smith, *Uneven Development*.

16. Willcocks, "Injurious Insects," 709–10.

17. Stuart, *Reports*, 26–27.

18. DUR, HIL 16, 40–47: Muḥammad Rushdī to Shīmī Bey (July 21, 1894); HIL 16, 66–76: Muḥammad Rushdī to Shīmī Bey (November 17, 1894).

19. Jallād, *Qāmūs al-idārah wa-l-qaḍā' (1889 Edition)*, 2, 552–53.

20. Ibid., 554.

21. The new commission was formed in August 1895 under the direction of 'Umar Luṭfī Pasha and Ya'qūb Artin Pasha. See "Dūdat al-quṭn," *al-Hilāl* Year 3, Part 24 (August 1, 1895): 916. The proceedings of the commission were published in *al-Qarārāt wa-l-manshūrāt al-ṣadirah min Majlis al-Nuẓẓār wa-min al-niẓārāt fī sannat 1895* (Cairo: al-Maṭba'ah al-Amīrīyah, 1896): 443–549.

22. Al-Liwā' Mukhtār Bāshā, "Dūdat al-quṭn wa-isti'ṣāluhā," *al-Muqtaṭaf*, 19 (Cairo: 1895), 602. *Al-Hilāl* encouraged its own readers to consult Mukhtār Pasha's tract on the cotton worm and follow his advice. "Dūdat al-quṭn wa-isti'ṣāluha," *al-Hilāl* Year 4, Part 9 (January 1, 1896), 358.

23. Stuart, *Egypt After the War*, 132–33.

24. See, for example, Brown, "Irrigation Department in Lower Egypt (1901)," 159.

25. Richards, "Technical and Social Change," 732.

26. Ibid., 733–35.

27. Ibid., 739. See also, Richards, *Egypt's Agricultural Development*, 87–92.

28. Eid, *La fortune immobilière*. See also, Jakes, "Boom, Bugs, Bust."

29. Richards, "Technical and Social Change," 737–38.

30. "Al-'ināyah bi-l-zirā'ah al-Miṣrīyah," *al-Muqaṭṭam* (April 7, 1898).

31. Goldberg, *Trade, Reputation, and Child Labor*, 45.

32. Willcocks, "Insects Injurious to the Cotton Plant," 17. Buḥayrah witnessed a 36.8% increase in cultivable land between 1894 and 1901, the largest increase of any province in the country during that period. Much of this new land was owned by two companies, the Behera Land Company and the Aboukir Land Company. 'Abbās, *al-Niẓām al-ijtimā'ī fī Miṣr*, 53.

33. Willcocks, like Mukhtār Pasha before him, singled out the adoption of a two-year rotation as the key factor in the explosion of insect populations. Willcocks, "Injurious Insects," 722.

34. Aḥmad Muḥarram, "Tashrī' al-jabr wa-l-ikrāh fī al-a'māl al-ikhtiyārīyah," *al-Mu'ayyad* (February 11, 1905).

35. "Al-Mashrū' al-quṭnī: al-ummah wa-l-ḥukūmah," *al-Liwā'* (March 1, 1905); "The Cotton Worm. Khedivial Decree," *EG* (March 1, 1905).

36. The original draft stipulated an age range between nine and seventeen. One of the few alterations in the final version was an upward adjustment to between ten and eighteen.

For the final text of the decree, which was promulgated on April 17, 1905, see Willcocks, "Insects Injurious to the Cotton Plant," 52–54. This first version of the decree only stipulated conscription for boys, but in practice both boys and girls were engaged in the campaigns.

37. Egypt. No. 1 (1906), *Reports by His Majesty's Agent (1905)*, 22.

38. Ibid.

39. The General Assembly ultimately ratified the draft decree with minimal changes. See Isma'īl, ed. *Maḥādir jalisāt al-jam'īyah al-'umūmīyah*, 329–49.

40. Ministry of the Interior, *Report on the Cotton Worm*, 27.

41. "Al-Mashrū' al-quṭnī: al-ummah wa-l-ḥukūmah," *al-Liwā'* (March 1, 1905).

42. Egypt. No. 1 (1906), *Reports by His Majesty's Agent (1905)*, 22.

43. Ibid.

44. Ibid.

45. Ministry of the Interior, *Report on the Cotton Worm*, 25.

46. At one point in the report, Machell puts the average wage between 1.5 and 2.5 piasters per child per day, but elsewhere his figures suggest that in some districts it may have been as little as one eighth that amount. Ibid., 25–27.

47. Ibid., 39.

48. DWQ, DAU 4003-022565: "Commission sur le coton" (March-April, 1908).

49. Ibid., Ḥussayn Kāmil to Muṣṭafá Fahmī (May 29, 1908).

50. Balls, "Concerning the Effect of Sub-Soil Water."

51. DWQ, MNW 0075-027819: Khedivial Agricultural Society to Council of Ministers (November 1908).

52. Egypt. No. 1 (1909), *Reports by His Majesty's Agent (1908)*, 21. See also, "The Unrest in Egypt. II. An Experiment That Failed," *London Times* (June 22, 1910).

53. DWQ, DAU 4003-022565: P. W. Machell to Inspection [*sic*] General of Irrigation (December 12, 1909). It was later determined that the pink boll worm was likely an invasive species that had arrived in a shipment of cotton seed from India. See W. D. Hunter, "The Pink Boll Worm," *Science* 45, no. 1160 (March 23, 1917): 293–94.

54. Egypt. No. 1 (1910), *Reports by His Majesty's Agent (1909)*, 3.

55. John A. Todd, "The Uses of Egyptian Cotton," *Cairo Scientific Journal* IV, no. 40 (January 1910): 10–17.

56. Ibid., 14.

57. Ibid., 15.

58. Ibid., 17.

59. On regulation and "reputation," see Goldberg, *Trade, Reputation, and Child Labor*; Goldberg, "Historiography of Crisis." In stressing the importance of regulation for quality, Goldberg identifies a crucial shift in the political economy of Egyptian cotton. He also argues, however, that "there is no evidence pointing to a crisis, and what appears to be a decline in natural productivity was due to a calculated shift in the composition of the

Egyptian cotton crop." Goldberg is certainly correct that the later adoption of a longer-staple, lower-yielding seed strain is the key to understanding output per feddan after 1910, but it was the "agricultural crisis" he sets out to debunk that precipitated that shift in the first place.

60. Egypt. No. 1 (1911), *Reports by His Majesty's Agent* (*1910*), 27; Owen, *Cotton and the Egyptian Economy*, 194.

61. TNA, FO 371/893: Edward Grey, "Parliamentary Debates" (June 13, 1910).

62. DWQ, DAU 4003-031001: Ronald Graham to Gerald Dudgeon (March 19, 1911); Dudgeon to Charles Dupuis (March 19, 1911); Dupuis to Dudgeon (March 20, 1911).

63. DUR, HIL 7, 302–3: Muḥammad Saʿīd to ʿAbbās Ḥilmī II (August 9, 1911).

64. DWQ, DAU 4003-031001: "Awrāq bayānāt wa-iḥṣā'iyāt Wizārat al-Dākhilīyah al-akhīrah ḥawla al-qaḍā' ʿalá dūdat al-quṭn" (1912).

65. This intensification of enforcement appears in the Interior Ministry's district-level administrative registers as a sudden and dramatic increase in the rate of disciplinary hearings for village headmen. The two most common offenses were: *ihmāl aʿmāl al-dūdah* (ignoring the worm measures) and *ihmāl aʿmāl al-munāwabah* (ignoring the irrigation rotations). See, for example, Dār al-Maḥfūẓāt al-Qawmīya (DMQ): *Daftar 'Urnīk 32, Ḥawādith al-bilād, ʿamalīyat Markaz Dakarnas bi-Mudīrīyat al-Daqhalīya*, Storeroom 5, Shelf 13, Number 1113.

66. DWQ, DAU 4003-022565: "Note: On the deterioration of the cotton crops in the Delta," (December 13, 1909); Inspection [*sic*] General of Irrigation, Lower Egypt to Cotton Commission (December 21, 1909).

67. DWQ, DAU 4003-031001: Wizārat al-Dākhilīyah, "Manshūr Nimrah 11 Dūdah" (November 11, 1912).

68. See, for example, DWQ, WA 0069-009895: Petition from "Fallāḥ" to Sulṭān Ḥussāyn Kāmil (December 26, 1914).

69. DWQ, DAU 4003-0171025: Acting Director-General of the Department of Agriculture to the Ministry of Public Works (June 16, 1913).

70. Schanz, *Cotton in Egypt*, 73.

71. Maṣlaḥat al-Zirāʿah, *Kutayyib fī dūd al-quṭn wa-ṭuruq al-waqāyah minhā* (Cairo: al-Maṭbaʿah al-Amīrīyah, 1912), 30.

72. In a particularly glaring instance of this contrast, Cromer encouraged peasants to borrow from the Agricultural Bank in the very same Fayyūm speech in which he first announced the government's deliberations over the cotton-worm campaigns. "Khuṭbat al-Lūrd Krūmar," *al-Mu'ayyad* (February 5, 1905).

73. Egypt. No. 1 (1910), *Reports by His Majesty's Agent* (*1909*), 13.

74. Egypt. No. 1 (1911), *Reports by His Majesty's Agent* (*1910*), 20.

75. LMA, MS 17908/2 (Part 1), Minutes of Local Committee for Egypt No. 2: "Minutes of a Meeting of the Local Board held on the 23rd November 1905."

76. Ibid.: "Minutes of a Meeting . . . on 13th June 1907."

77. Ibid.: "Minutes of a Meeting . . . on 5th December 1907" and "Minutes of a Meeting . . . on 19th December 1907."

78. LMA, MS 17908/3, Minutes of Local Committee for Egypt No. 3: "Minutes of a Meeting . . . on 27th August 1908."

79. Having made a loan in December 1906 to Najīb Fahmī Maṭar for £18,000 on the basis of a faulty land valuation, the Gresham was forced to foreclose and hire one of its valuation experts to run the estate until it was sold off for £7,500 in February 1911. Ibid.

80. FO 371/891: "L'Égypte à l'Encan," *La Bourse Egyptienne* (February 16, 1910).

81. Ministry of Justice, *Report* (*1905*), 49.

82. Arminjon, "Les enseignements de la crise financière."

83. Egypt. No. 1 (1911), *Reports by His Majesty's Agent* (*1910*), 20.

84. Egypt. No. 1 (1910), *Reports by His Majesty's Agent* (*1909*), 13.

85. Ibid.

86. Egypt. No. 1 (1911), *Reports by His Majesty's Agent* (*1910*), 20.

87. TNA, FO 141/531/2: Cheetham to Grey (September 5, 1914).

88. Egypt. No. 1 (1911), *Reports by His Majesty's Agent* (*1910*), 20.

89. Hunter, *Power and Passion*, 239–40.

90. Tollefson, *Policing Islam*, 59; Mansfield, *British in Egypt*, 77–79, 191–92.

91. TNA, FO 371/1114: Resolution from "the Egyptian Committee," (July 14, 1911); "Kitchener," *La Bourse d'Orient* (no date) enclosed in Charles Marling to Grey (July 24, 1911); International Arbitration and Peace Association to Grey (July 19, 1911).

92. Ronald Storrs, *Orientations* cited in Richmond, *Egypt*, 168.

93. Egypt. No. 1 (1910), *Reports by His Majesty's Agent* (*1909*), 12.

94. Owen, *Cotton and the Egyptian Economy*, 218.

95. Egypt. No. 1 (1913), *Reports by His Majesty's Agent* (*1912*), 5.

96. DWQ, MNW 0075-042894: Nāẓir al-Ḥaqqānīyah, "Mashrūʿ al-qānūn al-mutaʿalliq bi-inshāʾ Maḥākim al-Akhṭāṭ: īdāḥ (April 1912).

97. Esmeir, *Juridical Humanity*.

98. DWQ, MNW 0075-042894. By 1914, the Ministry of Justice had established 235 cantonal courts. Egypt. No. 1 (1914), *Reports by His Majesty's Agent* (*1913*), 52.

99. Thorburn, *Musalmans and Money-Lenders*, 102.

100. Barrier, "Punjab Alienation of Land Bill"; Mamdani, *Define and Rule*.

101. Talbot, "Punjab Under Colonialism," 6.

102. Barrier, "Punjab Alienation of Land Bill"; Mufakharul Islam, "Punjab Land Alienation Act."

103. Egypt. No. 1 (1913), *Reports by His Majesty's Agent* (*1912*), 4.

104. "Chamber of Commerce. President's Speech. Five Feddan Law Criticised," *EG* (March 1, 1913); MEC, GB 165-0055 Sir Milne Cheetham Collection, File 3: Private letters and telegrams to and from Lord Kitchener, 1912–13.

105. TNA, FO 371/1364: Cheetham to Grey (July 29, 1912).

106. Egypt. No. 1 (1913), *Reports by His Majesty's Agent (1912)*, 48.

107. Ibid., 4.

108. Ministry of Justice, *Report (1912)*, 29.

109. TNA, FO 141/531/2: Arnold Morley, Viscount Esher, J.F.F. Horner, and T. F. Stevens to Edward Grey (August 14, 1912).

110. Owen, *Middle East in the World Economy*, 224.

111. TNA, FO 371/1364: Cheetham to Grey (September 21, 1912).

112. Ibid.

113. F. T. Rowlatt, "The Agricultural Bank: Adjournment of the Meeting. Director's Report," *EG* (March 13, 1913).

114. Crédit Foncier Égyptien, *Rapports (1908)*.

115. ING Bank, Baring Brothers Papers, 203127: "Mortgage Company of Egypt. Issue of Debentures" (January 1912); LMA, MS 17908/3: "Companies in Egypt: Mortgage Company of Egypt: A Large Field for Investment—Increase of Capital," *EG* (May 20, 1909). The second trustee was his nephew John Baring, 2nd Baron Revelstoke, who was then senior partner at Baring Brothers & Co.

116. ING Bank, Baring Brothers Papers, 203127: "Mortgage Company of Egypt. Issue of Debentures" (January 1912).

117. ING Bank, Baring Brothers Papers, 203127: Messrs. Norton, Rose, Barrington & Co. to Lord Revelstoke (July 29, 1913).

118. Ibid.: Cromer to Revelstoke (August 1, 1913).

119. "The Agricultural Bank of Egypt and the Mortgage Company of Egypt," *The Economist* (November 15, 1913): 1086.

120. ING Bank, Baring Brothers Papers, 203127: Messrs. Norton, Rose, Barrington & Co. to Lord Revelstoke (March 13, 1914).

121. See, for example, Egypt. No. 1 (1906), *Reports by His Majesty's Agent (1905)*, 50.

122. See also, Barak, *On Time*, 76.

CHAPTER 8

1. Abū Bakr Luṭfī, "al-Iḥtilāl al-maddī: al-bank al-zirāʿī wa-l-fallāḥ," *Miṣr al-Fatāh* (September 25, 1909).

2. Luṭfī, "al-Iḥtilāl al-maddī."

3. Ibid.

4. DUR, HIL 6, 208–209: Muḥammad Saʿīd to AHII (September 25, 1909).

5. Luṭfī, "al-Iḥtilāl al-maddī."

6. Anderson, *Imagined Communities*, 5. In a similar vein, Partha Chatterjee has suggested that "we have all taken the claims of nationalism to be a *political* movement much too literally and much too seriously." Chatterjee, *Nation and Its Fragments*, 6.

7. Said, *Orientalism*, 240.

8. El Shakry, *Great Social Laboratory*; Gasper, *Power of Representation*; Jacob, *Working Out Egypt*; Pollard, *Nurturing the Nation*; Ryzova, *Age of Efendiyya*.

9. Chatterjee, *Nationalist Thought*.

10. In her brilliant study of Iraq in the first half of the twentieth century, Sara Pursley identifies in the development agenda of Iraqi nationalists a similar concern to undertake a governmental project of subject formation that they understood the British mandate to have abdicated. See Pursley, *Familiar Futures*, 57–78.

11. Davis, *Challenging Colonialism*; Beckert, *Empire of Cotton*. For an alternative critique of Davis, see Vitalis, *When Capitalists Collide*. Vitalis too argues that Davis's effort to portray Muḥammad Ṭal'at Ḥarb as an industrial developmentalist *avant la lettre* is misplaced. He does so, however, by first accepting Davis's interpretation of Ḥarb's programmatic statements and then exploring how poorly Ḥarb's business activities in the interwar era conformed to those supposed objectives. For Vitalis, Ḥarb's political career and his involvement in the nationalist movement were largely instrumental to his pursuits as a rent-seeking capitalist. I suggest here that an alternative reading of Ḥarb's ideas, like those of his contemporaries, might point toward a different critical history of struggles over decolonization in the interwar years.

12. This I take to be the meaning of Marx's statement that the "belated scientific discovery that the products of labour, in so far as they are values, are merely the material expressions of the human labour expended to produce them, marks an epoch in the history of mankind's development, but by no means banishes the semblance of objectivity possessed by the social characteristics of labour." Marx, *Capital, Vol. 1*, 167.

13. Henderson, *Value in Marx*, 13. See also, Roberts, *Marx's Inferno*, 96–97.

14. Marx, *Capital, Vol. 1*, 167.

15. DUR, HIL 6, 56–57: Muḥammad Sa'īd to AHII (April 13, 1909).

16. Mansfield, *British in Egypt*, 194; Rothstein, *Egypt's Ruin*, 363.

17. TNA, FO 371/892: Gorst to Grey (May 6, 1910); Gorst to Mallet (May 7, 1910); Gorst to Grey (May 20, 1910); Gorst to Hardinge (May 22, 1910); Gorst to Mallet (May 29, 1910).

18. "Extremists v. Government," *Egyptian Gazette* (*EG*) (March 24, 1910); "Government v. Extremists," *EG* (March 29, 1910).

19. *Al-'Alam*, an Arabic synonym for *al-Liwā'*, ran its first issue on March 7, 1910. Mīkhā'īl, *al-Ṣaḥāfah al-Miṣrīyah*, 87.

20. "Suspension of 'Al Alam,' " *EG* (March 21, 1910). The paper was suspended from March 19 to May 19, 1910. During that time the National Party employed a different paper, *al-Sha'b*, as its official organ with Jāwīsh as its editor.

21. 'Abd al-'Azīz Jāwīsh, "al-Ḥurūb al-silmīyah," *al-'Alam* (May 26, 1910).

22. "Les Guerres Pacifiques," enclosed in TNA, FO 371/892: Gorst to Mallet (May 29, 1910).

23. See Qunaybir, *'Abd al-'Azīz Jāwīsh*; Lockman, "Exploring the Field"; Jāwīsh, *al-'Ālam al-Islāmī*.

24. Jāwīsh, "al-Ḥurūb al-silmīyah."

25. Ibid.

26. Jāwīsh was referring here to the boycott of American goods and services launched by the Chinese public in May 1905 to protest the Chinese Exclusion Act of April 27, 1904. See, Lew-Williams, *Chinese Must Go*, 212–13.

27. See, Çetinkaya, *Young Turks and the Boycott Movement*, Chapter 2.

28. On the Swadeshi movement, see Goswami, "Swadeshi to Swaraj"; Goswami, *Producing India*; Sarkar, *Swadeshi Movement*; Sartori, *Bengal in Global Concept History*.

29. Jāwīsh, "al-Ḥurūb al-silmīyah."

30. Ibid.

31. Goswami, "Swadeshi to Swaraj," 624.

32. Jāwīsh, "al-Ḥurūb al-silmīyah."

33. On Jāwīsh's involvement in debates about sectarian identity and the question of minority representation in a future nation state, see Omar, "Minority as Microbe."

34. That infatuation had been abruptly dispelled when, in the spring of 1910, Roosevelt delivered a pair of speeches, first at the new Egyptian University in Cairo and subsequently at the Guildhall in London, in which he praised the occupation for its accomplishments and denounced the National Party's calls for Egyptian self-rule as "a noxious farce." See, Roosevelt, "Law and Order in Egypt"; Roosevelt, "British Rule in Africa."

35. "Aʿmāl al-muḥtallīn fī Miṣr," *al-ʿAlam* (July 6, 1910; July 20, 1910; July 28, 1910).

36. Ibid. (July 6, 1910).

37. Ibid. (July 28, 1910).

38. Ibid.

39. Ibid. (July 6, 1910).

40. Muḥammad Zakī ʿAlī, "Wasāʾil al-istiqlāl: al-rijāl wa-l-māl," *al-ʿAlam* (May 31, 1910; June 3, 1910; June 9, 1910; June 16, 1910; June 27, 1910; June 30, 1910; July 19, 1910).

41. Ibid., (May 31, 1910).

42. Ibid.

43. Ibid. (June 16, 1910).

44. Ibid. (June 27, 1910).

45. Ibid. (June 30, 1910).

46. Ibid.

47. Ibid.

48. Ibid.

49. Muḥammad Zakī ʿAlī, "Wasāʾil al-istiqlāl: al-rijāl wa-l-māl (4): al-māl! al-māl!" *al-ʿAlam* (June 16, 1910).

50. Al-Rāfiʿī, *Mudhakkirātī*.

51. Ibrahim, *Copts of Egypt*, 56–58; Pennington, "Copts in Modern Egypt," 160; Bayly, "Representing Copts and Muhammadans"; Omar, "Minority as Microbe."

52. TNA, FO 371/1113: Milne Cheetham to Edward Grey (May 6, 1911).

53. Al-Mu'tamar al-Miṣrī, *Majmū'at a'māl al-mu'tamar*, 132.

54. Naḥḥas was born in 1876 and received his doctorate in Paris in 1897. For a detailed exposition of his writings and thought during the interwar era, see Goldberg, *Trade, Reputation, and Child Labor*, Chapter 5.

55. Yūsuf Naḥḥās, "Tarjamat taqrīr muqaddam li-l-mu'tamar al-Miṣrī min Yūsuf Naḥḥās Bey duktūr fī al-ḥuqūq 'an ḥālat Ṃisr al-iqtiṣādīyah wa-l-mālīyah," in Al-Mu'tamar al-Miṣrī, *Majmū'at a'māl al-mu'tamar*, 137.

56. Ibid.

57. Ibid.

58. Ibid.

59. Ibid., 136.

60. Ibid.

61. Ibid., 133.

62. Ibid., 135.

63. Ibid., 138.

64. FO 371/1113: Foreign Office note by "R.P.M." (May 22, 1911): "The organising committee of the Congress exercised great discretion, and the president, Riaz Pasha, kept in touch with the Ministry of the Interior throughout. The speeches were moderate in tone, and practically no debate was allowed."

65. Al-Mu'tamar al-Miṣrī, *Majmū'at a'māl al-mu'tamar*, 134.

66. Ibid., 139.

67. Ibid., 138.

68. Al-Rāfi'ī, *Niqābāt al-ta'āwun al-zirā'īyah*, 187–88.

69. Luzzatti, "International Institute of Agriculture," 655.

70. 'Umar Luṭfī, "al-Ta'āwun al-mālī" in Al-Mu'tamar al-Miṣrī, *Majmū'at a'māl al-mu'tamar*, 148.

71. Ibid., 140–41. Luṭfī established the first syndicate in the village of Shubrā al-Namlah in Gharbīyah Province in May 1910. See, 'Umar Bey Luṭfī, "Awwal niqābah zirā'īyah fī Miṣr," *al-'Alam* (May 25, 1910).

72. Ibid., 141. See also, Jakes, "Boom, Bugs, Bust."

73. On this new discourse of scientific farming, see Gasper, *Power of Representation*, Chapter 4.

74. One of the most striking features of the probate inventories cited in Chapter 3 is the frequency with which they list both loans within the village and co-ownership of essential livestock and machinery. See DWQ, MM 2016-002449 through 002474. On practices of cooperative labor, see Ghosh, *Imam and Indian*, 134–68.

75. DUR, HIL 16, 66–76: Muḥammad Rushdī to Muḥammad Sa'īd Shīmī Bey (November 17, 1894).

76. Beckert, *Empire of Cotton*; Davis, *Challenging Colonialism*; Tignor, *State, Private Enterprise, and Economic Change.*

77. Ḥarb, *'Ilāj Miṣr al-iqtiṣādī*, 31.

78. Ibid.

79. Ibid., 33.

80. Ibid., 113.

81. Ibid., 159.

82. Ibid., 34.

83. Ibid., 33.

84. My approach to the historically specific character of comparative thought and the transposability of cooperative "models" as a response to the lived unevenness of global capitalist and colonial restructuring draws on Goswami, "Modular Nation Form"; Goswami, " 'Provincializing' Sociology."

85. Indeed, his sweeping narrative of "revolt after revolt until national redemption" would later help to form the worldview of the young military cadets who "put his history to work in real life" in the Free Officers' Revolt of 1952. See Di-Capua, *Gatekeepers of the Arab Past*, 220–27.

86. Al-Rāfiʿī, *Mudhakkirātī*, 25.

87. Aḥmad Luṭfī, "Muqaddimat al-Kitāb" in Al-Rāfiʿī, *Niqābāt al-taʿāwun al-zirāʿīyah*, و.

88. Mill, "Civilization," 134.

89. Al-Rāfiʿī, *Niqābāt al-taʿāwun al-zirāʿīyah*, 115.

90. Aḥmad Luṭfī, "Muqaddimat al-Kitāb," ج.

91. Al-Rāfiʿī, *Niqābāt al-taʿāwun al-zirāʿīyah*, 160, 168.

92. Ibid., 178-179. See also Chapter 5 and Legrand, *Les crises de 1907 et 1908.*

93. Al-Rāfiʿī, *Niqābāt al-taʿāwun al-zirāʿīyah*, 176–87.

94. Ibid., 263–64.

95. Ibid. For the reports of these two committees, see DWQ, MNW 0075-016866: "Mudhakkirat Niẓārat al-Mālīyah ʿan sharikāt al-taʿāwun."

96. Ibid., 204.

97. Ibid.

98. ʿUmar Luṭfī, "Awwal niqābah zirāʿīyah fī Miṣr," *al-ʿAlam* (May 25, 1910).

99. TNA, FO 141/469/4: Gerald Dudgeon, "Note on the Agricultural Co-operation Movement with Respect to Egypt" (May 1913).

100. Al-Rāfiʿī, *Niqābāt al-taʿāwun al-zirāʿīyah*, 274.

101. In his memoirs, al-Rāfiʿī reproduces a letter from Farīd (dated April 22, 1913) in which the latter had encouraged his protégé to keep working on his study and warned, "I have learned from reading the newspapers that Kitchener will begin working on [cooperation] in order to attract the people towards himself and towards the occupation." Al-Rāfiʿī, *Mudhakkirātī*, 36.

102. Al-Rāfiʿī, *Niqābāt al-taʿāwun al-zirāʿīyah*, 286.

103. Ibid., 298.

104. The Law on Cooperation was passed in June 1914. TNA, FO 141/469/4: "The Present Situation with Regard to Cooperation."

105. Al-Rāfiʿī, *Niqābāt al-taʿāwun al-zirāʿīyah*, 305.

106. Ibid., 302.

CONCLUSION

1. On the distinction between freedom and agency, see Roberts, *Marx's Inferno*, 96–97; Roberts, "Idea of Emancipation."

2. McIlwraith, "Declaration of a Protectorate."

3. TNA, FO 371/1970: Cheetham to Grey (November 5, 1914).

4. L. G. Roussin, "The Present Monetary Regime in Egypt," *L'Égypte Contemporaine* (February 1924): 1; Ministère des Finances, *Documents relatifs à la guerre (1914–15)*, 2.

5. Goldberg, "Peasants in Revolt"; Anderson, "Egyptian Labor Corps."

6. TNA, FO 371/3199: W. E. Brunyate, "Note by the Acting Financial Adviser on the Budget of 1918" (March 1918).

7. Ministère des Finances, *Documents relatifs à la guerre (1916–1917)*, 878.

8. Rifaat, *Monetary System of Egypt*, 62.

9. Ibid., 63–65.

10. TNA, FO 371/3199: W. E. Brunyate, "Note by the Acting Financial Adviser on the Budget of 1918" (March 1918).

11. TNA, FO 371/2932: R. C. Lindsay to High Commissioner (November 25, 1917).

12. Manela, *Wilsonian Moment*. In identifying the movements and revolutions of the postwar moment as "Wilsonian," Manela largely obscures the long prior history of anticolonial thought and practice and thereby attributes the idea of self-determination to Wilson himself.

13. Barak, *On Time*, 186.

14. TNA, FO 371/3711: Reginald Wingate, "Notes of an Interview with His Highness the Sultan" (December 12, 1918).

15. TNA, FO 371/3714: Cheetham to Foreign Office (March 9, 1919).

16. Ibid.: Cheetham to FO (March 10, 1919).

17. TNA, FO 371/3715: Cheetham to Lord Curzon (March 22, 1919); Al-Rāfiʿī, *Thawrat 1919*, 1, 118–19.

18. TNA, FO 371/3714: Cheetham to FO (March 11, 1919).

19. Cromer, *Abbas II*, xx.

20. Barak, *On Time*, 190–200; Brown, *Peasant Politics*, 206–7; Goldberg, "Peasants in Revolt"; Schulze, "Colonization and Resistance."

21. MEC, GB 165-0055, Milne Cheetham Collection, File 5: Graham to Cheetham (April 16, 1919).

22. Ministère des Finances, *Documents relatifs à la guerre (1919)*, 1878–79.

23. TNA, FO 141/745/6: "Air Intelligence Summary" (March 25, 1919); Beinin and Lockman, *Workers on the Nile*, 93; Killingray, "Air Power," 430. See also, Satia, "Defense of Inhumanity."

24. Ministère des Finances, *Documents relatifs à la guerre (1919)*, 1887.

25. Cheetham Collection: Graham to Cheetham (April 16, 1919).

26. Quoted in Mansfield, *British in Egypt*, 231.

27. For an excellent synthesis of existing scholarship on 1919 that manages to capture some of the richness and variety of political thought and practice, see Chalcraft, *Popular Politics*, 206–15. See also, Omar, "Rule of Strangers"; Berque, *Egypt: Imperialism and Revolution*, 316.

28. Milner, *England in Egypt*, 436.

29. Egypt. No. 1 (1921), *Report of the Special Mission to Egypt*, 15–16.

30. Warburg, " 'Three-Legged Stool.' "

31. Aaron Jakes, "The Myth of Egypt's Liberal Constitution," *Egypt Independent* (April 8, 2012); DWQ, MNW 0075-016890: Ministère de la Justice, Comité Consultatif de Legislation, "Séances des 5, 6, 7, 12, 13 et 14 Novembre, 1922."

32. Gramsci, *Prison Notebooks*, 160.

33. Shokr, "Beyond the Fields."

BIBLIOGRAPHY

ARCHIVAL SOURCES

Egypt

DWQ: *Dār al-Wathā'iq al-Qawmīyah* (Egyptian National Archives), Cairo

WA (0069)	Wathā'iq 'Ābdīn (Papers of the 'Ābdīn Palace)
MNW (0075)	Majlis al-Nuẓẓār wa-l-Wuzarā' (The Council of Ministers)
MGS (1033)	Maḥkamat al-Gharbīyah al-Shar'īyah (Shar'ī Court of Gharbīyah Province)
MCC (1179)	Records of the Mixed Court of Cairo
MCM (1181)	Records of the Mixed Court of Manṣūrah
DD (2001)	Dīwān al-Dākhilīyah (Ministry of the Interior)
MM (2016)	Mudīrīyat al-Manūfīyah (Records of Manūfīyah Province)
MG (2017)	Mudīrīyat al-Gharbīyah (Records of Gharbīyah Province)
DM (3003)	Dīwān al-Mālīyah (Ministry of Finance)
DAU (4003)	Dīwān al-Ashghāl al-'Umūmīyah (Ministry of Public Works)

DMQ: *Dār al-Maḥfūẓāt al-Qawmīyah* (Egyptian Public Records Office), Cairo

Dafātir Ḥawādith al-Bilād (Registers of Village Incidents)

England

TNA: The National Archives

FO Foreign Office Papers

CAB Cabinet Papers

PRO Domestic Records of the Public Record Office

BL: The British Library

IOR India Office Records

Lord Ripon Papers

DUR: Durham University Library

ʿAbbās Ḥilmī II Collection (unit titles listed as written in the catalogue)

HIL 6 (Ministry of Interior I)

HIL 7 (Ministry of Interior II)

HIL 15 (Muhammad Saʿid Shimi Bey)

HIL 16 (Shimi Bey's Collaborators)

HIL 52 (al-Azhar)

HIL 61 (Dinshawi Incident)

HIL 260 (Husain Nassar, Ali Sulaiman, Muhammad Rushdi)

MEC University of Oxford, Middle East Centre Archives

GB 165-0035: Harry Boyle Papers

GB 165-0055: Milne Cheetham Papers

GB 165-0122: Eldon Gorst Papers

GB 165-0148: Andrew Holden Papers

The Bank of England Archive

ING Bank Archive

Baring Brothers Papers

LMA London Metropolitan Archives, Guildhall Business Archives

IOB Imperial Ottoman Bank Papers

Gresham Life Assurance Society Papers

LSE London School of Economics Archive

Ionian Bank Papers

BBA Barclay's Bank Archive

Anglo-Egyptian Bank Papers

India

Uttar Pradesh State Archives (Lucknow, India)

SELECTED JOURNALS AND NEWSPAPERS

ARABIC PERIODICALS

al-Ahālī

al-Ahrām

al-ʿAlam

al-Baṣīr

al-Fallāḥ

al-Hilāl

al-Jarīdah

al-Jawāʾib al-Miṣrīyah

al-Liwāʾ

al-Minbar

Miṣr

Miṣr al-Fatāh

al-Muʾayyad

al-Muqaṭṭam

al-Muqtaṭaf

al-Quṭr al-Miṣrī

al-Rāʾid al-Miṣrī

al-Shaʿb

al-Siyāsah al-Muṣawwarah

al-Waqāʾiʿ al-Miṣrīyah

al-Waṭan

al-Ẓāhir

al-Zirāʿah

OTHER PERIODICALS

Blackwood's Magazine

La Bourse Égyptienne

The Cairo Scientific Journal

The Economist

L'Egypte Contemporaine

The Egyptian Gazette

Le Figaro

Financial News

Financial Review of Reviews

Louisiana Courier-Journal

The New York Times

The Statist

The Times of London

The Washington Post

Yearbook of the Khedivial Agricultural Society

OTHER PUBLISHED SOURCES CITED

'Abbās, Ra'ūf. *al-Niẓām al-ijtimāʿī fī Miṣr fī ẓill al-milkīyāt al-zirāʿīyah al-kabīrah, 1837–1914*. Cairo: Dār al-Fikr al-Ḥadīth, 1973.

'Abd al-Fattāḥ, Fatḥī. *al-Qaryah al-Miṣrīyah: dirāsah fī al-milkīyah wa-ʿalāqāt al-intāj*. al-Qāhirah: Dar al-thaqāfah al-jadīdah, 1973.

'Azabāwī, 'Abdallah Muḥammad. *'Umad wa-mashāyikh al-qurá wa-dawruhum fī al-mujtamaʿ al-Miṣrī fī al-qarn al-tāsiʿ ʿashr*. Cairo: Dār al-Kitāb al-Jāmʿī 1984.

Abbas, Raouf, and Assem El-Dessouky. *The Large Landowning Class and the Peasantry in Egypt, 1837–1952*. Translated by Amer Mohsen and Mona Zikri. Syracuse, NY: Syracuse University Press, 2012.

Abū 'Arjah, Taysīr. *Al-Muqaṭṭam: jarīdat al-iḥtilāl al-Brīṭānī fī Miṣr*. Cairo: Al-Hay'ah al-Miṣrīyah al-ʿĀmmah li-l-Kitāb, 1997.

Abul-Magd, Zeinab. *Imagined Empires: A History of Revolt in Egypt*. Berkeley: University of California Press, 2013.

Ahmad, Feroz. "Great Britain's Relations with the Young Turks 1908–1914." *Middle Eastern Studies* 2, no. 4 (July 1966): 302–29.

Ahuja, Ravi. *Pathways of Empire: Circulation, 'Public Works' and Social Space in Colonial Orissa (c. 1780–1914)*. Hyderbad: Orient BlackSwan, 2009.

Al-Barūdī, Muḥammad. *Dalīl al-ʿumdah*. Cairo: Maṭbaʿat al-Sharqī, 1899.

Al-Iskandārī, ʿAbd al-Laṭīf Shukrī. *Dalīl al-Manūfīyah*. Cairo: Maṭbaʿat al-Sharqī, 1900.

Al-Masaddī, Muḥammad Jamāl al-Dīn. *Dinshawāy*. al-Qāhirah: Maṭbaʿat dār al-kutub wa-l-wathā'iq al-qawmīyah, 2006.

Al-Mu'tamar al-Miṣrī. *Majmūʿat aʿmāl al-mu'tamar al-Miṣrī al-awwal*. Cairo: al-Maṭbaʿāh al-Amīrīyah, 1911.

Al-Musallamī, Ibrāhīm ʿAbdallah. *Aḥmad Ḥilmī: sajīn al-ḥurrīyah wa-l-ṣaḥāfah*. Cairo: al-Hay'ah al-Miṣrīyah al-ʿammah li-l-kitāb, 1993.

Al-Rāfiʿī, ʿAbd al-Raḥman. *Mudhakkirātī*. Cairo: Mu'assasat Akhbār al-Yawm, 1989.

———. *Niqābāt al-taʿāwun al-zirāʿīyah: niẓāmuhā wa-tārīkhuhā wa-thamarātuhā fī Miṣr wa-Ūrūbā*. Cairo: Maṭbaʿat al-Nahḍah al-Adabīyah, 1914.

———. *Thawrat 1919: tārīkh Miṣr al-qawmī min sannat 1914 ilá sinnat 1921*. Vol. 1, al-Qāhirah: Dār al-shaʿb, 1968.

Al-Sayyid, Afaf Lutfi. *Egypt and Cromer: A Study in Anglo-Egyptian Relations*. New York: Frederick A. Praeger, 1969.

Al-Wakīl, Ḥamdī. *Milkīyat al-arāḍī fī Miṣr khilāla al-qarn al-tāsiʿ ʿashr*. al-Qāhirah: al-Hayʿah al-Miṣrīyah al-ʿammah li-l-kitāb, 2000.

Alexander, John Romich. *The Truth About Egypt*. London: Cassell and Company, 1911.

Alger, George W. *Report to His Excellency Herbert H. Lehman, Governor of the State of New York*. New York: New York State Insurance Department, 1934.

Ali, Imran. *The Punjab Under Imperialism, 1885–1947*. Princeton, NJ: Princeton University Press, 1988.

Amin, Shahid. "Gandhi as Mahatma: Gorakhpur District, Eastern UP, 1921–2." In *Selected Subaltern Studies*, edited by Ranajit Guha and Gayatri Chakravorty Spivak, 288–348. New York: Oxford University Press, 1988.

———. *Sugarcane and Sugar in Gorakhpur: An Inquiry into Peasant Production for Capitalist Enterprise in Colonial India*. Delhi: Oxford University Press, 1984.

Anderson, Benedict R. *Imagined Communities: Reflections on the Origin and Spread of Nationalism*. London: Verso, 1991.

Anderson, Kyle J. "The Egyptian Labor Corps: Workers, Peasants, and the State in World War I." *International Journal of Middle East Studies* 49, no. 1 (February 2017): 5–24.

Annuaire de la Finance Égyptienne. Alexandria: Société de Publications Égyptiennes, 1907.

Armbrust, Walter. *Mass Culture and Modernism in Egypt*. Cambridge: Cambridge University Press, 1996.

Arminjon, Pierre. *La Situation economique et financière de l'Égypte*. Paris: Librarie Jerirale de Droit & le Jurisprudence, 1911.

———. "Les enseignements de la crise financière égyptienne actuelle et le bilan économique de l'Égypte." *Revue Économique Internationale* (February 1909): 265–302.

———. *The Present Financial Crisis in Egypt.* Translated by Robert L. Devonshire. London: Waterlow and Layton, 1907.

Arrighi, Giovanni. *Adam Smith in Beijing: Lineages of the Twenty-First Century.* New York: Verso, 2007.

———. *The Geometry of Imperialism: The Limits of Hobson's Paradigm.* London: Verso, 1983.

———. *The Long Twentieth Century: Money, Power, and the Origins of Our Times.* New York: Verso, 1994.

Ashley, Richard. "Three Modes of Economism." *International Studies Quarterly* 27, no. 4 (December 1983): 463–96.

Badawī, Aḥmad Aḥmad. *Maʿ al-ṣuḥufī al-mukāfiḥ Aḥmad Ḥilmī.* Cairo: Maktabat Nahḍat Miṣr, 1957.

Badrawi, Malak. *Political Violence in Egypt 1910–1924: Secret Societies, Plots and Assassinations.* Richmond, Surrey: Curzon Press, 2000.

Baer, Gabriel. *A History of Landownership in Modern Egypt, 1800–1950.* London: Oxford University Press, 1962.

———. *Studies in the Social History of Modern Egypt.* Publications of the Center for Middle Eastern Studies. Chicago: University of Chicago Press, 1969.

Balibar, Etienne. "Is There a 'Neo-Racism'?" In *Race, Nation, Class: Ambiguous Identities,* edited by Etienne Balibar and Immanuel Maurice Wallerstein, 17–28. London: Verso, 1991.

Ball, Terence. "The Formation of Character: Mill's 'Ethology' Reconsidered." *Polity* 33, no. 1 (Autumn 2000): 25–48.

Balls, William Lawrence. *Egypt of the Egyptians.* New York: Charles Scribner's Sons, 1916.

———. "A Summary of Present Information Concerning the Effect of Sub-Soil Water on the Cotton Crop with a Scheme for Systematic Observations." In *Yearbook of the Khedivial Agricultural Society for 1909,* edited by Khedivial Agricultural Society. Cairo: National Printing Press, 1910.

Banaji, Jairus. "Capitalist Domination and the Small Peasantry: Deccan Districts in the Late Nineteenth Century." *Economic and Political Weekly* 12, no. 33/34 (1977): 1375–404.

Banerjee, Himadri. *The Agrarian Society of the Punjab.* Delhi: Manohar, 1982.

Barak, On. *On Time: Technology and Temporality in Modern Egypt.* Berkeley: University of California Press, 2013.

Barakāt, ʿAlī. *Taṭawwur al-milkīyah al-zirāʿīyah fī Miṣr wa-atharuhu ʿalá al-ḥarakah al-siyāsīyah, 1813–1914.* Cairo: Dār al-Thaqāfah al-Jadīdah, 1977.

Baron, Beth. *Egypt as a Woman: Nationalism, Gender, and Politics.* Berkeley: University of California Press, 2007.

———. "The Making and Breaking of Marital Bonds in Modern Egypt." In *Women in Middle Eastern History*, edited by Nikki R. Keddie and Beth Baron. New Haven, CT: Yale University Press, 1991.

Barrier, Norman G. "The Formulation and Enactment of the Punjab Alienation of Land Bill." *The Indian Economic and Social History Review* II, no. 2 (April 1965): 145–65.

Bayly, C. A. "Representing Copts and Muhammadans: Empire, Nation, and Community in Egypt and India, 1880–1914." In *Modernity and Culture from the Mediterranean to the Indian Ocean, 1890–1920*, edited by Leila Tarazi Fawwaz, C. A. Bayly, and Robert Ilbert, 158–203. New York: Columbia University Press, 2002.

Beckert, Sven. "Emancipation and Empire: Reconstructing the Worldwide Web of Cotton Production in the Age of the American Civil War." *The American Historical Review* 109, no. 5 (December 2004): 1405–38.

———. *Empire of Cotton: A Global History*. New York: Alfred A. Knopf, 2014.

Beinart, William, and Lotte Hughes. *Environment and Empire*. Oxford: Oxford University Press, 2007.

Beinin, Joel. *Workers and Peasants in the Modern Middle East*. Cambridge: Cambridge University Press, 2004.

Beinin, Joel, and Zachary Lockman. *Workers on the Nile: Nationalism, Communism, Islam, and the Egyptian Working Class, 1882–1954*. Princeton, NJ: Princeton University Press, 1987.

Bell, Duncan. *Reordering the World: Essays on Liberalism and Empire*. Princeton, NJ: Princeton University Press, 2016.

Bentham, Jeremy. *An Introduction to the Principles of Morals and Legislation*. New York: Hafner Press, 1948.

Berque, Jacques. *Egypt: Imperialism and Revolution*. Translated by Jean Stewart. New York: Praeger Publishers, 1972.

Birla, Ritu. *Stages of Capital: Law, Culture, and Market Governance in Late Colonial India*. Durham, NC: Duke University Press, 2009.

Blunt, Wilfrid Scawen. *Atrocities of Justice Under British Rule in Egypt*. London: T. Fisher Unwin, 1906.

———. *My Diaries: Being a Personal Narrative of Events, 1888–1914*. 2 vols. New York: Alfred A. Knopf, 1921.

Bose, Sugata. *Credit, Markets, and the Agrarian Economy of Colonial India*. Delhi; New York: Oxford University Press, 1994.

———. *Peasant Labour and Colonial Capital: Rural Bengal since 1770*. The New Cambridge History of India. Cambridge; New York: Cambridge University Press, 1993.

Bottomore, Tom. *A Dictionary of Marxist Thought*. Oxford: Blackwell, 1991.

British Chamber of Commerce of Egypt. *List of Financial, Manufacturing, Transport and Other Companies Established in Egypt*. Alexandria, 1901.

Brown, Nathan. "Brigands and State Building: The Invention of Banditry in Modern Egypt." *Comparative Studies in Society and History* 32, no. 2 (1990): 258–281.

———. *Peasant Politics in Modern Egypt: The Struggle Against the State*. New Haven, CT: Yale University Press, 1990.

———. "Who Abolished Corvée Labour in Egypt and Why?" *Past and Present*, no. 144 (August 1994): 116–37.

Brown, R. Hanbury. "Administration Report of the Irrigation Department in Lower Egypt for 1901." In *Report upon the Administration of the Public Works Department for 1901*, edited by Public Works Ministry. Cairo: National Printing Department, 1902.

———. *History of the Barrage at the Head of the Delta of Egypt*. Cairo: F. Diemer, 1896.

Brown, Wendy. *Undoing the Demos: Neoliberalism's Stealth Revolution*. New York: Zone Books, 2015.

Bruner, Robert F., and Sean D. Carr. *The Panic of 1907: Lessons Learned from the Market's Perfect Storm*. Hoboken, NJ: John Wiley & Sons, 2007.

Buck-Morss, Susan. "Envisioning Capital: Political Economy on Display." *Critical Inquiry* 21, no. 2 (1995): 434–67.

Cain, P. J., and A. G. Hopkins. *British Imperialism, 1688–2000*. 2nd ed. New York: Longman, 2002.

Çaliskan, Koray. *Market Threads: How Cotton Farmers and Traders Create a Global Commodity*. Princeton, NJ: Princeton University Press, 2010.

Callon, Michel. "The Embeddedness of Economic Markets in Economics." In *The Laws of the Markets*, 1–57. Oxford: Blackwell, 1998.

Campos, Michelle. *Ottoman Brothers: Muslims, Christians, and Jews in Early Twentieth-Century Palestine*. Stanford, CA: Stanford University Press, 2011.

Catanach, I. J. *Rural Credit in Western India, 1875–1930: Rural Credit and the Co-operative Movement in the Bombay Presidency*. Berkeley: University of California Press, 1970.

Çetinkaya, Y. Doğan. *The Young Turks and the Boycott Movement: Nationalism, Protest and Social Class in the Formation of Modern Turkey*. London: I. B. Tauris, 2013.

Chalcraft, John. "The Coal Heavers of Port Saʿid: State-Making and Worker Protest, 1869–1914." *International Labor and Working-Class History*, no. 60 (Fall 2001): 110–24.

———. "Counterhegemonic Effects: Weighing, Measuring, Petitions and Bureaucracy in Nineteenth-century Egypt." In *Counterhegemony in the Colony and Postcolony*, edited by John Chalcraft and Yaseen Noorani, 179–203. New York: Palgrave Macmillan, 2007.

———. "Engaging the State: Peasants and Petitions in Egypt on the Eve of Colonial Rule." *International Journal of Middle East Studies* 37 (2005): 303–25.

———. *Popular Politics in the Making of the Modern Middle East*. Cambridge: Cambridge University Press, 2016.

———. *The Striking Cabbies of Cairo and Other Stories: Crafts and Guilds in Egypt, 1863–1914*. Albany: SUNY Press, 2004.

Charlesworth, Neil. "The Myth of the Deccan Riots of 1875." *Modern Asian Studies* 6, no. 4 (1972): 401–21.

———. *Peasants and Imperial Rule: Agriculture and Agrarian Society in the Bombay Presidency, 1850–1935*. Cambridge: Cambridge University Press, 1985.

Chatterjee, Partha. *The Nation and Its Fragments: Colonial and Postcolonial Histories*. Princeton, NJ: Princeton University Press, 1993.

———. *Nationalist Thought and the Colonial World: A Derivative Discourse*. Minneapolis: University of Minnesota Press, 1986.

Chaudhuri, Meghna. "A Measure of Value: Life, Land and Agrarian Finance in India, 1830–1960." Ph.D. thesis, New York University, 2020.

Chhabria, Sheetal. *Making the Modern Slum: The Power of Capital in Colonial Bombay*. Seattle: University of Washington Press, 2019.

Clapham, John. *The Bank of England: A History*. Cambridge: Cambridge University Press, 1944.

Clément, Anne Marie. "Fallāḥin on Trial in Colonial Egypt: Apprehending the Peasantry through Orality, Writing, and Performance (1884–1914)." Ph.D. diss., University of Toronto, 2012.

Cole, Juan *Colonialism and Revolution in the Middle East: Social and Cultural Origins of Egypt's 'Urabi Movement*. Princeton, NJ: Princeton University Press, 1993.

Coles, Charles Edward. *Recollections and Reflections*. London: Saint Catherine Press, 1918.

Colvin, Auckland. *The Making of Modern Egypt*. 3rd ed. London: Seeley, 1906.

Cook, Eli. *The Pricing of Progress: Economic Indicators and the Capitalization of American Life*. Cambridge, MA: Harvard University Press, 2017.

Coronil, Fernando. "Beyond Occidentalism: Toward Nonimperial Geohistorical Categories." *Cultural Anthropology* 11, no. 1 (1996): 51–87.

———. *The Magical State: Nature, Money, and Modernity in Venezuela*. Chicago: University of Chicago Press, 1997.

Cottrell, P. L. *British Overseas Investment in the Nineteenth Century*. London: Macmillan Press, 1975.

Crecelius, Daniel. "Nonideological Responses of the Egyptian Ulama to Modernization." In *Scholars, Saints, and Sufis: Muslim Religious Institutions in the Middle East Since 1500*, edited by Nikki R. Keddie, 167–210. Berkeley: University of California Press, 1972.

Crédit Foncier Égyptien. *Rapports du Conseil d'Administration et des Censeurs, Résolutions de l'Assemblée: Exercice 1908*. Cairo: Imprimerie Ch. Emmanuel, 1909.

Cromer, Earl of (Evelyn Baring). *Abbas II*. London: Macmillan and Co., 1915.

———. *Modern Egypt*. Vol. II, New York: The Macmillan Company, 1908.

———. *Political and Literary Essays, 1908–1913*. London: Macmillan and Co., 1913.

Crouchley, Arthur Edwin. *Investment of Foreign Capital in Egyptian Companies and Public Debt*. New York: Arno Press, 1977.

Cunningham, Alfred. *To-day in Egypt: Its Administration, People and Politics*. London: Hurst & Blackett, 1912.

Cuno, Kenneth M. *The Pasha's Peasants: Land, Society, and Economy in Lower Egypt, 1740–1858*. New York: Cambridge University Press, 1992.

Dasūqī, ʿĀṣim. *Kibār mullāk al-arāḍī al-zirāʿīyah wa-dawruhum fī al-mujtamaʿ al-Miṣrī, 1914–1952*. Cairo: Dār al-Shurūq, 2007.

Davis, Eric. *Challenging Colonialism: Bank Miṣr and Egyptian Industrialization, 1920–1941*. Princeton, NJ: Princeton University Press, 1983.

Davis, Mike. *Late Victorian Holocausts: El Niño Famines and the Making of the Third World*. London; New York: Verso, 2001.

Dawson, Michael C. "Hidden in Plain Sight: A Note on Legitimation Crises and the Racial Order." *Critical Historical Studies* 3, no. 1 (2016): 143–61.

Dawson, Michael C., and Emily A. Katzenstein. "Survey Article: Articulated Darkness: White Supremacy, Patriarchy, and Capitalism in Shelby's *Dark Ghettos*." *The Journal of Political Philosophy* 27, no. 2 (2019): 252–268.

Der Matossian, Bedross. *Shattered Dreams of Revolution: From Liberty to Violence in the Late Ottoman Empire*. Stanford, CA: Stanford University Press, 2014.

Derr, Jennifer. *The Lived Nile: Environment, Disease, and Material Colonial Economy in Egypt*. Stanford, CA: Stanford University Press, 2019.

Deutscher, Isaac. *Stalin: A Political Biography*. New York: Vintage, 1960.

Dewey, Clive. "The Influence of Sir Henry Maine on Agrarian Policy in India: A Centennial Reappraisal." In *The Victorian Achievement of Sir Henry Maine*, edited by Alan Diamond, 353–75. Cambridge: Cambridge University Press, 1991.

Di-Capua, Yoav. *Gatekeepers of the Arab Past: Historians and History Writing in Twentieth-Century Egypt*. Berkeley: University of California Press, 2009.

East India (Deccan Riots Commission). *Copy of the Report of the Commission Appointed in India to Inquire into the Causes of the Riots Which Took Place in the Year 1875, in the Poona and Ahmednagar Districts of the Bombay Presidency*. London: George Edward Eyre and William Spottiswoode, 1878.

Egypt. No. 1 (1895). *Report on the Finances, Administration, and Condition of Egypt, and the Progress of Reforms*. London: Harrison and Sons, 1895.

Egypt. No. 1 (1896). *Report on the Finances, Administration, and Condition of Egypt, and the Progress of Reforms*. London: Harrison and Sons, 1896.

Egypt. No. 1 (1903). *Reports by His Majesty's Agent and Consul-General on the Finances, Administration, and Condition of Egypt and the Soudan in 1902*. London: Harrison and Sons, 1903.

Egypt. No. 1 (1904). *Reports by His Majesty's Agent and Consul-General on the Finances, Administration, and Condition of Egypt and the Soudan in 1903*. London: Harrison and Sons, 1904.

Egypt. No. 1 (1905). *Reports by His Majesty's Agent and Consul-General on the Finances, Administration, and Condition of Egypt and the Soudan in 1904*. London: Harrison and Sons, 1905.

Egypt. No. 1 (1906). *Reports by His Majesty's Agent and Consul-General on the Finances, Administration, and Condition of Egypt and the Soudan in 1905*. London: Harrison and Sons, 1906.

Egypt. No. 1 (1907). *Reports by His Majesty's Agent and Consul-General on the Finances, Administration, and Condition of Egypt and the Soudan in 1906*. London: Harrison and Sons, 1907.

Egypt. No. 1 (1908). *Reports by His Majesty's Agent and Consul-General on the Finances, Administration, and Condition of Egypt and the Soudan in 1907*. London: Harrison and Sons, 1908.

Egypt. No. 1 (1909). *Reports by His Majesty's Agent and Consul-General on the Finances, Administration, and Condition of Egypt and the Soudan in 1908*. London: Harrison and Sons, 1909.

Egypt. No. 1 (1910). *Reports by His Majesty's Agent and Consul-General on the Finances, Administration, and Condition of Egypt and the Soudan in 1909*. London: Harrison and Sons, 1910.

Egypt. No. 1 (1911). *Reports by His Majesty's Agent and Consul-General on the Finances, Aministration, and Condition of Egypt and the Soudan in 1910*. London: Harrison and Sons, 1911.

Egypt. No. 1 (1913). *Reports by His Majesty's Agent and Consul-General on the Finances, Administration, and Condition of Egypt and the Sudan in 1912*. London: Harrison and Sons, 1913.

Egypt. No. 1 (1914). *Reports by His Majesty's Agent and Consul-General on the Finances, Administration, and Condition of Egypt and the Sudan in 1913*. London: Harrison and Sons, 1914.

Egypt. No. 1 (1921). *Report of the Special Mission to Egypt*. London: His Majesty's Stationery Office, 1921.

Egypt. No. 2 (1890). *Further Correspondence Respecting the Finances and Condition of Egypt*. London: Harrison and Sons, 1890.

Egypt. No. 3 (1891). *Report on the Administration and Condition of Egypt and the Progress of Reforms*. London: Harrison and Sons, 1891.

Egypt. No. 3 (1892). *Report on the Administration, Finances, and Condition of Egypt and the Progress of Reforms*. London: Harrison and Sons, 1892.

Egypt. No. 6 (1888). *Copy of a Despatch from Sir E. Baring Inclosing a Report on the Condition of the Agricultural Population in Egypt*. London: Harrison and Sons, 1888.

Egypt. No. 15 (1885). *Reports on the State of Egypt, and the Progress of Administrative Reforms*. London: Harrison and Sons, 1885.

Eid, Alfred. *al-Tharwah al-ʿaqārīyah li-l-quṭr al-Miṣrī wa-diyūnuhu al-maʿqūdah ʿalá rahn ʿaqārī.* Cairo: Maṭbaʿat al-Maʿārif, 1909.

———. *La fortune immobilière de l'Égypte et sa dette hypothécaire.* Paris: Félix Alcan, 1907.

El Shakry, Omnia S. *The Great Social Laboratory: Subjects of Knowledge in Colonial and Postcolonial Egypt.* Stanford, CA: Stanford University Press, 2007.

Elden, Stuart. *Foucault's Last Decade.* Cambridge, UK: Polity Press, 2016.

Ellis, Matthew. *Desert Borderland: The Making of Modern Egypt and Libya.* Stanford, CA: Stanford University Press, 2018.

Elson, Diane. "The Value Theory of Labour." In *Value: The Representation of Labour in Capitalism*, edited by Diane Elson, 115–80. London: Verso, 2015.

Elyachar, Julia. *Markets of Dispossession: NGOs, Economic Development, and the State in Cairo.* Durham, NC: Duke University Press, 2005.

Engels, Friedrich. "Speech at the Graveside of Karl Marx." In *The Marx-Engels Reader*, edited by Robert C. Tucker, 681–82. New York: W. W. Norton, 1978.

Esmeir, Samera. *Juridical Humanity: A Colonial History.* Stanford, CA: Stanford University Press, 2012.

———. "The Work of Law in the Age of Empire: Production of Humanity in Colonial Egypt." Ph.D. diss., New York University, 2005.

EzzelArab, AbdelAziz. "The Fiscal and Constitutional Program of Egypt's Traditional Elites in 1879: A Documentary and Contextual Analysis of 'al-Lāʾiḥa al-Waṭaniyya' ("The National Program")." *Journal of the Economic and Social History of the Orient* 52 (2009): 301–24.

Fahmy, Khaled. *All the Pasha's Men: Mehmed Ali, His Army, and the Making of Modern Egypt.* Cambridge: Cambridge University Press, 1997.

———. *In Quest of Justice: Islamic Law and Forensic Medicine in Modern Egypt.* Berkeley: University of California Press, 2018.

Fahmy, Ziad. *Ordinary Egyptians: Creating the Modern Nation through Popular Culture.* Stanford, CA: Stanford University Press, 2011.

Federici, Silvia. *Wages Against Housework.* Bristol: Falling Wall Press, 1975.

Feis, Herbert. *Europe, the World's Banker, 1870–1914.* Clifton, NJ: Augustus M. Kelley, 1974.

Foucault, Michel. *The Birth of Biopolitics: Lectures at the Collège de France 1978–1979.* Translated by Graham Burchell. New York: Picador, 2008.

———. *Security, Territory, Population: Lectures at the Collège de France 1977–1978.* Translated by Graham Burchell. New York: Picador, 2007.

Frankel, Oz. *States of Inquiry: Social Investigations and Print Culture in Nineteenth Century Britain and the United States.* Baltimore: Johns Hopkins University Press, 2006.

Fraser, Nancy. "Behind Marx's Hidden Abode: For an Expanded Conception of Capitalism." *New Left Review*, no. 86 (March-April 2014): 55–72.

———. *Fortunes of Feminism: From State-Managed Capitalism to Neoliberal Crisis.* London: Verso, 2013.

———. "Legitimation Crisis? On the Political Contradictions of Financialized Capitalism." *Critical Historical Studies* 2, no. 2 (Fall 2015): 157–89.

Fraser, Nancy, and Rahel Jaeggi. *Capitalism: A Conversation in Critical Theory*. Cambridge, UK: Polity Press, 2018.

Gasper, Michael. *The Power of Representation: Publics, Peasants, and Islam in Egypt*. Stanford, CA: Standford University Press, 2009.

Genell, Aimee M. "Empire by Law: Ottoman Sovereignty and the British Occupation of Egypt, 1882–1923." Ph.D. diss., Columbia University, 2013.

Gershoni, Israel, and James P. Jankowski. *Egypt, Islam, and the Arabs: The Search for Egyptian Nationhood, 1900–1930*. New York: Oxford Unviersity Press, 1986.

———. *Redefining the Egyptian Nation, 1930–1945*. Cambridge: Cambridge University Press, 1995.

Gesink, Indira Falk. *Islamic Reform and Conservatism: Al-Azhar and the Evolution of Modern Sunni Islam*. London: Tauris Academic Studies, 2010.

Ghosh, Amitav. *The Imam and the Indian*. Delhi: Permanent Black, 2002.

Gilmartin, David. *Blood and Water: The Indus River Basin in Modern History*. Berkeley: University of California Press, 2015.

Goldberg, David Theo. *The Racial State*. Malden, MA: Blackwell, 2002.

Goldberg, Ellis. "The Historiography of Crisis in the Egyptian Political Economy." In *Middle East Historiographies: Narrating the Twentieth Century*, edited by Israel Gershoni, Amy Singer, and Hakan Erdem, 183–207. Seattle: University of Washington Press, 2006.

———. "Peasants in Revolt—Egypt 1919." *International Journal of Middle East Studies* 24, no. 2 (May 1992): 261–80.

———. *Trade, Reputation, and Child Labor in Twentieth-Century Egypt*. New York: Palgrave Macmillan, 2004.

Goldschmidt, Arthur. "The Egyptian Nationalist Party, 1892–1919." In *Political and Social Change in Modern Egypt: Historical Studies from the Ottoman Conquest to the United Arab Republic*, edited by P. M. Holt, 308–33. London: Oxford University Press, 1968.

Gorman, Anthony. *Historians, State, and Politics in Twentieth Century Egypt: Contesting the Nation*. London: Routledge, 2003.

Goswami, Manu. "From Swadeshi to Swaraj: Nation, Economy, and Territory in Colonial South Asia, 1870 to 1907." *Comparative Studies in Society and History* 40, no. 4 (October 1998): 609–36.

———. *Producing India: From Colonial Economy to National Space*. Chicago: University of Chicago Press, 2004.

———. " 'Provincializing' Sociology: The Case of a Premature Postcolonial Sociologist." *Political Power and Social Theory* 24 (2013): 145–75.

———. "Rethinking the Modular Nation Form: Toward a Sociohistorical Conception of Nationalism." *Comparative Studies in Society and History* 44, no. 4 (2002): 770–99.

Gramsci, Antonio. *Selections from the Prison Notebooks of Antonio Gramsci*. London: Lawrence and Wishart, 1971.

Gran, Peter. "Modern Trends in Egyptian Historiography: A Review Article." *International Journal of Middle East Studies* 9, no. 3 (October 1978): 367–71.

Granduillot, G. *Étude sur la crise Égyptienne*. Alexandrie: Établissements A. Mourès, 1909.

Guha, Ranajit. *Dominance Without Hegemony: History and Power in Colonial India*. Cambridge, MA: Harvard University Press, 1997.

———. *A Rule of Property for Bengal: An Essay on the Idea of Permanent Settlement*. Durham, NC: Duke University Press, 1996.

Hall, A. R., ed. *The Export of Capital from Britain: 1870–1914*. London: Routledge, 2012.

Hammad, Hanan. "Between Egyptian 'National Purity' and 'Local Flexibility': Prostitution in al-Mahalla al-Kubra in the First Half of the 20th Century." *Journal of Social History* 44, no. 3 (Spring 2011): 751–83.

———. *Industrial Sexuality: Gender, Urbanization, and Social Transformation in Egypt*. Austin: University of Texas Press, 2016.

Hamzah, Dyala. "From 'Ilm to Ṣiḥāfa or the Politics of the Public Interest (maṣlaḥa): Muḥammad Rashīd Riḍa and His Journal al-Manār (1898–1935)." In *The Making of the Arab Intellectual: Empire, Public Sphere and the Colonial Coordinates of Selfhood*, edited by Dyala Hamzah, 90–127. London: Routledge, 2013.

Hanīn, Girgis. *al-Aṭyān wa-l-ḍarā'ib fī al-quṭr al-Miṣrī* [1904], edited by Muḥammad Sābir 'Arab. Cairo: al-Hay'ah al-Miṣrīyah al-'Āmmah li-l-Kitāb, 2008.

Hanioglu, M. Sukru. *The Young Turks in Opposition*. New York: Oxford University Press, 1995.

Hanley, Will. *Identifying with Nationality: Europeans, Ottomans, and Egyptians in Alexandria*. New York: Columbia University Press, 2017.

Hansen, Bent. "Interest Rates and Foreign Capital in Egypt Under British Occupation." *Journal of Economic History* XLIII, no. 4 (December 1983): 867–84.

Ḥarb, Muḥammad Tal'at. *'Ilāj Miṣr al-iqtiṣādī wa-mashrū' bank al-Miṣrīyīn aww bank al-ummah* [1912]. Cairo: Maṭba'at Dār al-Kutub, 2002.

Hardiman, David. *Feeding the Baniya: Peasants and Usurers in Western India*. Delhi: Oxford University Press, 1996.

Harvey, David. *Justice, Nature, and the Geography of Difference*. Oxford: Blackwell Publishers, 1996.

———. *The Limits to Capital*. New and fully updated ed. New York: Verso, 2006.

———. *Paris, Capital of Modernity*. London: Routledge, 2003.

———. *Spaces of Capital: Towards a Critical Geography*. New York: Routledge, 2001.

———. *The Urban Experience*. Baltimore: Johns Hopkins University Press, 1989.

Hay, Colin. "Crisis and the Structural Transformation of the State: Interrogating the Process of Change." *British Journal of Politics and International Relations* 1, no. 3 (1999): 317–44.

Henderson, George L. *California and the Fictions of Capital*. Philadelphia: Temple University Press, 2003.

———. "Nature and Fictitious Capital: the Historical Geography of an Agrarian Question." *Antipode* 30, no. 2 (1998): 73–118.

———. *Value in Marx: The Persistence of Value in a More-Than-Capitalist World*. Minneapolis: University of Minnesota Press, 2013.

Higher Committee for Agrarian Reform. *Silent Struggle Between the Egyptian Fellah and Mohamed Aly Dynasty*. Cairo: HCAR Press Department, 1954.

Hilferding, Rudolf. *Finance Capital: A Study of the Latest Phase of Capitalist Development*. London: Routledge Press, 2006.

Hobsbawm, Eric. *The Age of Empire, 1875–1914*. New York: Vintage Books, 1989.

Hobson, J. A. *Imperialism: A Study*. New York: James Pott & Company, 1902.

Holt, Elizabeth M. *Fictitious Capital: Silk, Cotton, and the Rise of the Arabic Novel*. New York: Fordham University Press, 2017.

Hont, Istvan. *Jealousy of Trade: International Competition and the Nation-State in Historical Perspective*. Cambridge, MA: Belknap Press, 2005.

Hopkins, A. G. "The Victorians and Africa: A Reconsideration of the Occupation of Egypt, 1882." *The Journal of African History* 27, no. 2 (1986): 363–91.

Hudson, Peter James. *Bankers and Empire: How Wall Street Colonized the Caribbean*. Chicago: University of Chicago Press, 2017.

Hunter, Archie. *Power and Passion in Egypt: A Life of Sir Eldon Gorst 1861–1911*. London: I. B. Tauris, 2007.

Hunter, Robert. *Egypt Under the Khedives 1805–1879: From Household Government to Modern Bureaucracy*. Pittsburgh, PA: University of Pittsburgh Press, 1984.

Ibrahim, Vivian. *The Copts of Egypt: The Challenges of Modernisation and Identity*. London: I. B. Tauris, 2011.

Islamoğlu, Huri, and Çağlar Keyder. "Agenda for Ottoman History." *Review* 1, no. 1 (Summer 1977): 31–56.

Isma'īl, Ḥamāda Maḥmūd, ed. *Maḥādir jalisāt al-jam'īyah al-'umūmīyah (1885–1909)*. Vol. 1. Cairo: Maṭba'at Dār al-Kutub, 2011.

Iyer, Samantha Gayathri. "The Paradox of Poverty and Plenty: Egypt, India, and the Rise of U.S. Food Aid, 1870s to 1950s." Ph.D. diss., University of California, Berkeley, 2014.

Jacob, Wilson Chacko. *Working Out Egypt: Effendi Masculinity and Subject Formation in Colonial Modernity, 1870–1940*. Durham, NC: Duke University Press, 2011.

Jakes, Aaron. "Boom, Bugs, Bust: Egypt's Ecology of Interest, 1882–1914." *Antipode* 49, no. 4 (2017): 1035–59.

———. "The Scales of Public Utility: Agricultural Roads and State Space in the Era of the British Occupation." In *The Long 1890s in Egypt: Colonial Quiescence, Subterranean Resistance*, edited by Marilyn Booth and Anthony Gorman, 57–86. Edinburgh: Edinburgh University Press, 2014.

Jakes, Aaron, and Ahmad Shokr. "Finding Value in Empire of Cotton." *Critical Historical Studies* 4, no. 1 (Spring 2017): 107–36.

Jallād, Fīlīb bin Yūsuf. *Qāmūs al-idārah wa-l-qaḍā'* [1889 edition]. 3 vols. Cairo: Maṭba'at Dār al-Kutub, 2003.

Jāwīsh, 'Abd al-'Azīz. *al-'Ālam al-Islāmī.* Istabul: Dār al-Khilāfah al-Islāmīyah, 1912.

Jessop, Bob. "Spatial Fixes, Temporal Fixes and Spatio-Temporal Fixes." In *David Harvey: a Critical Reader*, edited by Noel Castree and Derek Gregory, 142–66. Oxford: Blackwell Publishing, 2006.

———. *State Power: A Strategic-Relational Approach.* Cambridge, UK; Malden, MA: Polity Press, 2008.

———. *State Theory: Putting the Capitalist State in its Place.* Cambridge, UK: Polity Press, 1990.

Kamel Pasha, Moustafa. *Égyptiens et Anglais.* Paris: Perrin et Cie., 1906.

———. "What the National Party Wants: Speech Delivered on 22nd October 1907 in the Zizinia Theatre at Alexandria." Cairo: *Egyptian Standard*, 1907.

Kāmil, Muṣṭafá. *Kitāb al-mas'alah al-sharqīyah.* Miṣr: Maṭba'at al-Ādāb, 1898.

Karabell, Zachary. *Parting the Desert: The Creation of the Suez Canal.* New York: Vintage Books, 2003.

Karakişla, Yavuz Selim. "The 1908 Strike Wave in the Ottoman Empire." *Turkish Studies Association Bulletin* 16, no. 2 (September 1992): 153–77.

Karam, Fu'ād, ed. *al-Niẓārāt wa-l-wizārāt al-miṣrīyah.* Vol. I. Cairo: al-Hay'ah al-Miṣrīyah lil-Kitāb, 1994.

Karl, Rebecca E. *The Magic of Concepts: History and the Economic in Twentieth-Century China.* Durham, NC: Duke University Press, 2017.

Kayali, Hasan. *Arabs and Young Turks: Ottomanism, Arabism, and Islamism in the Ottoman Empire, 1908–1918.* Berkeley: University of California Press, 1997.

Kazziha, Walid. "The Jarīdah-Ummah Group and Egyptian Politics." *Middle Eastern Studies* 13, no. 3 (October 1977): 373–85.

Kemmerer, Edwin W. "The Fiscal System of Egypt." *Publications of the American Economic Association* 1, no. 3 (August 1900): 189–216.

———. *Report on the Agricultural Bank of Egypt to the Secretary of War and to the Philippine Commission.* Washington, DC: Government Printing Office, 1906.

Khan, Noor-Aiman. *Egyptian-Indian Nationalist Collaboration and the British Empire.* New York: Palgrave Macmillan, 2011.

Kholoussy, Hanan. *For Better, For Worse: The Marriage Crisis That Made Modern Egypt.* Stanford, CA: Stanford University Press, 2010.

———. "Monitoring and Medicalising Male Sexuality in Semi-Colonial Egypt." *Gender & History* 22, no. 3 (November 2010): 677–91.

Khuri-Makdisi, Ilham. *The Eastern Mediterranean and the Making of Global Radicalism*. Berkeley: University of California Press, 2010.

Killingray, David. " 'A Swift Agent of Government': Air Power in British Colonial Africa, 1916–1939." *The Journal of African History* 25, no. 4 (1984): 429–44.

Koselleck, Reinhart. "Crisis." *Journal of the History of Ideas* 67, no. 2 (April 2006): 357–400.

Kwak, James. *Economism: Bad Economics and the Rise of Inequality*. New York: Pantheon, 2017.

Landes, David S. *Bankers and Pashas: International Finance and Economic Imperialism in Egypt*. Cambridge, MA: Harvard University Press, 1958.

Leary, David E. "The Fate and Influence of John Stuart Mill's Proposed Science of Ethology." *Journal of the History of Ideas* 43, no. 1 (January-March 1982): 153–62.

Lefebvre, Henri. *The Production of Space*. Oxford, UK: Blackwell, 1991.

Legrand, F. *Les fluctuations des prix et les crises de 1907 et 1908 en Égypte*. Nancy: Imprimerie Type-Lytho J. Coube, 1909.

Lenin, V. I. *Essential Works of Lenin: "What Is to Be Done?" and Other Writings*. New York: Dover Publications, 1987.

———. "Imperialism: The Highest Stage of Capitalism." http://www.marxists.org/archive/lenin/works/1916/imp-hsc/.

Levy, Jonathan. *Freaks of Fortune: The Emerging World of Capitalism and Risk in America*. Cambridge, MA: Harvard University Press, 2012.

Lévy, M. Edwin. "Les événements de 1907 et la situation actuelle de l'Égypte." *L'Égypte Contemporaine* III, no. 12 (Nov. 1912): 503–30.

Lew-Williams, Beth. *The Chinese Must Go: Violence, Exclusion, and the Making of the Alien in America*. Cambridge, MA: Harvard University Press, 2018.

Lockman, Zachary. *Contending Visions of the Middle East: The History and Politics of Orientalism*. 2nd ed. Cambridge: Cambridge University Press, 2004.

———. "Exploring the Field: Lost Voices and Emerging Practices in Egypt, 1882–1914." In *Histories of the Modern Middle East: New Directions*, edited by Israel Gershoni, Hakan Erdem, and Ursula Woköck, 137–54. Boulder, CO: Lynne Rienner, 2002.

———. "Imagining the Working Class: Culture, Nationalism, and Class Formation in Egypt, 1899–1914." *Poetics Today* 15, no. 2 (Summer 1994): 157–90.

———. "The Social Roots of Nationalism: Workers and the National Movement in Egypt, 1908–19." *Middle Eastern Studies* 24, no. 4 (October 1988): 445–59.

Ludden, David E. *Agricultural Production and South Asian History*.2nd ed. New Delhi; Oxford; New York: Oxford University Press, 2005.

———. "Orientalist Empiricism: Transformations of Colonial Knowledge." In *Orientalism and the Postcolonial Predicament*, edited by Carol Breckenridge and Peter Van der Veer, 250–78. Philadelphia: University of Pennsylvania Press, 1993.

Lugard, Frederick John Dealtry. *The Dual Mandate in British Tropical Africa*. Edinburgh: William Blackwood and Sons, 1922.

Luṭfī al-Sayyid, Aḥmad. *Turāth Aḥmad Luṭfī al-Sayyid*. Cairo: Maṭbaʿat Dār al-Kutub wa-l-Wathāʾiq al-Qawmīyah, 2008.

Luxemburg, Rosa. *The Accumulation of Capital* [1913]. Translated by Agnes Schwarzschild. New York: Routledge, 2003.

Luzzatti, Luigi. "The International Institute of Agriculture." *The North American Review* 182, no. 594 (May 1906): 651–59.

Lyons, H. G. *The Cadastral Survey of Egypt, 1892–1907*. Cairo: National Printing Department, 1908.

Mabrūk, Muḥammad. "al-Bank al-ahlī al-Miṣrī wa-dawruhu fī al-iqtiṣād al-Miṣrī." Cairo University, 2011.

Maine, Henry Sumner. *Ancient Law: Its Connection to the History of Early Society* [1861]. Middletown, NY: Pantianos Classics, 2017.

———. *Popular Government* [1885]. Indianapolis: Liberty Fund, 1976.

———. *Village-Communities in the East and West* [1871]. London: John Murray, 1895.

Malm, Andreas. *Fossil Capital: The Rise of Steam Power and the Roots of Global Warming*. London: Verso, 2016.

Mamdani, Mahmood. *Citizen and Subject: Contemporary Africa and the Legacy of Late Colonialism*. Princeton, NJ: Princeton University Press, 1996.

———. *Define and Rule: Native as Political Identity*. Cambridge, MA: Harvard University Press, 2012.

Manela, Erez. *The Wilsonian Moment: Self-Determination and the International Origins of Anticolonial Nationalism*. Oxford: Oxford University Press, 2007.

Mansfield, Peter. *The British in Egypt*. New York: Holt, Rinehart and Winston, 1971.

Mantena, Karuna. *Alibis of Empire: Henry Maine and the Ends of Liberal Imperialism*. Princeton, NJ: Princeton University Press, 2010.

———. "The Crisis of Liberal Imperialism." In *Victorian Visions of Global Order: Empire and International Relations in Nineteenth-Century Political Thought*, edited by Duncan Bell, 113–35. Cambridge: Cambridge University Press, 2007.

Marʿī, Ḥassan. *Riwāyat al-Azhar wa-qaḍīyat Ḥamādah Bāshā*. Cairo, 1909.

Marlowe, John. *Cromer in Egypt*. New York: Praeger, 1970.

Marx, Karl. *Capital: A Critique of Political Economy, Volume 1*. Translated by Ben Fowkes. London: Penguin Books, 1976.

———. *A Contribution to the Critique of Political Economy*. New York: International Publishers, 1970.

———. *Grundrisse: Foundations of the Critique of Political Economy*. London: Penguin Books, 1973.

Mathew, Johan. *Margins of the Market: Trafficking and Capitalism Across the Arabian Sea*. Berkeley: University of California Press, 2016.

McIlwraith, Malcolm. "The Declaration of a Protectorate in Egypt and Its Legal Effects." *Journal of the Society of Comparative Legislation* 17, no. 1/2 (1917): 238–59.

Mehta, Uday Singh. *Liberalism and Empire: A Study in Nineteenth-Century British Liberal Thought*. Chicago: University of Chicago Press, 1999.

Merrifield, Andy. *The New Urban Question*. London: Pluto Press, 2014.

Mestyan, Adam. *Arab Patriotism: The Ideology and Culture of Power in Late Ottoman Egypt*. Princeton, NJ: Princeton University Press, 2017.

———. "Domestic Sovereignty, Aʿyan Developmentalism, and Global Microhistory in Modern Egypt." *Comparative Studies in Society and History* 60, no. 2 (2018): 415–45.

Metcalf, Thomas. *Aftermath of Revolt: India 1857–1970*. Princeton, NJ: Princeton University Press, 1964.

Mies, Maria. *Patriarchy and Accumulation on a World Scale: Women in the International Division of Labor*. 3rd ed. London: Zed Books Ltd., 2014.

Mīkhāʾīl, Ramzī. *al-Ṣaḥāfah al-Miṣrīyah wa-l-ḥarakah al-waṭanīyah*. Cairo: al-Hayʾah al-Miṣrīyah al-ʿĀmmah li-l-Kitāb, 1995.

Mikhail, Alan. *Nature and Empire in Ottoman Egypt: An Environmental History*. Cambridge: Cambridge University Press, 2011.

Milgate, Murray, and Shannon C. Stimson. *After Adam Smith: A Century of Transformation in Politics and Political Economy*. Princeton, NJ: Princeton University Press, 2009.

Mill, John Stuart. "Civilization" [1836]. In *Dissertations and Discussions*, 130–67. London: George Routledge & Sons, 1910.

———. *Collected Works of John Stuart Mill, Vol. 2–3: Principles of Political Economy*. Indianapolis: Liberty Fund, 2006.

———. "Considerations on Representative Government" [1861]. In *Collected Works of John Stuart Mill, Volume XIX: Essays on Politics and Society*, edited by J. M. Robson, 371–613. Toronto: University of Toronto Press 1977.

———. "Essays on Some Unsettled Questions of Political Economy" [1844]. In *Collected Works of John Stuart Mill, Vol. 4: Essays on Economics and Society, 1824–1845*, edited by J. M. Robson, 229–339. Indianapolis: Liberty Fund, 2006.

Mill, John Stuart, and Jeremy Bentham. *Utilitarianism and Other Essays*. New York: Penguin, 1987.

Miller, Isaac. "The Egyptian Financial Crisis of 1907: Capitalism and Regulation Under Fragmented Colonialism." M.A. thesis, American University in Cairo, 2015.

Milner, Alfred. *England in Egypt*. London: Edward Arnold, 1892.

Ministère de l'Intérieur. *Essai de statistique générale de l'Égypte*. Le Caire: Typographie de L'État, 1879.

Ministère des Finances. *Recueil des documents relatifs à la guerre publiés au 'Journal Officiel' du 1er Août 1916 au 31 Juillet 1917*. Le Caire: Imprimerie Nationale, 1920.

———. *Recueil des documents relatifs à la guerre publiés au 'Journal Officiel' du 1er Août 1918 au 31 Juillet 1919*. Le Caire: Imprimerie Nationale, 1920.

———. *Recueil des documents relatifs à la guerre publiés au 'Journal Officiel' du 3 Août 1914 au 31 Juillet 1915*. Le Caire: Imprimerie Nationale, 1920.

Ministry of Finance (Egypt). *Projet de péréquation de l'impôt foncier en Égypte, récapitulation par village*. Cairo: Imprimérie Nationale, 1897.

Ministry of Justice. *Report for the Year 1905 Presented by the Judicial Adviser*. Cairo: National Printing Department, 1906.

———. *Report for the Year 1909 Presented by the Judicial Adviser*. Cairo: National Printing Department, 1910.

———. *Report for the Year 1912 Presented by the Judicial Adviser*. Cairo: Government Press, 1913.

Ministry of the Interior. *Report on the Cotton Worm, 1905*. Cairo: Al-Mokattam Printing Office, 1906.

Minkin, Shane. "Documenting Death: Inquests, Governance and Belonging in 1890s Alexandria." In *The Long 1890s in Egypt: Colonial Quiescence, Subterranean Resistance*, edited by Marilyn Booth and Anthony Gorman, 31–56. Edinburgh: Edinburgh University Press, 2014.

———. *Imperial Bodies: Empire and Death in Alexandria, Egypt*. Stanford, CA: Stanford University Press, 2019.

Mitchell, Timothy. *Carbon Democracy: Political Power in the Age of Oil*. London: Verso, 2011.

———. *Colonising Egypt*. Berkeley: University of California Press, 1991.

———. "Fixing the Economy." *Cultural Studies* 12, no. 1 (January 1998): 82–101.

———. *Rule of Experts: Egypt, Techno-Politics, Modernity*. Berkeley: University of California Press, 2002.

———. "Society, Economy, and the State Effect." In *State/Culture: State-Formation after the Cultural Turn*, edited by George Steinmetz. Ithaca, NY: Cornell University Press, 1999.

Moore, Jason. *Capitalism in the Web of Life: Ecology and the Accumulation of Capital*. New York: Verso, 2015.

———. "Ecology, Capital, and the Nature of Our Times: Accumulation and Crisis in the Capitalist World-Ecology." *Journal of World-Systems Research* 17, no. 1 (2011): 108–47.

———. "Transcending the Metabolic Rift: A Theory of Crises in the Capitalist World-Ecology." *The Journal of Peasant Studies* 38, no. 1 (2011): 1–46.

———. "Wall Street Is a Way of Organizing Nature." *Upping the Anti* 12 (2011): 47–61.

Mufakharul Islam, M. "The Punjab Land Alienation Act and the Professional Moneylenders." *Modern Asian Studies* 29, no. 2 (1995): 271–91.

Nagano, Yoshiko. "The Agricultural Bank of the Philippine Government, 1908–1916." *Journal of Southeast Asian Studies* 28, no. 2 (September 1997): 301–23.

National Bank of Egypt. *National Bank of Egypt, 1898–1948*. Cairo: N.B.E. Printing Press, 1948.

Noyes, Alexander Dana. *Forty Years of American Finance: A Short Financial History of the Government and People of the United States Since the Civil War, 1865–1907*. New York: G. P. Putnam's, 1909.

———. "A Year After the Panic of 1907." *The Quarterly Journal of Economics* 23, no. 2 (February 1909): 185–212.

Odell, Kerry A., and Marc D. Weidenmier. "Real Shock, Monetary Aftershock: The 1906 San Francisco Earthquake and the Panic of 1907." *The Journal of Economic History* 64, no. 4 (December 2004): 1002–27.

Ollman, Bertell. *Alienation: Marx's Conception of Man in Capitalist Society*. Cambridge: Cambridge University Press, 1971.

Omar, Hussein. "Arabic Thought in a Liberal Cage." In *Beyond Muslim Liberalism*, edited by Faisal Devji and Zaheer Kazmi. London: Hurst, 2016.

———. "Minority as Microbe: Secularism, Sectarianism, and Sovereignty in English-Occupied Egypt." (forthcoming).

———. "The Rule of Strangers: Empire, Islam and the Invention of 'Politics,' 1867–1914." Ph.D. diss., University of Oxford, 2016.

Owen, Edward Roger John. "The Cairo Building Industry and the Building Boom of 1897–1907." In *Colloque international sur l'histoire du Caire*, 337–50. Cairo: General Egyptian Book Organization, 1972. .

———. *Cotton and the Egyptian Economy, 1820–1914: A Study in Trade and Development*. Oxford: Clarendon Press, 1969.

———. "Egypt and Europe: From French Expedition to British Occupation." In *Studies in the Theory of Imperialism*, edited by Edward Roger John Owen and Robert B. Sutcliffe, 195–205. London: Longman, 1972.

———. "Imperial Policy and Theories of Social Change: Sir Alfred Lyall in India." In *Anthropology and the Colonial Encounter*, edited by Talal Asad, 223–45. London: Ithaca Press, 1975.

———. "The Influence of Lord Cromer's Indian Experience on British Policy in Egypt 1883–1907." In *Middle Eastern Affairs*, no. 4 (St. Antony's Papers, no. 17), edited by Albert Hourani, 109–139. London: Oxford University Press, 1965.

———. *Lord Cromer: Victorian Imperialist, Edwardian Proconsul*. Oxford: Oxford University Press, 2004.

———. "The Middle East in the Eighteenth Century—An 'Islamic' Society in Decline?: A Critique of Gibb and Bowen's Islamic Society and the West." *British Society for Middle Eastern Studies. Bulletin* 3, no. 2 (1976): 110–17.

———. *The Middle East in the World Economy, 1800–1914*. London: I. B. Tauris, 2002.

———. "Studying Islamic History." *The Journal of Interdisciplinary History* 4, no. 2 (Autumn 1973): 287–98.

Pennington, J. D. "The Copts in Modern Egypt." *Middle Eastern Studies* 18, no. 2 (April 1982): 158–79.

Pincus, Steve. "Neither Machiavellian Moment nor Possessive Individualism: Commercial Society and the Defenders of the English Commonwealth." *American Historical Review* 103, no. 3 (June 1998): 705–36.

Pitts, Jennifer. *A Turn to Empire: The Rise of Imperial Liberalism in Britain and France*. Princeton, NJ: Princeton University Press, 2005.

Platt, D. C. M. *Britain's Investment Overseas on the Eve of the First World War: The Use and Abuse of Numbers*. New York: St. Martin's Press, 1986.

Polanyi, Karl. *The Great Transformation: The Policial and Economic Origins of Our Time*. Boston: Beacon Hill, 1957.

Pollard, Lisa. "Egyptian by Association: Charitable States and Service Societies, Circa 1850–1945." *International Journal of Middle East Studies* 46 (2014): 239–57.

———. *Nurturing the Nation: The Family Politics of Modernizing, Colonizing and Liberating Egypt*. Berkeley: University of California Press, 2005.

Pomeranz, Kenneth. *The Great Divergence: China, Europe, and the Making of the Modern World Economy*. Princeton, NJ: Princeton University Press, 2000.

Postel, Charles. *The Populist Vision*. Oxford: Oxford University Press, 2009.

Postone, Moishe. *Time, Labor, and Social Domination: A Reinterpretation of Marx's Critical Theory*. New York: Cambridge University Press, 1993.

Poulantzas, Nicos. *State, Power, Socialism*. New ed. London: Verso, 2000.

Public Works Ministry. *Report upon the Administration of the Public Works Department for 1899*. Cairo: National Printing Department, 1900.

Pursley, Sara. *Familiar Futures: Time, Selfhood, and Sovereignty in Iraq*. Stanford, CA: Stanford University Press, 2019.

Quataert, Donald. *Social Disintegration and Popular Resistance in the Ottoman Empire, 1881–1908: Reactions to European Economic Penetration*. New York: New York University Press, 1983.

Qunaybir, Sālim ʻAbd al-Nabī. *Al-Ittijāhāt al-siyāsīyah wa-al-fikrīyah wa-al-ijtimāʻīyah fī al-adab al-ʻArabī al-muʻāṣir: ʻAbd al-ʻAzīz Jāwīsh 1872–1929*. Benghazi: Dār Maktabat al-Andalus, 1968.

Ralph, Michael. *Forensics of Capital*. Chicago: University of Chicago Press, 2015.

Ratcliffe, S. K. *Sir William Wedderburn and the Indian Reform Movement*. London: George Allen & Unwin Ltd., 1923.

Ricardo, David. *The Principles of Political Economy and Taxation*. New York: E. P. Dutton & Co., 1912.

Richards, Alan. *Egypt's Agricultural Development, 1800–1980*. Boulder, CO: Westview Press, 1982.

———. "Technical and Social Change in Egyptian Agriculture, 1890–1914." *Economic Development and Cultural Change* 26, no. 4 (July 1978): 725–45.

Richmond, J.C.B. *Egypt, 1798–1952: Her Advance Towards a Modern Identity*. New York: Columbia University Press, 1977.

Rieker, Martina E. "The Sa'id and the City: Subaltern Spaces in the Making of Modern Egyptian History." Ph.D. diss., Temple University, 1997.

Rif'at, 'Abd al-Fattāḥ Afandī. *Wājibāt al-'umdah*. Cairo: Maṭba'at al-Ma'ārif, 1901.

Rifaat, Mohammed Ali. *The Monetary System of Egypt: An Inquiry into Its History and Present Working*. London: George Allen & Unwin Ltd., 1935.

Rivlin, Helen. *The Agricultural Policy of Muḥammad 'Alī in Egypt*. Cambridge, MA: Harvard University Press, 1961.

Roberts, William Clare. "The Idea of Emancipation after Postcolonial Theory." *Interventions* 19, no. 6 (2017): 747–63.

———. *Marx's Inferno: The Political Theory of Capital*. Princeton, NJ: Princeton University Press, 2016.

Robinson, Cedric. *Black Marxism: The Making of the Black Radical Tradition*. Chapel Hill: University of North Carolina Press, 2000.

Robinson, Ronald, and John Gallagher. *Africa and the Victorians: The Climax of Imperialism in the Dark Continent*. New York: St. Martin's Press, 1961.

Rodgers, Mary Tone, and James E. Payne. "How the Bank of France Changed U.S. Equity Expectations and Ended the Panic of 1907." *The Journal of Economic History* 74, no. 2 (2014): 420–48.

Roitman, Janet. *Anti-Crisis*. Durham, NC: Duke University Press, 2014.

Roosevelt, Theodore. "British Rule in Africa: Address Delivered at the Guildhall, London, May 31, 1910." London, 1910.

———. "Law and Order in Egypt: An Address Before the National University in Cairo, March 28, 1910." Cairo University, 1910.

Rosenberg, Emily *Financial Missionaries to the World: The Politics and Culture of Dollar Diplomacy, 1900–1930*. Durham, NC: Duke University Press, 2003.

Rothstein, Theodore. *Egypt's Ruin: A Financial and Administrative Record*. London: A. C. Fifield, 1910.

Roux, François Charles. *Le Coton en Égypte*. Paris: Librairie Armand Colin, 1908.

Ryzova, Lucie. *The Age of Efendiyya: Passages to Modernity in National-Colonial Egypt*. Oxford: Oxford University Press, 2014.

Ṣabrī, 'Abd al-'Azīz. *Ḥadīth al-'umad*. Manṣūrah: Maṭba'at Liyūnīdā Vinayyarī wa-Akīhi, 1916.

Safran, Nadav. *Egypt in Search of Political Community: An Analysis of the Intellectual and Political Evolution of Egypt, 1804–1952*. Cambridge, MA: Harvard University Press, 1961.

Said, Edward. *Orientalism*. New York: Vintage Books, 1994.

Sarkar, Sumit. *The Swadeshi Movement in Bengal: 1903–1908*. New ed. Delhi: Permanent Black, 2010.

Sartori, Andrew. *Bengal in Global Concept History: Culturalism in the Age of Capital*. Chicago: University of Chicago Press, 2008.

———. "The British Empire and Its Liberal Mission." *The Journal of Modern History*, no. 78 (September 2006): 623–42.

———. "Global Intellectual History and the History of Political Economy." In *Global Intellectual History*, edited by Samuel Moyn and Andrew Sartori. New York: Columbia University Press, 2013.

———. *Liberalism in Empire: An Alternative History*. Berkeley: University of California Press, 2014.

Satia, Priya. "The Defense of Inhumanity: Air Control and the British Idea of Arabia." *The American Historical Review* 111, no. 1 (February 2006): 16–51.

Saul, S. B. *The Myth of the Great Depression, 1873–1896*. London: Macmillan, 1969.

Saul, Samir. *La France et l'Égypte de 1882 à 1914: Intérêts économiques et implications politiques*. Paris: Comité pour l'histoire économique et financière de la France, 1997.

Sayer, Derek. *The Violence of Abstraction: The Analytic Foundations of Historical Materialism*. Oxford: Basil Blackwell, 1987.

Sayers, Richard S. *The Bank of England, 1891–1944*. Cambridge: Cambridge University Press, 1976.

Schanz, Moritz. *Cotton in Egypt and the Anglo-Egyptian Sudan*. Scheveningen: 9th International Cotton Congress, 1913.

Schölch, Alexander. *Egypt for the Egyptians! The Socio-political Crisis in Egypt, 1878–1882*. London: Ithaca Press, 1981.

Schulze, Reinhard C. "Colonization and Resistance: The Egyptian Peasant Rebellion, 1919." In *Peasants and Politics in the Modern Middle East*, edited by Farhad Kazemi and John Waterbury, 171–202. Gainesville: University of Florida Press, 1991.

Schumpeter, Joseph. "The Crisis of the Tax State." In *The Economics and Sociology of Capitalism*, edited by Richard Swedberg, 99–140. Princeton, NJ: Princeton University Press, 1991.

Scott, David. "Colonial Governmentality." *Social Text*, no. 43 (Autumn 1995): 191–220.

Scott, James C. *Against the Grain: A Deep History of the Earliest States*. New Haven, CT: Yale University Press, 2017.

———. *The Art of Not Being Governed: An Anarchist History of Upland Southeast Asia*. New Haven, CT: Yale University Press, 2009.

———. *The Moral Economy of the Peasant: Rebellion and Subsistence in Southeast Asia*. New Haven, CT: Yale University Press, 1976.

———. *Seeing Like a State: How Certain Schemes to Improve the Human Condition Have Failed*. New Haven, CT: Yale University Press, 1998.

———. *Weapons of the Weak: Everyday Forms of Peasant Resistance*. New Haven, CT: Yale University Press, 1985.

Scott, Joan Wallach. "Women in The Making of the English Working Class." In *Gender and the Politics of History*, 68–90. New York: Columbia University Press, 1988.

Scott-Moncrieff, Colin. *A'māl al-rayy fī sannat 1885–1886*. Translated by Ibrāhīm Muṣawwir. Cairo: Maṭbaʿat al-Muqtaṭaf, 1887.

Seigel, Micol. "Beyond Compare: Comparative Method after the Transnational Turn." *Radical History Review*, no. 91 (Winter 2005): 62–90.

Seikaly, Sherene. *Men of Capital: Scarcity and Economy in Mandate Palestine*. Stanford, CA: Stanford University Press, 2016.

Selim, Samah. *The Novel and the Rural Imaginary in Egypt, 1880–1985*. New York: Routledge, 2004.

Semmel, Bernard. *The Rise of Free Trade Imperialism: Classical Political Economy, the Empire of Free Trade, and Imperialism*. Cambridge: Cambridge University Press, 1970.

Shafiee, Katayoun. *Machineries of Oil: An Infrastructural History of BP in Iran*. Cambridge, MA: MIT Press, 2018.

Shafīq, Aḥmad. *Mudhakkirātī fī niṣf qarn*. 4 vols. Vol. 3. Cairo: al-Hay'ah al-ʿĀmmah li-l-Kitab, 1998.

Shalabī, ʿAlī. *al-Rīf al-Miṣrī fī al-niṣf al-thānī min al-qarn al-tāsiʿ ʿashar, 1847–1891*. al-Qāhirah: Dār al-Maʿārif, 1983.

Shamir, Ronen. *Current Flow: The Electrification of Palestine*. Stanford, CA: Stanford University Press, 2013.

Sharīf, Muḥammad Ḥāmid. *Ḥādithat Dinshawāy: wa-ṣadāhā fī al-adab al-ʿarabī al-ḥadīth wa-l-ṣaḥafah al-ʿarabīyah*. al-Qāhirah: al-Hayʿah al-Miṣrīyah al-ʿāmmah li-l-kitāb, 2006.

Shechter, Relli. *Smoking, Culture, and Economy in the Middle East: The Egyptian Tobacco Market 1850–2000*. Cairo: American University in Cairo Press, 2006.

Shokr, Ahmad. "Beyond the Fields: Cotton and the End of Empire in Egypt, 1919–1956." Ph.D. diss., New York University, 2016.

Sladen, Douglas. *Egypt and the English*. London: Hurst and Blackett, 1908.

Slobodian, Quinn. *Globalists: The End of Empire and the Birth of Neoliberalism*. Cambridge, MA: Harvard University Press, 2018.

———. "How to See the World Economy: Statistics, Maps, and Schumpeter's Camera in the First Age of Globalization." *Journal of Global History* 10, no. 2 (July 2015): 307–32.

Smith, Adam. *An Inquiry into the Nature and Causes of the Wealth of Nations*. New York: The Modern Library, 1994.

Smith, Neil. *Uneven Development: Nature, Capital, and the Production of Space* [1984]. 3rd ed. Athens: University of Georgia Press, 2008.

Sohn-Rethel, Alfred. *Intellectual and Manual Labor: A Critique of Epistemology*. Atlantic Highlands, NJ: Humanities Press, 1978.

Sohrabi, Nader. *Revolution and Constitutionalism in the Ottoman Empire and Iran*. Cambridge: Cambridge University Press, 2011.

Stokes, Eric. *The English Utilitarians and India*. Delhi: Oxford University Press, 1989.

Stoler, Ann Laura. "Tense and Tender Ties: The Politics of Comparison in North American History and (Post) Colonial Studies." *The Journal of American History* 88, no. 3 (Dec. 2001): 829–65.

Strachey, John, and Richard Strachey. *The Finances and Public Works of India From 1869 to 1881*. London: Kegan Paul, Trench, & Co., 1882.

Stuart, Villiers. *Egypt After the War: Being the Narrative of a Tour of Inspection (Undertaken Last Autumn)*. London: John Murray, 1883.

———. *Reports Respecting Reorganization in Egypt*. London: Harrison and Sons, 1883.

Sullivan, Eileen P. "Liberalism and Imperialism: J. S. Mill's Defence of the British Empire." *Journal of the History of Ideas* 44, no. 4 (October-December 1983): 599–617.

Talbot, Ian. "The Punjab Under Colonialism: Order and Transformation in British India." *Journal of Punjab Studies* 14, no. 1 (Spring 2007): 3–10.

Taymūr, Ḥussayn. *al-Būrṣah wa-tijārat al-quṭn*. Cairo: Maṭba'at al-Fajjālah, 1917.

Thorburn, Septimus S. *Musalmans and Money-Lenders in the Punjab*. Edinburgh: W. Blackwood, 1886.

Tiberi, Mario. *The Accounts of the British Empire: Capital Flows from 1799 to 1914*. Burlington, VT: Ashgate, 2005.

Tignor, Robert L. "British Agricultural and Hydraulic Policy in Egypt, 1882–1892." *Agricultural History* 37, no. 2 (April 1963): 63–74.

———. "The 'Indianization' of Egyptian Administration under British Rule." *The American Historical Review* 68, no. 3 (Apr. 1963): 636–61.

———. "Lord Cromer: Practitioner and Philosopher of Imperialism." *The Journal of British Studies* 2, no. 2 (May 1963): 142–59.

———. *Modernization and British Colonial Rule in Egypt, 1882–1914*. Princeton, NJ: Princeton University Press, 1966.

———. *State, Private Enterprise, and Economic Change in Egypt, 1918–1952*. Princeton, NJ: Princeton University Press, 1984.

Toledano, Ehud. "Social and Economic Change in the 'Long Nineteenth Century.'" In *The Cambridge History of Egypt*, edited by M. W. Daly, 252–84. Cambridge: Cambridge University Press, 1998.

Tollefson, Harold. "The 1894 British Takeover of the Egyptian Ministry of Interior." *Middle Eastern Studies* 26, no. 4 (October 1990): 547–60.

———. *Policing Islam: the British Occupation of Egypt and the Anglo-Egyptian Struggle over Control of the Police, 1882–1914*. Westport, CT: Greenwood Press, 1999.

Tucker, Judith. *Women in Nineteenth-Century Egypt*. Cambridge: Cambridge University Press, 1985.

Van Dieren, Edouard. *Considerations sur les avantages et la sécurité des placements hypothécaires en Égypte*. Bruxelles: Alliance Typographique, 1897.

Vitalis, Robert. *When Capitalists Collide: Business Conflict and the End of Empire in Egypt*. Berkeley: University of California Press, 1995.

Vogel, Lise. *Marxism and the Oppression of Women: Toward a Unitary Theory*. Chicago: Haymarket Books, 2013.

Warburg, Gabriel. "The 'Three-Legged Stool': Lampson, Faruq, and Nahhas, 1936–1944." In *Egypt and the Sudan*, edited by Gabriel Warburg. London: Frank Cass, 1985.

Washbrook, David. "Law, State and Agrarian Society in Colonial India." *Modern Asian Studies* 15, no. 3 (July 1981): 649–721.

Wedderburn, William. "Agricultural Banks for India." Bombay: Bombay Gazette Steam Press, 1884.

———. "Paper to Be Read at a Meeting of the Manchester Chamber of Commerce on Friday, 19th October 1883." In *Copy of Correspondence Respecting Agricultural Banks in India*, edited by House of Commons. London: Henry Hansard and Son, 1887.

White, Richard. *Railroaded: The Transcontinentals and the Making of Modern America*. New York: W. W. Norton & Company, 2012.

Willcocks, F. C. "Injurious Insects." In *Text-Book of Egyptian Agriculture*, edited by G. P. Foaden and F. Fletcher. Cairo: National Printing Department, 1910.

———. "Insects Injurious to the Cotton Plant in Egypt, Part I." In *Yearbook of the Khedivial Agricultural Society, Cairo, 1905*. Cairo: National Printing Press, 1906.

Willcocks, Sir William. *Sixty Years in the East*. Edinburgh: W. Blackwood, 1935.

Willcocks, Sir William, and J. I. Craig. *Egyptian Irrigation*, Vol. I. 3rd ed. London: E. & F. N. Spon, 1913.

———. *Egyptian Irrigation*, Vol. II. 3rd ed. London: E. & N. Spon, 1913.

Williams, Raymond. "Base and Superstructure in Marxist Cultural Theory." *New Left Review*, no. 82 (November-December 1973): 3–16.

Willis, Walter H., and R. J. Barrett, eds. *The Anglo-African Who's Who and Biographical Sketch-Book*. London: George Routledge & Sons, 1905.

Wood, Ellen Meiksins. "The Separation of the Economic and Political in Capitalism." *New Left Review*, no. 127 (1981): 66–95.

Zayn al-Dīn, Ismāʿīl. *al-Zirāʿah al-Miṣrīyah fī ʿahd al-iḥtilāl al-Brīṭānī*. Cairo: al-Hay'ah al-ʿĀmmah li-l-Kitāb, 1995.

Zimmerman, Andrew. *Alabama in Africa: Booker T. Washington, the German Empire, and the Globalization of the New South*. Princeton, NJ: Princeton University Press, 2010.

———. " 'What Do You Really Want in German East Africa, Herr Professor?' Counterinsurgency and the Science Effect in Colonial Tanzania." *Comparative Studies in Society and History* 48, no. 2 (2006): 419–61.

NOTE ON ILLUSTRATIONS

The engraved illustrations that appear in the chapter headings are taken from the stock certificates of ten Egyptian companies established during the period covered by this study. All of these documents are held in the collection of the author. Below is a list of the certificates that correspond to these images:

Introduction	The Egyptian Land Investment Company, One Founder's Share (1905).
Chapter 1	Société Anonyme du Béhera, Ten Ordinary Shares (1899).
Chapter 2	The Commercial and Estates Company of Egypt, One Founder's Share (1904).
Chapter 3	The Agricultural Bank of Egypt, One Ordinary Share (1903).
Chapter 4	The United Egyptian Lands, Limited, One Deferred Share (1907).
Chapter 5	North Egypt Land Company, Limited, Twenty Ordinary Shares (1905).
Chapter 6	The Cairo Electric Railways and Heliopolis Oases Company, One Founder's Share (1906).
Chapter 7	The Anglo-Egyptian Land Allotment Company, One Founder's Share (1906).
Chapter 8	The Upper Egypt Irrigation Company, Two Ordinary Shares (1910).
Conclusion	The Anglo-Belgian Company of Egypt, Limited, One Ordinary Share (1907).

INDEX

Page references followed by *f* or *t* refer to figures or tables, respectively.

'Abbas Hilmi II: on the 'Azhar strike, 185–187; on fears of constitutionalism and revolution, 168–170; Gorst reconciliation with, 174–175, 182, 184; Istanbul visit (1908), 167–168; Kamil rivalry with, 117; Ministry of Interior Secret Police and, 183–184; nationalism and, 114–115, 168–169, 185; opposition to British occupation by, 58, 61, 68–69, 71–73, 121, 270n70. *See also* khedivial spy network

'Abduh, Shaykh Muhammad, 185

Abdulhamid II, Sultan, 167, 181

Aboukir Land Company, 294n32

'Adhra' Dinshaway (The Virgin of Dinshaway; Haqqi), 136

administrative primers, 77–78, 78*f*

Agricultural Bank of Egypt: Cromer's public promotion of, 114; demise of, 214–217; enforcement of loans by, 200–201; explosive growth of, 102, 103*f*; in the financial crisis, 160; formation of, 42, 86, 93–96, 102–103, 103*f*; interest rates of, 101, 104, 200, 216; loan defaults after 1907, 208–211, 296n72, 297n79; as mechanism for creating large class of smallholders, 95–96, 104, 212; as model for other countries, 103, 195; National Bank of Egypt and, 101–102; nationalist criticisms of, 220, 238, 241; as sole source of loans to cooperatives, 243; special concessions of, 94–95

agricultural cooperatives: al-Rafi'i on British approach to, 240, 243, 302n84, 302n101; British attempts to control, 242–243; in cotton cultivation, 236, 237, 301n74; nationalist movement on, 162–163, 165–166, 234–237, 242–244, 247; proposals for during financial crisis, 162–163, 165–166

agricultural depression (1894), 96–97

Agriculture, Department of, 206–207

al-Ahram, 68, 76, 124, 157, 161, 181

al-'Alam, 225, 228–229, 242, 299n20

'Ali Yusuf, Shaykh, 71, 116–117, 172, 279n14, 291n84

Allenby, Edmund, 251

Anderson, Benedict, 28, 220, 229, 282n88

Anglo-Egyptian Banking Company, 155, 277n114

Anglo-French Agreement (1904), 114

Arrighi, Giovanni, 256n19, 272–273n17, 273n20
Artin Pasha, Ya'qub, 294n21
Ashley, Richard, 257n40
al-'Ashri, al-Siba'i, 81–82, 271n109
Aswan Dam, 105, 109
'azaba root, 268–269n34
Azharis: as proponents of mass mobilization, 188; as vanguard in 1919 demonstrations, 250
Azhar strike (1909), 184–188, 291n89, 291n100, 292n116
Azhar Union Society (*jam'iyat ittihad al-Azhar*), 186–187, 189, 190
azmah, meaning of, 141–142, 283n11. *See also* financial crisis (1907)

Baer, Gabriel, 52, 271n101
Balibar, Étienne, 293n9
Bank of Egypt, 277n114
Bank of France, 148–149
banks and banking: as agents of "material occupation," 219–220; Agricultural Bank of Egypt formation, 42, 86, 93–96, 102–103, 103*f*; agricultural cooperatives, 162–163, 165–166, 234–237, 240, 242–244, 247; attempts to mitigate financial crisis, 149–150, 152; call for government loan for, 151; Cassa di Sconto e di Risparmio closure and, 155–156; drain of wealth thesis, 233–234; Eid study on property valuation, 110–111; global money supply constriction (1906), 148; increasing land values and, 104–105; indebtedness and, 98–101, 99*t*, 110, 222; lack of central banks in Egypt and the United States, 148; landed property as a financial asset and, 53, 88–89, 266n122, 273n21; land survey statistics and, 96–98; moneylenders, 40, 89–92, 95, 100, 210; mortgage-insurance complex, 106–111; national capital formation, 220, 223–224; nationalist proposals for a national bank, 148, 165, 231–232, 234–235, 237–238, 243–244; syndicate formation efforts, 150, 152, 162, 225–226, 234–235; usufructory loans, 100, 275n75; Wedderburn bank model, 93–96, 280n46. *See also* European capital; financial crisis (1907); *names of individual banks*
Baring, Evelyn, 7, 255n1. *See also* Cromer, Evelyn Baring, Earl of
Baring, John, 2nd Baron Revelstoke, 298n115
Barry, E. W. H., 145
al-Barudi, Muhammad, 77, 80
base-superstructure metaphor: deterministic interpretations of, 257n41; as a feature of British colonial discourse, 26, 182; Marx's use of, 14
Basic Law (1866), 63–64
Beckert, Sven, 262n10
Behera Land Company, 277n125, 294n32
Bentham, Jeremy, 19, 23
birsim (clover), 207
Blignières, Ernest de, Marquis, 49
Blunt, Wilfrid Scawen, 72, 128–129
La Bourse Égyptienne, 210
Boyle, Harry, 120–121, 170, 194, 285n49
Brigandage Commissions, 65–66, 67
British Chamber of Commerce, 139–140
British occupation: 'Abbas Hilmi II and, 58, 61, 68–69, 71–73, 167–169, 182, 184, 187, 270n70; Agricultural Bank and, 42, 86, 93–96, 102–103, 103*f*, 214–217; agriculture regulated in, 206–208, 212–214; Blunt's criticism of, 128–129; as colonial laboratory, 6, 10, 25–26, 41, 86, 89, 95, 102–103, 182–183, 192, 195–196, 205, 208, 211, 212, 231; corvée and, 47–51, 265n106;

cotton-leaf worm infestations and, 197–204, 205, 294nn32–33, 294–295n36, 296n65; crackdown on opposition (1910), 224–225; Cromer's annual reports on, 2, 45–46, 70, 98, 104, 110, 118, 121, 125, 128, 202–203, 279n8; Dinshaway incident (1906), 129–137, 282n88, 282n93; economic narrative by, 1–2, 5–8, 114–118, 116*t*, 124–125, 170–171; economic peripheralization and, 6–7, 11–12, 27, 58–59, 222, 299n11; Egyptian currency in, 248–249, 264n69; after Egyptian default on loans, 37; as failing by its own criteria, 142–143; on fanaticism, 131, 134–136, 137, 139–140, 154–155; in financial boom, 104–111, 122–127; "gilded speech" of, 9, 27, 117–118, 128; Gorst's annual reports, 159, 173, 238; increasing coercive powers of, 2, 130, 132–133, 183–184, 190, 222, 224, 251; independence, qualified, 252–253; justification for, 2, 6–8, 32–34, 38–41, 133–135, 159, 161, 246–247; under Kitchener, 211–215, 275n73; land valuation and taxation, 96–101, 108, 110–111, 297n79; local politics and, 6, 41–42, 61, 64, 70, 75, 82, 83, 136, 176, 268n20; nonintervention policy during crisis, 142–143, 151–154, 157–159, 241, 286n96; on opposition, 115, 133–136, 191–192; peasant defaults and, 208–211, 296n72, 297n79; on peasant indebtedness, 6, 89–96, 193–194, 196–197, 213–214, 217; peasants blamed for crop declines, 193–197, 201–202, 205, 213–214; policy of conciliation and, 182–184, 290n68; prosperity versus sovereignty in, 27–28; protectorate declaration, 2–3, 248, 255n8, 255n11; protests after World War I and, 250–252; smallholders as focus of, 34–35, 96–97, 217, 261–262n9, 262n13; as transformative, 3–4, 8–9; on village cooperatives, 242–243; violence against opposition, 133–134, 187, 189–190, 224, 251, 292n120; during World War I, 248–249. *See also* colonial economism; Cromer, Evelyn Baring, Earl of; Gorst, Sir John Eldon; Interior, Ministry of; Justice, Ministry of; opposition to British occupation; Public Works, Ministry of; racism; social transformation

Brown, Nathan, 47–48, 265n93

Brown, R. Hanbury, 121

Buck-Morss, Susan, 258, 258n51, 259n64

Bullock, G. M., 129–130

al-Bustani, Yusuf, 155

cab drivers: Alexandria strike (1906), 176; Cairo strike (1907), 178, 289n52

Caisse de la Dette Publique, 44, 50

Caisse Hypothécaire, 107

Campbell-Bannerman, Sir Henry, 151

cantonal courts, 212–213

capitalism: accumulation in, 4, 13, 19, 20, 28, 239, 257n36; in agriculture, 88–89, 104, 212; British vision of peasantry and, 6, 34–35, 86, 91, 94, 252; capitalist production of nature, 13, 196, 293–294n15; constraints on accumulation, 19–20; economic history and history of, 11–12; economism and, 11–14, 223, 257n40; exploitation and expropriation in, 12–13, 34–35, 257n35; national capital and, 223–224, 230, 232, 236, 239, 254; nationalist movement and, 120–127, 150–155, 156–157, 161–163, 179, 180*f*, 219–221, 223–224, 226, 234, 237, 239, 299n11; new approaches to critical theory of, 11–13, 15–16; property consolidation in, 88–89, 273n21; social relations under, 13–15, 17–18, 36, 143, 196, 223; spatial fix in, 87,

272n13; study of, 11–13. *See also* colonial economism; economism
Cassa di Sconto e di Risparmio, 150, 155–156, 157
Cassel, Ernest, 101
certificate of poverty, 81, 271n106
Chatterjee, Partha, 298n6
Cheetham, Milne, 215, 232
children: applied entomology literature for, 208; conscription of peasant children, 201–204, 203*f*, 294–295n36, 295n46; uncompensated labor of, 34–35
"the circle of brotherhood," 71, 73. *See also* khedivial spy network
civilization: as criterion for politics, 22–23, 25–26, 240; as developmental trajectory, 4
Clarke, Frederick S., 46, 48, 265n83
coal heavers of Port Said strike (1882), 175
Coles, Charles, 101
colonial economism: civilizational progress in, 4, 22–23, 25–26, 240; credit for peasants and, 6, 42, 86, 92–93, 95–96, 111, 193–197, 209–211; Cromer and, 2–3, 194–195; defined, 4–6, 25–27; Dinshaway incident as rejoinder to, 118, 132–133; economism and, 4–5; financial crisis and critiques of, 164–166, 173–175; "gilded speech" as name for, 9, 27, 117–118; as hostile projection, 247; in justification for occupation, 6–8; liberalism and, 5, 18–27; Muhammad Rushdi on, 59, 74; peasant characteristics assumed in, 5–6, 41–42, 46, 86, 96, 165, 170, 194, 208, 221–223, 235; political participation and, 6, 41–42, 57, 60–61, 69–71, 169–171; racial narratives in failures of, 218, 240; Shimi Bey critique of, 61; smallholders and, 6, 34–35, 48, 86, 89, 96, 111, 196, 200, 217; strikes as practical rejoinder to, 177–179; during World War I, 249–250
Committee for Union and Progress, 167, 180–181
commodity exchange, 17, 20
comparison: in anticolonial thought, 119, 128, 143, 156–157, 164, 167–168, 174, 191, 220, 225–228, 239–241, 244–245, 302n84; colonial rule and, 10, 40, 93, 95, 256n25, 284n19; economic history and, 11, 257n30, 262n10; between Egypt and India, 25, 38, 40, 42, 43, 86, 89, 90, 91–92, 94, 95, 97, 102–103, 191, 197, 211, 213, 226–228, 256n25, 263n54; between Egypt and Ireland, 119, 128, 191, 220, 241, 245; between Egypt and the Philippines, 103, 195; between Egypt and the United States, 88, 128, 148, 152, 156–157, 174
conservatism: Henry Maine and, 24–25, 29, 90, 194, 211; of the Khedive's spies, 75; theories of British rule and, 24–25, 42, 90–93, 96, 193–197, 212–213, 217–218, 247–248
Considerations on Representative Government (Mill), 23
Considerations sur les avantages et la sécurité des placements hypothécaires en Égypte (Van Dieren), 104–105
Consultative Chamber of Delegates, 63
cooperation: establishment of cooperatives and agricultural syndicates, 235–236, 239–244; in Mill's conception of civilization, 22–23, 240; in nationalist thought, 163, 234
Coptic Christians, 188, 232–233
Coptic Conference (Asyut, 1911), 232–233
corruption: Cromer's "three Cs" and, 49–50, 65; nationalist press allegations of British, 120–121; reported by Khedive's spies, 73–74, 76–79, 98

Cortelyou, George B., 157
corvée: British efforts to distinguish from child labor in cotton-worm campaigns, 202; Cromer's "three Cs" and, 49–50; French on, 50–51; "Nile corvée," 51–52, 266n112, 266n115; payment of laborers and, 50, 51–52; peasant flight over, 62–63; prior to the British occupation, 36, 47–48, 49; social class inequalities in, 48–50; ʿumdah enforcement of, 62; unpopularity of, 47, 50, 265n106, 266n115
cotton cultivation: agricultural cooperatives and, 236, 237; as "background" to the occupation, 28, 260n112; conscription of peasant children, 34–35, 201–204, 203*f*, 262n13, 294–295n36, 295n46; cotton-leaf worm and, 197–204, 198*f*, 203*f*, 205, 294nn32–33, 295n46; declining yields and quality, 196–197, 201–202, 204–208, 229, 238, 295–296n59; as Egypt's "real wealth," 162, 236; in financial crisis, 147, 157, 161, 162, 284n38; foreign lending impact, 222; future independence and, 166; imams instructing peasants on, 207–208; irrigation water distribution, 39–40, 45–47, 77, 199–200; peasant debt and, 59, 196–197; pink bollworm, 205, 207, 295n53; price increase in late 1890s, 105; prior to the British occupation, 36; progress measured in terms of, 45–46; regulations and punishments for, 201–204, 207, 294–295n36, 296n65; smallholder importance in, 34–35, 96, 217, 262n10, 262n13; speculation and rigging of futures market for, 120–121, 284n24; United States production and, 37, 56, 96–97; violence in, 62–63, 268n15, 273n21. *See also* corvée; irrigation
cotton-leaf worm: British indictment of Egyptian self-government and, 205; conscription of peasant children and, 201–204, 203*f*, 294–295n36, 295n46; as ecological manifestation of class inequality in credit markets, 200–201; infestations, 197–199, 198*f*; peasant smallholders blamed for damage by, 200–202, 205, 294nn32–33
courbash (*kurbaj*), 49–50
craft guilds, 176
Crédit Foncier (France): as dominant mortgage bank in Egypt, 105, 277n122; in the financial crisis, 160, 216, 234, 277n122; Wedderburn's agricultural bank and, 94
Crédit Lyonnais, 150, 152
Cromer, Evelyn Baring, Earl of: on abolition of village elections, 70–71, 79, 83; Agricultural Bank of Egypt, 95–96, 101, 208, 216, 296n72; budget cuts by, 43–44; colonial economism and, 3–7; on corvée, 49, 52; cotton-leaf worm regulations and, 201–204, 207; Dinshaway incident (1906), 129–130, 133; Dufferin report and, 41–43; Fayyum address (1905), 113–114, 116, 124; financial crisis and, 149, 155; financial stability assurances, 127, 128–129, 134; on foreign capital investment, 7, 53; on Gorst's concessions, 182; irrigation reconstruction, 44–47, 55; on land distribution, 124–125; on land tax, 96–98; on Mortgage Company of Egypt, 216; on opposition to British occupation, 2, 72, 121, 136, 139–140, 194; on peasant indebtedness, 42, 89, 92–93, 98–101, 99*t*; on property law, 53–56, 96–97; on provincial administration, 65, 67–68, 70–71, 75; on racial particularities, 26–27, 42–43, 95, 208, 212; raised to peerage, 255n1; resignation of, 149, 155, 285n49; self-enrichment by, 120–121; smallholder policies of, 86, 95–96; on social classes,

41–43, 111, 120, 208; on streamlining government, 3, 255n11; theory of imperial rule, 2–3, 4, 7, 10, 25–27, 41–43
Cuno, Kenneth M., 268n22

Dalil al-'Umdah (*The 'Umdah's Guidebook*; al-Barudi), 77, 80
Davis, Eric, 288n18
Deccan Riots, 90, 93
Delta Barrage, 44–45
depressions: agricultural depression (1894), 96–97; First Great Depression (1873-1896), 85, 87–88, 272–273n17
al-Din Pasha, Muhammad Sa'd, 73–74
Dinshaway incident (1906): Ahmad Hilmi's role in publicizing, 130–131, 132, 135; British defense of tribunal, 133–135; British interpretation of, 129, 131; concept of "the people" and, 136, 282n88; as counternarrative to colonial economism, 118, 133; description of event, 129; National Party's use of petitions and, 136–138, 137*f*; outcome and executions, 132; polarized responses to, 133–137, 282n88, 282n93; press reports on, 130–131; special tribunal for, 129–132
"Dual Control," Anglo-French, 41
Dudgeon, Gerald, 242–243
Dufferin, Earl of (Frederick Temple): on bankruptcy as outcome of Oriental despotism, 39; on corporal punishment, 49–50; Cromer's disagreements with, 41–43, 263n54; "General Report," 38–41, 55–56, 257nn40–41; on mortgage credit and protective legislation, 40, 42; Organic Law (May 1883), 38; Stuart report on peasant indebtedness, 89–90, 92–93; on taxation, 49–50, 54, 96; on village elections, 41–42, 60–61, 64; on the virtues of Egyptian smallholders, 39
Dunlop, Douglas, 176–177

the economic: as discrete domain, 16–17; as distinct from "the economy," 16, 258n51, 258n54; emergence of political economy and, 17–18; as proxy for public approval, 45–46, 112, 114–117, 116*f*, 128, 134; relation to the political, 18–23, 27–31, 112, 118, 122, 133, 136, 143, 161–162, 164–166, 169–171, 175, 177–179, 181, 219–220, 221–222, 223, 224, 225–228, 231, 232, 233–235, 237–238, 246–247, 248, 252–254
economism: changes in meaning of, 10–11; critical social theory and, 10–13; defined, 11; as mode of regulation, 14, 18, 254; neoliberalism and, 11; as recurrent feature of social thought inside the history of capitalism, 13–15, 223, 257n40; in theory and history, 5–6, 10–15. *See also* colonial economism
economistic behavior, 165, 183, 221–223
"the economy": emergence of, 15, 258n44, 258n57; as statistical abstraction, 17–18
Egypt, prior to British occupation: corvée, 36, 47–48, 49; insolvency of, 33, 37, 233–234; irrigation in, 36, 44, 56–57; under Isma'il Pasha, 37, 44, 54, 63–64, 176, 267n10; under Mehmed Ali Pasha, 36–37, 43, 53–54, 62–63, 96–97; provincial administration in, 62–64; rise of large landholders, 33–36; under Tawfiq Pasha, 68
Egyptian Conference (Heliopolis, 1911), 232–236
Egyptian Gazette: on the Azhar strike, 185; on Cromer's Fayyum speech, 114; on the Dinshaway incident, 134–135; on the economic irrationality of the Egyptian fellah, 193–194; on the Egyptian fellah, 193–194; on the financial crisis, 143, 148,

155, 157–158; on the law students' strike, 177; optimism of, during the boom, 85, 124–125, 128; on political parties, 172
Egyptian Mortgage Insurance Company, 107
Egyptian Revolution (1919), 250–252
Eid, Alfred, 110–111, 278n136
Ellis, Matthew, 270n70
Elyachar, Julia, 20
Empire of Cotton (Beckert), 34, 262n10
Engels, Friedrich, 257n41
English republicanism, 20
Esmeir, Samera, 213, 265n93, 268n15, 273n21
ethology, 21
European capital: agricultural banks and, 94–95; British allegations of fanaticism and, 137, 139–140; calling in loans from Egypt, 149; as constraint on independence, 164–166, 219–220, 231, 233–234, 238; Egyptian farm mortgages as fix for, 86, 87; Egyptian mortgage investment boom, 104–106; Eid study on property valuation, 110–111; estimates of, 272n9, 273n20; fickle nature of, 8–9, 127; First Great Depression and, 85, 87–88, 272–273n17; Haussmannization and, 37, 87, 272n14; in India, 93–96; interest rates and, 86, 109–110, 144–146, 216, 284n27; in joint-stock companies, 144–146, 284n24; large landholders and, 85–86, 106–110, 209, 297n79; lending to the Egyptian government, 1, 7, 36–37, 44; from life insurance companies, 106–111; as means of exploitation, 122–123; peasant indebtedness reports and, 98–101, 99*t*, 110; property law standardization and, 6, 53–55; smallholders and, 6, 35, 94, 95–96, 106; to the United States, 87–88, 147–148, 273n20; urban properties and, 144; valuation experts, 108, 297n79; Wedderburn bank model, 93–96
Fahmi Pasha, Mustafa, 68, 269n48
fanaticism: as alleged effect of material duress, 218, 247; attributed to material prosperity, 139; as British explanation for popular politics, 26–27, 69, 183, 190, 196; as justification for Dinshaway sentences, 131, 133–137; as repellent to foreign capital, 154–155, 183, 225
Farahat, 'Abd al-Hamid, 76
Farid, Muhammad, 168, 225, 232, 240, 302n101
Fayyum address (Cromer, 1905), 113–114, 116, 124
feddans: Five Feddan Law, 213–215, 241, 275n73; of large landholders, 34, 66, 98, 109, 111; in loans to smallholders, 101–102, 111; in requirements for 'umdahs and shaykhs, 270n59; as standard unit of land, 261n8
"fetishism of the commodity," as argument about unfreedom, 223, 299n12
financial boom: Arabic novels and, 255n14; building on agricultural land in, 126; colonial economism and, 6–8; economic instability in, 126–127; expectations of affluence in, 124–126; exports of European capital and, 84, 86, 87–89; intensification of rural inequality and, 110–111; investment boosters and, 104–106; land surveys and, 96–98; as obstacle to occupation's critics, 9–10, 112, 115, 118, 119, 122; peasant indebtedness and investors, 98–101, 99*t*, 110; social improvement lacking in, 122–123
financial crisis (1907), 141–166; agricultural commodity price fluctuations in, 161–162, 163; American interventionist response, 156–159; attempts to mitigate market crash, 149–150; British nonin-

tervention policy in, 142–143, 151–154, 157–159, 241, 286n96; call for government action, 151–152; as dress rehearsal for the Great Depression, 256n21; generalized character of, 162–163; investor confidence loss as cause of, 150, 154–155; justification of occupation and, 142–143, 159, 161; nationalist movement in, 29–30, 161–166, 173–174; nationalists blamed for, 9, 150–151, 153; newspapers on, 141, 143, 148–152; peasants and servants in, 157, 159–161, 241; political party formation in, 172–173; profiteering during, 216, 234; San Francisco earthquake (1906) and, 146–147; social dislocation resulting from, 159–161; Theodore Roosevelt as example in, 148, 156–157, 229; underlying mechanism of, 143–146, 145*f*, 162, 284n24; uneven class dynamics of, 209–211
Findlay, Charles, 134, 139
Five Feddan Law: as "complement" to acceleration of foreclosure procedures, 214; as opportunity for village moneylenders, 241; as pretext for concessions to the Agricultural Bank, 215; Punjab Alienation of Land Bill and, 213; statistics on rural lending and, 275n73
"flesh pots," 84, 272n5
La fortune immobilière de l'Égypte et sa dette hypothécaire (Eid), 110–111, 278n136
Foster, E. W. P., 45, 47, 277n125
Foucault, Michel, 18
Fourteen Points (Wilson), 250
France: Anglo-French Agreement (1904), 114; Anglo-French "Dual Control," 41; on corvée abolition, 49–50, 265n106; Crédit Foncier and, 94, 105, 216, 234
Fraser, Nancy, 12
Free Officers' Revolt (1952), 302n85
Garstin, William, 51–52, 56–57, 65, 121, 216
gender, capitalism and, 13, 257n37, 262n14
"General Resumé of the Occurrence at Denshawai, June 13, 1906," 131
Gesink, Indira Falk, 291n89
Ghali Pasha, Butrus, 190, 191
"the gilded river," 233
"gilded speech," 9, 27, 117–118, 128
Goldberg, Ellis, 295–296n59
Gorst, Sir John Eldon: on the Agricultural Bank, 210–212; appointed as Consul-General of Egypt, 149; as British adviser to Ministry of Interior, 67, 70, 74–77; death of, 211; on declining cotton yields, 205; on experiment in self-government, 192, 195–196, 205, 211; financial crisis response of, 150, 152, 154–155, 157–159, 164, 173–175; on increasing state coercive powers, 183–184, 189; on Jewish deportation, 224–225; Khedive's reconciliation with, 174–175, 182, 184; local election abolition by, 61; on nationalist movement, 170, 183, 192; on peasant defaults, 210–211; policy of conciliation, 182–184, 290n68
Goswami, Manu, 227
Graham, Ronald, 168–170, 191–192, 293n128
Gramsci, Antonio, 14–15, 18, 254
Gresham Life Assurance Society, 107–110, 209, 284n27, 297n79
Grey, Edward, 134, 137, 139, 192

halaqat (network of village markets), 212
Hamadah, Dasuqi, 80
Hamadah Pasha, Khalil, 187
Hansen, Bent, 272n9
Haqqi, Mahmud Tahir, 136
Harb, Muhammad Tal'at, 162–163, 221, 222, 237–239, 299n11
Hardinge, Arthur, 51, 69, 266n115

Harvey, David, 87, 266n122, 272n13, 294n15
Harvey, George, 293n128
Haussmann, Eugène, Baron, 37
Haussmannization, 37, 87
Higher Council (of the Azhar), 185, 187
al-Hilal, 112, 123, 280n33, 294n22
Hilmi, Ahmad: on British rigging of cotton futures market, 120–121; on "gilded speech," 9, 27, 117–118; investigative reporting on Dinshaway incident, 130–132, 135; on national purchasing syndicate formation, 162; on petitioning as means of popular representation, 137, 138*f*; on wealth versus social improvement, 122–123, 135
History of Landownership in Modern Egypt (Baer), 52
hizb, meanings of, 171
hizb al-Ingliz (euphemism for collaborators), 171
Hizb al-Ummah (the People's Party), 172, 174–175, 187, 188
al-Hizb al-Watani. *See* National Party
Holt, Elizabeth, 255n14

Ibrahim, al-Sayyid, 71
Ibrahim, Hafiz, 136
ikhtilal (deliberate misspelling of "the occupation"), 73–74, 75
'Ilaj Misr al-iqtisadi (Egypt's Economic Cure; Harb), 237
Imagined Communities (Anderson), 28, 220
imperialism: autonomy and, 244; capitalism and, 6–9, 104, 221; as class exploitation on a world stage, 179, 226; economic nationalism and, 165, 222; financialization and, 256n19; political party formation and, 171
imperial liberalism, 23–24
Imperial Ottoman Bank (IOB), 106–107, 110, 145, 155
India: Agricultural Bank of Egypt debated in, 102–103; as comparative model for British rule in Egypt, 10, 43, 95, 211, 213; hierarchy of racial types in, 23, 92; Mill on, 21; peasant indebtedness in, 90–92, 93–96; Punjab, 91–92; rural usury in, 90–91; social transformation in, 25, 260n103; Swadeshi movement in, 226–227; Wedderburn bank model for, 93–96
Indian Revolt (1857), 90
interest rates: Agricultural Bank and, 101, 104, 200; bank criteria in setting, 109–111; Bank of England, 147; class inequalities in, 91, 111, 196–197, 200, 208, 293–294n15; in the financial boom, 143–146; in the financial crisis, 148–149, 160, 241; foreign capital and, 86, 109–110, 144–146, 284n27; Islam and, 135; by local moneylenders, 95; multiple determinants of, 91; on National Bank's experimental loans, 102; rising productivity induced by, 200; on urban development, 145–146
Interior, Ministry of: Brigandage Commissions, 65–66, 67; British influence over, 59–61, 64–71, 73–76, 269n47; forced relocation of peasants by, 64–67, 83; Gorst as adviser to, 67–71, 74–77; incompetence, corruption, and depravity in, 73–74, 76–79; peasants' petitions and, 61–63, 79–83, 271n109; 'umdah accountable to British, 77–79. *See also* khedivial spy network; village shaykhs
Ionian Bank, 84, 105–106
irrigation: Anglo-Indian engineers and, 43–45, 96, 264n63; Aswan Dam, 105; class inequality in, 39; Delta Barrage repairs, 44–45; distribution of, 39–40, 46–47, 77, 80, 199–200; insider trading by engineers, 120–121; local abuse of control over, 89; in Ottoman administration,

43; perennial, 43, 48, 50; prior to British occupation, 36, 44, 56–57; rising water tables and salinity from, 204; smallholders and, 111, 193–194, 200. *See also* corvée
al-Iskandari, ʿAbd al-Latif Shukri, 32
Ismaʿil Pasha: Consultative Chamber of Delegates, 63–64; craft guilds and, 176; default on loans by, 37; irrigation repairs neglected by, 44; labor policies of, 267n10; on landed property, 54–55; *muqabalah* policy of, 54
istiʿmar, dual meaning of, 32–35
ʿ*izbah* (plural, ʿ*izab*), redefinition of, 66–67, 268–269n34, 269n39

Japan, First Great Depression (1873-1896) and, 87–88
al-Jaridah: British praise for, 154, 172; on collective action, 189; on the financial crisis, 141, 155, 161; on national industrialization, 237; National Party and, 172, 174–175; support for the Azhar strike, 189
Jawdat, Ismaʿil Bey, 71–72, 75
Jawish, Shaykh ʿAbd al-ʿAziz, 189–190, 224–227, 228, 300n26
joint-stock companies, 7, 144–146, 284n24
Justice, Ministry of: appointment of a British adviser, 68; cantonal courts in, 212–213; class inequalities in, 80–81; Mixed Courts, 40, 85, 104, 210–211, 214–215, 267n129; role of ʿumdahs in, 77–78, 78*f*, 80; Shariʿah Courts, 100, 275n76

kafr, 268–269n34. See also ʿ*izbah*
Kamil, ʿAli Fahmi, 173–174
Kamil, Muhammad Afandi, 71
Kamil, Mustafa: on British response to crisis, 164; death of, 168; *al-Liwaʿ* founder, 117; opposition to British occupation, 117, 118–119, 168; rivalry with the Khedive, 117; on takeover of the Interior, 269n47; on "the Eastern Question," 142. *See also* National Party (*al-Hizb al-Watani*)
al-Khayri, Muhammad, 76
khedivate: British on insolvency of, 33; elite and elitist character of, 268n25; origin of, 35–37; peasant petitions in, 61–63, 79–83, 271n109; three Cs of despotism in, 65. *See also* ʿAbbas Hilmi II; Interior, Ministry of; Ismaʿil Pasha; Tawfiq Pasha
Khedivial Agricultural Society, 201, 204–205, 207, 242
Khedivial Decree of April 15, 1891 (on landed property), 52
Khedivial Law School students' strike (1906), 176–177
khedivial spy network: ʿAbbas Hilmi II and, 58, 61, 71–77, 184, 270n70; on British influence in the interior, 58–60, 71, 73–75; on British policy impoverishing the country, 59, 96, 119–120, 237; conservative views of, 61, 75–76; on corruption and depravity, 72–73, 76–77, 98; countersurveillance against, 77, 184; on occupation and personal gain, 74, 76, 247; on the occupation's economic narrative, 96, 119–120; opposition to British rule and, 72, 75, 82–83
Kitchener, Herbert, 211–215, 275n73
Koselleck, Reinhart, 283n12

Labor Corps, 248–249
laissez-faire, 14, 18, 156, 175
Land and Mortgage Company Limited (British), 94, 105
land tax: in the agricultural depression (1894), 96–97; corvée and surcharge on, 50–51; Dufferin on, 40, 49–50, 54, 96; in India, 93; inequality of, 40, 96–97;

under Mehmed Ali Pasha, 62–63, 96–97; origin of, 53–54; rural usury and, 90; shaykhs as collectors, 62–64; survey and reassessment of (1894), 96–98; village collectors (sayarif) as agents of Agricultural Bank, 94, 102. *See also* property; property values
Lang, Robert Hamilton, 112
large landholders: banks not foreclosing on, 209, 297n79; corvée and, 48, 49–50; in Eid study on property valuation, 110–111; European loans to, 85–86, 106–110, 209, 297n79; expanding after peasant flight, 63; feddans of, 34, 66, 98, 109, 111; as impediment to reforms, 39; *'izbah* system and, 66; labor and water appropriation by, 39–40, 46–47; Mortgage Company of Egypt and, 216; Oriental despotism and, 217; in prior accounts of British rule, 33–34; property law and, 52–55, 123–124, 265n129; rise of, 33–36
Larkworthy, Falconer, 84–85, 105–106, 139
Legrand, F., 144, 160, 163
LeGrelle, Charles, 67
Lenin, Vladimir I., 11
liberal political theory, 5, 14, 18, 20–21, 23–24
liberal universalism, 24–25, 53, 154, 212
life insurance company investments, 106–111
Life Society, 188–189, 190–191
al-Liwa': on 'Ali Yusuf controversy, 279n14; on the Azhar strike, 187, 189; on the Dinshaway incident, 131, 132; on fanaticism, 135, 139, 154; on the financial crisis, 151, 154–155, 162; on financial instability, 126–127; on "gilded speech," 9; on independence, 112; on polarization of the press, 116; on political parties, 174; as rival to *al-Mu'ayyad*, 117; on torture, 135; on wealth distribution in the boom, 116, 128
Lockman, Zachary, 136
Lowe, H. A, 205
Lutfi, Abu Bakr, 219–221, 224
Lutfi, Ahmad, 240–241
Lutfi, 'Umar Bey, 163, 220–221, 235, 239–242, 294n21
Lutfi al-Sayyid, Ahmad, 154, 172, 174–175, 188–189
Luzzatti, Luigi, 235–236

Machell, Percy W., 131–132, 202, 204, 295n46
Maine, Henry Sumner, 24–25, 26, 29, 90, 194, 211
Manela, Erez, 303n12
Mansfield, Peter, 283n10
Mansur, Ahmad Afandi, 71
Mantena, Karuna, 24, 28
Manual Trade Workers Association (*jam'iyat al-sana'i'al-yadawiyah*), 189
Mar'i, Hassan, 291n100
Marlowe, John, 283n10
Marx, Karl Heinrich, 14, 17, 20, 223, 257n41, 299n12
Marxist thought, 11, 14–15
mass mobilization. *See* opposition to British occupation
Mazlum Pasha, Ahmad, 58, 71
McIlwraith, Malcolm, 214
Mehmed Ali Pasha: irrigation and transportation structures, 43; land distribution corruption, 53–54, 96–97; military-fiscal regime of, 36, 62–63; peasant petitions to, 63–64
mercerization, 205
Mestyan, Adam, 268n25
Mies, Maria, 13
Mill, John Stuart, 21–24, 25–26, 35, 240
Miller, Isaac, 283n10

Milner, Alfred, 26, 43, 216, 251–253
Milward, Robert Harding, 106
al-Minbar (newspaper), 133, 136, 281n74
al-Minbar (political party), 172
Misr al-Fatah (newspaper), 177, 179, 187–188, 219, 224
Mitchell, Timothy: on abstraction, 17–18; conflation of "the economy" with "the economic," 17–18; on cotton production as background, 28; on financial crisis, 283n10; on historicity of "the economy," 15; on landed property, 52–53, 273n21; reading of occupation as liberal universalism, 25, 52–53. *See also* "fetishism of the commodity," as argument about unfreedom; Mantena, Karuna
Mixed Courts, 40, 85, 104, 210–211, 214–215, 267n129
Modern Egypt (Cromer), 95
moneylenders: Agricultural Bank and, 200; Five Feddan Law and, 214; Greek and Levantine, 89–90, 95, 100; Hindu, 92; National Bank of Egypt and, 101; village, 40, 210
Mortgage Company of Egypt, 216, 298n115
al-Mu'ayyad: on Azhar strike, 186; criticism of occupation, 116–117; on Dinshaway incident, 131–133; on interest rates, 135; on nationalism, 68; National Party and, 171; on peasant blame for cotton-leaf worm, 201; on rising land prices, 125–126, 128; spy network and, 71; on Theodore Roosevelt, 156
Mubarak, 'Ali, 49, 56
mudirs, 32, 51, 60, 65, 74–76
Muhammad, Isma'il, 80
Mukhbir, 'Abd al-Halim Afandi, 71
muqabalah (quid pro quo), 54
al-Muqattam: on the Dinshaway incident, 131, 134–135; in financial crisis, 151–152, 153–154, 157, 159; on the National Party's subscriptions, 173; on political party proliferation, 173; support for occupation, 116, 128
Musalmans and Money-Lenders (Thorburn), 92, 213

Nahhas, Yusuf, 221, 233–235, 301n54
al-Nashrah al-idariyah (*The Administrative Bulletin*), 78
Nassar, Hussayn Afandi, 71, 76
Nasser, Gamal Abdel, 34
national bank (*masraf watani*), calls for, 165, 231–232, 234–235, 237–238, 243–244
National Bank of Egypt, 101–102, 150, 248–249, 286n82
nationalism, nature of, 28–29, 220–224, 298n6, 299n11
nationalist movement: 'Abbas Hilmi II and, 167–170, 184; on agricultural cooperatives, 162–163, 165–166, 234–237, 242–244, 247; blamed for financial crisis, 150–151, 153; boycotts as inspiration, 226–227, 228, 300n26; Butrus Ghali Pasha assassination, 191; capitalism and, 221–224, 226, 237, 239, 299n11; constitution and independence demands, 139, 168, 221, 228–229, 253, 282n98; convergence of classes and interests in, 136–137, 177–179, 188–191, 237; Copts in, 232–233; on diversifying productive activity, 222, 230–231, 234; financial crisis impact on, 29–30, 161–166, 173–174; on foreign lending increasing poverty, 222–223; government surveillance of, 184, 190, 293n128; history of (by al-Rafi'i), 239–240; interventionist state demand, 148, 156–157, 228–229; mass mobilization in, 189–190, 227–228; on national bank formation, 165, 231–232,

234–235, 237–238, 243–244, 247; national capital need, 162–163, 222–223, 232, 236, 237–239, 248; Paris Peace Conference and, 250–251; petitioning by, 136–137, 138*f*, 168, 250; postwar protests, 250–251; on preserving wealth within the country, 220, 223–224, 230; protests after World War I, 250–251; on subject formation, 221, 299n10; Swadeshi movement and, 226–227; syndicate formation efforts in, 150, 152, 162, 225–226, 234–236. *See also* opposition to British occupation

National Party (*al-Hizb al-Watani*): ʻAbbas Hilmi II and, 72, 168, 187; in the Azhar strike, 186–187, 189; calls for constitution, 167–168; charter and platform of, 171–174, 279n16; in the financial crisis, 150–151, 153; Kamil in, 117, 172, 269n47, 279n16; in mass mobilization, 177, 189–190, 220, 228; People's Night Schools, 189; petitioning by, 136–137, 138*f*, 167–168; on preserving wealth within the country, 220; rift in party, 225; Theodore Roosevelt on, 300n34; village cooperatives by British and, 243–244; vision of national improvement, 228–229

al-Nawawi, Shaykh Hassunah, 187

neoliberalism, 11, 22, 257n33

New Order (for the Azhar), 185–186

newspapers and journals: Azhar strike and, 185–187, 189; on British occupation, 121–122, 134–136; on Dinshaway incident, 130–131; polarization in, 115–116. *See also names of individual newspapers and journals*

Nicholson, Frederick A., 102

"Nile corvée," 51–52, 266n112, 266n115. *See also* corvée

Nimr, Faris, 116

Niqabat al-taʻawun al-ziraʻiyah (*Agricultural Cooperative Syndicates*; al-Rafiʻi), 240

Noyes, Alexander Dana, 146

Nubar Pasha, 64–66, 69–70

Omar, Hussein, 171, 256n23

opposition to British occupation: by ʻAbbas Hilmi II, 58, 61, 68–69, 71–73, 121, 270n70; Azhar strike (1909), 184–188, 291n89, 291n100, 292n116; Blunt's warning to Cromer, 128–129; boycotts, 226–227, 228, 300n26; British crackdown on (1910), 183–184, 191–192, 224–225; British portrayals of, 115, 133–136, 191–192; calls for constitution, 139, 168, 228–229, 245, 253, 282n98; calls for interventionist state, 148, 156–157; class and group convergence in, 136–137, 177–179, 188–191, 237; Cromer on, 2, 72, 121, 136, 139–140, 194; Cromer's Fayyum address and, 114–115, 116, 120; cultural changes in, 188–189; Dinshaway incident and, 130–131; Gorst's concessions, 182–184, 290n68; industrial enterprise promotion, 222, 237–238; by Kamil, 117, 118–119, 168; in khedivial spy network, 61–63, 71–77, 117–118; material prosperity challenges, 119–120, 122–123; national bank proposal, 165, 220, 231–232, 234–235, 237–238, 243–244, 248; national independence demand, 139, 168, 221, 228–229, 253, 282n98; petitioning by, 136–137, 138*f*, 167–168, 250; political parties, 171–175; protests after World War I, 250–251; on retaining land ownership by Egyptians, 219–220; on sovereign rights, 27–28, 115, 119; Swadeshi movement (India) and, 226–227; violence against, 133–134, 187, 189–190, 224, 292n120; on wealth from rising land prices, 125–126; on Westerners residing

in Egypt, 186. *See also* khedivial spy network; nationalist movement
Organic Law of May 1883, 38
Oriental despotism: bankruptcies attributed to, 38–41; beneficiaries of, 217; as British distortion, 254; British justice compared to, 46, 55, 76, 83, 244; village elections and, 64
Orientalist exceptionalism, 5, 11, 95
Ottoman Empire: calls for constitution, 167–169, 171; Egypt's increasing autonomy from, 1, 36; irrigation infrastructures and, 43; land tenure and, 53–54, 62; revolutionary influences from, 180–181, 190–191, 226; in World War I, 248; Young Turks' revolt, 167–168
Owen, Roger, 12, 34, 256n19, 264n63, 264n76, 283n10

Palmer, Edwin, 98–101, 99*t*
Paris Peace Conference (1919), 250–251
patriotism (*wataniyah*), 61, 115
peasant indebtedness: Agricultural Bank of Egypt and, 96–97, 214–215; bank direct loans and, 85–86; bank foreclosures (1910), 209–211, 296n72, 297n79; British policies and, 27, 34, 98; British racial explanation of, 193–194, 196–197, 213–214, 217; class designations for loan terms, 196–197; Cromer on, 42, 92–93; debt cycle in 1894 slump, 59; Dufferin on, 40–41, 42; Eid study on property valuation, 110–111; Five Feddan Law and, 214–215, 241, 275n73; Gorst on, 210–211; in India, 90–92, 93–96; landless peasants and, 27, 92, 125, 217; moneylenders, 89–90, 95, 210; National Bank of Egypt and, 101–102, 150; Palmer study on, 98–101, 99*t*, 110; racialization of, 92; rising productivity required in, 200–201; rural usury, 90–91, 160, 241; Stuart report on, 89–90; usufruct practice, 275n75; in Wedderburn bank model, 93–96; women as creditors, 100, 275n77
peasantry (fallahin): assessment of occupation by, 47; blamed for crop declines, 193–197, 201–202, 205; British focus on, 34–35, 96–97, 217–218, 262n13; colonial economism and, 5–6, 41–42, 46, 86, 96, 165, 170, 194, 208, 221–223, 235; conscription of children of, 201–204, 203*f*, 294–295n36, 295n46; corvée and, 47–52; cotton-leaf worm damage and, 199–201, 207–208, 294nn32–33; Cromer's assessment of, 41–43; expectations during economic boom, 124–125; in financial crisis (1907), 157, 159–161, 241; Five Feddan Law and, 213–215, 241, 275n73; forced relocation of, 64–67, 83; landless, 27, 92, 125, 217; land survey and reassessment, 96–98, 110, 274n63; local government and, 62–64, 65, 69–71, 75–78, 199, 268n22; under Mehmed Ali Pasha, 36–37; peasant flight from state demands, 62–63, 66; petitions by, 61–63, 79–83, 271n109, 286n91; punishments for not obeying regulations, 201, 202, 207, 296n65; pursuit of economic gain attributed to, 59, 74, 112, 221–223, 246–247; rising land prices and, 80, 85, 104–105, 124–126; in rural cooperation, 235–236, 240; village elections, 41–42, 60–61, 62–64, 70–71, 83; violence against, 62–63, 79–82, 268n15, 273n21; during World War I, 248–249. *See also* racism; smallholders
"People's Night Schools," 189
People's Party (*Hizb al-Ummah*), 172, 174–175, 187, 188
petitioning: as nationalist technique for

representing public opinion, 136–137, 138*f*, 167–168, 250; by peasants, 61–63, 79–83, 271n109, 286n91; via telegraph, 167–168
Philippines, 103, 195
pink bollworm, 205, 207, 295n53. *See also* cotton-leaf worm
Polanyi, Karl, 17
political parties: political sociability in, 173; proliferation of, 171–175; strikes and protests of, 175–179. *See also names of individual political parties*
Press Law revival (1910), 183, 189–190, 224–225, 290n79
Principles of Political Economy (Mill), 21–22, 35
property: capitalism and consolidation of, 53–55, 88–89, 273n21; circulation of financial capital and, 88–89; corruption and, 76, 80–81, 96–97, 98; as domain of sovereign power, 273n21; Eid study on property valuation, 110–111; extended to facilitate expropriation, 54–55, 267n129; Five Feddan Law, 213–215, 241, 275n73; land grants by Mehmed Ali dynasty, 36, 96–97; land survey and reassessment, 96–98; preserving ownership inside Egypt, 219–220, 230; redistribution of land, 34–35, 237; standardization of, 6, 52–53, 267n129; state-owned land auctions, 123–125, 220. *See also* land tax; property values
property values: in financial crisis, 159–160; increasing, 80, 85, 104–105, 124–126; of urban properties, 144, 160. *See also* land tax
prostitution, 81–82, 271n108
protectorate declaration, 2–3, 214, 255n8
Public Instruction, Ministry of, 43
public utility: land expropriation and, 53–55; as object of government, 44, 56; in Ottoman statecraft, 56–57, 267n137
Public Works, Ministry of: Anglo-Indian engineers appointed to, 43, 44; "British justice" and, 46, 55; corvée and, 47–52; cotton yields and, 45, 199–200; Department of Agriculture established in, 206; employees' strike (1919), 251; as feeder for company boards, 108, 216; under the khedivate, 36–37, 39, 43, 49; landed property and, 54–55, 267n129; market manipulation and, 120–121; rental value survey, 97–98; road building, 56–57; water distribution and, 44–47, 80
Punjab: Alienation of Land Bill (1900), 92, 213; indebtedness of peasants in, 91–92; "Punjab school" of administration, 211, 213–214. *See also* India
Pursley, Sara, 299n10

qintar/kantar, 264n76
qirat, 261n8
al-qurawiyin (villagefolk), 213

racism: academic, 293n9; capitalism and, 13; colonial economism and, 5–6, 22, 25–26, 42–43, 60, 92, 95, 103, 139, 165, 183, 194–195, 247; critical responses to, 74, 221, 227–228, 245; Egypt as laboratory and, 25–26, 89, 192, 195–196, 205, 208; explanation for policy shifts and, 217–218; inter-imperial comparison and, 103, 195; in Orientalist exceptionalism, 5, 11, 95
al-Rafi'i, 'Abd al-Rahman, 232, 239–241, 243–245
al-Ra'id al-Misri (newspaper), 120
real abstraction, 18, 143, 283n13
Reeves, John, 106–107

rental value survey, 97, 110, 274n63
Riaz Pasha, Mustafa, 50, 69, 301n64
Ricardo, David, 19
Richards, Alan, 200
Rif'at, 'Abd al-Fattah, 78, 78*f*
"the ring of valor and manly virtue," 71, 73. *See also* khedivial spy network
"Rising Generation" (youth organization), 136
Riyad, Muhammad Afandi, 71
Roosevelt, Theodore, Jr., 103, 148, 156–159, 229, 300n34
Rothstein, Theodore, 7
Roux, Charles, 265n106
Rowlatt, F. T., 215
Rule of Experts (Mitchell), 15
rural administration: Brigandage Commissions, 65–66, 67; British relocation of rural population, 64–67; British reorganization of, 59–61; "General Report" by Dufferin, 38–41, 55–56, 257nn40–41; responsible for executing British designs, 60; village elections, 41–42, 60–61, 62–64, 70–71, 83. *See also* Interior, Ministry of; Justice, Ministry of; village shaykhs
Rushdi, Hussayn, 212–213
Rushdi, Muhammad: casts doubt on the expertise of British surveyors, 98; on the economistic character of social life under British rule, 59, 74; on Egypt's underdevelopment as cotton plantation, 58–59, 96, 237; on Gorst's plans for the Ministry of Interior, 74–75; on peasant indebtedness, 58–59; on the spy network, 71, 73; on state-building, 117

Sabri Pasha, Mahmud, 32–33
Sa'id, Muhammad (minister of the interior), 206, 291n84
Sa'id Pasha, Muhammad (Ottoman *wali*), 97
Salim 'Abdullah, Fatimah Bint, 80
Salvago, C. M. (banking house), 101
San Francisco earthquake (1906), 146–147
Sarruf, Ya'qub, 116
Sartori, Andrew, 17, 261n126
Saul, S. G., 272–273n17
Schumpeter, Joseph, 17
Scott, James C., 256n21
Scott, John, 68, 261–262n9, 269n45
Scott-Moncrieff, Colin, 43–45, 48, 51, 56
self-interest, 5–6, 23–24, 60, 165, 183, 221–223
sexual violence, 81–82, 271n108
al-Sha'b, 299n20
Shafiq Pasha, Ahmad, 185
Shakir, Shaykh Muhammad, 190
Shari'ah Courts, 100, 275n77
shaykh al-mashayikh, 62
Shimi Bey, Muhammad Sa'id, 59–61, 71–77, 117, 184, 291n84
Shukri Pasha, Mahmud, 129, 131
smallholders: bank foreclosures (1910), 209–211; in British proposals for economic development, 34–35, 39, 96, 193–197, 217, 262n13; colonial economism and, 6, 111–112, 217–218; cotton-leaf worm and, 199–200; credit system and debt cycle, 59, 85–86; debt burden among, 99–101, 99*t*; figured as male property owner, 34–35, 262n14; in the financial crisis, 159–161, 238; Five Feddan Law and, 214–215, 241, 275n73; irrigation water distribution and, 39–40, 46–47, 80, 199–200; loans to, 102–103, 106; misconstrued as virtuous other to agrarian capitalism, 34–35, 261–262n9; property valuation (Eid study), 110–111; reassessment of land taxes and, 97, 110, 274n63.

See also agricultural cooperatives; peasant indebtedness; peasantry (fallahin)
Smith, Adam, 18, 19–21, 259n64
social classes: Agricultural Bank of Egypt and, 104; British occupation and, 123–124, 226; capitalist-laborers, 91; corvée and, 47–50; Cromer on, 41–43; European capital and, 106–109; in histories of the occupation, 33–34; interest rate inequalities and, 91, 111, 196–197, 200, 208, 293–294n15; irrigation water distribution and, 39–40, 46–47; in the justice system, 81; loan terms and, 85–86, 102–103, 106–110, 196–197, 208–211; peasant indebtedness and, 98–101, 99*t*; property ownership and, 53–54, 89, 123–124; role of, in nationalist movement, 136–137, 177–179, 188–191, 225–228, 237; social relations in capitalism, 13–15, 17–18, 36, 143, 196, 223. *See also* large landholders; peasantry (fallahin); smallholders
social transformation: from colonial rule, 3–4, 21–22, 85, 122–123; in the economic boom, 9–10, 118; in the financial crisis, 143; generalized, 30, 223, 261n126; in India, 25, 260n103; lack of social improvements, 122; pursuit of economic gain as effect of, 59, 74, 76, 112, 221–223, 246–247; self-interested individualism as outcome of, 165, 235, 240
Society for Islamic Progress, 224
Society for Modern Youth, 190–191
soil salinity, 204
spy network. *See* khedivial spy network
"state effect," 83, 272n112
"Statute on ʿUmdahs and Shaykhs," 70, 75
strikes: by Azhar students (1909), 184–188, 291n89, 291n100, 292n116; by cab drivers of Alexandria (1906), 176; by cab drivers of Cairo (1907), 178, 289n52; by cigarette workers (1899), 176; as claims to self-representation, 177–178; by coal heavers of Port Said (1882), 175; convergence of interests in, 177–179, 188–191; by immigrant laborers, 176; increasing frequency of, 178; by Khedivial Law School students (1906), 176–177; Ottoman Empire (1908), 180–181; as practical rejoinder to colonial economism, 177–179; by tramway workers (1908), 181; violence against, 187, 189–190, 292n120
Stuart, Villiers, 89–90, 92, 197, 199
Suares, Ralph (banking house), 101
Sudan, Anglo-Egyptian conquest of, 105, 158, 211, 253
Suez Canal, 37, 191, 253, 266n108
Sulayman, ʿAli Afandi, 71, 74
Swadeshi movement (India), 226–228
synchronic essentialism, 221

tahazzub (partisanship), 171
"The Tala Outrage." *See* Dinshaway incident (1906)
Tawfiq Pasha, 68
taxation. *See* land tax
Thorburn, Septimus, 92, 213
"three Cs" of khedivial despotism, 49–50, 65
Tignor, Robert, 283n10
Todd, John A., 205–206
tramway workers' strike (1908), 181

ʿumdahs: abuse of administrative responsibilities, 80–82; British and, 65, 69–71; disciplinary measures for, 78–79, 296n65; judicial authority of, 77; methods of circumventing selection criteria for, 75–76; qualifications for, 270n59; responsibilities of, 77–79, 78*f*, 80, 212, 271n106; tradition of, 62, 64. *See also* village shaykhs

unions (*ittihad*): Committee for Union and Progress, 167, 180–181; meaning of, 181; in the Ottoman Empire, 181; as a principle of labor militancy and mass mobilization, 170, 188–189, 225; striking Azharis and, 186–187, 189–191
United States: as comparative example of state intervention, 174; cotton crop impact on Egypt, 37, 58, 96–97; on Egypt as a model for Philippine policy, 103, 195; European capital investment in, 87–88, 147–148, 273n20; financial crisis (1907), 146–148, 152; First Great Depression (1873–1896) and, 87–88, 148; mortgage-insurance instruments in, 107; San Francisco earthquake (1906), 146–147; Theodore Roosevelt, 103, 148, 156–159, 229, 300n34
ʿUrabi revolt, 64, 89, 197
usufruct, 53, 100, 275n75; land taxes and, 53; sharʿi mortgages, 100, 275n75
utilitarianism, 19, 23–24, 26

valuation experts, 108, 297n79
Van Dieren, Edouard, 104–105, 139, 278n127
Viennese Union Bank, 156
village elections: abolition of, 70–71, 83; British perception of Egyptians and, 41–42, 60–61; under the Mehmed Ali dynasty, 62–64; parallels with craft guilds, 176
village shaykhs: appointment of, 69–71, 75–76, 268n22, 270n59; British commentaries on, 65, 69; continuity in, 268n22; description of, 62–64; election of, 63–64; responsibilities of, 75, 77–78, 78*f*, 199. See also *ʿumdahs*; village elections
village syndicates, 234–236. *See also* agricultural cooperatives
violence: in agricultural labor, 268n15, 273n21; in the countryside under the khedivate, 62–63; as a feature of the brigandage commissions, 67–68; in local administration, 81–82; recourse to by the occupation, 133–134, 187, 189–190, 224, 292n120; sexual, 81–82, 271n108
Vitalis, Robert, 299n11

Wafd party, 250, 251
al-Wardani, Ibrahim Nasif, 191
wataniyah (patriotism), 61, 115
The Wealth of Nations (Smith), 19
Wedderburn, William, 93–96, 101–102, 108, 280n46
Willcocks, F. C., 201, 294nn32–33
Willcocks, William, 44–45, 97, 108, 110
Wilson, Thomas Woodrow, 250, 303n12
Wingate, Francis Reginald, 250
women: conscription of girls, 294–295n36; as creditors, 100, 275n77; forced marriage of, 279n14; sexual violence against, 81–82, 271n108; in small family farms, 35, 262n14; uncompensated labor of, 34–35
Wood, Ellen Meiksins, 17

Young Turks' revolt, 167
Yusuf, Shaykh ʿAli, 71, 172, 186, 279n14. See also *al-Muʾayyad*

Zaghlul, Saʿd, 250
al-Zahir (newspaper): on banks as agents of crisis, 152; on the Dinshaway incident, 131; on the financial crisis as an expression of abstract interdependence, 165; on nationalists as potential repellents to foreign capital, 154; on price-gouging during the crisis, 163; on Theodore Roosevelt, 157
Zaki ʿAli, Muhammad, 221, 229–232
Zaydan, Jurji, 280n33

The authorized representative in the EU for product safety and compliance is:
Mare Nostrum Group
B.V Doelen 72
4831 GR Breda
The Netherlands

www.ingramcontent.com/pod-product-compliance
Lightning Source LLC
Chambersburg PA
CBHW031846220426
43663CB00006B/510
* 9 7 8 1 5 0 3 6 1 2 6 1 7 *